Robust Intelligent Systems

T0138154

Alfons Schuster

Editor

Robust Intelligent Systems

 Springer

Editor

Alfons Schuster
School of Computing and Mathematics
University of Ulster at Jordanstown
Northern Ireland, UK
a.schuster@ulster.ac.uk

ISBN: 978-1-84996-765-5   e-ISBN: 978-1-84800-261-6
DOI: 10.1007/978-1-84800-261-6

British Library Cataloguing in Publication Data
A catalogue record for this book is available from the British Library

© Springer-Verlag London Limited 2010
Apart from any fair dealing for the purposes of research or private study, or criticism or review, as permitted under the Copyright, Designs and Patents Act 1988, this publication may only be reproduced, stored or transmitted, in any form or by any means, with the prior permission in writing of the publishers, or in the case of reprographic reproduction in accordance with the terms of licences issued by the Copyright Licensing Agency. Enquiries concerning reproduction outside those terms should be sent to the publishers.
The use of registered names, trademarks, etc., in this publication does not imply, even in the absence of a specific statement, that such names are exempt from the relevant laws and regulations and therefore free for general use.
The publisher makes no representation, express or implied, with regard to the accuracy of the information contained in this book and cannot accept any legal responsibility or liability for any errors or omissions that may be made.

Printed on acid-free paper

Springer Science+Business Media
springer.com

Preface

Our time recognizes robustness as an important, all-pervading feature in the world around us. Despite its omnipresence, robustness is not entirely understood, rather difficult to define, and, despite its obvious value in many situations, rather difficult to achieve.

One of the goals of this edited book is to report on the topic of robustness from a variety and diverse range of fields and perspectives. We are interested, for instance, in fundamental strategies nature applies to make systems robust—and arguably "intelligent"—and how these strategies may hold as general design principles in modern technology. A particular focus is on computer-based systems and applications. This in mind, the book has four main sections:

Part I has a look at robustness in terms of underlying technologies and infrastructures upon which many computer-based "intelligent" systems reside and investigates robustness on the hardware and software level, but also in larger environments such as the Internet and self-managing systems. The contributions in Part II target robustness in research areas that are inspired by biology, including brain-computer interfaces, biological networks, and biological immune systems, for example. Part III involves the exciting field of artificial intelligence. The chapters here discuss the value of robustness as a general design principle for artificial intelligence, stressing its potential in areas such as humanoid robotics and image processing. In a way, Part IV does the omnipresent nature of robustness justice by lifting it beyond earthly confines into the vastly inspiring and equally challenging space domain, scrutinizing its impact for space mission success, space system design, and bio-regenerative life support systems.

I would like to express my sincerest thankfulness to all authors contributing to this book for their dedicated efforts. The support, guidance, and help I received from Beverley Ford, Helen Desmond, and Frank Ganz at Springer, and from Springer itself, throughout this project was exceptional—thank you very much! I am also delighted to say thank you to the following individuals for their assistance in the review process of this edited book: Dr. Dewar Finlay, Dr. David Glass, Dr. Kieran Greer, Dr. Alexander Grigorash, Dr. Christian Hölscher, Dr. Neil Lester, Dr. Gaye Lightbody, Dr. George Moore, Professor Shahid Masud, Dr. Jürgen Vogel, Dr. Martin Stetter, and Dr. Philip Taylor.

Belfast, February 2008   Alfons Schuster

Contents

Part III   Robustness in Artificial Intelligence Systems

Part IV   Robustness in Space Applications

Contributors

Uwe Aickelin
School of Computer Science, University of Nottingham, NG8 1BB,
United Kingdom, uxa@cs.nott.ac.uk

Brendan Allison
Institute of Automation, University of Bremen, D-28359 Bremen, Germany,
allison@iat.uni-bremen.de

Cecilio Angulo
Automatic Control Department, Technical University of Catalonia, 08034
Barcelona, Spain, cecilio.angulo@upc.edu

David Bustard
University of Ulster, School of Computing and Information Engineering,
Coleraine, Co. Londonderry BT52 1SA, Northern Ireland, dw.bustard@ulster.ac.uk

Steve Cayzer
Hewlett Packard Labs, Bristol, BS34 8QZ, United Kingdom, steve.cayzer@hp.com

Mathäus Dejori
Siemens Corporate Research, Intelligent Vision and Reasoning Princeton, NJ, USA,
mathaeus.dejori@siemens.com

Jordi Duatis
NTE, 08186 Barcelona, Spain, jordid@nte.es

Martin Fuchs
University of Vienna, Faculty of Mathematics, 1090 Vienna, Austria,
martin.fuchs@univie.ac.at

Daniela Girimonte
European Space Agency, Advanced Concepts Team, 2201 Noordwijk,
The Netherlands, daniela.girimonte@esa.int

Bernhard Graimann
Institute of Automation, University of Bremen, D-28359 Bremen, Germany,
graimann@iat.uni-bremen.de

Axel Gräser
Institute of Automation, University of Bremen, D-28359 Bremen, Germany,
ag@iat.uni-bremen.de

Julie Greensmith
School of Computer Science, University of Nottingham, NG8 1BB, United
Kingdom, jqg@cs.nott.ac.uk

Rosa Laura Zavala Gutierrez
University of South Carolina, Department of Computer Science and Engineering
Columbia, SC 29208, USA, zavalagu@engr.sc.edu

Michael Huhns
University of South Carolina, Department of Computer Science and Engineering
Columbia, SC 29208, USA, huhns@engr.sc.edu

Dario Izzo
European Space Agency, Advanced Concepts Team, 2201 Noordwijk,
The Netherlands, dario.izzo@esa.in

Gaye Lightbody
University of Ulster, School of Computing & Mathematics, Newtownabbey, Co.
Antrim BT37 0QB, Northern Ireland, g.lightbody@ulster.ac.uk

Thorsten Lüth
Institute of Automation, University of Bremen, D-28359 Bremen, Germany,
lueth@iat.uni-bremen.de

Olaf Maibaum
German Aerospace Center, Department of Simulation and Software Technology,
D-38108 Braunschweig, Germany, olaf.maibaum@dlr.de

Christian Mandel
Institute of Computer Science, University of Bremen, D-28359 Bremen,
Germany, cmandel@uni-bremen.de

Giorgio Metta
University of Genoa, Department of Communication, Computer and System Sciences 16145 Genoa, Italy, giorgio.metta@iit.it

Sergio Montenegro
German Aerospace Center, Institute of Space Systems, D-28359 Bremen, Germany,
sergio.montenegro@dlr.de

Andreas Nägele
Siemens Corporate Technology, Department of Information and Communications,
D-81730 Munich, Germany, andreas.naegele.ext@siemens.com

Arnold Neumaier
University of Vienna, Faculty of Mathematics, 1090 Vienna, Austria
arnold.neumaier@univie.ac.at

Francesco Nori
Italian Institute of Technology, 16163 Genoa, Italy, francesco.nori@iit.it

Pere Ponsa
Automatic Control Department, Technical University of Catalonia, 08034 Barcelona, Spain, pedro.ponsa@upc.edu

Vicenç Puig
Automatic Control Department, Technical University of Catalonia 08034 Barcelona, Spain, vicenc.puig@upc.edu

Danijela Ristić
Institute of Automation, University of Bremen, D-28359 Bremen, Germany, ristic@iat.uni-bremen.de

Giulio Sandini
Italian Institute of Technology, 16163 Genoa, Italy, giulio.sandini@iit.it

Alfons Schuster
University of Ulster, School of Computing & Mathematics, Newtownabbey, Co. Antrim BT37 0QB, Northern Ireland, a.schuster@ulster.ac.uk

Roy Sterritt
University of Ulster, School of Computing & Mathematics, Newtownabbey, Co. Antrim BT37 0QB, Northern Ireland, r.sterritt@ulster.ac.uk

Martin Stetter
Siemens Corporate Technology, Department of Information and Communications, D-81730 Munich, Germany, stetter@siemens.com

Thomas Terzibaschian
German Aerospace Center, Department of Optical, Information Systems, D-12489 Berlin, Germany, thomas.terzibaschian@dlr.de

Diana Valbuena
Institute of Automation, University of Bremen, D-28359 Bremen, Germany, valbuena@iat.uni-bremen.de

Jürgen Vogel
European Media Laboratory, D-69118 Heidelberg, Germany, juergen.vogel@eml.org

Jörg Widmer
DoCoMo Communications, Laboratories Europe, D-80687 Munich, Germany widmer@docomolab-euro.com

Roger Woods
Queen's University Belfast, School of Electronics, Electrical Engineering & Computer Science, Belfast BT3 9DT, Northern Ireland, r.woods@qub.ac.uk

Part I
Robustness in Computer Hardware, Software, Networks, and Protocols

Chapter 1
Robustness in Digital Hardware

Roger Woods and Gaye Lightbody

Abstract The growth in electronics has probably been the equivalent of the Industrial Revolution in the past century in terms of how much it has transformed our daily lives. There is a great dependency on technology whether it is in the devices that control travel (e.g., in aircraft or cars), our entertainment and communication systems, or our interaction with money, which has been empowered by the onset of Internet shopping and banking. Despite this reliance, there is still a danger that at some stage devices will fail within the equipment's lifetime. The purpose of this chapter is to look at the factors causing failure and address possible measures to improve robustness in digital hardware technology and specifically chip technology, giving a long-term forecast that will not reassure the reader!

1.1 Introduction

The electronics market has been driven by the incredible growth in silicon density whereby the number of transistors on a single device doubles every 18–24 months, relating to an annual growth of 58%. This is commonly referred to as Moore's Law and is a relationship that is still holding some 30 years from the initial observation. By 2010, the silicon technology roadmap [Allan et al., 2002] estimates that chip sizes will be in the region of 4 billion transistors while reaching clock rates of 10 GHz; this will be expected to exceed 50 GHz by 2017 [IRTS, 2003]. Naturally, this increase in silicon density opens up a wealth of capabilities, permitting extremely complex functions to be implemented as a complete system-on-a-chip (SoC) instead of as a collection of individual components. In real terms, this has driven a number of consumer markets and the computer industry. High-tech products and devices such as digital TV, DVDs, stereos, PCs, PDAs, notebooks, and mobile telephones are all the result of these advances. In addition to area and speed

R. Woods
School of Electronics, Electrical Engineering and Computer Science, ECIT, Queen's University Belfast, Queen's Island, Queen's Road, Belfast, BT3 9DT, Northern Ireland
email: r.woods@qub.ac.uk

A. Schuster (ed.), *Robust Intelligent Systems,* DOI: 10.1007/978-1-84800-261-6_1,
© Springer-Verlag London Limited 2008

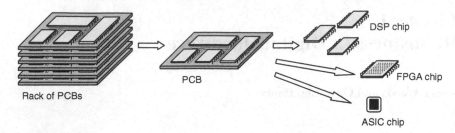

DSP chip

PCB

FPGA chip

Rack of PCBs

ASIC chip

Fig. 1.1 Evolving hardware technologies

gains, reductions in power consumption have also been achieved. This is illustrated in Fig. 1.1, which shows a rack of printed circuit boards (PCBs) being replaced by a single PCB, or in some cases, a single chip such as a Digital Signal Processor microprocessor (DSPμ), a Field Programmable Gate Array (FPGA), or an Application Specific Integrated Circuit (ASIC). A more detailed description of these will be given within this chapter.

Whereas the shrinking of the dimensions of silicon technology provides more transistors as well as making them go faster and consume less power, it also causes problems with regard to robustness. As stated within this book, a robust system is widely viewed to be *a system that tolerates faults*. We are now dealing with robustness on several fronts. Firstly, with shrinking technology we are now coping with progressively sensitive transistors whose effects have to increasingly be dealt in the design process [Phillips, 2007]. Secondly, the methodologies needed to design advanced silicon chips have not matured at the same rate as the increase in silicon density. This has resulted in a gap between the rate of growth in silicon density (58%) to the rate of increase in transistors implemented per staff-month (21%), commonly referred to as the *design productivity gap* [Rowen, 2002], as illustrated in Fig. 1.2.

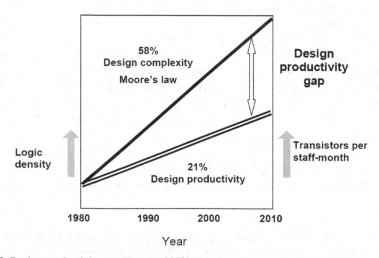

Fig. 1.2 Design productivity gap [Rowen, 2002]

Thirdly, the design problem has changed. More than a decade ago, a single chip represented a component of a system but now the chip can represent the full system itself, hence *system-on-chip*, involving a number of technologies ranging from sensors to technology for receiving data signals. These technologies typically involve different design approaches, and additional care is needed as they can interfere with each other. Lastly, there is also an expectation that electronic devices will not fail, which was a strong selling point over the less reliable mechanical and analog technology. This is increasingly becoming more difficult to achieve as both the technology becomes more unpredictable and the tools lag behind the methodology.

The purpose of the chapter is to address some of the issues regarding robustness of hardware, specifically digital hardware. The aim is to present an insight and discussion on the elements of digital hardware system design that provide a level of robustness. It starts with a brief discussion of issues of robustness in hardware highlighting increasing device complexity. The chapter then focuses on hardware technologies and describes the characteristics of various types of hardware platforms, namely ASIC, DSPμ, microprocessors, and FPGA. The description also gives details of their structure and programming model with a particular focus on robustness. The next section covers the types of faults that can occur in silicon hardware and the design and operation techniques available to avoid these faults. The latter sections will then give an overview of the approaches currently available for proving hardware robustness ranging from the highly practical to some of the more exotic solutions. Finally, the chapter will conclude by considering the future problems caused by process variations and the challenges this will create.

1.2 Digital Hardware Technologies

In the evolution of silicon technology over the past 40 years, a number of different types of hardware technologies have emerged and can be generally classified as being either ASIC, programmable based designs (DSPμ, microprocessors), or as FPGAs. A brief description of each is given in Fig. 1.3.

The first offerings were the 74 series logic chips in the 1960s, which were the building block for many "budding techies" up to recently. This was followed by the first microprocessor, the Intel 4004 processor in 1971, which along with microcontrollers have now formed the core for many applications with lower bandwidth requirements. The concept of developing custom large-scale integration (LSI) components emerged in the 1970s, but the development of the programmable logic array (PLA) in 1978 and the first FPGA in 1984 was the start of an increasing interest in programmable hardware structures. Remarkably, this was followed by a renaissance of developing dedicated hardware implementations or ASICs in the late 1980s.

The first aspect is to highlight that silicon fabrication works on the principle that each chip will meet the specification for which it was designed. Therefore, a margin of error is built into each design such that it is guaranteed to work at the required specification. To this end, two specifications are typically catered for, the *industrial* one and the more rigorous *military* specification; these represent the

Processor based design

- Microprocessors, DSPμ, reconfigurable processors
- Designed for flexibility of operation
- Very wide range of applications
- Markets can vary widely, e.g. space applications or in products with a long life span
- Reliability and robustness are key specifically:
  ○ diversity
  ○ cohesiveness
  ○ coupling
  ○ and the notion of recovery

FPGA chip

- Software *and* the hardware are reprogrammable
- Captures some of the aspects of ASIC along with the programmable notion of software
- This allows an additional layer of robustness by providing means for:
  ○ redundancy
  ○ restoration
  ○ self healing and self repair

ASIC chip

- Created for a single or limited range of purposes
- Best performance in terms of speed, silicon area and power consumed
- High volume markets where performance and unit cost critical
- Typically a one-off design
- Little consideration in the design process for robustness largely as the technology will probably be superseded in a number of years or even months!
- Time-to-market critical

Fig. 1.3 Basic technology comparison

worst-case conditions at which the device will operate. Heat is a key issue as it decreases device speed and can accelerate possible chip malfunctions but it can be taken into account in the design and simulation stages. The major focus on *right first time* design is driven by the spiraling costs of *masks*, which are the result of the design process and are used to fabricate the chip. Typically, they cost $1M to create [LaPedus, 2007]; a price that is incurred whether they are needed for a small number of prototypes or for a full deployment of a million devices. Even so, yet as many as 55% of designs are failing to pass first silicon [Robertson, 2004] therefore incurring a great loss of money and time!

In addition to the highly pessimistic design process, another interesting feature impacting robustness was first observed by Tsugio Makimoto of Sony. It was coined *Makimoto's wave* and is illustrated in Fig. 1.4. Makimoto observed that system construction seemed to be swinging between *standardization* where silicon chips were created as standard parts (e.g., TTL chips, microprocessors, and then FPGAs) and *customization* in the form of LSI and ASICs developed for single or a restricted

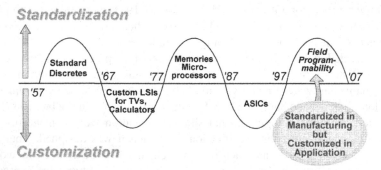

Fig. 1.4 Makimoto's wave (Source: Electronics Weekly, January, 1991)

range of applications. For the *standardized* part, the key attribute was usability across a range of applications implying *granularity* in the form of a building block that could be used to build a larger function for a range of applications, therefore also supporting *diversity*. The customized solution implies a limited range of applications, therefore robustness is not a key criteria either in terms of the application range needed or, indeed, the lifetime of the product.

1.2.1 More Detailed Description of Technology

In the previous section, the various types of technologies were briefly outlined. This section provides a more detailed overview and their current status.

Microprocessors currently have clock rates of 4 GHz, and recent predictions under the International Technological Roadmap for Semiconductors [IRTS, 2003] suggest clock rates will exceed 50 GHz by 2017. Whereas these performance figures are staggering, it must be remembered that the microprocessor has a von Neumann architecture where computations are performed in a serial fashion, not ideal for highly parallel algorithms. It could be argued that the inefficiency is an acceptable price to pay for the high levels of programmability that the microprocessor offers, but energy considerations are becoming a critical design factor in many applications and this level of inefficiency cannot be tolerated. The programming route is via high-level software platforms and, as the user will no doubt be well aware, this platform has a wide application base. Evolutions over the past decade include *hyper-threading* [Koufaty and Marr, 2003] supported on the Intel Pentium 4 device and the evolution of multiple processors on a single die.

DSPμs are dedicated hardware platforms that are based on a different underlying architecture from the microprocessor, namely the Harvard architecture, which uses separate buses for instructions and data and has physically separate storage memories for program and data. The device is programmed in much the same fashion as the microprocessor and is applied largely in the DSP market as a commodity part. An overview of DSP architectures can be found in [Glossner et al., 2000] and [Tan and Heinzelman, 2003]. The major innovations in DSPμs include very long instruction words (VLIW) and single input multiple data (SIMD) architectural changes [Rui et al., 2003]. These innovations are possible due to the computational needs of many DSP computations.

FPGAs have emerged from being glue logic components in the early 1980s to offering complete processing platforms for complex systems. They offer programmability, but unlike the microprocessor/DSPμ, this involves changing the hardware architecture of the device. This offers a number of advantages from a robustness perspective. If the FPGA is used as part of a system, it is possible to reconfigure the hardware and operation to overcome faults caused either in the design stage or as a result of malfunction. Given that the device comprises a lot of similar cells that can be migrated to different parts of the device, it does introduce the possibility of *self-healing* [Andraka and Brady, 2002, Samudrala et al., 2004, Gokhale et al., 2006]. However, a key aspect of digital design implementation is the standardization and verification of designs, which the concept of *self-healing* acts against.

ASICs and toward system-on-chip (SoC) involve a detailed and costly design process plus the costs to produce the mask for fabrication. A number of variations include *standard cell*, which comprises cells of pre-designed logic blocks and *structured ASIC*, which is a more modern version of gate array technology where the structure is mostly developed and the only custom fabrication step is the definition of the interconnection. The one-off costs called non-recurrence engineering (NRE) costs can be amortized into the component cost when volumes are large. Thus the nature of the designs are such that they are heavily restricted, as the name suggests, and little thought will have gone into making the designs robust unless the application directly requires it. In this case, particular choices may be made to use, for example, radiation hard fabrication technologies if the applications require this level of protection, or even to duplicate circuitry [Hollander et al., 1995, Lacoe et al., 2000, Ruano et al., 2007].

ASSP (application specific standard product) (includes emerging platforms such as, for example, reconfigurable DSPs) have also emerged. It is clear from the descriptions above that there is no single suitable technology; ASSPs combine the *fixed architecture* structure of microprocessors or DSPμs but provide some level of hardware programmability to allow the processor to be customized to the specific application. This represents the new types of technologies hinted at in the post-2007 part of the Makimoto wave, which are largely standardized but which can be customized for specific applications.

In truth, a lot of variations of these classifications are beginning to appear. For example, FPGAs now have embedded microprocessors such as the Xilinx MicroBlaze and the Altera NIOS processor, which can be customized for specific applications. DSPμs are also becoming complex SoC platforms with dedicated hardware units for high-performance wireless communications and other functions. IBM has been developing platforms with embedded FPGAs and Intel has been embedding DSP engines within their RISC (reduced instruction set computer) technology. It is clear that hybrids are beginning to emerge allowing users to select architectures based on system requirements and making it difficult to categorize the technologies in the classical way that has been done here. These technologies are best compared against time-to-market, performance, price, ease of development, energy efficiency, as well as a number of other emerging factors, such as radiation hardware, ability to incorporate legacy designs, and upgradability and, of course, robustness.

1.3 Issues with Testing and Verifying Digital Hardware

Digital design is subject to faults in PCB or chip design formats due to errors in the manufacturing process. It is therefore essential that the circuit is tested both prior to delivery to the customer and also prior to operation in normal day-to-day use. From a manufacturing point-of-view, it is important to carry out *fault analysis* to detect where the fault has occurred in order to isolate any production problems. However, it is typical that faults will occur and a certain level of faults will be tolerated, thus it falls on the designer to create a series of tests that will allow *fault detection* thereby establishing whether a fault has occurred in order that the producer can eliminate faulty chips/PCBs and thus remove them at production.

In electronic design generally but IC design specifically, there are a number of causes of faults. These are classified as:

Open Circuit where the circuit connection is broken thus causing an "open" circuit. This can occur due to *electric migration* where the electric fields are so strong that the metal atoms migrate thereby causing a break in the connection and also due to *current overstress* where large currents make the wire lift from the silicon thereby breaking the connection and once again causing an open circuit.

Short Circuit which can be caused by defects in the fabrication material used (e.g., silicon oxide) or in the fabrication process itself where the mask used to create the transistors is not aligned properly. The result is that correct isolation is not provided and a short circuit can occur thereby causing malfunction.

Latch Up which is a special condition that can happen in CMOS (complementary metal oxide semiconductor) circuits where transient currents force CMOS gates to be stuck at a value, thereby preventing it from changing as required. It can be a temporary condition that terminates upon removal of the inputs or a condition that requires a full system reset or even replacement of damaged parts.

Single Event Upsets (SEU), which are errors induced by radiation effects when charged particles, typically from cosmic rays, lose energy by ionizing the silicon material through which they pass, leaving behind a wake of electron-hole pairs. Two types of radiation have been identified as the primary cause of SEUs in semiconductor devices: alpha particle radiation (which has now been largely avoided by higher-purity package materials) and atmospheric neutrons, originating from the effects of cosmic rays hitting the Earth's atmosphere, which remain the primary cause for SEU effects today. Typically, they appear as transient logic pulses or manifest themselves as bit changes in memory or flip-flop storage. They tend to be transient soft errors and are not destructive to the technology.

1.3.1 Static Faults

The static faults, which broadly speaking tend to be physical defects and electrical faults, are dealt with at the design stage and can be tested at manufacture and in some cases during normal operation by applying the *built-in self test* (BIST) sequence prior to operation. A physical fault will manifest as a logical fault that can be either static or dynamic. The dynamic faults appear at certain times and are usually caused by timing faults. This should be catered for within the design cycle and should be avoided. Static faults are logical faults and possibly due to one of the effects listed above and thus must be checked. The designer can incorporate the impact of these faults using a number of models.

One of the most common mechanisms that is also used commercially is the *stuck-at model*, which assumes that the logic gates will be *stuck-at-0* or *stuck-at-1* as a result of the physical defects and electrical faults. Therefore, the aim is to generate a test sequence that will reveal the error by producing an incorrect sequence at the output of the chip or circuit due to the presence of the fault. From a design perspective, we do this by stipulating the *stuck-at* condition and then determining which input sequences will produce the errored output sequence. We test every *stuck-at* condition in the circuit and generate a test file, which will then detect a percentage of the errors. This is known as *fault coverage*.

The relationship between faults and yield is given in Fig. 1.5. If the production yield of fault-free circuits on a wafer is Y, then $Y = 0$ means that all circuits are faulty and $Y = 1$ means that all circuits are fault free. If FC is the fault coverage, then $FC = 0$ means that tests do not detect any faults and $FC = 1$ means that tests detect all possible faults. Thus, the defect level (DL) is given by the graph outline. It is easy to determine that a higher fault coverage is desirable with typical production lines ($Y = 0.7 - -0.8$).

The major difficulty with generating this test file to provide the fault coverage is that the designer has only a very limited access to the circuit in terms of inputs and outputs. In a chip, this will only be provided through the input and output pins and with multi-layered boards, and it is now becoming increasingly difficult to even monitor individual chips without adding test connections; this is costly in terms of area and increases the risk of design failure due to their very existence.

Two terms that are an important measure in fault detection and design for test are *observability*, which is used to indicate how well the state of a signal on an internal node may be detected on the output pins, and *controllability*, which describes the

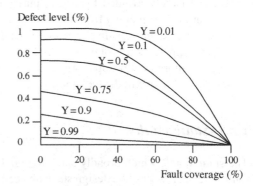

Fig. 1.5 Relationship between defect level and fault coverage [Hurst, 1988]

Fig. 1.6 Variation in observability and controllability in silicon chips

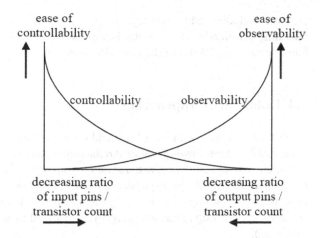

case with which a particular internal signal value can be set by applying signals to the input pins. Figure 1.6 shows how these values vary in a silicon chip.

The main problem is that as complexity grows, the number of logic levels between input and output grows, meaning that large proportions of the transistors can be neither tested nor observed. The designer's job is thus to add additional circuitry that makes the internal nodes more controllable and observable. This can be done by using a scan path to the circuit allowing the nodes to be linked into one big scan path in addition to their normal operation. This is now a standard within the IEEE, called the "IEEE boundary-scan standard 1149", and can be used at board level as well as chip level.

1.3.2 Dynamic Faults

There is a well-established mechanism for robustness in IC design with regard to static faults, as the chip manufacturer will normally insist that a chip design will be delivered in terms of the mask sets, etc., along with the necessary test data to provide 95% minimum fault coverage, i.e., 0.95 for Fig. 1.5. This value is used on the basis that their statistics tell them that 95% fault coverage is usually good enough to ensure that *no* chips sent from the production line will contain faults. However, dynamic faults are more problematic and represent a much greater problem with regard to robustness.

With regard to CMOS latch up, literature tends to suggest that a lot of problems can be avoided by using specific technology fixes and by giving careful attention to CMOS outputs, their loading, and the stresses applied to them in order to avoid the high transient currents that cause the problem [Naughton and Tyler, 2005, Boselli and Duvvury, 2005]. However, the SEU issue is becoming much more critical as the effect is greater as transistors are effectively becoming smaller compared with the particles as the technology scales. It is of particular concern for airborne or space industries because of the increased risk in higher atmospheres. A lot of vendors are now including additional test circuits to test for these errors as the circuit is operating [Hollander et al., 1995, Hentschke et al., 2002, Makihara et al., 2003, Samudrala et al., 2004, Golshan and Bozorgzadeh, 2007].

1.4 Robustness Approaches

Robustness was defined in this book and elsewhere and summarized as possessing some or all of the following features: *redundancy, compensation, diversity, mechanical robustness, granularity, restoration (cognitive), cohesion and coupling, recovery, self-healing, self-repair (physical)*. From the authors' perspective, the following aspects feature strongly in the design and realization of digital circuitry namely *redundancy, diversity, granularity, recovery*, as well as *self-healing* and *self-repair* (physical).

1.4.1 Redundancy

Typically, redundancy is applied for two reasons in digital hardware implementation, namely for *improved design performance* and for *test purposes*.

1.4.1.1 Redundancy for Design Performance

Redundancy can be employed at many levels in hardware. At the system level, redundancy is directly related to cost and will be avoided unless there is a strong application need for it. For example, the equipment may be either remotely or inconveniently located making repair a costly exercise as the equipment is difficult to access. In this case, several modules may be co-located along with the necessary test circuitry to ensure correct detection of the errored state. The circuitry can be either switched on live, i.e., *hot insertion*, or turned on when the equipment is in reset mode, i.e., temporarily turned-off.

Given that redundancy capability for design can be exploited at the system level as suggested above, there is little requirement to deliberately introduce redundancy in the components described in Section 1.2.1 as this will involve additional silicon area and therefore increase component cost. There are a few exceptions to this. For example, the circuit in Fig. 1.7(a) implements the digital function $f = A.\overline{B}.D + B.C.D$.

However, when the input B changes, as shown, both AND gates can temporarily give a "0" thus giving an output of "0", which is not logically correct. This can be avoided by adding a *redundant* gate, shown in shading in Fig. 1.7(b), which always ensures a logical 1 to the OR when B changes ensuring a constant "1" and avoiding any glitching problems that may result. These types of redundancy techniques are employed for specific design quality reasons but should be avoided because the techniques used to perform static testing of the circuit in Fig. 1.7(a) are now complicated

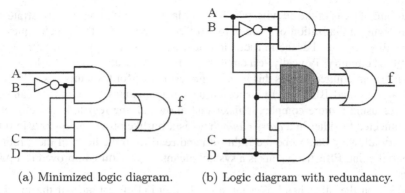

(a) Minimized logic diagram.   (b) Logic diagram with redundancy.

Fig. 1.7 Redundancy in logic design

by the addition of the gate in Fig. 1.7(b). In some cases, this level of application can make the circuits untestable.

FPGAs, on the other hand, offer an alternative to employing redundancy due to their internal structure. As highlighted earlier, the FPGA structure typically comprises a series of logic cells that can be interconnected in different ways by programming the interconnection. FPGAs are sold on the basis of discrete chip sizes, which simply scales the number of available resources. With fixed resources within a chosen device, some level of unused logic may exist, which the designer can exploit to provide redundancy.

1.4.1.2 Test Circuitry

As was highlighted in Section 1.3, testing is becoming an increasingly difficult task as transistor counts increase. For this reason, test is now part of the design cycle, and there is an increased "emphasis" on *design for test*, i.e., introducing redundant circuitry with the aim of making the circuit more testable. The key diagram in this discussion is Fig. 1.6, which shows that our ability to control and observe internal circuitry is decreasing as the ratio of input and output pins to transistor count decreases, making it ever more difficult to obtain adequate fault coverage as design complexity grows. A truer description of this graph would show a large proportion of the chip that we can neither control nor observe from a testing point of view. It is vital that we continue to demonstrate that electronics is a robust technology, thus there is a very strong need to increase these levels and achieve the necessary fault tolerance.

Design for testability is typically based on three concepts, employing ad-hoc techniques, scan path, and built-in self test (BIST). Ad hoc as the Latin suggests is employing design methods that are suitable for the design under consideration. This includes obvious things like the introduction of test points that allow the designer to get data into the heart of the circuit and also to observe output from the same or similar point; isolation of key circuits, e.g., the clock allowing the designer to enter a test clock as opposed to the normal clock; adding additional circuitry to allow bypassing of parts of the circuits, which is similar to the use of test points; strategies for allowing initialization of circuits in a different mode. All these techniques are reasonably obvious, but the introduction of test points and bypass circuitry infers additional circuitry. Typically, test circuitry will constitute an extra 10% silicon area, which is a unrequited cost as this area is only ever used for test purposes.

Scan path and BIST are two specific design techniques for testing. Scan path involves using a more complex register that allows all the registers in a circuit to be connected together in a *daisy chain*. This is a bit like providing *tunnels* into the circuitry allowing data to be fed right into and read from the heart of the circuit at a desired point. Effectively, this is a system means of providing improved test point access.

BIST, on the other hand, is a more crude method of testing. All the previous techniques involve creating the hardware and the necessary data streams to provide the testing of the circuitry. BIST employs a *random number generator* to produce a huge amount of data that is then fed into the circuit and a *signature analysis circuit* to capture the output data produced by the circuit under test, producing a final signature, namely a binary word. If any test problem has occurred, then the signature produced will be different, or strictly speaking, will have a very small statistical chance of being the same! All of the above methods involve introducing redundant circuitry with the aim of making the circuitry more testable and thus more robust.

Redundancy also features strongly in methods to protect against SEUs. Here, Triple Mode Redundancy (TMR) can be applied to allow a majority vote, that is, the logic is repeated three times and the outputs compared with a choice made for the two that are the same, providing that there is not a failure in the voting logic itself [Andraka and Brady, 2002, Samudrala et al., 2004]. Naturally, such extreme measures would be more applicable in safety critical scenarios and applications most susceptible to SEU effects.

1.4.2 Diversity

The notion of diversity can be best described in Makimoto's wave in Fig. 1.4, which shows how the various technology evolutions have swung between standardization and customization. As the name suggests, customization implies building hardware that has a very restricted application focus, whereas the standard components such as FPGAs and microprocessors can be applied to a diverse range of applications. The provision of suitable programming environments for both these technologies has meant a wide and varied range of applications. For example, most recently there has been a huge interest in employing FPGAs for scientific computing applications as acceleration to arrays of processors and companies such as Silicon Graphics and Cray who built their reputation of building processor chips are now offering processor/FPGA platforms. The attraction of being able to construct highly parallel architectures for some scientific applications gives huge potential.

The microprocessor itself has had a wide and varied application environment. For example, processors are now starting to be used quite widely in the automobile industry to provide the range of applications and comforts required by many drivers today. A whole genera of computer music has now been created where the composer is now using computers, typically Apple Macs, as instruments. This is only to name but a few applications. It should not be underestimated that this diversification is based on the inherent reliability of the technology, which relies heavily on the design principles described in the previous section.

1.4.3 Granularity

When we talk about granularity of a design, it can mean any one of a number of things. If the application scales, can the design scale with it? There are a number of levels of granularity. At the highest level, this could be a matter of using more PCBs to meet the system demands or adding additional chips. As we go down the level of granularity, it would mean enabling greater performance output from the chip designs. Here, performance enhancement could be met by retargeting the design to a more powerful technology, maybe the current FPGA devices or latest ASIC foundry technology. But true design scalability is a multidimensional challenge that has fueled a research area devoted to parameterizable design and *design for reuse* strategies. The following section will detail some of the key issues in need of consideration when undertaking a fully parameterizable design. The benefits of rising to these challenges is also discussed with emphasis given on how design practices such as these aim to add robustness to chip development.

1.4.3.1 Design Reuse—IP Cores

The increase in transistor count, leading to the incorporation of an entire system on a single device, has resulted in an exceptionally complex design route with component heterogeneity escalating problematic issues regarding chip design and in particular test and verification. As highlighted earlier, the design productivity gap of Fig. 1.2 means that we must think of dramatically different ways of constructing systems. Specifically, this means treating the design process in a more abstract fashion by representing designs as comprising components that, if possible, can be reused from existing designs.

The concept of creating a system in this modular fashion has effectively created an industry in third-party products referred to as silicon Intellectual Property (IP) cores, also known as virtual circuits (VCs). These range from actual silicon layout known as *hard cores* through to *soft cores*, which can be in the form of efficient code targeted to programmable DSP or RISC processors, or dedicated cores captured in a Hardware Description Language (HDL). Effectively, *design for reuse* methodologies provide flexibility allowing designs targeted to one project to be applied to another one with different specifications.

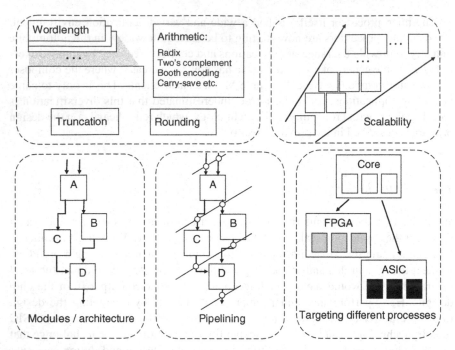

Fig. 1.8 IP parameters

The key aspect in developing IP cores is the concept of identifying the parameters needed for the general usage of the cores, as demonstrated in Fig. 1.8. Parameterization leads to a library of cores that can be targeted to a range of specifications, without the need to alter the internal workings of the code. The system should effectively allow a number of parameters to be fed into the top level of the code and then passed down through the different levels of abstraction of the code to the lowest levels [Shannon, 2002, Lightbody et al., 2003]. Obviously, considerable effort is needed at the architecture level to develop this parameterizable circuit architecture. This initial expense in terms of time and effort undoubtedly hinders the expanded use of *design for reuse* principles but could result in savings in the long run.

In Fig. 1.8, design aspects such as arithmetic effects, i.e., type of arithmetic used namely fixed or floating point representations, need to be defined as a parameter. *Pipelining*, which is a design technique to speed up performance, can be applied but it has timing implications. The cores must also be able to be applied across a range of platforms, which, as the earlier description showed, can vary quite dramatically in terms of their internal architecture. Identifying the key parameters and then designing the IP core for them requires a detailed understanding of the range of implementations in which the core may be used. The aim is to balance flexibility with the additional workload and resulting benefits. This is important as over-parameterization of a design not only affects the development time but also affects the verification and testing so to ensure that all permutations of the core have been considered [Gajski et al., 2000].

1.4.4 Recovery, Self-healing, Self-repair

Generally speaking, electronic systems are designed for usually a short life span when compared with mechanical products because of trends in product aging, i.e., yesterday's design. In addition, newer technology is emerging at such a pace that the performance gain of the new technology is such that the need to reconfigure or self-heal older technology is not worth the cost of adding the extra functionality to achieve this. However, this assumes that in the construction of such systems, the specification is fully defined and does not need to be altered at a later stage of the design flow. Given the nature of recent systems, the design process is now viewed as one that is constantly evolving.

Thus, the programmable nature of certainly microprocessor and, more recently, FPGAs present a highly attractive, low-risk proposition for system designers. A heterogeneous platform comprising processors and FPGAs will have a worse performance profile in terms of power-area-speed performance, but this drop-off in performance can be put against the added advantage of reconfigurability allowing change during the design cycle and, indeed, afterward. From an engineering perspective, this represents a good engineering safety net, but as the title of this section indicates, users have taken this to a further extreme effectively, with circuits that will self-repair or self-heal [Gokhale et al., 2006, Andraka and Brady, 2002, Samudrala et al., 2004].

1.4.4.1 FPGA Reconfiguration

The opportunity offered by the reconfigurability property of FPGAs is very appealing. It is first worthwhile explaining the operation of FPGAs to see what level of self-healing the device offers. Most FPGAs are based on static random access memory (SRAM). The basic principle is that the FPGA is programmed exactly like a memory, but rather than storing the information as in a conventional memory, the FPGA uses the data to program circuitry that performs the required function. Thus, reprogramming the memory is effectively changing the function. The programming information is created by the design tools that correctly mimic the function that the user programmed into the tools.

One of the main issues with processors is that they are very inefficient. Typically, [Hennessey and Patterson, 1996] in their famous text indicated that most computationally complex applications spend 90% of their execution time in only 10% of their code, and the instructions in this 10% of the code will vary from application to application. The attraction of being able to dramatically increase this level of performance by programming the architecture to match the performance requirements holds a great attraction from a power-area-speed perspective. The concept was captured by the notion of FPGA Custom Computing Machines (FCCMs) for which a dedicated conference has been run every year in Napa, California.

1.4.4.2 The Self-repair Rationale

FCCMs typically comprise FPGAs connected to a microprocessor that stores the reconfiguration data necessary to convert the FPGA into the required functional engine. The system can either be pre-designed to cope with a number of modes of operation, thus there is either a required sequence of reconfiguration of the device or the reconfiguration is triggered by the hardware itself to load the best configuration data to match the needs of the device. The reconfiguration can either be performed by completely reprogramming the device or partially reconfiguring it [Sezer et al., 1998]. The problem with full reconfiguration is that the device can be unoperational for up to several milliseconds. In a real application where the data needs to be processed in the region of millions of cycles per second, this means the temporary storage of a considerable amount of data. In addition, the rate at which reconfiguration takes place can then be counter-productive as the graph in Fig. 1.9 indicates. This graph was produced for a key image processing function in image compression and shows that even though the FPGA implementation is much faster than the processor implementation, the reconfiguration time required means that it will only be efficient after a certain time.

Researchers have gotten around this limitation in a number of ways, firstly by performing *partial reconfiguration*, which involves changing part of the programming information of the FPGA while it is still operating and actually designing the circuits to allow this to happen. This involves splitting the application into a number of sequential stages. Each of these stages could then be implemented on the FPGA in turn, with the device being reconfigured between stages to support the next operation. Alternatively or in addition to partial reconfiguration, the amount of reconfiguration information could be compressed therefore speeding up reconfiguration [Compton and Hauck, 2002].

The real panacea would be to develop a system where the designer does not have to worry about creating the programming and that the device would reconfigure itself. These systems are known as evolvable systems [Stoica et al., 2001] and are an active area of research. Researchers have been building truly evolvable systems for a range of applications by exploiting the reconfigurability property of FPGAs. Whereas this is attractive from an implementation perspective, it is laden with trou-

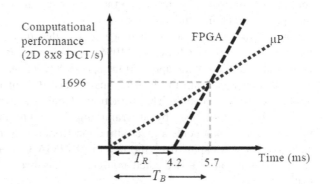

Fig. 1.9 Impact of reconfiguration time for a "8X8 2D discrete cosine transform (DCT)" implementation

ble for an engineer. For example, how can you be sure that the system has correctly reconfigured? This questions the concept of whether there is an ideal specification system that a product will work to or whether the user is prepared to accept a system that will vary in quality of operation. We think that this has to be sold to the public, but some of the discussion in the summary about where technology is evolving to may influence this argument.

1.5 Summary

The chapter has considered the robustness of hardware systems covering a range of topics including *redundancy, diversity, granularity, recovery*, as well as *self-healing* and *self-repair* (physical). The discussion has been given from an engineering perspective, arguably with a word of caution about the opportunities of reconfigurable FPGAs to employ self-healing or self-repair properties. The reality is that up to now, this additional level of functionality has been a luxury, and it should also be realized that the designer is responsible to ensure the correct operation of any circuitry, even circuitry added with the good intention to make it robust! The long-term future presents some interesting problems though. Reliability has been key to Moore's Law, but future indications suggest that upcoming technologies will start to be very unreliable due to the variation in performance of the transistors as a result of shrinking dimensions [Constantinescu, 2003]. We will then just have to work with the reality of dramatic transistor speed variation or transistors that may not work at all. Self-healing and self-repair may then be required steps in the design process. From an engineering perspective, this is a horrendous nightmare that might be best avoided, thus signaling an end to Moore's Law?

References

Allan, A., Edenfeld, D., Joyner, W.H., J., Kahng, A., Rodgers, M., and Zorian, Y. (2002). 2001 Technology Roadmap for Semiconductors. *Computer*, 35(1):42–53.

Andraka, R. and Brady, J. (2002). Low complexity method for detecting configuration upsets in SRAM-based FPGAs. In *Proceedings 5th International Conference on Military and Aerospace Programmable Logic Devices*, volume B4, Maryland, USA.

Boselli, G. and Duvvury, C. (2005). Trends and challenges to ESD and Latch-up designs for nanometer CMOS technologies. *Microelectronics and Reliability*, 45(9–11):1406–1414.

Compton, K. and Hauck, S. (2002). Reconfigurable computing: a survey of systems and software. *ACM Computer Survey*, 34(2):171–210.

Constantinescu, C. (2003). Trends and challenges in VLSI circuit reliability. *IEEE Micro*, 23(4):14–19.

Gajski, D., Wu, A.-H., Chaiyakul, V., Mori, S., Nukiyama, T., and Bricaud, P. (2000). Essential issues for IP reuse. In *Proceedings of the ASP-DAC 2000 Design Automation Conference, Asia and South Pacific*, pages 37–42, January 25–28, Yokohama, Japan. IEEE Standards Office.

Glossner, J., Moreno, J., Moudgill, M., Derby, J., Hokenek, E., Meltzer, D., Shvadron, U., and Ware, M. (2000). Trends in compilable DSP architecture. In *Workshop on Signal Processing Systems (SIPS'2000)*, pages 181–1999, October 11–13, Lafayette, LA, USA. IEEE Press.

Gokhale, M., Graham, P., Wirthlin, M., and Johnson, D. (2006). Dynamic reconfiguration for management of radiation-induced faults in FPGAs. *International Journal of Embedded Systems*, 2(1):28–38.

Golshan, S. and Bozorgzadeh, E. (2007). Single-event-upset (SEU) awareness in FPGA routing. In *Proceedings 44th Confenrence on Design Automation*, pages 330–333. ACM Press, New York.

Hennessey, J. and Patterson, D. (1996). *Computer Architecture: A Quantitative Approach*. Morgan Kaufmann Publishers Inc., New York.

Hentschke, R., Marques, F., Lima, F., Carro, L., Susin, A., and Reis, R. (2002). Analyzing area and performance penalty of protecting different digital modules with Hamming code and triple modular redundancy. In *Proceedings 15th Symposium on Integrated Circuits and Systems Design*, pages 95–100, September 9–14, Porto Alegre, RS, Brazil. IEEE Computer Society.

Hollander, H., Carlson, B., and Bennett, T. (1995). Synthesis of SEU-tolerant ASICs using concurrent error correction. In *Proceedings 5th Great Lakes Symposium on VLSI*, pages 90–93, March 16–18, Washington, USA. IEEE Computer Society.

Hurst, S. (1988). *VLSI Testing: digital and mixed analogue/digital techniques*. IEE, Savoy Place, London.

IRTS (2003). International roadmap for semiconductors. http://www.itrs.net/.

Koufaty, D. and Marr, D. (2003). Hyperthreading technology in the netburst microarchitecture. *IEEE Micro*, 23(2):56–65.

Lacoe, R., Osborn, J., Koga, R., Brown, S., and Mayer, D. (2000). Application of hardness-by-design methodology to radiation-tolerant ASIC technologies. *IEEE Transactions on Nuclear Science*, 47(6):2334–2341.

LaPedus, M. (2007). Open-silicon to drive down mask costs. *EE Times Online*. http://www.eetimes.com/showArticle.jhtml?articleID$=$198900081.

Lightbody, G., Woods, R., and Walke, R. (2003). Design of a parameterizable silicon intellectual property core for QR-based RLS filtering. *IEEE Transactions on Very Large Scale Integration (VLSI) Systems*, 11(4):659–678.

Makihara, A., Sakaide, Y., Tsuchiya, Y., Arimitsu, T., Asai, H., Iide, Y., Shindou, H., Kuboyama, S., and Matsuda, S. (2003). Single-event effects in 0.18/spl mu/m CMOS commercial processes. *IEEE Transactions on Nuclear Science*, 50(6):2135–2138.

Naughton, J. and Tyler, M. (2005). Best methods to minimize latch-up sensitivities in semiconductor circuits. In *IEEE Workshop on Microelectronics and Electron Devices*, pages 95–98, April 15, Boise, Idaho, US. IEEE Standards Office.

Phillips, I. (2007). When less means more; and more, the-same? In *IEEE International Symposium on Industrial Embedded Systems*, July 4–6, Lisbon, Portugal. IEEE Industrial Electronics Society.

Robertson, C. (2004). Silicon modeling of nanometer systems-on-chip. In *Proceedings 4th IEEE International Workshop on System-on-Chip for Real-Time Applications*, pages 19–22, July 19–21, Banff, Canada. IEEE Computer Society.

Rowen, C. (2002). Reducing SoC simulation and development time. *Computer*, 35(12):29–34.

Ruano, O., Reyes, P., Maestro, J., Sterpone, L., and Reviriego, P. (2007). An experimental analysis of SEU sensitiveness on system knowledge-based hardening techniques. In *IEEE Conference on Design and Diagnostics of Electronic Circuits and Systems (DDECS'07)*, pages 1–6, April 11–13, Krakow, Poland. IEEE Press.

Rui, S., Ying, H., Dong-Hui, W., Tie-Jun, Z., Qian, Y., and Chao-Huan, H. (2003). A 32-bit hybrid microprocessor design for multimedia applications. In *Proceedings 5th International Conference on ASIC*, page (2.3), Beijing, China, October 21–24. IEEE Press.

Samudrala, P., Ramos, J., and Katkoori, S. (2004). Selective triple Modular redundancy (STMR) based single-event upset (SEU) tolerant synthesis for FPGAs. *IEEE Transactions on Nuclear Science*, 51(5, Part 4):2957–69.

Sezer, S., Woods, R., Heron, J., and Marshall, A. (1998). Fast partial reconfiguration for FCCMs. In *Proceedings of the IEEE Symposium on FPGAs for Custom Computing Machines (FCCM'98)*, page 318, Washington, DC. IEEE Computer Society.

Shannon, L. (2002). *Impact of Intellectual Property Cores on Field Programmable Gate Array Designs*. National Library of Canada.

Stoica, A., Zebulum, R., Keymeulen, D., Tawel, R., Daud, T., and Thakoor, A. (2001). Reconfigurable VLSI architectures for evolvable hardware: from experimental field programmable transistor arrays to evolution-orientedchips. *IEEE Transactions on Very Large Scale Integration (VLSI) Systems*, 9(1):227–232.

Tan, E. J. and Heinzelman, W. B. (2003). DSP architectures: past, present and futures. *SIGARCH Computer Architecture News*, 31(3):6–19.

Chapter 2
Multiagent-Based Fault Tolerance Management for Robustness

Rosa Laura Zavala Gutierrez and Michael Huhns

Abstract Despite the use of software engineering best practices and tools, it would be very risky to assume that the software that is developed today is fault-free. Moreover, we have to consider the fact that the software could face unexpected situations not considered during its design. Robustness is a highly desirable and sometimes indispensable software requirement, especially for critical systems, where the consequences of a system failure can be catastrophic. This chapter outlines existing fault tolerance techniques, followed by a discussion of the potential that multiagent systems have to enhance the design of robust, fault-tolerant systems, thereby improving large-scale, critical, and complex system reliability.

2.1 Introduction

Making software robust—i.e., enabling it to be performed without failure under a wide range of conditions—has always been a desirable outcome, particularly in critical applications (e.g., control of aircraft, chemical plants, nuclear plants, financial transactions, or medical assistance) where the consequences of software failing go beyond simply annoying the users, and can cause huge financial losses, serious injuries, or the loss of life. The importance of software as an important contributor to catastrophic events has been well documented (e.g., [Leveson, 1995]).

There is a large compendium of work in software engineering addressing the problem of producing reliable and robust software systems. Methods, processes, technologies, and tools have been proposed for good software design and development. These approaches have been very beneficial in improving our ability to produce better software. Nevertheless, despite significant contributions, the ever increasing complexity and pervasiveness of software systems creates the need for continuous improvement. Additionally, the more dependable software systems

R.L.Z. Gutierrez
Department of Computer Science and Engineering, University of South Carolina, 301 Main Street, Columbia, SC 29208, USA
email: zavalagu@engr.sc.edu

A. Schuster (ed.), *Robust Intelligent Systems,* DOI: 10.1007/978-1-84800-261-6_2,
© Springer-Verlag London Limited 2008

become, the more dependence is placed on them. As a consequence, there is always a search for innovative new approaches to software development that provide ways to significantly increase reliability and robustness. Recent efforts include self-adaptive software and autonomic computing. The area of self-adaptive software [Laddaga et al., 2001, Laddaga, 1999] studies techniques for developing software that modifies its behavior when self-evaluation indicates that it is not accomplishing what it is intended to do, or when better functionality or performance is possible. Techniques usually include planning, monitoring or dynamic model-checking, and machine learning. Autonomic computing [Kephart and Chess, 2003], an initiative started by IBM in 2001, aims to engineer self-managing computer systems that regulate themselves much in the same way our autonomic nervous system regulates and protects our bodies. IBM's main objectives are to reduce the total cost of ownership of systems and to find better ways of managing their increasing complexity. One of the main properties of a system from the viewpoint of autonomic computing is a self-healing ability: it must be able to recover from routine and extraordinary events that might cause some of its parts to malfunction. Other important properties are self-configuring, self-protecting, and self-optimizing.

Clearly, these areas address similar issues and both point toward the development of autonomous and robust computer systems. Although they represent very desirable visions for computing and software development, none of them has really made it into conventional systems development. Complete self-adaptive or autonomic systems do not yet exist.

Related work in software engineering, particularly in software fault tolerance, can provide valuable contributions and should be part of the basis for the development of autonomous, self-adaptive, and robust systems. In order to make software systems more robust, it is necessary to incorporate into them a strategy for tolerating software faults. However, the field itself has not yet developed to its full and there are several unresolved issues. More research is needed to be conducted on software fault tolerance, and existing techniques need to be enhanced and improved before it can be used as a basis for more complex systems. As Randell [Randell, 2000] recently pointed out, software fault tolerance is still somewhat controversial as historically the main software engineering research challenge has been to find ways of developing error-free software, rather than managing faults. Software fault tolerance techniques have only been used for a few critical systems with very high reliability requirements [Bishop, 1995], as opposed to error-avoidance software engineering techniques that are used for the development of every software system—at least to some degree.

Design diversity is the most explored and used approach for achieving software fault tolerance. It exploits the idea of synergy, that is, that the whole is greater than the sum of its parts. Or as stated in [DeMarco and Lister, 1987], the production of a team is greater than that of the same people working independently. Diversity is ubiquitous in human activity, for example, in an informal context, you can have someone else check your arithmetic in a complex calculation. Social insects provide also examples of the use of diversity for achieving robustness in their tasks. Experiments with swarms of honey bees [Seeley et al., 2006] and ants [Smith, 2006] revealed that they use teams of expert members to locate and choose their nest site collectively. The authors in [Seeley et al., 2006] concluded that a relevant factor to the success of bees at making collective judgments is that the scout bees are organized in a way that promotes diversity of knowledge within the group. "The wisdom of crowds" [Hempel, 2006], a popular Web 2.0 term, refers to the fact that two heads are better than one, and that still more heads will yield even better results. The implementation of diversity into software development is done by having multiple program versions (different, independently developed programs with the same functionality) for a particular task in order to provide tolerance to faults in any one of them. Several issues arise when trying to put the strategy into practice:

- How can different versions be obtained without incurring a high-cost solution?
- What is the efficient way to combine the diverse programs to really take advantage of their redundant functionality without adding much complexity to the system?
- How can diversity among the programs be ensured so that a good coverage of faults is achieved? At what level should diversity be introduced? How much diversity is needed for a particular problem or a specific desired level of reliability?
- How can the efficacy of the approach be measured quantitatively?

The idea of diversity for robustness has also been explored in the design of intelligent applications. The use of multiple heuristics for constraint solving has been explored to design robust algorithms that perform well across a range of problems, models, and instances [Vidotto et al., 2005]. Artificial intelligence (AI) practitioners have recently agreed on the importance of integrated approaches as one of the main directions that should be explored in AI research [Brachman, 2006]. They want to investigate how different methodologies can be incorporated into robust applications and used synergistically; for example, combining or integrating the outputs of multiple neural classifiers in pattern recognition problems. Previous work investigated the use of multiagent systems to incorporate design diversity into conventional software systems [Huhns et al., 2003a,b] and [Zavala Gutierrez and Huhns, 2003, 2004]. Agents having different algorithms, but similar responsibilities produce the redundancy. Possible modes that agents can use in order to reach consensus, the focus being in the use of agents only for the decision procedure, have been defined in [Huhns et al., 2003a, Zavala Gutierrez and Huhns, 2004].

Extending that work, this chapter introduces a multiagent-based framework for fault tolerance management. The main goal is to address the elements of such a framework that agents can manage, besides a voting procedure, in order to obtain a better gain from such a system. This chapter first presents the concepts of software fault tolerance as an introduction to the field, as well as a review of the existing work on design diversity. Then, it provides a review of previous work on multiagent-based diversity for robustness. Then, it addresses the elements of a diverse system that can be managed dynamically by a multiagent system. The chapter concludes with a discussion of issues that need to be addressed and research directions.

2.2 Software Dependability

Dependability is defined as that property of a computer system that allows reliance to justifiably be placed on the service it delivers. The service delivered by a system is its behavior as it is perceived by its user(s); a user is another system (human or physical) that interacts with the former [Laprie et al., 1992]. Figure 2.1 [Avizienis et al., 2000, Laprie et al., 1992, Laprie, 1995] depicts the concept of dependability in terms of threats to, attributes of, and the means by which dependability is attained.

2.2.1 Threats: Faults, Errors, and Failures

Faults are flaws in a system that can be caused by different reasons such as an incorrect specification or an incorrect implementation. Errors and failures are the consequences of encountering the faults during operation or execution of the system. The faults may be either transient or omnipresent. More specifically, a system failure occurs when the delivered service deviates from fulfilling the system function, the latter being what the system is aimed at. An error is an anomaly in the system state that is liable to lead to subsequent failure. A fault is the adjudged or hypothesized cause of an error. The manifestation of a fault will produce errors in the state of the system, which could lead to a failure [Randell, 2000, Laprie, 1995, Parhami, 1988].

2.2.2 Attributes: Software Reliability and Robustness

Software reliability is the probability that the software will work without failure for a specified period of time. It is the failure-free operation of a computer program for a specified time in a specified environment [Musa et al., 1987]. Besides the attributes listed in Fig. 2.1, other secondary attributes can be defined. An example of a specializing secondary attribute is robustness (i.e., dependability with respect to external faults, such as erroneous inputs), which characterizes a system reaction to a specific class of faults [Avizienis et al., 2000].

The required level of reliability in a system depends on the effects that runtime errors might produce. Critical systems, for instance, mission-critical, safety-critical,

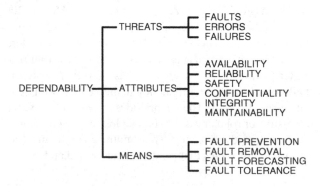

Fig. 2.1 The
dependability tree

business-critical, have very high reliability requirements because errors during execution can lead to catastrophic consequences. For other, non-critical systems, the consequences of a small number of errors during performance may be acceptable.

Safety-critical systems are those where loss of life or environmental disaster must be avoided (e.g., power, chemical, and nuclear plant control, radiation therapy, and military radars). Mission-critical systems stress mission completion (e.g., spacecraft and aircraft control). Business-critical systems are responsible for keeping a business operating (e.g., banking, stocks, and trading). All these instances of critical systems have very high reliability requirements, because errors during performance could have catastrophic consequences. For other, non-critical systems, the cost or consequences of a small number of errors during performance may be acceptable.

2.2.3 Means: Prevention, Detection and Removal, Tolerance, and Forecasting

Variations in the emphasis on the different attributes of dependability directly affect the appropriate balance of the techniques (fault prevention, tolerance, detection and removal, and forecasting) to be employed in order to make the resulting system dependable [Avizienis et al., 2000]. It is important to notice that the existing techniques to achieve dependability do not have to be used in exclusion of each other; they can be used as complementary strategies.

Fault prevention or avoidance is achieved with the use of good software engineering practices. However, human errors cannot be avoided during development, resulting in bugs in the resultant software product. For fault removal, verification and validation techniques are used to discover and remove faults in a system before it is released. Fault forecasting uses statistical techniques to estimate how many faults remain in the system as well as how severe their effects might be. This information is useful to decide if the system can be released or if more fault detection and removal is needed. Even after testing, it is probable that a product will still contain faults. Moreover, even if the software performs to its specification (it does not contain any faults) and the tests for verification consider exceptional cases, it is impossible to anticipate all the possible scenarios under which the system will operate. Therefore, we need to consider the fact that the software application will face unexpected situations. With fault tolerance, the system is designed so that neither faults nor unexpected situations result in system failure.

2.3 Robust Software

The concept of software robustness has varying definitions in the literature. The main differences being whether it is part of the more general concept of dependability and whether it implies resilience to faults in the code. The different approaches entail distinct ways to achieve software robustness, according to what the goal is.

Anderson [Anderson, 1985] states that dependability and robustness are the key attributes of a resilient computing system—a system capable of providing dependable service to its users over a wide range of potentially adverse circumstances. He defines a robust computer system as one that retains its ability to deliver service in conditions that are beyond its normal domain of operation, whether due to harsh treatment, or unreasonable service requests, or misoperation, or the impact of faults, or lack of maintenance. This conceptualization situates software robustness separate from dependability. Most of the definitions of software robustness, though, refer to it as a specialized secondary attribute of dependability. The following are probably two of the most widely accepted definitions:

- Software robustness is the ability of a software product to remain in service and perform correctly despite the occurrence of errors that are attributable to hardware, software, or even people [Fraser et al., 2005].
- Software robustness is the ability of a software product to function correctly or coherently in a changing environment, in the presence of invalid or conflicting inputs, and in the presence of situations not considered during its design. Software reliability is a wider concept, which includes robustness. It is the probability of error-free operation of an application [Sommerville, 1995].

The different means to achieve robustness that can be found in the literature vary according to what problems are targeted, and include:

- All software fault tolerance techniques, if the definition of robustness is taken literally and also if overcoming faults in the code is a goal.
- Exception handling to tolerate exceptional cases. Dependability cases [Maxion and Olszewski, 1998] have been proposed as a technique to deal with a programmer's inadequate coverage of exceptional conditions. The aim is to improve exception-handling coverage.
- The robust software approach in [Pullum, 2001] includes only nonredundant software that properly handles input-related problems, i.e., out-of-range inputs, inputs of the wrong type, and inputs in the wrong format.

The software robustness approach taken in the rest of this chapter corresponds with robustness in the context of dependability with software fault tolerance techniques, particularly design diversity (see next section), as a mean to achieve it.

2.3.1 Software Fault Tolerance

One way to reduce the number of software failures caused by faults or unexpected situations (e.g., erroneous inputs), and thus enhance software dependability, is to use software fault tolerance. Software fault tolerance techniques aim at enabling a system to continue operation even when the software faults remaining in the system after its development or other unexpected situations are encountered during execution.

Techniques for achieving software fault tolerance fall into one of two categories.

1. Single-version software. A single program implementation with one or more of the following capabilities: self-checking, atomicity of actions, exception handling, error detection and recovery.
2. Multiple-version software (design diversity). Multiple, diverse software versions are used to provide tolerance to faults in any one of the versions. The term "version" in this context is different from "version" in a general software context. It refers to different, independently developed programs with the same functionality. Diversity can be applied to a function, a process, or the whole system. Usually, the more relevant components, the ones with a high probability of faults, or the ones with highest usage, are chosen to be made redundant.

The incorporation of fault tolerance should complement, not discard, the use of other strategies (prevention, verification, and validation procedures).

Design Diversity

Motivation

Design diversity is an approach based on the idea of synergy, that is, that the whole is greater than the sum of its parts, or that a group of agents can outperform an individual on a consistent basis [Hasling, 1975].

An interesting example of robust collective decision-making found in nature is the choice of a nesting site by a swarm of honey bees. When a hive gets too crowded, its queen and half the hive will swarm to a nearby tree and quietly wait while several hundred scouts go house hunting. To explore the decision-making process, [Seeley et al., 2006] conducted a series of experiments. They labeled all 4,000 bees in a swarm and recorded the scouts reporting on their site visits. They offered bees both mediocre and superb nest sites. Although the superior site was never the first one found, it was almost always chosen.

The bees use a quorum-sensing mechanism that allows them to choose the best site but avoids any need for them to do arithmetic and is highly robust to occasional defective bees. A scout bee "votes" for a site by waggle dancing for it; the better the housing site, the stronger the waggle dance, which prompts other scouts to visit the recommended site. If they agree that it is a good choice then they also dance to advertise the site and revisit it frequently. Scouts committed to different sites compete to attract uncommitted scouts to their sites, but because the bees grade their recruitment signals in relation to site quality, the scouts build up most rapidly at the best site. Somehow the bees at each site monitor their numbers there so that they know whether they have reached the threshold number (quorum) and can proceed to initiating the swarm's move to this site.

These group decision-making methods include several key elements: an open forum of ideas, frank "discussions", and friendly competition, promoting diversity of knowledge and independence of opinions among a group's members, and aggregating the opinions in a way that meets time constraints yet wisely exploits the breadth of knowledge within the group [Seeley et al., 2006, Smith, 2006].

Similar research [Smith, 2006] shows that ants also locate and choose their nest site collectively. Just as for honeybees, ants supporting a site recruit new members at different exponential growths proportional to the average of some quality measure of the site. Eventually, the ants pushing the site with greatest average range-vote will dominate and a quorum method cuts off debate once enough ants have assembled at the winner site.

In a different context, Shapley and Grofman [Shapley and Grofman, 1984] give an example of a team of weather experts who have the task of collectively producing a weather forecast. If they all have different expertise and their reputation can be asserted by looking at their past performance, how should the contributions of these experts be combined to achieve the most accurate possible result and outperform any expert individual performance?

Suppose that the particular task is to predict whether or not it is going to rain. Assuming independence of contributions and equal probability of occurrence of the two possible results, Shapley and Grofman showed that the best way to maximize the probability of an accurate team prediction is to use weighted voting with weights in proportion to $\log(p_i/(1 - p_i))$, where p_i is the probability of forecaster i making a correct decision. For a particular example of a five-member team with reliabilities of 0.9, 0.9, 0.6, 0.6, and 0.6, the corresponding weights are 0.392, 0.392, 0.072, 0.072, and 0.072, respectively. Weighted majority voting provides a group reliability of 0.927, which is higher than that of any single expert and also higher than unweighted majority voting, which has a group probability of only 0.877.

Implementation into Fault Tolerance Strategies

The implementation of diversity into software development is done by having multiple diverse, usually independently developed, programs for a particular task in order to provide tolerance to faults in any one of them. Recovery blocks and N-version programming (NVP) are the two originally established design diverse software fault tolerance techniques. They both require at least two different implementations for the same problem. Each different implementation is referred to in the literature as a module, version, variant, or alternate.

The recovery blocks technique [Randell, 1995, 1975] is based on the use of acceptance testing (AT) and backward recovery. In AT, an acceptance test evaluates the correctness of a program output. Figure 2.2 illustrates the structure and operation of the recovery block technique.

The versions are invoked in some specified order (e.g., ranked by their service and reliability). After each version is executed, the test to check correctness is run, and the next version is executed only if the test fails. In some cases, backward recovery is performed upon failure of the test by a version and before invoking the next version. If none of the versions can produce a correct result (i.e., a result accepted by AT), an exception is raised.

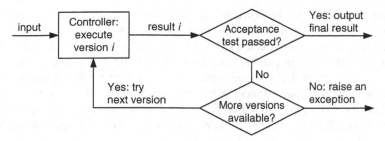

Fig. 2.2 Operation of the recovery blocks scheme

In NVP, *n* versions are executed in parallel, and the final result depends on a generic decision algorithm that implements some voting mechanism with the results delivered by the versions. If the voting mechanism cannot produce a result (e.g., the number of matching outputs required for success is not met), an exception is raised [Avizienis and Chen, 1977, Avizienis and Kelly, 1984, Avizienis, 1995]. Figure 2.3 illustrates the structure and operation of the NVP technique. NVP is the most used approach to software fault tolerance [Sommerville, 1995]. It has been used in practice in some systems, particularly for critical systems with very high reliability requirements [Bishop, 1995], including railway interlocking and train control [Anderson and Hagelin, 1981], reactor protection [Voges et al., 1982], and Airbus flight controls [Traverse, 1988].

The recovery blocks and NVP approaches are based solely on AT and voting, respectively. Hybrid techniques that combine both concepts have also been suggested. The consensus recovery block (CRB) [Scott et al., 1983] technique operates as NVP, but in the case that the voter cannot decide on a result, the results are evaluated in some specified order using AT, and the first to pass the test is taken as the correct output. N-self checking programming (NSCP) [Laprie et al., 1990, 1987] works in one of two modalities. The first modality makes use of AT and is also referred to as acceptance voting (AV) scheme [Lyu, 1996]. In AV, the versions are executed in parallel, and their results are evaluated by an acceptance test, and only accepted results are provided to a voter for the final decision. In the second

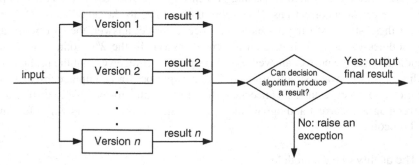

Fig. 2.3 Operation of the NVP scheme

modality of the NSCP, n versions are executed in pairs, and the results of each pair are compared and passed to the final voter only if they agree. In the NVP with a tie-breaker and an acceptance test (NVP-TB-AT) technique [Tai et al., 1993], three versions are executed in parallel, and the results of the first two that finish their execution are compared. If the results match, their common result is assumed correct and taken as final output. Otherwise, the program waits for the slowest version to finish, and the results from all the versions are submitted to a majority voter. Finally, AT is performed on the majority result before being output as the correct outcome.

Relevant Issues

Diversity can be enforced by using different designs, programming teams, programming languages, software engineering practices, etc. The goal being that the different versions will fail independently. However, there is a lack of methods to measure quantitatively the independence among redundant versions and the diversity they provide. Empirical evidence questions the hypothesis that redundant software versions developed by deliberatively enforcing diversity might fail in a statistically independent manner [Knight and Leveson, 1986]. Nevertheless, almost all design diversity software fault tolerance experiments have reported some degree of reliability improvement [Avizienis and Kelly, 1984].

2.4 Multiagent-Based Fault Tolerance Management

2.4.1 The Problem

Multiple software versions or modules that provide alternative means of exhibiting the same functionality can increase robustness if (i) combined they provide a wider coverage of the space of correct solutions and (ii) the strengths of each are exploited and the weaknesses of each are compensated or covered. However, it is a challenge to design the software system so that it can accommodate the additional modules and take advantage of their redundant functionality.

More formally, a system consisting of n modules whose result is assumed to be either correct or incorrect has 2^n possible input states to the adjudicator. Only in one of these states is it impossible to produce a correct answer, the case when all the modules in the system give an incorrect answer. In the 2^n-1 other cases, the adjudicator has the correct answer in the set of inputs it receives, but the problem of finding it is not always straightforward. There might be, for example, consensus on identical incorrect results. It is necessary that the adjudicator be able to distinguish between agreed correct and agreed incorrect results. Several factors will affect the final outcome:

- The quality of each module.
- The variety in the reliabilities of the modules.

- The degree of independence among the modules, specifically, the failure coverage (or, on the other side, the correctness) of their ensemble.
- The output space cardinality.
- The mechanism used to produce the final result based on the individual contributions of each module.

Consider, for example, a diverse system composed of 3 modules with reliabilities of 0.96, 0.97, and 0.98. If these close-to-perfect modules exhibit high failure dependence (they tend to fail under the same scenarios), we might not obtain a significant increase in reliability regardless of their high individual reliabilities. Now consider the case of a diverse system composed of 3 less accurate modules with reliabilities of 0.8, 0.6, and 0.65. Suppose that the 20% of time that the first one fails, the other two are correct (no matter their mediocrity). Then there is the case of perfect coverage and, if exploited adequately, the system could achieve 100% correctness. Clearly, in this case the best solution would be to always execute the first module alone, and only in the case that it does not pass an acceptance test (assuming an AT can be created for the particular domain), make use of the other modules.

Unfortunately, it is almost always the case that the reliability of the modules is not known exactly, much less the diversity among them or their failure coverage. The problem lies in how to configure the redundant system so that the design space is optimally explored and to successfully provide the highest failure coverage possible as allowed by the diversity of the modules.

2.4.2 Previous Work on Multiagent Systems for Reaching Agreement on a Solution

Possible modes in which the agents can reach consensus are listed in Table 2.1 [Huhns et al., 2003a, Zavala Gutierrez and Huhns, 2004].

A preprocessing approach would consist of the agents choosing, at the beginning, which agent(s) are going to perform the task. There are three strategies applicable to this approach:

- Randomly picking an agent to perform the task. This is equivalent to a lottery. The output would be based solely on the results from that agent. Any bugs or errors in the agent would not be caught or corrected. The lottery method would be appropriate in a system where all agents have the same capabilities or in a system with a relatively large number of correct agents and the probability of

Table 2.1 Approaches for combining agents' functionalities

Preprocessing	Postprocessing
Random/lottery	Performance-based
Auction election/criteria selection	Voting
Team	Collaboration
	Incremental

selecting an appropriate agent is high. Communication overhead would be low as it would be needed only for determining the winner of the lottery.

- Selecting an agent by auction or voting (using information such as reliability and past performance of modules). Because this is a single-input, single-output subsystem, an agent's desire to perform a task would be based on mitigating factors the agent knows or can deduce about itself, such as speed, complexity, and reputation. These factors would help in determining which agent is chosen to perform each task. It would be the means for determining the agent's bid in an auction or the value (or weight) of an agent's vote in an election. This method, while also based on a single agent's response, is a more intelligent choice because justifying factors are involved in the selection. The domain is similar to that of the lottery method.

- Distributing the task among the agents. This strategy consists in distributing the task to be performed into subtasks assigned to individual agents. The individual agents would be responsible for processing only a subset of the original task. The subsets would then be collected and combined to contribute to the single answer required by the system. This methodology would increase speed as far as the processor goes. If all agents are equally competent, then this method is practical for a large problem that could be divided into smaller subsets. The problem of selecting an agent to perform a task, as well as distributing a task among different agents, has been largely discussed in previous distributed AI and multiagent systems literature, beginning with the Contract Net Protocol and extending through market approaches, auctions, and distributed planning [Smith, 1988, Martin et al., 1999, Cheyer and Martin, 2001].

A postprocessing approach would consist of all the agents performing the task, followed by a decision on which one produced the best result. There are four strategies applicable to this approach:

- Taking the result of the agent whose processing was the fastest. A domain in which the agents are sufficiently competent would be an appropriate one for this strategy.

- Choosing the result voted for by the most agents. This is different from the voting scheme above, in that the proposed output would be based on a direct comparison of information. Agents would compare their results to other agents and a running tally kept. The result with the most votes is given as the final answer. To handle ties, a weight could be assigned to each agent based on additional factors such as speed and reputation.

- Making a decision only about controversial data subsets. This involves a collaboration strategy where data is compared between agents so that any common data subsets are kept and only a decision about controversial data subsets (result data not agreed upon) have to be made. The decision about any controversial subsets could be made by any of the methods mentioned. An average, a minimum, or a maximum could be computed and utilized by such collaboration methods.

- Incremental voting. An agent is selected by some means already discussed. One agent's result is compared with another's and, if they are the same, the result is forwarded. If the comparison is different or if more comparisons are desired, then more agents are included before a result is forwarded. A variation to this would be for agents to sample a subset of the data and compare results. Agents who differ from the majority are culled from the sampling, and comparisons continue until a single result emerges.

A combination of the preprocessing and postprocessing approaches could also be used. For example, more than one agent could be selected using either a random or a voting preprocessing approach, and the result would then be selected using one of the postprocessing approaches. The preprocessing approaches by themselves are not representative of a design diversity robustness approach; however, they are useful when combined with a postprocessing approach.

2.4.3 The Framework

This section provides a multiagent-based framework for fault tolerance management and continues earlier contributions by [Huhns et al., 2003a] and [Zavala Gutierrez and Huhns, 2004]. The goal is to address the elements of such a framework that agents can manage, besides the voting procedure, in order to obtain a better gain from such a system. Existing developments and issues for each are also discussed.

2.4.3.1 Selection of the Modules

The task of choosing how many modules and which ones are going to be used can be automated, and any of the strategies applicable to the preprocessing approach (see previous section) can be used. Factors influencing this decision include known attributes of the modules (e.g., speed, complexity, and reliability), known dependencies among them, as well as the acceptable level of reliability for the diverse system—if available. This task is interconnected, in fact, with the next one (configuring the system), but a separate discussion facilitates understanding.

Related research includes [Donald et al., 1989], where the authors study appropriate sizes for groups to perform best. There is an extreme number that a group should hold, although this is not an exact number and should be applied to the different circumstances. A group generally stops being a group at about 10 to 15 members, after that the classification can be noted as an assembly (where members do more waiting around than not) or a mob (where members are out of control). Efforts have also been made to address the issues of measuring and ensuring diversity and failure independence among the redundant modules [Lyu and Avizienis, 1991, Lyu et al., 1992, Mitra et al., 1999, Becker and Corkill, 2007]. In [Lyu et al., 1992], the authors characterize software diversity from different points of view (e.g., structural diversity, fault diversity, and failure diversity) in the search for a means to quantify software diversity. Model-based or structural diversity is defined according to the attributes of the module: source lines of code, function points, nested loops, etc. The purpose of fault diversity is to demonstrate the differences between the faults introduced by the programming teams in the software development process. Failure diversity shows the differences in the failure behaviors of a certain combination of versions. The design diversity metric proposed by Mitra et al. in [Mitra et al., 1999] corresponds with fault diversity. They define fault diversity with respect to a fault pair (f_i, f_j), d_{ij}, as the probability that the versions i and j do not produce identical error patterns, in response to a given input sequence when f_i and f_j affect versions i and j, respectively. Based on this, they further define a design diversity metric, D, between two versions as the expected value of the diversity with respect to different fault pairs equation (2.1).

$$D = \sum_{f_i, f_j} P(f_i, f_j) d_{i,j} \tag{2.1}$$

Similarly, in [Becker and Corkill, 2007], the authors develop a Bayesian network model that facilitates analysis of confidence integration of contributions from multiple agents. But, as the authors point out, while it may be reasonable to assume that the accuracy of the individual contributions might be known, assuming all of the dependencies among them is known is unrealistic. The metric provided by Mitra suffers also from inapplicability due to unrealistic assumptions, namely, to know the response of the modules with respect to all possible fault pairs.

Although it is likely that the ideal outcome of total failure independence does not hold, assuming versions will fail independently greatly facilitates reliability measurement of the diverse system. For a given diverse system S and a set of versions V, if all n versions from V must function correctly for system success, the system reliability $R(S)$ is given by equation (2.2). This would be the case when all versions are used and unanimity is required to produce the final result. If successful functioning of any of the n versions from V will result in system success, the system reliability is given by equation (2.3). This measurement also represents the probability that any inconsistency will be detected (although not necessarily corrected). For a k-out-of-n system, the reliability is given by equation (2.4), where S_i is a system that requires exactly i versions from V to function correctly for system success and its reliability is given by equation (2.5). $C_i^n(V)$ in equation (2.5) corresponds with all the possible combinations of size i from V.

$$R(S) = \prod_{v \in V} R(v) \tag{2.2}$$

$$R(S) = 1 - \prod_{v \in V} (1 - R(v)) \tag{2.3}$$

$$R(S) = \sum_{i=k}^{n} R(S_i) \tag{2.4}$$

$$R(S_i) = \sum_{C \in C_i^n(V)} \prod_{v \in C} R(v) \prod_{v \in (V-C)} 1 - R(v) \tag{2.5}$$

2.4.3.2 System Configuration and Adjudication of Results

Existing fault tolerance strategies (see Section 2.3.1) are based on the use of acceptance testing (AT) and/or a voting mechanism. Each strategy, as well as each of the postprocessing approaches described in Section 2.4.2, corresponds with one of the many combinations that can be done with the n modules and these two components (AT and voter). A better exploration of the design space and dynamic configuration of the system architecture using such elements can provide increased robustness of the software.

The voting mechanisms that have been used for the process of adjudication that computes an output based on the results provided by multiple redundant modules are:

- Majority voter [Avizienis and Chen, 1977, Avizienis and Kelly, 1984] and [Lyu, 1996]: selects the result given by the majority of the modules, i.e., $(n + 1)/2$.
- Consensus or plurality voter [Vouk et al., 1993]: the result with the largest agreement number is chosen as the correct answer. If there are several outputs with the same agreement number, the tie can be broken in several ways
- Maximum likelihood voter (MLV) [Kim et al., 1996]: takes the reliability of each software version into consideration and determines the most likely correct answer.
- Weight-based or reputation-based voter [Grosspietsch and Silayeva, 2003, Turlapati and Hulms, 2005]: models and manages different quality levels of the versions. This is achieved by associating a weight factor or reputation with each version and updating it dynamically according to the version performance.

Other voting strategies should also be explored. A new voting strategy that has yet not been used in software fault tolerance, based on the quorum-sensing mechanism that allows bees and ants to choose the best site, could work by computing a confidence value of the current result during the voting procedure (based, for example, in individual agents' reliabilities or self-confidence). If the value reaches a threshold, then it can be assumed that a reliable outcome has been determined (a quorum has been reached) and the voting process stops. In [Smith, 2006], the author defines a range voting mechanism as an implementation of the quorum-sensing mechanism of the bees. The focus is not on application to fault tolerance, but it could be adapted to that domain.

2.4.3.3 Evaluation of Fault Tolerance Strategies

One of the most difficult tasks in the design of a fault-tolerant mechanism is evaluating its efficacy. In most of the cases, only qualitative analysis are used. The use of fault injection has been suggested as a means to improve the level of empirical knowledge regarding design-diverse systems [Townend and Xu, 2002]. The goal is to determine how well the fault tolerance mechanisms work by fault simulations. Fault injection involves the deliberate insertion of faults into an operational system to determine its response. Faults can be introduced either through direct alteration of source code or by the perturbation of data flows to achieve the effects of faults indirectly.

Agents in a multiagent-based software fault tolerance system can make use of fault injection for different purposes, e.g., evaluation of the different design configurations when exploring the design space, assignment of fault rates, failure coverages, and reliabilities, etc.

2.5 Discussion

The future of programming promises more robust systems with less effort on the developers. Autonomic computing, self-adaptive computing, and similar efforts have all common visions about the development of autonomous and robust computer systems. Still, a lot of work needs to be done to form the ground for these approaches. Software fault tolerance provides part of the ground needed but needs more research, too.

This chapter presented an introduction to the field of software fault tolerance and, in particular, design diversity as a strategy to achieve it. It discussed the elements that would form part of a multiagent-based design diversity approach for software robustness. Details of how exactly a system would work were not provided but rather pointed to the existing developments. This represents a strategic refocus rather than an innovative new approach and leaves the room open for contributions. Although each individual aspect of our approach has been the focus of much research, integrating these aspects into a multiagent-based autoconfigurable system is unprecedented.

The cost of having to develop n modules for a single task has largely been pointed out as a shortcoming of design diversity. This problem will be lessened with the expansion of the use of component- and service-oriented paradigms, as well as open source communities of developers such as those that employ crowdsourcing [Hempel, 2006]. In the IBM manifesto for autonomic computing [Fraser et al., 2005], its success is linked to the use of open standards, open source code, and open technologies in general.

References

Anderson, H. and Hagelin, G. (1981). *Computer Controlled Interlocking System*. Ericsson Review No 2.

Anderson, T. (1985). *Resilient Computing Systems*. Collins, London, UK.

Avizienis, A. (1995). The methodology of n-version programming. In Lyu, M. R., editor, *Software Fault Tolerance*, pages 23–46. John Wiley & Sons, New York.

Avizienis, A. and Chen, L. (1977). On the implementation of N-version programming for software fault tolerance during execution. In *Proceedings of the 1st IEEE International Computer Software and Applications Conference (COMPSAC'77)*, pages 149–155, 8–11 November, Chicago. IEEE Computer Society.

Avizienis, A. and Kelly, J. P. J. (1984). Fault tolerance by design diversity: Concepts and experiments. *Computer*, 17:67–80.

Avizienis, A., Laprie, J.-C., and Randell, B. (2000). Fundamental concepts of dependability. In *Proceedings of the 3rd IEEE Information Survability Workshop (ISW-2000)*, pages 7–12, 20–21 December, Boston. IEEE Computer Society.

Becker, R. and Corkill, D. (2007). Determining confidence when integrating contributions from multiple agents. In *Proceedings of the 6th International Joint Conference on Autonomous Agents and Multi-Agent Systems (AAMAS'07)*, pages 449–456. The International Foundation for Autonomous Agents and Multiagent Systems (IFAAMAS).

Bishop, P. (1995). Software fault tolerance by design diversity. In Lyu, M., editor, *Software Fault Tolerance*, pages 211–229. John Wiley & Sons, New York.

Brachman, R. J. (2006). (AA)AI more than the sum of its parts. *AI Magazine*, 27(4):19–34.

Cheyer, A. and Martin, D. L. (2001). The open agent architecture. *Autonomous Agents and Multi-Agent Systems*, 4(1/2):143–148.

DeMarco, T. and Lister, T. (1987). *Peopleware: productive projects and teams*. Dorset House Publishing Co., Inc., New York.

Donald, L., Keller, S., and Calhoun, C. (1989). *Sociology*. Alfred A. Knopf, New York.

Fraser, S., Campara, D., Chilley, C., Gabriel, R., Lopez, R., Thomas, D., and Utas, G. (2005). Fostering software robustness in an increasingly hostile world. In *Proceedings of the 20th ACM SIGPLAN conference on Object-oriented programming, systems, languages, and applications (OOPSLA'05)*, pages 378–380, 16–20 October, San Diego. ACM.

Grosspietsch, K. E. and Silayeva, T. A. (2003). An adaptive approach for n-version systems. In *Proceedings of the 17th International Symposium on Parallel and Distributed Processing (IPDPS'03)*, page 215.1, Nice, France. IEEE Computer Society.

Hasling, J. (1975). *Group Discussion and Decision Making*. Thomas Y. Crowell Company, New York.

Hempel, J. (2006). Crowdsourcing: Milk the masses for inspiration. *Business Week*. 25 September.

Huhns, M. N., Holderfield, V. T., and Zavala Gutierrez, R. L. (2003a). Achieving software robustness via large-scale multiagent. In Garcia, A., Lucena, C., Zambonelli, F., Omicini, A., and Castro, J., editors, *Software Engineering for Large-Scale Multi-Agent Systems*, volume 2603 of *Lecture Notes in Computer Science*, pages 199–215. Springer, Berlin Heidelberg.

Huhns, M. N., Holderfield, V. T., and Zavala Gutierrez, R. L. (2003b). Robust software via agent-based redundancy. In *Proceedings of the 2nd International Joint Conference on Autonomous Agents and Multiagent Systems (AAMAS'03)*, pages 1018–1019. ACM.

Kephart, J. O. and Chess, D. M. (2003). The vision of autonomic computing. *Computer*, 36(1): 41–50.

Kim, K., Vouk, M., and McAllister, D. (1996). An empirical evaluation of maximum likelihood voting in failure correlation conditions. In *Proceedings of the 7th International Symposium on Software Reliability Engineering (ISSRE'96)*, pages 330–339, White Plains, NY. IEEE Computer Society.

Knight, J. and Leveson, N. (1986). An experimental evaluation of the assumption of independence in multi-version programming. *IEEE Trans. Software Engineering*, 12:96–109.

Laddaga, R. (1999). Guest editor's introduction: Creating robust software through self-adaptation. *IEEE Intelligent Systems*, 14(3):26–29.

Laddaga, R., Robertson, P., and Shrobe, H., editors (2001). *Self-Adaptive Software, 2nd International Workshop (IWSAS'01), Revised Papers*, volume 2614 of *Lecture Notes in Computer Science*, Balatonfüred, Hungary. Springer, New York.

Laprie, J. (1995). Dependable computing: Concepts, limits, challenges. In *Special Issue of the 25th IEEE International Symposium on Fault-Tolerant Computing*, pages 42–54, Pasadena, CA.

Laprie, J., Avizienis, A., and Kopetz, H., editors (1992). *Dependability: Basic Concepts and Terminology*. Springer-Verlag, New York.

Laprie, J. C., Arlat, J., Beounes, C., Kanoun, K., and Hourtolle, C. (1987). Hardware and software fault tolerance: definition and analysis of architectural solutions. In *Proceedings of the 17th International Symposium Fault-Tolerant Computing*, pages 116–121, Pittsburgh, PA. ACM.

Laprie, J.-C., Béounes, C., and Kanoun, K. (1990). Definition and analysis of hardware- and software-fault-tolerant architectures. *Computer*, 23(7):39–51.

Leveson, N. G. (1995). *Safeware: System Safety and Computers*. ACM, New York.

Lyu, M., editor (1996). *Handbook of Software Reliability Engineering*. McGraw-Hill and IEEE Computer Society, New York.

Lyu, M. and Avizienis, A. (1991). Assuring design diversity in N-version software: A design paradigm for N-version programming. In Meyer, J. and Schlichting, R., editors, *Proceedings of the 2nd IFIP International Working Conference on Dependable Computing for Critical Applications (DCCA-2)*, pages 197–218, Tucson, Arizona, USA. Springer-Verlag, New York.

Lyu, M., Chen, J., and Avizienis, A. (1992). Software diversity metrics and measurements. In *Proceedings of the 16th IEEE Annual International Computer Software and Applications Conference (COMPSAC'92)*, pages 69–78, 21–25 September, Chicago. IEEE Computer Society.

Martin, D., Cheyer, A., and Moran, D. (1999). The open agent architecture: a framework for building distributed software systems. *Applied Artificial Intelligence*, 13(1/2):91–128.

Maxion, R. A. and Olszewski, R. T. (1998). Improving software robustness with dependability cases. In *28th International Symposium on Fault-Tolerant Computing (FTCS'98)*, pages 346–355, Munich, Germany. IEEE Computer Society.

Mitra, S., Saxena, N. R., and McCluskey, E. J. (1999). A design diversity metric and reliability analysis for redundant systems. In *Proceedings of the 1999 IEEE International Test Conference (ITC'99)*, page 662, Washington, DC. IEEE Computer Society.

Musa, J. D., Iannino, A., and Okumoto, K. (1987). *Software reliability: measurement, prediction, application*. McGraw-Hill, Inc., New York.

Parhami, B. (1988). From defects to failures: a view of dependable computing. *SIGARCH Computer Architecture News*, 16(4):157–168.

Pullum, L. L. (2001). *Software fault tolerance techniques and implementation*. Artech House, Inc., Norwood, MA.

Randell, B. (1975). System structure for software fault tolerance. In *Proceedings of the International Conference on Reliable Software*, pages 437–449, Los Angeles, California. ACM.

Randell, B. (1995). The evolution of the recovery block concept. In Lyu, M., editor, *Software Fault Tolerance*, chapter 1, pages 1–22. John Wiley & Sons, New York.

Randell, B. (2000). Turing memorial lecture–facing up to faults. *Computer*, 4(2):95–106.

Scott, K., Gault, J., and McAllister, D. (1983). The consensus recovery block. In *Total Systems Reliability Symposium*, pages 3–9, Gaithersburg, MD. IEEE Computer Society.

Seeley, T. D., Visscher, P. K., and Passino, K. M. (2006). Group decision making in honey bee swarms. *American Scientist*, 94:220–229.

Shapley, L. S. and Grofman, B. (1984). Optimizing group judgmental accuracy in the presence of interdependence. *Public Choice*, 43:329–343.

Smith, R. G. (1988). The contract net protocol: High-level communication and control in a distributed problem solver. *IEEE Transactions on Computers*, C-29(12):1104–1113.

Smith, W. D. (2006). Ants, bees, and computers agree range voting is best single-winner system. Technical report, Temple University, Department of Mathematics.

Sommerville, I. (1995). *Software Engineering*. Addison-Wesley, Reading, MA, 5th edition.

Tai, A., Meyer, F., and Avizienis, A. (1993). Performability enhancement of fault-tolerant software. *IEEE Transactions on Reliability*, pages 227–237.

Townend, P. and Xu, J. (2002). Assessing multi-version systems through fault injection. In *Proceedings of the 7th IEEE International Workshop on Object-Oriented Real-Time Dependable Systems (WORDS'02)*, pages 105–112, San Diego, CA. Computer Society.

Traverse, P. (1988). Airbus and ATR system architecture and specification. *Software Diversity in Computerised Control Systems*, pages 95–104.

Turlapati, R. and Huhns, M. N. (2005). Multiagent reputation management to achieve robust software using redundancy. In *Proceedings of the IEEE/WIC/ACM International Conference on Intelligent Agent Technology (IAT'05)*, pages 386–392, Compiegne, France. Computer Society.

Vidotto, A., Brown, K. N., and Beck, J. (2005). Robust constraint solving using multiple heuristics. In Creaney, N., editor, *Proceedings of the 16th Irish Artificial Intelligence and Cognitive Science Conference (AICS'05)*, page 871, Coleraine, Northern Ireland. University of Ulster.

Voges, U., Fetsch, F., and Gmeiner, L. (1982). Use of microprocessors in a safety-oriented reactor shutdown system. In Lauber, E. and Moltoft, J., editors, *Reliability in Electrical and Electronic Components and Systems*, pages 493–497. North-Holland Publishing Company, Amsterdam, The Netherlands.

Vouk, M., McAllister, D., Eckhardt, D., and Kim, K. (1993). An empirical evaluation of consensus voting and consensus recovery block reliability in the presence of failure correlation. *Journal of Computer and Software Engineering*, 4:367–388.

Zavala Gutierrez, R. L. and Huhns, M. N. (2003). Achieving software robustness via multiagent-based redundancy (extended abstract). In Das, R. and Walsh, W., editors, *Proceedings of the IJCAI-03 Workshop on AI and Autonomic Computing: Developing a Research Agenda for Self-Managing Computer Systems*, Acapulco, Mexico. IBM.

Zavala Gutierrez, R. L. and Huhns, M. N. (2004). On building robust web service-based applications. In Cavedon, L., Maamar, Z., Martin, D., and Benatallah, B., editors, *Extending Web Services Technologies: The Use of Multi-Agent Approaches*, chapter 14, pages 293–310. Kluwer Academic Publishing, New York.

Chapter 3
A Two-Level Robustness Model
for Self-Managing Software Systems

David Bustard and Roy Sterritt

Abstract Potentially, software quality can be improved significantly by constructing systems that are self-managing. Such systems monitor both their internal state and operating environment during execution, and respond, as necessary, to any significant changes or problems detected. This chapter considers the role of robustness in the design and operation of self-managing systems. Robustness is discussed in relation to other general requirements of ideal systems and a basic design pattern developed. The resulting model includes a two-level user interface for communication with self-managing systems, which is illustrated with word processing and Web browser examples.

3.1 Introduction

Historically, software development has often been associated with striving for perfection. [Brooks, 1975], for example, describes the challenge of programming in the following terms:

The computer resembles the magic of legend.... If one character, one pause, of the incantation is not strictly in proper form, the magic doesn't work. Human beings are not accustomed to being perfect, and few areas of human activity demand it. Adjusting to the requirement for perfection is, I think, the most difficult part of learning to program.

In practice, however, such perfection is rarely, if ever, achieved. There are many factors contributing to this failing, including three stubborn issues where the possibility of improvement seems limited. The first is that software cannot be tested exhaustively and so often contains faults, both at the point of delivery and in subsequent use. These range from imperfections that are inconvenient to users, to

D. Bustard
School of Computing and Information Engineering, Faculty of Computing & Engineering, University of Ulster, Coleraine, Co. Londonderry BT52 1SA, Northern Ireland
email: dw.bustard@ulster.ac.uk

A. Schuster (ed.), *Robust Intelligent Systems,* DOI: 10.1007/978-1-84800-261-6_3,
© Springer-Verlag London Limited 2008

situations that can cause physical harm. The second factor is that, even if implementation problems are avoided, the functionality provided may not meet the requirements of all users. This is partly because not all users can be consulted in the design process but, more significantly, user needs may conflict [Boehm, 1996, Hoh et al., 2001]. For example, an interface that is suitable for experienced users may be unsuitable for novices and vice versa. Finally, even if software is fault-free and satisfies all users at some point in its development, circumstances will change, as time passes, and the software become less acceptable as a result.

The apparent conclusion is that it is impossible to build perfect software using the traditional approach implied. There is, however, an emerging alternative strategy that may lead to significant improvement; that approach is to create software that is *self-managing*. In particular, this means designing it to detect and repair its own faults, adapt to the needs of different users, and self-align to changing circumstances. Such an approach is currently receiving considerable attention in conferences and in industry, especially through IBM's *autonomic computing* initiative [Horn, 2001, IBM, 2005].

Building software that routinely embodies all of the currently identified self-managing properties is, however, a long-term goal, implying that advances will have to be achieved in stages [Kephart and Chess, 2003, Kephart, 2005]. Arguably, the most important requirement is to create software that users can *trust* [Nelson, 1990, Avizienis et al., 2004]. In particular, this means having software that does not collapse unexpectedly, leaving users uncertain about what has been lost or what recovery action is necessary; in other words, software should be *robust*. Essentially, robust software will protect itself against most threats and be able to recover smoothly should any fault occur.

This chapter considers how robustness might be improved using a self-managing architecture. The approach taken is to consider robustness in the wider context of system "perfection" to help ensure that its contribution is consistent with other improvements and general system requirements. The next section examines the requirements for perfection in more detail, identifying seven main properties that conveniently spell out the mnemonic PERFECT (the "R" is for "Robustness").

Section 3.3 suggests a basic structure for PERFECT software looking in particular at the implications of supporting robustness. A two-level service model is developed, as summarized in Fig. 3.1, in which a computer-based *service supplier*

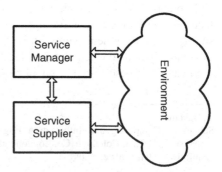

Fig. 3.1 Two-level service model summary

element is overseen by a *service manager* element that is responsible for monitoring the service in relation to requirements and current conditions, taking control action, as necessary.

The model is essentially the same as the structure of an IBM *autonomic element* [IBM, 2005] and an *S1 subsystem* in Beer's Viable System Model [Beer, 1984]. One significant innovation, however, as described in Section 3.3, is to reflect this two-level structure in the user interface. Section 3.4 illustrates the proposed structure with two examples. The first is a word processor, looking specifically at Microsoft Word; the second is a Web browser, particularly Mozilla Firefox. The conclusion indicates how the ideas presented might be taken forward.

3.2 PERFECT Software

Earlier work [Bustard and Sterritt, 2006] identified a set of general requirements for self-managing systems. In this section, these requirements are developed further and presented in a way that spells out the mnemonic PERFECT, as an *aide-mémoire*. In summary, it is proposed that a self-managing system should be:

- *Proactive*, in taking initiative to improve the system.
- *Effective*, in implementing what users require or expect.
- *Robust*, in coping with error situations and facilitating recovery.
- *Flexible*, in empowering users to tailor the system to their preferences.
- *Easy to use*, in taking initiative on a user's behalf to facilitate system use.
- *Cautious*, in taking account of risks and making allowance for recovery.
- *Transparent*, in revealing the reasoning behind system actions and options.

Although what follows presents these requirements individually, they are inevitably interconnected and that quickly becomes evident from the discussion. Thus, in practice, the requirements need to be taken into account holistically in an implementation. Note also that the requirements are largely user-focused. This seems reasonable as satisfying users should also be the main concern of developers. Some of these user-oriented properties may also be beneficial to developers, however, especially in relation to facilitating maintenance.

3.2.1 Proactive

The essence of self-managing systems is that they take action in support of system objectives without direct user control; that is, they are *proactive*. For example, in any application managing data, a system might usefully perform a periodic check on the integrity of that data without the user explicitly requesting the check.

Conceptually, therefore, self-managing systems consist of two parts that operate concurrently: (i) a *service supply* component, with which the user interacts to access system functionality; and (ii) a *service manager* component that monitors and supports the service component (see Fig. 3.1). The management component will periodically examine the state of the system and its environment, making adjustments as necessary. So, for example, internally, if data is found to be inconsistent, the problem might be reported to the user and help provided to resolve it. Similarly, if the data that is used internally is linked to information in an external source, and a relevant change is detected, necessary adjustments would be made. These might be handled automatically, if practical, or implemented in consultation with the user.

3.2.2 Effective

All systems need to be *effective* in the sense of satisfying explicit and implicit user requirements. With a self-managing structure, it is possible to add extra value by monitoring how a system is used in practice and refining both the functionality provided and its means of access.

Monitoring would include recording system errors and user faults. Having an automatic assessment of user behavior is particularly valuable for systems that are created incrementally, in an evolutionary cycle, as is currently popular in agile software development [Abrahamsson et al., 2003, Cockburn, 2002]. This pattern of development involves the building of successive versions of an application by learning from each release. The monitoring of effectiveness is beneficial to users in helping to achieve a product that is tuned to their needs. Such monitoring is also important to developers, as it allows them to assess how a system is actually being used in relation to their expectations. Moreover, when a system fails, error reports can be generated promptly and accurately, with little effort from the user and developer.

One potential obstacle, however, is the cost of monitoring user activity. If observation is at a detailed level, then there is a risk of performance being affected, which some users may find unacceptable [O'Reilly et al., 2005]. More importantly, many users may be uncomfortable about having their activity monitored at all, especially if there is concern about how the gathered information is used. As a result, current systems will usually not collect information about user activity without explicit approval. So, for example, if a Microsoft Office application fails, details of the problem will only be returned to Microsoft if the user gives permission.

Not all aspects of effectiveness can be inferred from user behavior so it is also desirable to enable users to give explicit feedback of any apparent shortcomings or potential issues. This feedback might be initiated by the user or by the system itself, depending on circumstances. For example, if a system collapses, then the user may be invited to supply relevant information as well as approving the transmission of an automatically generated error report.

3.2.3 Robust

The general expectation is that all systems should be *robust*. That is, they should be largely fault-free and designed to protect themselves from accidental or malicious harm. When a fault occurs, user activity should not be disrupted unduly and a smooth recovery facilitated. The faults themselves must, of course, be reported to users and developers as necessary. In self-managing systems, fault-reporting can occur at several levels. If, for example, the fault has been caused by users supplying inappropriate data, then the mistake would be explained to them and perhaps also logged for reporting to developers in case this is a commonly occurring problem. On the other hand, if the fault is internal, caused by an implementation error, then the developers alone need to be informed. In principle, users do not have to be involved if the error has not affected them, but, as indicated in Section 3.2.2, users may have to give permission for the information to be recorded and transmitted.

In situations where faults are not anticipated and the system fails, then a "graceful" recovery is expected [Bentley, 2005]. This means that control should appear to remain with the system, which will then explain to the user what damage, if any, has been caused, and how recovery can be achieved. Once again, an error report should be returned to the developers, summarizing the system state and the actions that led to the failure. Another aspect of robustness is the automatic repair of faults. In effect, this now occurs routinely through the auto-update mechanism on most computers connected to the Internet. In particular, serious problems, such as security risks, may have to be repaired quickly. Typically, this would involve (i) the developers creating a new version of the system or a repair "patch"; (ii) placing it in a location that the system checks periodically for updates; and (iii) downloading the update and installing it. In principle, such an update is close to "perfection" in that the fault can often be repaired without user effort, and indeed without user knowledge. Unfortunately, in practice, this strategy is only fully acceptable if the update is certain to have no side effects that create difficulties for the user. Clearly, developers cannot provide such guarantees, so again there is a need for users to collaborate in approving changes and in deciding when they should occur to avoid interference with current work.

3.2.4 Flexible

From the discussion of requirements so far, it is clear that while self-management can bring benefits, there is also an inherent risk of negative side effects for the user. This suggests that self-managing systems should obtain user approval before taking on most responsibilities; that is, while the system may be able to take full responsibility for particular operations, the actual degree of involvement should be agreed with the user. In this way, self-managing systems take on the role of a "good servant", following orders, passively providing information and guidance, and stepping in if a significant problem arises. The self-management options available to a user should be clearly laid out, with most self-management activity switched off by default. The exceptions would be basic system monitoring and reaction to significant threats or actual faults.

3.2.5 Easy to Use

It is expected that all systems should be *easy to use*, with self-management bringing additional benefit. Traditionally, this requirement is associated with minimizing the effort required to understand system functions and use them effectively [Gilb, 1988]. As discussed already, in relation to other requirements, self-managing systems can take initiative in monitoring user activity, draw conclusions about the significance of particular operations, and make adjustments dynamically. Some operating systems, for example, offer to hide icons on a desktop that have not been used recently. Similarly, some applications dynamically adjust initial menu choices to those operations that are used frequently. Such support, while well-meaning, can be irritating to users so although many users welcome the flexibility to tailor systems to their preferences, few want tailoring to be automatic. Thus, for example, although Microsoft only introduced self-adjusting (personalized) menus in Office 2000, they were never popular and are not used in Office 2007. The overall implication is that self-managing systems should passively monitor user activity and provide summaries for users to interpret. "Ease of use" could then be improved by presenting such summaries in a clear form, with additional relevant information and advice available on request.

3.2.6 Cautious

The general message emerging from the discussion so far is that self-management has a role in monitoring user activity and assisting in recovery from failure, but otherwise a passive approach is needed because of the risk of making changes that have unwelcome side effects. So another desirable aspect of self-managing systems is that they should be *cautious*; that is, they should be aware of the risks involved in making changes and take precautions accordingly. In particular, after any change, it seems prudent for the system to monitor resulting behavior in case problems have been caused that do not appear immediately.

Realistically, it is impossible to foresee the impact of all changes so, where possible, changes should be reversible. Thus, for example, if a new version of a system is installed but a fault is found on running acceptance tests, it should be possible to revert to the original version. If the fault is found later, after data specific to the new version has been created, then reversal may be much more difficult. In general, version reversal can only be achieved if it is anticipated when the system is first designed.

Overall, there is a balance between the risk associated with making a change and the risk of not doing it. For example, a security patch may be so important to the well-being of many users that it should be implemented automatically even if some face problems as a result. One strategy is to classify the importance of potential changes so that in critical situations the system can act autonomously to install them. Unfortunately, autonomy is itself a risk as it might be exploited by virus software. A detailed risk analysis is therefore desirable in implementing any self-management facility in order to achieve the best risk balance overall.

3.2.7 Transparent

The requirements discussed so far reveal a tension between the potential benefits of allowing a system to perform operations independently and anxiety over the risk of what might go wrong as a result. To reduce this anxiety, self-managing systems should be *transparent*, in that they should explain the implications of any activity they undertake on behalf of a user. This might be provided before an activity is approved or after an activity has been completed. In the latter case, this means keeping a history of self-management actions taken within a system, including all monitoring performed and its impact.

A self-managing system reacts to changes in its operating environment and in its own internal state. The measurements that are being taken are effectively based on models of these areas and they too need to be explained to users in as much detail as necessary to inspire confidence. Generally, it is expected that users will be provided with some form of display in which the state of the system and its environment is portrayed, indicating expected performance and highlighting problem areas.

3.2.8 Robustness Revisited

From a user perspective, robustness is probably the most important system property on which to concentrate, as improvement could reduce user loss in the event of failure and reduce user effort in recovering from failure. It is also beneficial to developers as increased robustness will inspire greater user confidence in the product and so improve its perceived quality.

As this section has indicated, however, improving user confidence also means avoiding some of the negative secondary risks associated with self-management and, in particular, ensuring that the user retains the feeling of being in control. The next section presents an abstract architecture intended to meet these needs and expectations, illustrated with two commonly used applications.

3.3 Two-Level Robustness Model

The analysis of requirements in Section 3.2 suggests some of the internal structure associated with the *service manager* and *service supplier* components of the two-level system model summarized in Fig. 3.1. Figure 3.2 adds this detail to this model by dividing both the *service supplier* and *service manager* into two parts.

For the service supplier the parts are (i) a *service interface* through which the system services are accessed; and (ii) a *service state*, holding information about the current operational condition of the service. For the service manager, the two parts are (i) the *control panel*, through which manager options are selected and the current and historical states of the service examined; and (ii) the *service monitor* responsible for observing the state of the service and its operating environment and reporting their condition through the control panel.

Fig. 3.2 Two-level service
model

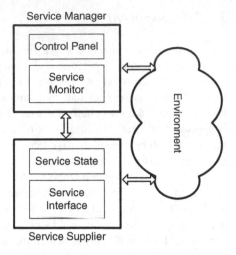

As an illustration of this structure, consider the case of a service offered through a specific application executing on a single user computer that has access to the Internet. In general, the state of the service would be represented by (i) the current point (or points) of execution of the application; (ii) the collective internal data of the application; and (iii) details of any external data involved. This information, if saved, could be used to restart the application after failure. The frequency of saving would be selected by the user through the control panel. Also, the time of the last saving might be shown here, together with other key information about the monitored state of the application and its environment. Such information could include, for example, details of memory used and space available in internal and external storage.

To minimize the link between the service manager and service supplier, knowledge of all but the key indicators of the service state might be kept within the service supplier, by having the supplier component save and restore its own state under direction from the manager component.

From the user perspective, interaction with the application is through the service supplier and the service manager, which execute concurrently. By implication, the user is able to observe the state of the application as it executes and interact with the service while monitoring takes place. In some circumstances, it may also be desirable to allow suspension of the service supplier by switching control to the service manager. This is equivalent to a request to "speak to the supervisor" and might be triggered if the user suspects that there is a fault in the application that the service monitor has not detected. This would be particularly useful if the application "hangs", ignoring input and making no apparent progress.

If the application collapses because of an internal failure, then control would be transferred automatically to the service manager, which would then assist the recovery process. This would typically mean restarting the application at the last saved point but it may also be desirable to check for a more recent version of the application to download. A record of the failure would also be retained within the control panel, with the service manager helping to report such details to the application developers. In particular, the user might want to supplement the description of the failure by explaining what was being attempted when the application failed and offer ideas on possible causes.

This model achieves improved robustness through handling all failure in the same controlled way, as a "call to the supervisor". The next section looks at the implications of using such a model in two commonly occurring application areas.

3.4 Examples

If the model proposed in Section 3.3 is indeed the basis of a better design for all applications, then its benefits should be evident from an analysis of its likely impact on existing applications. This section looks at two types of application that are used daily in an office environment, a *word processor* and a *Web browser*, to consider the potential advantages of each being implemented using the two-level service architecture outlined.

3.4.1 Word Processor Example

Microsoft Word was first introduced in 1983 [Wikipedia, 2007] and is now the most successful word processor on the market. Over that period it has been refined to improve its usability, which includes better response to failure. Failure may result from faults in Word or in its environment, such as problems with memory or the power supply. Word's approach to handling such problems is similar to that proposed in the two-level service model, namely to take periodic snapshots of the system state and use these to facilitate recovery. The apparent advantages of the proposed two-level service model over the Microsoft Word approach (in Office 2007 in a Windows XP environment) are as follows:

- *The two-level model makes user control visible at the highest level of the application.* In Word, such control tends to be in lower-level menus and grouped with application level options. Figure 3.3, for example, shows the screen for setting various choices associated with saving files, one of which is the frequency with which recovery backups are made. Many users may not even be aware that such a facility exists, relying entirely on the default settings.
- *The two-level model includes an explanation of the control options available.* In Word, little explanation is offered. For example, in relation to taking backup snapshots, the interval can be adjusted from 1 to 120 minutes but there is no guidance on how to make the choice. The default interval is 10 minutes, which has been standard for many years, despite advances in memory technology and the expectation that, on average, users will lose 5 minutes worth of typing following a failure. One minute seems best for users, to minimize typing loss, but machine constraints may make selection of a higher value more desirable. In a

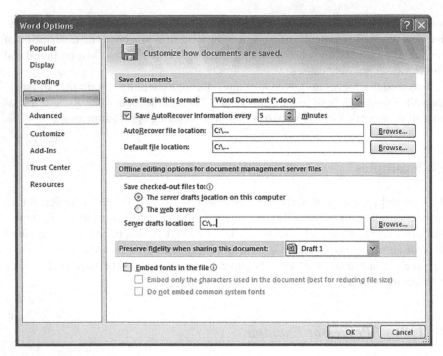

Fig. 3.3 "Save Options" screen in Word 2007

small experiment, setting the value to "1 minute" on a one-year old standard PC, and observing system behavior over a few weeks, there were no obvious user problems, but longer-term wear-and-tear on the disk might be an issue.

- *The two-level model can handle most failures within the application.* If Word fails, all problems are handled at the operating systems level. For example, if Word "hangs" (not responding), the only option is to ask the operating systems to close it, but being outside the Word application means that data may be lost, as indicated in the message shown in Fig. 3.4. In the two-level model, failures at the service supplier level are directed to the service manager. Should it fail, however, the operating system would have to become involved. It is important, therefore, that the service manager component be very reliable.
- *The two-level model allows users to add a commentary to fault reports.* If Word fails, a standard report is sent to Microsoft (see Fig. 3.5). This has the advantage that the user can send the report with just one mouse click but excludes the user from adding context information and ideas about possible causes of the failure.
- *In the two-level model, recovery from failure is attempted immediately.* In Word, recovery only occurs when the application is reactivated. At that point, Word searches for AutoRecover files and, if any are present, recovers the files and displays them for the user to examine. This search occurs every time Word is opened. The main disadvantage here, however, is that users need to be aware that

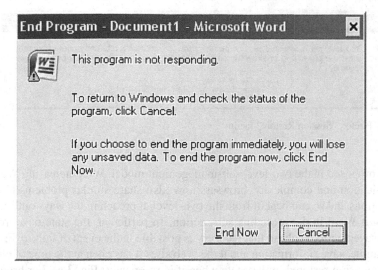

Fig. 3.4 "No-Response" dialogue box for Windows 2007

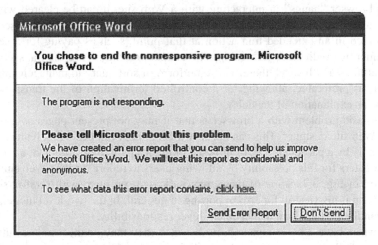

Fig. 3.5 "Error Report" dialogue box for Windows 2007

this is how recovery is implemented as there is no explanation given at the point of failure.

3.4.2 Web Browser Example

A Web browser, such as *Internet Explorer, Firefox*, or *Opera*, is similar in structure to most other applications. That is, like Microsoft Word, browsers mix functional and management activities in a single piece of software, rather than separate them

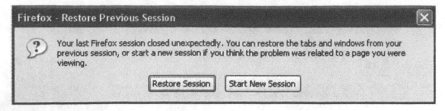

Fig. 3.6 Firefox "Session Restore" facility

out, as proposed in the two-level self-management model. With increasing Web site sophistication and complexity, browsers now also share similar problems to other applications and so can benefit from the two-level approach in the ways outlined for Microsoft Word in the preceding sub-section. In particular, the state of a browser can be saved periodically so that recovery is possible in the event of failure. Firefox, for example, saves information about the Web sites it has open at the time of closure and the session restored to that state when it is re-opened (Fig. 3.6). For browsers, there is less data involved so saving and restoring a state is more straightforward.

If a browser "hangs" in interacting with a Web site, it can be cleared with the stop button if it fails to "time out". One difficulty, however, is that the user may be involved in an extended transaction at that point, such as paying for a service or product by credit card, so breaking the connection may leave the transaction in an uncertain state. Instead, therefore, some form of soft query to management level software is preferable, allowing for a controlled termination of the transaction or perhaps an explanation of the delay.

One basic problem with a browser is that it may not present pages as intended by the Web site designer. This can occur if the site is developed using features supported only by a particular type of browser, or even a particular version of a browser. Firefox caters for this possibility by allowing users to report "broken Web sites", as indicated in Fig. 3.7. Some of these may indicate a problem with Firefox so this mechanism is also useful for error reporting in general. In the two-level model, such error handling would be a management-level responsibility.

Browsers have a basic vulnerability because they may connect to sites that are "malicious". Sources of vulnerability include the use of:

1. *Pop-up windows* that appear on entry to a site.
2. *Cookies*, files created by a Web site to store information on a user's computer about use of that site.
3. *Plug-ins*, which add new capabilities to a browser, such as the ability to play audio or video clips. Examples include Macromedia Flash Player and Java.
4. The embedding of *JavaScript* in the underlying HTML code.

All of these facilities have perfectly legitimate uses and indeed may be essential for some sites. Because of their risk, however, they may be blocked, possibly by default, with the user giving explicit approval if any are needed (Fig. 3.8). Currently,

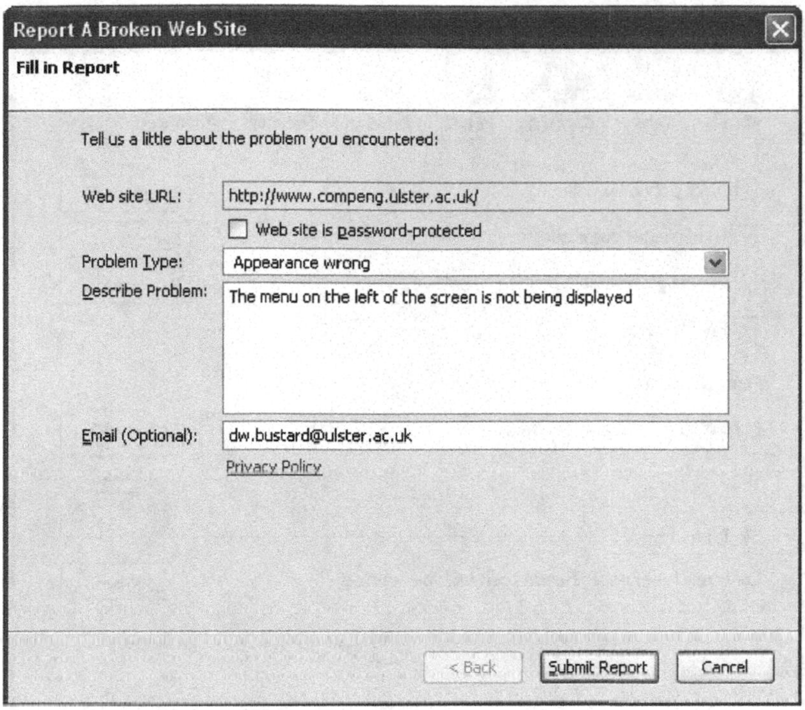

Fig. 3.7 "Broken Web Site" dialogue box for Firefox

management of these facilities is mixed with other functionality in browsers, so location in a two-level framework would again be beneficial.

Some plug-ins enhance the functionality of a browser and so conceptually extend the "service supplier" part of the application. Likewise, the same mechanism may extend the service management part. One good example is *McAfee SiteAdvisor* [McAfee, 2007], which was developed in 2005 by a small start-up at MIT, before being taken over in 2006 by McAfee. SiteAdvisor uses Web crawlers to examine sites on the Internet and rate them as:

- *green*, safe, with no significant problems found;
- *yellow*, caution, if tests reveal some minor security or nuisance issues or the site has had past security issues; or
- *red*, warning, if tests and manual analysis reveal serious issues to consider before accessing the site. This includes misusing supplied e-mail addresses or including malware in downloads.

Following a Web search, using an established engine such as *Google, Yahoo*, or *Ask Jeeves*, the presented page of links is analyzed and tags added to each link. A green, yellow, or red tag is attached if the site has been rated by SiteAdvisor; otherwise a question mark is used. The report for dubious sites can be examined in detail before entry, but for most users all sites graded yellow or red would probably

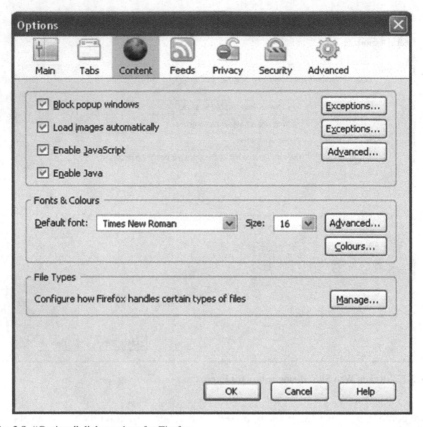

Fig. 3.8 "Options" dialogue box for Firefox

be avoided. Currently, this is about 10% of those assessed. Significantly, this facility works much like the proposed two-level model might behave, in that it involves management monitoring superimposed on functional behavior.

Another problem is that Web sites that use JavaScript may not be coded correctly, causing difficulties for the browser. Firefox highlights such problems through an *error console* (previously called JavaScript console), as illustrated in Fig. 3.9.

This is another management-level concern and one that can benefit from being integrated with general error control. In particular, this information might be combined with the broken Web site report, illustrated in Fig. 3.7.

For most users, information about underlying coding problems on Web pages is irrelevant to them and should instead be reported to the owners of the Web site. The same is true of pages that have unsatisfactory content, including broken links. Broken links do not cause the browser to fail but indicate a maintenance problem on the server hosting the Web sites. This is currently a significant concern across the Internet [Tian et al., 2004] and is yet another example of where a monitoring management layer is beneficial. In this case, it means monitoring the pages in a

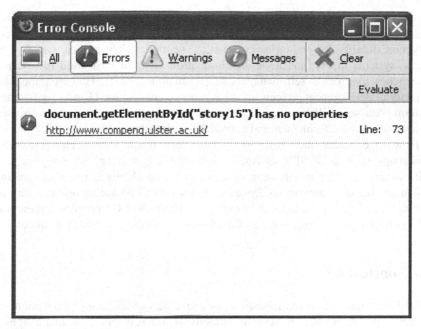

Fig. 3.9 Firefox "Error Console"

Web site periodically to ensure that all links are live and then initiating repair if any are found to be faulty [Bustard et al., 2007].

3.5 Additional Thoughts on Self-Managing Systems and Software

As has been highlighted earlier in this chapter, self-managing systems and self-managing software came to the forefront in applied and industrial research in 2001 with IBM's Autonomic Computing initiative. Other related research initiatives have followed; including N1 (Sun) [Sun, 2002], Adaptive Infrastructure (HP) [HPWorld, 2003], Dynamic Systems Initiative (Microsoft) [Microsoft, 2004], Adaptive Network Care (Cisco) [IBM and Cisco, 2003], Proactive Computing (Intel) [Want et al., 2003], and Autonomic Networking (Motorola) [Strassner, 2008], as well as joint academic and industrial led initiatives such as autonomic communications, biological inspired computing, and organic computing. This proliferation of initiatives highlights the understanding of the need for self-managing systems and self-managing software, while at the same time the many different initiatives may be considered to highlight that there is no foundational approach to creating such systems and software.

In terms of foundational disciplines to develop such systems, artificial intelligence, catastrophe theory, connectionism, control theory (digital, analog, closed/

open loop), cybernetics, decision theory, dependency management, expert systems, game theory, information theory, mathematical optimization, operations research, polycontexturality, second-order cybernetics, semiotics, synergetics, sociosynergetics, systems theory, and trade-off elimination have all been used in research approaches to provide self-management [Lightstone, 2007]. However, the vast majority of development projects aimed at specific areas of the IT industry (storage systems, databases, Web servers, network infrastructure, telephony) have focused on a subset of these techniques and approaches [Lightstone, 2007].

How to engineer such software is still very much a research topic, with workshops such as ICSE's SEAMS (Software Engineering for Adaptive and Self- Managing Systems) [Cheng et al., 2007] and IEEEs EASe (Engineering of Autonomic and Autonomous Systems) [EASe, 2006] providing research forums in which possible approaches can be explored. The PERFECT properties presented in this chapter provide requirements for what self-managing software should entail.

3.6 Conclusion

This chapter has considered robustness as one aspect of achieving "perfection" in the development of software systems. Effectively, it has been argued that a significant improvement in robustness can be achieved by implementing software with a self-managing structure and taking into account the general requirements of such systems. Specifically, this means creating systems with a two-level structure, separating the services offered by the system from the monitoring and control of the achievement of those services.

This chapter has introduced the idea of bringing this two-level structure up to the user interface and discussed the basic design structure and operation of the resulting software. The approach was illustrated by considering its implication for a word processor (Microsoft Word) and browser (Mozilla Firefox). This analysis suggested that the two-level self-management structure had the potential to improve robustness, especially in relation to systems collapsing or hanging.

The key to making this structure successful is in ensuring that the service management component of every system is extremely reliable. Further implications of the structure are currently being investigated both in relation to robustness and the general properties and expectations of self-management.

Acknowledgments This work was undertaken through the Centre for Software Process Technologies, which is supported by the EU Programme for Peace and Reconciliation in Northern Ireland and the Border Region of Ireland (PEACE II).

References

Abrahamsson, P., Warsta, J., Siponen, M., and Ronkainen, J. (2003). New directions on agile methods: A comparative analysis. In *Proceedings of the 25th International Conference on Software Engineering*, pages 244–254, 3–10 May, Portland, OR. IEEE Computer Society.

Avizienis, A., Laprie, J., Randell, B., and Landwehr, C. (2004). Basic concepts and taxonomy of dependable and secure computing. *IEEE Transactions on Dependable and Secure Computing*, 1(1):11–33.

Beer, S. (1984). The viable system model: Its provenance, development, methodology and pathology. *Journal of the Operational Research Society*, 35:7–26.

Bentley, P. (2005). Investigations into graceful degradation of evolutionary developmental software. *Natural Computing*, 4:417–437.

Boehm, B. (1996). Identifying quality-requirement conflicts. *Software*, 13(2):25–35.

Brooks, F. (1975). *The Mythical Man-Month: Essays on Software Engineering*. Addison-Wesley Professional, Reading, MA.

Bustard, D., Moore, A., Higgins, D., and Ayre, D. (2007). Towards self-managing web sites: The link integrity problem. In *Proceedings of 4th IEEE International Workshop on Engineering of Autonomic and Autonomous Systems*, pages 61–67. Tucson, AZ, IEEE Computer Society.

Bustard, D. and Sterritt, R. (2006). A requirements engineering perspective on autonomic systems development. In Parashar, M. and Hariri, S., editors, *Autonomic Computing: Concepts, Infrastructure, and Applications*. Taylor & Francis Group, Boca Raton, FL. CRC Press.

Cheng, B., de Lemos, R., Fickas, S., Garlan, D., Litoiu, M., Magee, J., Mulller, H., and Taylor, R. (2007). Seams 2007: Software engineering for adaptive and self-managing systems. In *International Workshop on Software Engineering for Adaptive and Self-Managing Systems (SEAMS '07)*, 20–26 May, Minneapolis, MN. IEEE Computer Society.

Cockburn, A. (2002). *Agile Software Development*. Pearson Education, 2nd edition.

EASe, I. (2006). *3rd IEEE International Workshop on Engineering of Autonomic & Autonomous Systems (EASe 2006)*. IEEE Computer Society, Potsdam, Germany, 24-30 March.

Gilb, T. (1988). *Principles of Software Engineering Management*. Addison Wesley Professional, Reading, MA.

Hoh, I., Boehm, B., Rodger, T., and Deutsch, M. (2001). Applying WinWin to quality requirements: A case study. In *Proceedings of the 23rd International Conference on Software Engineering*, pages 555–564, Toronto, Ontario, Canada. IEEE Computer Society.

Horn, P. (2001). Autonomic computing: Ibm perspective on the state of information technology. Technical report, IBM T.J. Watson Labs., NY. Presented at AGENDA 2001, Scottsdale, AR, http://www.research.ibm.com/autonomic/.

HPWorld (2003). Adaptive infrastructure. Technical report, Atlanta, GA.

IBM (2005). An architectural blueprint for autonomic computing. Technical report. White paper, 3rd edition.

IBM and Cisco (2003). Adaptive services framework. Technical report, IBM and Cisco Systems. White paper, Version 1.0.

Kephart, J. (2005). Research challenges of autonomic computing. In *In Proceedings of the 27th International Conference on Software Engineering*, pages 15–22, St. Louis, Missouri. IEEE Computer Society.

Kephart, J. and Chess, D. (2003). The vision of autonomic computing. *Computer*, 36(1):41–52.

Lightstone, S. (2007). Foundations of autonomic computing development. In *4th IEEE International Workshop on Engineering of Autonomic and Autonomous Systems (EASe 2007)*, pages 163–171, 26–29 March, Arizona. IEEE Computer Society.

McAfee (2007). http://www.siteadvisor.com.

Microsoft (2004). Dynamic systems initiative overview. Technical report, Microsoft Corporation. White paper, revised 15 November.

Nelson (1990). Fault tolerant computing: Fundamental concepts. *Computer*, 23(7):19–25.

O'Reilly, C., Bustard, D., and Morrow, P. (2005). The war room command console: shared visualizations for inclusive team coordination. In *Proceedings of the ACM 2005 Symposium on Software Visualization*, pages 57–65, 14–15 May, St. Louis, Missouri.

Strassner, J. (2008). Autonomic networking. In *5th IEEE International Workshop on Engineering of Autonomic and Autonomous Systems*, Belfast, Northern Ireland, 31 March–4 April. IEEE Computer Society. Accepted for publication.

Sun (2002). N1 - Introducing just-in-time computing. Technical report, Sun Microsystems. White paper.

Tian, J., Rudraraju, S., and Li, Z. (2004). Evaluating web software reliability based on workload and failure data extracted from server logs. *IEEE Transactions on Software Engineering*, 30(11):754–769.

Want, R., Pering, T., and Tennenhouse, D. (2003). Comparing autonomic and proactive computing. *IBM Systems Journal in Technology*, 42(1):129–135.

Wikipedia (2007). Microsoft word. http://en.wikipedia.org/wiki/Microsoft_ Word (last accessed October 2007).

Chapter 4
Robustness in Network Protocols and Distributed Applications of the Internet

Jürgen Vogel and Jörg Widmer

Abstract The Internet connects computers from all over the world for a fast and reliable exchange of data, e.g., from e-mail or Web applications. Considering its sheer size and heterogeneity, the Internet is the most complex computer system ever built. It has coped with a tremendous growth, has handled many critical situations, and, overall, does work quite well. This is because robustness was a major goal from the very beginning, which led to a network design that is self-regulatory, redundant, scalable, and updatable. In this chapter, we will discuss these design principles and the Internet's architecture, the core protocols IP and TCP, protocols for wireless communication, and applications such as the popular BitTorrent file exchange.

4.1 Introduction

The Internet is the most complex computer system ever built. The past two decades witnessed its exponential growth from a small research network to the dominating all-purpose communication infrastructure with an estimated number of 427 million computers that connect organizations, companies, and people from all over the world, totalling almost 2 billion users [ITU, 2007]. Besides its sheer size, the Internet is complex because of the heterogeneity of the supported hardware (from hand-held devices to supercomputers) and software (from e-mail to games). Moreover, it is self-organizing in the sense that there is no single Internet administration, and basically everyone is free to use and to contribute to its content and applications. And yet, the Internet does work quite well and has handled many critical situations such as natural disasters, terrorist attacks, and computer viruses.

This is possible because robustness, the property of a system to continue to function well despite changes in operating environment, was a major design goal from the very beginning [Clark, 1988]. The foundations of the Internet were developed in the 1970s on the initiative of the U.S. military. The goal of the original ARPANET,

J. Vogel

European Media Laboratory, Schloss-Wolfsbrunnenweg 31c, 69118 Heidelberg, Germany

email: juergen.vogel@eml.org

A. Schuster (ed.), *Robust Intelligent Systems,* DOI: 10.1007/978-1-84800-261-6_4,
© Springer-Verlag London Limited 2008

as it was called, was to connect and provide access to the scarce computing resources at that time in a way such that the network could survive the common failures of individual computers or communication lines. This chapter discusses how technologies and design principles of computer networks in general, and the Internet in particular, can provide such robustness. The chapter starts by introducing the general architecture of the Internet.

4.2 How the Internet Works

The Internet is a worldwide computer network that allows all attached devices to exchange data with each other. An Internet application such as e-mail generates data in the form of messages that need to be transported from its sender to the receiver(s) in a reliable, secure, fast, and efficient way.

4.2.1 Delivering Data

In case the sending and receiving computers, or *end systems*, are located within the same Local Area Network (LAN), data delivery is straightforward: A LAN is a broadcast medium, i.e., data is always received by all attached computers that decide whether it is intended for them or not. If sender and receiver are not within the same LAN, a system of intermediate network nodes is used. Each of these intermediate nodes is connected to some others, forming a network topology of nodes and the links that connect them. The task of the intermediate nodes is then to successively forward incoming data to appropriate neighboring nodes until the receiver is reached. This forwarding process is called *routing*. A prerequisite for routing is that all network nodes can be identified unambiguously by means of a unique address. For the Internet, the 32-bit IP address is used (or a symbolic name such as www.springer.com that is resolved by DNS to its IP address [Mockapetris, 1987]).

On its way, data like an e-mail or a Web document is fragmented into small packets (if necessary). By interleaving packets, network links can be utilized by different ongoing communication sessions in parallel, which optimizes the network's overall throughput. These packets can be routed through a network either by *virtual circuit routing* or *datagram routing* [Tanenbaum, 2002]. In the first case, an appropriate path between sender and receiver is established before the actual transmission, and each router included in this virtual circuit stores status information about the incoming and the outgoing link. Data packets carry an identifier of the virtual circuit they belong to, and all packets of a certain transmission follow the same path. On completion, the virtual circuit is terminated explicitly. One advantage of virtual circuits is that the routing algorithm needs to be executed only once. But if a link or node fails, a completely new virtual circuit has to be set up, and all status information that belongs to the broken circuit needs to be deleted from the routers.

In comparison, datagram routing handles each packet independently from other packets: Packets carry the receiver's address, and the routers decide for each incoming packet about the outgoing link. Thus, routers do not need to store any per-session status information, and packets of the same session may even take different paths to the receiver. Failed links or nodes are bypassed automatically, leading to a more robust data transport than with virtual circuits. These arguments led to the decision that the Internet should use datagram routing [Clark, 1988] (while the telephone network uses virtual circuits).

The link between two network nodes can be different physical media. In the Internet, end systems are often connected via copper wire (e.g., DSL) or wireless (e.g., WLAN), whereas routers are usually linked with high-speed fiber optics (e.g., SONET/SDH). Routers and links are installed and administered by so-called Internet Service Providers (ISPs). Each ISP is responsible for certain parts, or sub-networks, of the Internet. These subnetworks are connected to each other and explain the origin of the term *Internet*, which denotes a network of interconnected networks. The primary goal of the Internet therefore is to hide its complex and heterogeneous infrastructure from its users by transparent end-to-end data delivery [Clark, 1988].

4.2.2 Why Robustness Requires Special Attention

During transport, data faces many dangers. First, when transmitting a packet over a link, it can be corrupted by bit errors, i.e., one or more bits have "flipped" and are decoded with the wrong value, because of hardware errors or interference. For instance, two overlapping transmissions on the same broadcast medium (e.g., a WLAN) collide such that neither transmission can be received error-free. Or a strong magnetic field interferes with the electric signal on a copper wire and generates bit errors. Second, a router might receive more packets than it can process or than its outgoing links can carry. Even though each router has a buffer for storing such packets until they can be processed, this buffer will overflow if too many packets arrive over a longer period of time so that ultimately packets are lost. Third, a link or router might be damaged or fail completely so that one or more packets are lost. Fourth, similar to routers, a receiver might get more packets than it can handle, and overflowing packets are lost. Fifth, packets that belong to the same session might follow different paths through the network due to routing table updates, broken links, and crashed or overloaded routers. Besides delay jitter, this may cause packets to arrive in a different order than the one they were originally sent in. Sixth, routers with parallel processing capabilities might also accidentally change the order between two incoming packets. Seventh, the router's knowledge about the network topology might be outdated or wrong so that packets do not reach their destination and are lost. Eighth, packets might be declared as lost erroneously (because they arrive too late) and are retransmitted by the network's error control. As a result, duplicate packets arrive at the receiver. Finally, besides these technical error sources, we should not forget that humans make errors, e.g., when administrating routers. As [Anderson et al., 2003] phrase it, one should expect "malicious attack, misimplementation, and misconfiguration at every turn".

A network must address all these aspects appropriately to achieve robustness. Like other distributed systems, computer networks employ the following general techniques to prevent, detect, or repair errors [Gray, 1986]: (1) keeping the design simple, modular, and scalable, adding meta-data to and verifying input, e.g., using packet checksums to detect bit errors, (2) adapting to dynamic conditions with measurements and feedback loops, e.g., tuning the sending rate to the router's and the receiver's capacity, and (3) over-provisioning and installing redundant hardware resources, e.g., providing enough capacity to handle peak traffic loads.

4.2.3 Protocol Layers

A computer network integrates many functions for transmitting data safely and efficiently between two computers, e.g., packetization, routing, and error control. In the Internet, these network functions are implemented with a *layering* approach that organizes the entire network functionality in independent layers where each layer is responsible for certain parts of that functionality. Layers are built on top of each other such that a layer uses the functionality (or service) of the underlying layer to provide its own. Service requests and responses between two layers are exchanged via a standardized interface that hides the implementation details. The communication between two network nodes is realized by the pairwise exchange of information between the nodes' layers on the same level. Each layer has its own packet header that carries its information, e.g., the packet header of the routing layer contains IP addresses. The rules of this communication are defined by a network *protocol*.

The main advantage of this approach is that the complex task of designing, implementing, and testing a network can be broken down to basic functions that are largely independent from each other. Moreover, layers are designed such that they can be used for different network applications. A layer's implementation can also be modified independently as long as the interface and the encoding of packets remain the same. The Internet has a total number of five layers (from bottom-up): (1) The *physical layer* takes data in the form of a bit string and, using an appropriate encoding scheme, transmits it via the physical medium to the next node. (2) The *data link layer* controls this transmission, e.g., by preventing or repairing collisions if the physical medium uses broadcast, e.g., as in the case of WLAN. (3) The *network layer* routes packets from end system to end system, which is the task of the Internet Protocol (IP) [Postel, 1981a] together with specialized protocols for the exchange of routing and control information. (4) The *transport layer* connects the sending and the receiving application and comes in two specifications: the Transmission Control Protocol (TCP) [Postel, 1981b] sets up a reliable connection between the sender and the receiver, delivers all packets in the correct order, and adapts the sending rate to the resources available at both the receiver and the network using flow control and congestion control, respectively. In contrast, the alternative User Datagram Protocol

(UDP) [Postel, 1980] is connectionless, unreliable, and does not adapt the sending rate. (5) Finally, the *application layer* manages the application-level data exchange, e.g., to transfer a file from the sender's hard drive to the receiver's.

The first three layers are run by the so-called core network of routers and their links, whereas transport layer and application layer are the end system's responsibility. IP is the key element in this layering model: It hides the complexity and vast variety of the underlying infrastructure with its links, switches, gateways, routers, and subnetworks behind a very simple interface, so that applications do not need to know about the actual hardware that is used to transfer their data. At the same time, routers can pass through data without needing to know about the applications behind it. This twofold transparency makes the Internet flexible to integrate new networking or application technologies without having to adapt the entire network.

4.2.4 The Hourglass Design and the End-to-End Arguments

The functionality of IP is the least common denominator of the many different applications that build upon it. From the application's perspective, IP does not do much aside from transparent routing: Packets can be lost on the way or arrive out of order. In case the application requires robust, i.e., reliable and ordered transmissions, this has to be addressed either by the transport layer or the application itself. Moreover, IP does not give any guarantees or even feedback about the quality of the transmission in terms of data rate, packet loss rate, end-to-end delay, or delay jitter. All concurrent transmissions compete for the Internet's available resources, and IP aims to provide the best service it can achieve given the current network conditions. Therefore, the Internet is called a *best effort* network. In order to prevent possible resource conflicts between concurrent transmissions, service providers usually install significantly more resources than are used on average, a strategy called *over-provisioning*. In comparison, a network with guaranteed *quality of service* levels would require a different architecture. For instance, the telephone network reserves as many resources for each call as are required for a voice transmission and refuses a call if no resources are available.

The higher number of protocols below and above IP has led to the metaphor that the Internet layers resemble an *hourglass* where IP is the thin waist. Also, IP itself is rather simple and uses datagram routing where routers do not have to manage status information about individual data transmissions [Carpenter, 1996]. The motivation behind the hourglass design that places the complex functionality of transport and application layer at the end systems are the so-called *end-to-end arguments*: First, only the application has the complete knowledge to decide if and to what extent a certain feature is required [Saltzer et al., 1984]. For instance, an application for transmitting live-audio might be able to tolerate packet-loss and does not require a reliable delivery, whereas a file transfer should be completely reliable. Even if the network were able to guarantee reliability, an error might also occur at a higher layer, e.g., when storing the file on disk. Thus, the overall responsibility is in any case with the application. Second, keeping routers simple lowers the risk of failures within the network. Moreover, it lowers the cost of routers and makes it relatively cheap to scale the Internet by adding capacity [Coffman and Odlyzko, 2002]. Finally, a general and minimalistic design of the network increases the chances that a new and unanticipated application can be added without having to change the core network [Clark and Blumenthal, 2001]. These end-to-end arguments seek to move as much functionality from the network's core to the end systems as possible. But obviously, some functions such as routing must remain with the core.

Although many experts see the hourglass design as a major reason for the Internet's success story, there were always concerns whether it is actually the best approach. For instance, [Clark, 1988] feared that implementation errors at the end systems might threaten the correct functioning of the Internet—which is actually true nowadays, not only because of programming errors but mostly because of deliberate attacks that utilize functionality placed at the end systems. Over the years, the waist of the hourglass has also thickened as the Internet core has become more and more complex [Bush and Meyer, 2002] by continuously adding features to the routers, e.g., to support security or mobile nodes or to make the Internet more robust [Clark and Blumenthal, 2001]. It is even believed that an ever-increasing complexity of the Internet is almost inevitable because new features that address a certain issue always have side-effects that require follow-up changes, leading to a never-ending "complexity/robustness spiral" [Willinger and Doyle, 2002]. Many experts therefore argue that the Internet has evolved into a network that is overly complex, inefficient, and will sooner or later break down [Handley, 2006], unless some fundamental design changes or a completely new version will be implemented [Clark et al., 2002].

There is also debate over whether the Internet topology itself is robust or fragile. It was argued in [Albert et al., 2000] that the Internet has properties of a scale-free network. Such a network has node degrees that follow a power law distribution, i.e., connectivity in the network is provided by a few central nodes connected to many other nodes, while most nodes are connected to only a few other nodes. Scale-free networks are very robust against random failures but are very susceptible to attacks targeted at the well connected nodes. However, it seems that while the Internet's node degree distribution indeed follows a power law, connectivity is provided by backbone routers connected to relatively few other backbone routers, and high-degree nodes are found more toward the periphery of the Internet [Doyle et al., 2005]. Such a topological structure is much more resilient to targeted attacks than pure scale-free networks.

4.2.5 Distributing Functionality: Replication vs. Centralization

Computer networks and network applications are distributed systems of interconnected nodes where each node delivers a certain part of the functionality [Tanenbaum, 2002]. For instance, consider the World Wide Web (WWW): Web pages are retrieved with a browser application that runs on the user's end system n_c.

Once the user opens a page, n_c issues a Hypertext Transfer Protocol (HTTP) request that is transmitted over TCP/IP via a series of routers n_{r_i} to the Web server n_s where the page is hosted. The Web server n_s reacts by transmitting the requested page back to n_c. Because n_c merely displays Web pages generated elsewhere, it is denoted as *client* whereas n_s provides the actual content and is therefore called *server*, i.e., the client uses the server's functionality (or service). With respect to managing the application state, such a client-server (C/S) system has a *centralized architecture* because n_s is solely responsible for managing (and updating, if necessary) the Web page.

In contrast, in a *replicated architecture* certain functionality or data is available from two or more nodes. Data (or state) replication means that several nodes manage a local copy of the same data. This approach is also known as peer-to-peer (P2P). In a P2P version of the WWW, alternative Web servers exist that host the identical content. Together with an appropriate load-balancing algorithm that for each request selects the Web server with the lowest resource usage, the P2P approach can serve considerably more requests than can the single-server alternative. Moreover, it can be scaled easily by adding more nodes, whereas a single server has a firm limit. The P2P system is also more robust against the failures of individual nodes (or broken network links) because it continues to work as long as there is at least one reachable node. Its main disadvantage when compared with C/S is its higher complexity: When reading data from several potential source nodes (e.g., Web servers), a mechanism for selecting a specific one is required (e.g., a load-balancing algorithm). Moreover, when writing data, all sources have to be updated (e.g., for Web pages with dynamic content) such that the next request leads to the same result independent of which node responds to it. All these extra functionalities for P2P systems introduce potential points of failure if not designed and implemented carefully [Vogel, 2004].

4.2.6 Managing Replicated Data: Soft State vs. Hard State

Many Internet protocols and applications have their state replicated to a certain degree. In addition to Web servers, load-balancing architectures are common for scientific grid computing, search engines, and multiplayer online games. Another example is routing protocols where each router needs information about the Internet's topology. In general, data may change dynamically because a certain node inserts, modifies, or deletes (parts of) it. For instance, a router might discover a broken link and change its routing table. The node responsible for such a change then needs to notify all other nodes to keep all copies of the affected data synchronized. This can be done either by means of hard state or soft state synchronization. The *soft state* approach was first introduced under the notion of "fate sharing" [Clark, 1988], which means that each node that uses certain data should also share the responsibility to maintain it: Nodes periodically announce the current state of their local data copy by sending it to all other nodes. When receiving such an announcement, a node can discover new or updated data. The time span between two announcements is called report interval. Within a certain report interval, a node sends an announcement only when it did not yet receive a corresponding announcement of another node. Thus, on average only one announcement per report interval is sent. Data is deleted implicitly with a timeout: Each node saves the time of the last announcement for each part of the data. In case a certain data part is not announced for several report intervals, and the node has no further interest in that part, it times out and is deleted.

All announcements are transmitted unreliably so that it might happen that no announcement is sent in a report interval. But because all nodes listen for an announcement and are ready to send one in case it should not arrive, this happens only rarely (depending on the packet loss rate and the number of nodes). But even if it does happen, a lost announcement will be replaced eventually by one of a later report interval. If several announcements in a row fail to reach a node, it deletes data erroneously. However, this error will persist only temporarily until the next successful announcement reinstalls the data. Besides packet loss, node failures are survived, too, as long as there are enough nodes to announce all data. And a node that late-joins, i.e., is restarted after a crash or is started for the first time, is initialized automatically with the current state through the announcements. Summing up, the soft state approach is very robust because it implicitly repairs all error situations unless some permanent failure occurs [Raman and McCanne, 1999], and it scales well with the number of nodes because of its simple logic. Its main drawback is the high network load due to the periodic announcements, especially if the state is large. Moreover, the notification time until a change has reached all nodes is unpredictable and might be several report intervals long.

The alternative to soft state is the *hard state* approach where new data, updates, and deletes are propagated explicitly and immediately. All changes need to be transferred reliably so that either the transport or the application layer needs to employ a mechanism for detecting and repairing packet loss. Moreover, node failures have to be detected and handled explicitly because data no longer times out. And initializing new nodes with the current state requires an appropriate late-join algorithm [Vogel et al., 2003]. This chapter covers such hard state synchronization mechanisms in Section 4.6. Because all possible error situations need to be handled explicitly, and the required mechanisms need to interoperate, the hard state approach often results in a more complex system than does a soft state design [Vogel, 2004]. But when compared with the soft state approach, the network load is significantly lower, and the notification time for state changes is expected to be much less.

In the Internet, we can find examples for both approaches: Soft state is typically used in network protocols for routing (PIM, DSR) and signaling (IGMP, RSVP, SIP, RTP) that have relatively small amounts of replicated data and in distributed military battlefield simulations that have high demands on scalability and robustness [Morse, 1996]. Hard state approaches are common for distributed systems at the application level that have extensive states, e.g., distributed databases (Oracle) and version control systems (CVS).

4.3 Measuring the Internet's Robustness

The topology of the Internet with its built-in redundancy is quite robust against the failures of individual links or nodes. [Palmer et al., 2001] used measurements of the Internet's topology from the year 1999 to set up a simulation model they could analyze in that respect. Their simulations show that even when up to 11.6% of all links and 3.6% of all routers are deleted randomly from the network model, overall connectivity was still given, i.e., all end systems were still able to communicate with each other. However, they could also show that the Internet is more sensitive to failures within the so-called backbone where relatively few routers play a vital role: When one hundred from those routers with the highest number of incoming and outgoing links fail, the connectivity is more than halved.

[Jaiswal et al., 2003] conducted a large-scale evaluation of live TCP traffic in order to analyze the actual error rate in the Internet. For their study, all TCP traffic passing through the optical backbone of Sprint, a large ISP in the United States, was logged over a period of seven months. Their analysis reveals that only a very small fraction of all packets is affected by duplication (see Section 4.2.2 for a description of error types), i.e., up to 0.003%. Reordered packets are more frequent: between 0.03% and 0.72% of all packets are received out of order. And the number of lost packets is relatively large: between 1.54% and 5.18%. These numbers include all possible error sources along a packet's path from the sender to the receiver. In an earlier study of incoming and outgoing traffic at selected end systems, [Paxson, 1999] discovered that the vast majority of these lost packets can be attributed to overloaded routers, whereas only 0.02% of all packets have one or more bit errors at the physical layer and are therefore discarded. In a subsequent study of the Sprint backbone, [Markopoulou et al., 2004] evaluated the causes for general failures. Over a period of six month, thousands of error events occurred, of which 20% were link outages due to maintenance work, 21.6% router hardware errors, and 58.4% link hardware errors. However, because of the backbone's redundant resources, these errors did not affect the connectivity but merely increased the numbers of lost, reordered, and duplicated packets. All failures were repaired by the provider within hours.

Work by [Oppenheimer et al., 2003] studied the robustness of three large-scale Internet services that host portals, content, and newsgroups. Each of these services is accessed up to 100 million times per day so that an around-the-clock availability is crucial. In all three cases, this is achieved by a high degree of replication on multiple levels: Each functional part of a service (e.g., database storage) can be provided by many alternative nodes that are orchestrated by a load-balancing switch, and complete sites are replicated to different geographic locations (up to 2,000 nodes). For each service, the authors registered between 40 and 70 error events per month that were either caused by individual failures of the network, hardware or software components, or by human mistakes. Because of the redundancy described above, only between 14% and 27% of these errors were actually observable by the end users, i.e., resulted in the service being unavailable or behaving incorrectly. Interestingly, the authors attribute up to 50% of all visible errors to the human operators, with misconfigurations causing by far the most problems, as is also observed by

[Anderson et al., 2003]. The reason for this high rate is that the aforementioned redundancy mechanisms are mostly targeted at machine failures and do not cover human errors. Moreover, the authors found that the network connection of a service site is a single-point-of-failure that is responsible for between 18% and 80% of all visible errors. These could be prevented if several independent connections of different ISPs were used. In order to lower the overall error rate, the authors propose a mixture of testing, replication, self-healing (i.e., automatized system restarts), and in particular better tools and coordination for human operators.

4.4 A Closer Look at the Internet Protocols

The routing and the transport layer are the most basic components of the Internet architecture and define how the Internet operates. This section discusses protocol details and properties of the most widely used protocols.

4.4.1 Routing Protocols

The size and structure of the Internet requires a hierarchical organization of the networks it is composed of. This is reflected in the structure of IP addresses assigned to routers and end-hosts for routing purposes [Kleinrock and Kamoun, 1977]. Routers use longest prefix matching to determine which forwarding table entry to use to decide via which outgoing link to send a given packet. It is neither necessary nor possible to have routing table entries for each subnetwork or even each node in the Internet. Instead, address ranges are aggregated into a single entry. The most specific (i.e., longest) forwarding table entry that matches the beginning (prefix) of a packet's IP address is then used for the forwarding decision.

The Internet does not run a single routing protocol. Instead, separate networks run individual instances of routing protocols, called Interior Gateway Protocols (IGP), and these routing protocols can be different for each network. Routing between networks is made possible by the gateways connecting the networks. They export the (aggregated) routing information gathered by the IGP routing protocol and exchange this information with other gateways via so-called Exterior Gateway Protocols (EGP).

Routing protocols are quite robust against crash failures where router failure is complete and can thus easily be detected. However, failures that produce syntactically correct messages that are semantically incorrect are much harder to detect and protect against [Anderson et al., 2003]. It was a process of trial and error that resulted in the routing protocols commonly used today, and protocols were often redesigned or new protocols were invented when severe problems in the operation of the Internet became apparent. Today's routing protocols have to cope with several IP link failures per day, most of them transient and of the order of minutes [Iannaccone et al., 2002].

One of the most widely used IGPs is Open Shortest Path First (OSPF) [Moy, 1998]. OSPF routers use soft state to periodically exchange link state information with all other routers in the network, which allows each router to locally build an image of the complete network topology. Together with a shortest path algorithm, this information is used to construct the forwarding table entries. OSPF provides a mechanism to authenticate other routers and the routing messages they send before using their link state information as input. This provides some degree of protection against the inclusion of false routing state. Research on how to further improve OSPF's robustness continues, for example, through analysis on how to select OSPF link weights so as to best cope with link failures [Sridharan and Guerin, 2005].

Robustness of the core EGP of the Internet, the Border Gateway Protocol (BGP) [Rekhter et al., 2006], is even more critical to the operation of the Internet as a whole, and malfunctions and misconfigurations can leave large portions of the Internet disconnected. BGP is a path vector routing protocol, where routing decisions are made based on the complete path of networks that the route traverses. As a policy routing protocol, BGP gives networks, so-called autonomous systems (AS), the freedom to decide which route advertisements to accept and which to advertise. Because this routing protocol operates between different ISPs, enforcing policies that reflect political or economic considerations is much more important than simply finding the shortest path. Although BGP has worked quite well over the past years, there is growing concern how well it is suited to keep up with the growing size and complexity of the Internet [Handley, 2006]. Because policies are not advertised to other networks and no AS knows which advertised routes might be filtered by another AS, BGP has to try many different alternative paths before converging after a failure [Labovitz et al., 2000]. It also makes analysis and debugging of routing configurations a very hard task for network operators. This is particularly problematic, as manual configuration of the routing policies themselves is error prone. Making BGP more robust or replacing it with a more robust alternative is certainly one of the big research and engineering challenges for the coming years.

4.4.2 Transporting Data with TCP

Almost all data transported over the Internet is using the Transmission Control Protocol (TCP) [Postel, 1981b] that was first described by Cerf and Kahn in [Cerf and Kahn, 1974].[1] As mentioned before, the underlying IP protocol that TCP uses only provides the basic functionality of routing a data packet from source to destination. TCP adds to this a number of useful features, such as the retransmission of packets that were lost along the way, reordering of packets in case they arrive at the destination out-of-order, flow control to prevent the receiver's buffer from overflowing, and congestion control [Cerf and Kahn, 1974]. Having this functionality available significantly simplifies writing networked applications.

---

[1] In 2004, Cerf and Kahn won the ACM Turing Award (comparable with the Nobel Prize) "For pioneering work on internetworking, including the design and implementation of the Internet's basic communications protocols, TCP/IP, and for inspired leadership in networking."

Before transmitting any data, TCP establishes a connection between source and destination to ensure that no data is transmitted unless the receiver is in a ready state to accept this data. TCP uses sequence numbers in the packet header that indicate the number of bytes already transmitted. This allows the TCP receiver to bring the data back into the right order in case of out-of-order packet reception. The TCP receiver also sends an acknowledgment (ACK) for the highest sequence number that was received without gaps in the data stream. These ACKs can be used by the sender to detect loss of data in the network and trigger a retransmission if an expected ACK did not arrive within the anticipated time span. This timer-based mechanism is called Automatic Repeat-reQuest (ARQ).

Loss of data usually happens when router buffers in the Internet overflow and is taken by TCP as a sign of congestion. TCP's congestion control mechanism is clearly one of the most important features responsible for the robustness of the Internet. Surprisingly, it was not part of the original TCP specification but only included at a later stage [Jacobson, 1988, Allman et al., 1999]. The importance of congestion control was only realized after a series of congestion collapses of the Internet in the mid-1980s. Whereas early TCP specifications used flow control to protect the receiver from too many packets, they did nothing to protect the network itself. Even worse, in case many packets were lost because of congestion, TCP's retransmission policy would request immediate retransmission of these packets, which in turn were likely to be lost as well, further exacerbating the load of the network. The result was a network operating at full load, but where few packets actually reached their destination. To prevent Internet congestion collapse, TCP was extended to include a congestion window that determines the number of packets a TCP sender can send before requiring an ACK from the receiver (i.e., the number of packets that are currently *in* the network). The congestion window increases slowly (linearly) as long as packets are acknowledged but is decreased quickly (multiplicatively) in case a packet loss is detected. In case the packet loss rate is high due to congestion, this mechanism will quickly reduce TCP's sending rate and thus the network load, allowing the router buffers to empty before new traffic is inserted. A control-theoretic foundation for such flow-based congestion control was given in [Kelly et al., 1998]. The authors show that traffic flows can be regulated in a purely distributed manner to achieve network congestion control and some notion of fairness among flows.

Having congestion control embedded in the transport protocol was the easiest way to address the urgent problem of congestion collapse at hand. However, it was not necessarily a good decision from an architectural point of view [Handley, 2006]. First of all, it provides a specific granularity of fairness, namely at the flow level, as opposed to a host or network level. This has given rise to the use of multiple parallel flows, for example, in Web browsers or download accelerators to speed up downloads. In case the capacity bottleneck of a flow is in the network (as opposed to the end-host), using several flows will achieve a multiple of the throughput of that of a single flow. This works well as long as this feature is not too widespread but may reduce network efficiency and defeats the purpose of TCP's congestion control algorithm in case it is used by all end-hosts. A more important drawback of TCP congestion control is that it evidently only controls the congestion caused by TCP. UDP is much more suitable for applications such as the transport of streaming audio and video. Although a number of congestion control algorithms for such purposes have been proposed [Widmer et al., 2001], none of them have become a standard in the same way TCP's congestion control has, and it is up to the application developer to integrate a suitable congestion control mechanism (or not). Lastly, TCP congestion control does not scale well to the very high link capacities of GBit/s, likely to be seen in the future. Research efforts are under way to provide congestion control algorithms with a similar level of robustness as TCP but a higher dynamic range from slow to very high speed connections [Wei et al., 2006, Xu et al., 2004].

4.5 Wireless Networks

Wireless communication is certainly not a new topic, but it has become a very important one, given the proliferation of mobile devices particularly in the past 20 years. In addition to the popularity of cellular phones, wireless data communication (such as IEEE 802.11 WLAN [IEEE 802.11, 1999]) has become near ubiquitous and extends the reach of the Internet into the wireless domain. The characteristics of wireless communication, however, make it difficult to achieve a similar level of robustness of communication as in wired networks. This section discusses challenges on three different levels: how to achieve reliable communication over a wireless link, how to arbitrate access to the wireless medium between different transceivers, and how to extend the range of the network to enable communication between transceivers that are outside each other's radio range. Important concepts to achieve this are coding and self-organization. Although this text uses IEEE 802.11 as an example, similar considerations apply to many other types of wireless networks.

4.5.1 Communicating Reliably Over Wireless Links

Wireless links are significantly more error prone than are wired links due to a number of reasons such as interference from other devices, substantial variations in wireless channel conditions over time, limited available bandwidth (i.e., the frequency range available for a specific wireless technology), and the need to achieve high data rates despite all this.

IEEE 802.11, the most popular technology for wireless access to the Internet, operates in an unlicensed frequency range (the so-called ISM band). Not having to obtain a license to be able to operate a wireless network in this band has certainly contributed to the widespread adoption of this technology. However, its popularity also means competition between a large number of different technologies and devices. Bluetooth [IEEE 802.15.1, 2005], cordless phones, and even microwave ovens operate in the same frequency range.

Modulation (i.e., the modification of a carrier signal to carry information) and channel coding techniques (i.e., the addition of redundant data to detect and correct errors) help to protect against noise and interference. While they are also used for wired networks, they are of particular importance in a wireless environment. IEEE 802.11b, one of the physical layer specifications for 802.11, uses direct-sequence spread spectrum (DSSS) together with quadrature phase-shift keying (QPSK) [Proakis, 2000] for the modulation. DSSS provides robust communication in the presence of noise by spreading the signal over a wider frequency range or bandwidth than strictly necessary.[2] Data bits are converted into a (longer) series of redundant bits by multiplying the data bits with a pseudo-random sequence. The final sequence of bits is then converted into a waveform by shifting the phase of the carrier signal with respect to these bits. Four different possible phase shifts allow encoding of two bits at a time. The redundancy in the bit patterns that are transmitted provides error detection and correction capabilities, as the original bits can be recovered even if some of the transmitted bits are corrupted. The receiver knows the common spreading sequence used by the sender and can de-spread the signal. This way, only a signal that was multiplied with the exact same spreading sequence will add up coherently at the receiver, whereas any other signal is likely to be canceled out.

IEEE 802.11b can use different types of spreading sequences (which determine how long the bit sequences are that a generated from a single data bit) and different phase-shift keying schemes. The shorter these sequences and the more bits are encoded through phase-shift keying at the same time, the higher the data rate, but the more susceptible to interference the transmission becomes. IEEE 802.11b provides data rates in the range from 1 to 11 Mbit/s, whereas the newer IEEE 802.11g and 802.11a standards support data rates of up to 54 Mbit/s. An important concept to achieve good performance is therefore to adapt the data rate to the current conditions of the wireless channel. The Auto Rate Fallback (ARF) protocol [Kamerman and Monteban, 1997] developed by Lucent was the first commercial implementation of such a rate adaptation mechanism, and the design of even more efficient adaptation schemes is the focus of ongoing research (e.g., [Sadeghi et al., 2005]). Overall, robust wireless communication is made possible by adding redundancy in a controlled and adaptive manner.

4.5.2 Sharing the Wireless Link: Medium Access Control

Nodes with an 802.11 wireless interface usually access the Internet via an 802.11 access point that functions as a gateway between the wireless and the wired network. Despite the interference handling capabilities of the physical layer, it is desirable to only have a single node transmit at a time. In fact, having two or more 802.11 nodes

---

[2] Earlier versions of 802.11 use frequency-hopping spread spectrum instead of DSSS, where the carrier frequency changes quickly over time and thus spreads the signal over the whole spectrum, instead of adding pseudo-random noise to the data. This helps to cope with interference that is limited to a specific frequency range.

transmit in close proximity at the same time would cause so much interference that the decoding of the transmissions would fail. The medium access control (MAC) layer is responsible to arbitrate between multiple nodes that want to access the channel at the same time.

The most widely used MAC technique in 802.11 is the Distributed Coordination Function (DCF), based on carrier sense multiple access with collision avoidance (CSMA/CA) [IEEE 802.11, 1999]. It is self-organizing and requires no state about the number of participating nodes. In IEEE 802.11, a node that wants to transmit first has to listen to the channel to check if there is an ongoing transmission. If the channel is idle for a certain (short) amount of time, the node can transmit. Otherwise, it has to defer sending its packet until the end of the ongoing transmission. To avoid that multiple stations start sending immediately after an ongoing transmission ends, such nodes perform an additional backoff with random duration after the ongoing transmission ended. The node with the shortest backoff interval then accesses the channel first, while other nodes further defer their transmissions. Nevertheless, a collision of packets will still occur in case nodes choose the same backoff value. For this reason, the backoff interval is adapted in case such collisions occur.

This simple design allows nodes to join and leave the network (or simply fail) at any time without any need for further coordination. Furthermore, it does not require an access point to be present but allows for communication between two arbitrary nodes. One important use of such transmissions among peers is discussed in the next section. Some of the disadvantages of this simple design are that real-time communication and quality of service are not well supported. Also a number of network scenarios may result in a very unfair allocation of transmission opportunities among nodes [Nandagopal et al., 2000].

4.5.3 Multi-Hop Communication

In a network of wireless nodes, it may be that not all nodes are within the range of an access point or other nodes with which they want to communicate. However, such nodes can exchange packets by routing over one or multiple intermediate nodes. City-wide wireless mesh networks are one of the prominent example applications for multi-hop routing [Akyildiz et al., 2005, Bicket et al., 2005]. As in wired networks, this requires building routes that determine along which nodes packets will be forwarded.

The characteristics of wireless links together with the potential mobility of nodes makes routing in wireless networks a much harder problem than in wired networks. A high robustness against failures and a fast and low overhead mechanism to repair broken routes are very important requirements for a routing protocol to perform well. Besides a large number of academic proposals, the specification of such routing protocols is done by the Mobile Ad-hoc Networks working group of the Internet Engineering Task Force (IETF).

Routing protocols in wired networks proactively maintain routing tables by continuously exchanging routing update messages. A similar approach is taken by the

Optimized Link State Routing Protocol (OLSR) [Clausen and Jacquet, 2003], which floods the nodes of the wireless network with link state information that allows the nodes to learn about the full topology of the network. The nodes can then locally compute optimum paths to any other node. However, the continuous maintenance of these routes, even if they are not currently in use, consumes computing resources and, more importantly, network capacity and energy to send the routing updates. This is unproblematic for routers in wired networks but can be critical in wireless networks that have a lower capacity, and in which nodes, in particular mobile nodes, may be much more energy constrained.

One of the proposals that depart from the proactive routing paradigm is Ad Hoc On Demand Distance Vector (AODV) Routing [Perkins et al., 2003]. It builds a route only when a packet is to be sent to a destination for which no route exists yet. The route is maintained as long as packets flow along the route. In the absence of traffic, route information times out after a certain period of time, and the route has to be rebuilt anew when new packets for the same destination are to be sent at a later time. The route to a destination is established by flooding the network with a route discovery message. When this message reaches the destination, the destination sends a reply along the reverse path of the discovery message, which then establishes routing state information. Reactive routing based on the actual traffic demands lowers the load in the network when only a few specific routes are required or traffic demands are low. However, the reactive route discovery procedure introduces a significant delay before the route can be used for the first time, and the flooding mechanism may cause a higher amount of routing traffic than OLSR in case packets are frequently sent from many sources to many different destinations [Clausen, 2004].

Forwarding performance in wireless multi-hop networks can be significantly improved by exploiting the diversity of the wireless links, instead of trying to make them as stable as possible to be able to use the same protocol concepts as in wired networks. Cooperative diversity [Laneman et al., 2001, Laneman et al., 2004] is a very good example of making use of the specific nature of the wireless medium rather than trying to combat it. Instead of using the traditional notion of a link between two nodes together with ARQ in case of transmit failure, cooperative diversity exploits the broadcast nature of the wireless medium. In case other nodes overhear a transmission that is not successfully decoded by the destination, they may retransmit the packet on behalf of the original sender, if they have a better channel to the destination. Furthermore, helper nodes may send only some additional coded information, which, combined with the corrupted packet from the original sender, allows the destination to decode. Mechanisms based on these principles lower the overhead of retransmissions.

4.6 Distributed Applications

As described in Section 4.2.5, Internet applications and protocols often replicate (parts of) their data. Whereas data can be read from any copy, write operations concern all copies and need to be propagated from the originating node to all other nodes so that the replicated data can be synchronized. First, this section describes a distributed application where data is stable and only accessed with read operations. A second example then discusses interactive applications with concurrent read and write access.

4.6.1 File Distribution with BitTorrent

BitTorrent is a highly popular distributed application for transferring large files (e.g., software packages) from a source node n_S to multiple receiver nodes. The responsibility for such a file exchange is shared among all nodes N, i.e., a file f is not only downloaded from n_S but primarily from peer nodes that already have retrieved (parts of) f. Compared with the traditional server-based file hosting, this drastically lowers the distribution costs for n_S.

BitTorrent works as follows: f is split into small blocks of up to 1 MByte each. Then, a meta-data file f_m is generated that describes f and its blocks and that includes hash codes to check the integrity of downloaded blocks. The meta-data file f_m is placed on a public Web server where it can be found by so-called *leecher* nodes n_l that wish to download f. Besides f_m, n_l needs a list N_p of peer nodes with whom it can exchange blocks of f. To get an initial N_p, n_l contacts a so-called tracker node n_T whose address is also found in f_m. The tracker node n_T maintains the set N of all active nodes currently involved in f's distribution, which is denoted as *torrent*. Because N can be quite large with several thousand nodes, n_T selects a small random subset as N_p (typically with 50 nodes). Thus, each node has a different list of peer nodes N_p, and N_p changes over time as nodes continuously join and leave the torrent. All nodes within N_p communicate which blocks they can offer. From these, n_l downloads the rarest ones first. This selection policy seeks to achieve an even distribution of all blocks among N and tries to prevent that a torrent fails because the last node that possessed a certain block has left. It also increases the utilization of n_l's upload capacity because n_l will soon possess blocks that other nodes will likely want to download.

Now, n_l needs to find nodes from N_p that it can download from and sends download requests to all nodes n_k holding the desired blocks. Thus, it tries to download from as many nodes as possible. But these decide whether they are willing to upload to n_l by means of a modified *tit-for-tat* strategy [Cohen, 2003]: A node n_k uploads to n_l (1) if n_l has uploaded data to n_k in the past and (2) if n_l also offers one of the best upload rates to n_k. The first part ensures a friendly behavior of nodes because they will only be able to download if they upload at the same time. The second part maximizes the overall throughput. Node n_k periodically (every 10 seconds) revises the decision with whom to connect in order to find better download rates for itself. Moreover, every three rounds, one node is picked regardless of this rate in order to discover better connections by chance and to allow new nodes like n_l to receive their first block. As soon as n_l has successfully received its first block, it can start uploading to other nodes. If n_l has received the complete file f, it becomes a so-called *seed* with uploading connections only. From there on, n_l picks its connections such that its uploading rate is maximized.

For BitTorrent, being robust means that users are always able to discover, join, and complete a torrent even when nodes including the original seed continuously join and leave a torrent. Discovering and joining a torrent is achieved by communicating with a Web server and a tracker node, respectively, to retrieve a torrent's meta-data file f_m and a list of peers N_p. Besides being simple for the user, this controlled environment also makes it relatively easy to prevent corrupted or fake f_m [Pouwelse et al., 2005]. For better scalability and availability, both components are replicated to a (limited) number of sites. But they are still the most vulnerable part of the application: In a study evaluating the most important BitTorrent Web server and a large tracker over several months, [Pouwelse et al., 2005] show that temporary failures in either one of them significantly reduces the number of active torrents.

Whether a node can complete a torrent depends on two factors. First, it must sustain a sufficient number of peer nodes N_p to connect to. This is achieved by selecting the initial list N_p randomly and by continuously discovering new nodes through incoming download requests, so that the resulting graph of all nodes in N is highly connected. If the number of active nodes in N_p falls below a certain threshold, a node can also ask n_T for additional nodes. Second, all blocks must be available. The rarest first policy quickly creates a complete copy from the original seed and always replicates critical blocks at first. And the tit-for-tat policy favors older nodes (because with their uploads they have created more and more friends in N_p) so that they can successfully complete and become new seeds. Despite these mechanisms, [Izal et al., 2004] found that more than 80% of all downloads remained incomplete when they evaluated a popular torrent with more than 180,000 participating nodes over a period of five months. Even when considering that 60% of all incomplete downloads attribute to users canceling the download shortly after they have joined, this is still a large number. The reason for this might be an insufficient number of seeds: The longer a node stays in a torrent and remains active as a seed, the better it is for the overall performance of a torrent. But in practice, many users leave a torrent as soon as their download has completed: [Pouwelse et al., 2005] found that only 17% of all nodes stay longer than one hour after they have become a seed. For a typical file distribution, this means that after a highly active phase, where many users download a file right after it has been released, the number of nodes in a torrent gradually decreases until at some point a block is missing and the torrent dies. A possible solution could be to offer nodes not only incentives to upload while they are still leechers, i.e., with the tit-for-tat policy that gives good download rates to busy uploaders, but also when they remain as seed where no such reward exists. Another interesting finding from the studies of [Pouwelse et al., 2005] and [Izal et al., 2004] is that BitTorrent indeed achieves a high scalability regarding the number of torrents and the number of nodes within a torrent.

4.6.2 Distributed Interactive Applications

Interactive applications are mostly found in the domain of social software (or groupware) where a group of users (or community) exchanges information, creates documents, or works cooperatively over a computer network. Prominent examples are e-mail, chat, video conferences, software code development, wikis, distributed simulations, and multiplayer games. If such an application is implemented with a replicated architecture and concurrent read and write access, a major challenge is to keep all nodes synchronized [Sun et al., 1998]: Imagine a distributed graphics application that runs on two nodes n_i and n_j. The two users may change the color of the same rectangle at approximately the same: n_i sends a "set color blue" operation o_i to n_j, whereas n_j transmits a "set color green" operation o_j to n_i. Now, n_i receives o_j and changes its rectangle to green, and n_j sets its rectangle to blue. Obviously, n_i's and n_j's data copies now differ in color, i.e., they are inconsistent, because the network delay for transmitting o_i and o_j resulted in different execution orders.

For time-sensitive (or continuous) applications such as simulations or games, the network delay poses an additional risk. Here, data changes not only by user interaction but also with the passing of time, e.g., cars driving in a racing game. The result of an operation now heavily depends on its execution time, e.g., whether the car will successfully master a turn or not depends on when exactly the steering operation o_i is executed. This is problematic for distributed applications because all nodes other than n_i perceive a certain transmission delay and can execute the operation only some time after it has been issued while their local state has changed in the meantime, e.g., the car has driven on in the original direction.

Preventing such inconsistencies from reordered or delayed operations is the task of a *consistency control* algorithm. Simplified, consistency is achieved when all nodes eventually have the same application state, for instance, all users from the graphics example above either see a green or blue rectangle. Consistency control algorithms can be classified as either *pessimistic* or *optimistic*.

Pessimistic mechanisms prevent concurrent operations and grant write access only to a single node at a certain point in time. This can be done by a locking algorithm where exclusive access rights have to be obtained before a modification [Greenberg and Marwood, 1994]. Alternatively, operations can be serialized through a distinct controlling node: All operations are first sent to a specific node, which orders operations and then distributes them. This approach is common for virtual environments under the name of *dead reckoning* [Singhal and Zyda, 1999]. Dead reckoning is based on soft state, i.e., the controlling node sends periodic updates for the status of its objects. Pessimistic approaches therefore reduce the consistency control challenge to the ordering of operations that originate from a single source. Even though this technique is very effective, it has a major drawback: Because of the explicit or implicit exchange of access rights, direct interaction among users is restricted.

Optimistic approaches, on the other hand, allow users to issue concurrent operations and handle any inconsistencies that emerge in an efficient way. They work best under the assumption that inconsistencies are infrequent. A popular optimistic mechanism based on hard state synchronization is *serialization* [Sun et al., 1996]: All nodes execute all operations in a distinct order, e.g., in a total order on the basis of state vectors [Lamport, 1978] or execution times. Because a node n_i does not know which operations will be received, it cannot anticipate this order. Instead, an operation is executed as soon as it arrives. Additionally, all operations are stored in a history. In case n_i receives an operation o_j that would violate the total order when appended to the history, an inconsistency has occurred, and the correct order of the operations needs to be restored. This can be achieved by the following "undo/do/redo" algorithm [Sun et al., 1998]: All operations o_c that have been executed already but that o_j precedes are undone, then o_j is executed, and finally those operations are redone that were undone in the first step. Afterwards, the history is in the correct order again. This algorithm is very robust against the failure of individual nodes [Vogel, 2004] and provides good scalability because additional communication for the purpose of synchronization (e.g., as with locking) is not necessary. But the history might consume considerable memory space depending on the size and number of operations. It also requires that the application is able to undo all operations, which is especially difficult for continuous applications. For example, in a car racing game the numerous (side-)effects of steering and accelerating operations need to be undone.

Timewarp is a serialization algorithm without the complexity of undo [Mauve et al., 2004]: In addition to the operations, each node periodically saves a snapshot of the current application state. A node collects all operations during a certain period of time T, which is usually the inverse of the frames-per-second rate of continuous applications. These operations are then inserted into the history at the correct position, and the oldest one is marked as o_t. Operation o_t then determines the starting point of a so-called timewarp: First, the application state is set back to the youngest state saved before o_t should have been executed, and all newer states are removed from the history (as they are now outdated). After that, all operations following o_t are executed in a fast-forward mode until the end of the history is reached.

The timewarp algorithm is suitable for all kinds of applications and relatively easy to implement. One major drawback is the additional memory usage that is mostly determined by the frequency of state snapshots. Whereas a low frequency saves memory, it also increases the average number of operations to be processed for the execution of a timewarp. The size of the history can be limited by deleting those operations (and state snapshots) that have been successfully processed and acknowledged by all nodes [Vogel, 2004].

Besides consistency control, replicated applications with hard state synchronization require a *late-join* algorithm to initialize nodes that have missed some operations [Vogel et al., 2003] (soft state implicitly initializes late-joining nodes). Late-joins typically occur in error situations when a node has crashed and needs to be restarted or happen on a regular basis for applications that support interleaved online and offline work of users [Vogel et al., 2004]. Thus, the late-join algorithm plays a vital role for the application's robustness. First, it must select a node that should provide the initialization data to the late-joining node n_c. In principle, this can be any node that possesses the required data so that a selection strategy is required. One possibility is a timer-based selection: Each candidate sets a timer with a running time that depends on the network delay to n_c; the node with the timer that expires first is selected. Second, in which form should the initialization data be provided? A replay of the operation history gives n_c the complete picture of everything that has happened in the past and is very robust in combination with a history-based consistency control algorithm. But a replay also contains much information that is outdated, e.g., about objects that have been deleted in the meantime, and is not very efficient. Alternatively, a current state snapshot can be delivered to n_c. However, this might pose new consistency problems because n_c then cannot handle inconsistencies from operations older than the initializing state. A good compromise is therefore to initialize n_c with an older state and the following part of the operation history.

4.7 Summary

The Internet started in the mid-1970s with a handful of nodes and grew slowly to a few thousand nodes within ten years. Back then it was a more or less controlled environment where the attached nodes came mainly from academia and governmental organizations, the end users had a technical background, and the exchanged data was composed of files and messages. In that respect, the Internet of today looks quite different and has scaled to hundreds of millions of nodes and users, the vast majority of which have little technical understanding. The Internet is now also used for many different kinds of applications, including high-quality video streams, and has a huge economical, political, and everyday life impact. Nevertheless, its original design principles of layering with an hourglass shape, stateless datagram routing, self-regulated error and rate control algorithms, and high scaling and availability through redundancy remained mostly untouched.

Table 4.1 gives a summary of the different mechanisms for achieving robustness in the Internet. These mechanisms make the Internet very robust against the randomized failures of individual components. Such failures are mostly detected under a fail-stop assumption [Anderson et al., 2003]: If a component fails, it does so detectably, e.g., by means of a timeout that reveals the crash of a router to its neighbors, so that the built-in feedback regulation can adapt to the new situation and, e.g., route around the failed node. However, as the discussion in Section 4.3 indicated, other types of failures like manual misconfigurations that lead to syntactically correct but semantically erroneous protocol behavior are frequent and much harder to detect. The Internet is also quite vulnerable against intentional and organized attacks by malicious users that spy on sensitive data, bother others with spam mails, or stage denial of service attacks against the infrastructure by overwhelming routers or Web servers with artificial service requests. These observations led to the notion that the Internet is "robust yet fragile" at the same time [Doyle et al., 2005].

However, when addressing such failures with appropriate countermeasures, this adds to the endless complexity spiral [Willinger and Doyle, 2002], meaning that the more aspects are changed or added, the more vulnerable the whole system becomes to unanticipated issues or unintended side-effects, requiring even more changes. It is therefore questionable how long the current practice of incremental changes can be sustained, and many experts propose a fundamental redesign. As one possible technical solution, [Heylighen and Gershenson, 2003] argue that applying the principle of self-organization, which can be found in nature in many variations ranging from

Table 4.1 Mechanisms for achieving robustness

Mechanism	Explanation	Application
Modular design	Components with standardized interfaces keep design simple and allow easy updates and new applications	– Network hardware and protocol layers – Hourglass design
Redundancy	Duplicate functional instances or data to mask individual failures	– Redundant bit encoding (DSSS) – Routing with alternative paths – Replicating services (DNS), application data (database), or Web content (proxies) – Steady file replication with rarest-first and tit-for-tat strategies (BitTorrent) – Periodic data updates by soft state (routing protocols, dead reckoning) – Consistency control with serialization or timewarp – Installing state by late-join
Over-provisioning	Install enough resources for situations with exceptionally high demands	– Internet infrastructure (backbone and sub-networks) – Server farms (Web servers, search engines, online game platforms)
Self-regulation and feedback loops	Measure current state of environment and adapt to changing conditions	– Adapt bit encoding scheme to channel quality (IEEE 802.11) – Medium access control – Adapt sending rate to resources of receiver (flow control) and network (congestion control)
Active error monitoring	Discover and handle possible errors	– Checksum for detecting bit errors – Detect lost, reordered, and duplicate packets with sequence numbers – Timer-based retransmission of lost packets
Support for human operators	Prevent errors from misconfigurations or deliberate attacks	– Administrative tools for monitoring and configuration – Protection against misinformation by authentication and encryption

growing crystals to swarm intelligence of ants, would lead to more robust computer systems in general and the Internet in particular. For instance, packets could find the best way to their destination similar to ants to food sources by leaving trails that are reinforced with the number of individuals following them. Others, such as [Clark et al., 2002], are more concerned about the organizational aspects and recommend that a new architecture should include mechanisms to balance the different interests of the various stakeholders that are now present on the Internet. For instance, the Internet can only provide universal connectivity if different ISPs interoperate. But at the same time, ISPs are also economic competitors, which naturally limits their will to cooperate. A routing protocol therefore needs to address such conflicts and offer incentives for both competitors if they cooperate (similar to the tit-for-tat policy of BitTorrent).

References

Akyildiz, I., Wang, X., and Wang, W. (2005). Wireless Mesh networks: a survey. *Computer Networks*, 47(4):445–487.

Albert, R., Jeong, H., and Barabasi, A.-L. (2000). Error and attack tolerance of complex networks. *Nature*, 406:378–482.

Allman, M., Paxson, V., and Stevens, W. (1999). TCP Congestion Control. Internet Request For Comments, IETF, RFC-2581.

Anderson, T., Shenker, S., Stoica, I., and Wetherall, D. (2003). Design guidelines for robust Internet protocols. *ACM SIGCOMM Computer Communications Review*, 33(1):125–129.

Bicket, J., Aguayo, D., Biswas, S., and Morris, R. (2005). Architecture and evaluation of an unplanned 802.11b Mesh network. In *Proceedings of the 11th ACM Annual International Conference on Mobile Computing and Networking (MobiCom)*, pages 31–42, Cologne, Germany. ACM, New York, NY, USA.

Bush, R. and Meyer, D. (2002). Some Internet architectural guidelines and philosophy. Internet Request For Comments, IETF, RFC-3439.

Carpenter, B. (1996). Architectural principles of the Internet. Internet Request For Comments, IETF, RFC 1958.

Cerf, V. and Kahn, R. (1974). A protocol for packet network intercommunication. *IEEE Transactions on Communications*, 22(5):627–641.

Clark, D. (1988). The design philosophy of the DARPA Internet protocols. In *Proceedings of ACM SIGCOMM Symposium on Communications Architectures and Protocols*, pages 106–114, Stanford, CA, August 16–18. ACM, New York.

Clark, D. and Blumenthal, M. (2001). Rethinking the design of the Internet: the end to end arguments vs. the brave new world. *ACM Transactions on Internet Technology*, 1(1):70–109.

Clark, D., Wroclawski, J., Sollins, K., and Braden, R. (2002). Tussle in cyberspace: defining tomorrow's Internet. In *Proceedings of the 2002 ACM SIGCOMM Conference on Applications, Technologies, Architectures, and Protocols for Computer Communications*, pages 347–356, Pittsburgh, PA, August 19–23. ACM, New York.

Clausen, T. (2004). Comparative study of routing protocols for mobile ad hoc networks. Technical Report inria-00071448, INRIA, France.

Clausen, T. and Jacquet, P. (2003). Optimized Link State Routing Protocol (OLSR). Internet Request For Comments, IETF, RFC-3626.

Coffman, K. and Odlyzko, A. (2002). *Handbook of Massive Data Sets*, chapter Internet growth: is there a "Moore's Law" for data traffic?, pages 47–93. Kluwer Academic Publishers, Norwell, MA.

Cohen, B. (2003). Incentives build robustness in BitTorrent. In *Proceedings of Workshop on Economics of Peer-to-Peer Systems (P2PEcon)*, Berkeley, CA.

Doyle, J. C., Alderson, D., Li, L., Low, S. H., Roughan, M., Shalunov, S., Tanaka, R., and Willinger, W. (2005). The "robust yet fragile" nature of the Internet. *Proceedings of the National Academy of Sciences*, 102(41):14497–14502.

Gray, J. (1986). Why do computers stop and what can be done about it? In *Proceedings Symposium on Reliability in Distributed Software and Database Systems*, pages 3–12, Los Angeles, CA.

Greenberg, S. and Marwood, D. (1994). Real-time groupware as a distributed system: concurrency control and its effect on the interface. In *Proceedings of the 1994 ACM Conference on Computer Supported Cooperative Work*, pages 207–217, Chapel Hill, NC, October 22-26. ACM, New York.

Handley, M. (2006). Why the Internet only just works. *BT Technology Journal*, 24(3):119–129.

Heylighen, F. and Gershenson, C. (2003). The meaning of self-organization in computing. *IEEE Intelligent Systems*, 18(4):72–75.

Iannaccone, G., Chuah, C.-N., Mortier, R., Bhattacharyya, S., and Diot, C. (2002). Analysis of link failures in an IP backbone. In *Proceedings of the 2nd ACM SIGCOMM Workshop on Internet Measurment (IMW)*, pages 237–242, Marseille, France, November 6–8. ACM, New York.

IEEE 802.11 (1999). IEEE Standards for Information Technology – Telecommunications and Information Exchange between Systems – Local and Metropolitan Area Network – Specific Requirements – Part 11: Wireless LAN Medium Access Control (MAC) and Physical Layer (PHY) Specifications.

IEEE 802.15.1 (2005). IEEE Standard for Information technology – Telecommunications and information exchange between systems – Local and metropolitan area networks – Specific requirements. Part 15.1: Wireless Medium Access Control (MAC) and Physical Layer (PHY) Specifications for Wireless Personal Area Networks.

ITU (2007). Internet indicators: subscribers, users and broadband subscribers in 2006. Available at: http://www.itu.int/ITU-D/ICTEYE/.

Izal, M., Urvoy-Keller, G., Biersack, E., Felber, P., Hamra, A., and Garces-Erice, L. (2004). Dissecting BitTorrent: five months in a Torrent's lifetime. In *Proceedings of 5th Passive and Active Measurement Workshop (PAM)*, pages 1–11, Juan-les-Pins, France, April 19–20.

Jacobson, V. (1988). Congestion avoidance and control. In *ACM SIGCOMM, Stanford, CA*, pages 314–329.

Jaiswal, S., Iannaccone, G., Diot, C., Kurose, J., and Towsley, D. (2003). Measurement and classification of out-of-sequence packets in a tier-1 IP backbone. In *Proceedings of 22nd IEEE Computer and Communications Societies (INFOCOM)*, pages 1199–1209, San Francisco, CA, March 30–April 03.

Kamerman, A. and Monteban, L. (1997). WaveLAN II: a high-performance wireless LAN for the unlicensed band. Technical report, Bell Labs Technical Journal.

Kelly, F. P., Maulloo, A., and Tan, D. (1998). Rate control for communication networks: shadow prices, proportional fairness and stability. *Journal of the Operational Research Society*, 49(3):237–252.

Kleinrock, L. and Kamoun, F. (1977). Hierarchical routing for large networks, performance evaluation and optimization. *Computer Networks*, 1(3):155–174.

Labovitz, C., Ahuja, A., Bose, A., and Jahanian, F. (2000). Delayed internet routing convergence. In *Proceedings of ACM SIGCOMM, Stockholm, Sweden*, pages 175–187, Stockholm, Sweden, August 28–September 01.

Lamport, L. (1978). Time, clocks, and the ordering of events in a distributed system. *Communications of the ACM*, 21(7):558–565.

Laneman, J. N., Wornell, G. W., and Tse, D. (2001). An efficient protocol for realizing cooperative diversity in wireless networks. In *Proceedings of IEEE International Symposium on Information Theory (ISIT)*, page 294, Washington, D.C., June 24–29.

Laneman, J. N., Wornell, G. W., and Tse, D. (2004). Cooperative diversity in wireless networks: efficient protocols and outage behavior. *IEEE Transactions on Information Theory*, 50(12):3062–3080.

Markopoulou, A., Iannaccone, G., Bhattacharyya, S., Chuah, C., and Diot, C. (2004). Characterization of failures in an IP backbone. In *Proceedings of 23rd AnnualJoint Conference of the IEEE Computer and Communications Societies (INFOCOM'04)*, pages 2307–2317, Hong King, China, March 7–11.

Mauve, M., Vogel, J., Hilt, V., and Effelsberg, W. (2004). Local-lag and timewarp: providing consistency for replicated continuous applications. *IEEE Transactions on Multimedia*, 6(1): 45–57.

Mockapetris, P. (1987). Domain names–oncepts and facilities. Internet Request For Comments, IETF, RFC-1034.

Morse, K. (1996). Interest management in large-scale distributed simulations. Technical Report ICS-TR-96-27, Department of Information and Computer Science, University of California, Irvine, CA.

Moy, J. (1998). OSPF Version 2. Internet Request For Comments, IETF, RFC-2328.

Nandagopal, T., Kim, T., Gao, X., and Bharghavan, V. (2000). Achieving MAC layer fairness in wireless packet networks. In *Proceedings of the 6th Annual International Conference on Mobile Computing and Networking (MobiCom)*, pages 87–98, Boston, MA. ACM, New York.

Oppenheimer, D., Ganapathi, A., and Patterson, D. (2003). Why do Internet services fail, and what can be done about it? In *Proceedings of the 4th Conference on USENIX Symposium on Internet Technologies and Systems (USITS)*, Seattle, WA, USA, March 26-28. USENIX Association, Berkeley, CA.

Palmer, C., Siganos, G., Faloutsos, M., Faloutsos, C., and Gibbons, P. (2001). The connectivity and fault-tolerance of the Internet topology. In *Proceedings of Workshop on Network-Related Data Management (NRDM)*, Santa Barbara, CA.

Paxson, V. (1999). End-to-end Internet packet dynamics. *IEEE/ACM Transactions on Networking*, 7(3):277–292.

Perkins, C., Belding-Royer, E., and Das, S. (2003). Ad hoc On-Demand Distance Vector (AODV) Routing. Internet Request For Comments, IETF, RFC-3561.

Postel, J. (1980). User Datagram Protocol. Internet Request For Comments, IETF, RFC-768.

Postel, J. (1981a). Internet Protocol. Internet Request For Comments, IETF, RFC-791.

Postel, J. (1981b). Transmission Control Protocol. Internet Request For Comments, IETF, RFC-793.

Pouwelse, J. A., Garbacki, P., Epema, D. H. J., and Sips, H. J. (2005). The BitTorrent P2P file-sharing system: measurements and analysis. In *Proceedings of the 4th International Workshop on Peer-to-Peer Systems (IPTPS)*, Lecture Notes in Computer Science, pages 205–216, Ithaca, NY, February 24-25. Springer, Berlin/Heidelberg.

Proakis, J. (2000). *Digital Communications*. McGraw Hill Higher Education, New York.

Raman, S. and McCanne, S. (1999). A model, analysis, and protocol framework for soft state-based communication. In *Proceedings of the ACM SIGCOMM Conference on Applications, Technologies, Architectures, and Protocols for Computer Communication*, pages 15–25, Cambridge, MA, August 30-September 03. ACM, New York.

Rekhter, Y., Li, T., and Hares, S. (2006). A Border Gateway Protocol 4 (BGP-4). Internet Request For Comments, IETF, RFC-4271.

Sadeghi, B., Kanodia, V., Sabharwal, A., and Knightly, E. (2005). OAR: an opportunistic auto-rate media access protocol for ad hoc networks. *ACM Wireless Networks*, 11(1):39–53.

Saltzer, J., Reed, D., and Clark, D. (1984). End-to-end arguments in systems design. *ACM Transactions on Computer Systems*, 2(3):277–288.

Singhal, S. and Zyda, M. (1999). *Networked Virtual Environments: Design and Implementation*. Addison Wesley, Upper Saddle River, NJ.

Sridharan, A. and Guerin, R. (2005). Making IGP routing robust to link failures. In *Proceedings of the 4th International IFIP-TC6 Networking Conference*, pages 634–646, Waterloo, Ontario, Canada, May 2-6.

Sun, C., Jia, X., Zhang, Y., Yang, Y., and Chen, D. (1998). Achieving convergence, causality preservation and intention preservation in real-time cooperative editing systems. *ACM Transactions on Computer-Human Interaction*, 5(1):63–108.

Sun, C., Yang, Y., Zhang, Y., and Chen, D. (1996). Distributed concurrency control in real-time cooperative editing systems. In *Proceedings of the Asian Computing Science Conference, Singapore*, pages 85–95, Singapore, December 2-5.

Tanenbaum, A. (2002). *Computer Networks*. Prentice Hall, Upper Saddle River, NJ, 4th edition.

Vogel, J. (2004). *Consistency algorithms and protocols for distributed interactive applications*. PhD thesis, University of Mannheim, Germany.

Vogel, J., Geyer, W., Cheng, L.-T., and Muller, M. (2004). Consistency control for synchronous and asynchronous collaboration based on shared objects and activities. *Computer Supported Cooperative Work*, 13(5–6):573–602.

Vogel, J., Mauve, M., Hilt, V., and Effelsberg, W. (2003). Late join algorithms for distributed interactive applications. *ACM/Springer Multimedia Systems*, 9(4):327–336.

Wei, D. X., Jin, C., Low, S. H., and Hegde, S. (2006). Fast TCP: motivation, architecture, algorithms, performance. *IEEE/ACM Transactions on Networking*, 14(6):1246–1259.

Widmer, J., Denda, R., and Mauve, M. (2001). A survey on TCP-friendly congestion control. *IEEE Network Magazine "Control of Best Effort Traffic"*, 15(3):28–37.

Willinger, W. and Doyle, J. (2002). Robustness and the Internet: design and evolution. Available at: http://netlab.caltech.edu/internet/.

Xu, L., Harfoush, K., and Rhee, I. (2004). Binary increase congestion control for fast, long distance networks. In *Proceedings of 23rd Annual Joint Conference of the IEEE Computer and Communications Societies (INFOCOM'04)*, pages 2514–2524, Hong King, China, March 7–11. IEEE Press.

Part II
Robustness in Biology Inspired Systems

Part II
Robustness in Biology Inspired Systems

Chapter 5
Detecting Danger: The Dendritic Cell Algorithm

Julie Greensmith, Uwe Aickelin, and Steve Cayzer

Abstract The "Dendritic Cell Algorithm" (DCA) is inspired by the function of the dendritic cells of the human immune system. In nature, dendritic cells are the intrusion detection agents of the human body, policing the tissue and organs for potential invaders in the form of pathogens. In this research, an abstract model of dendritic cell (DC) behavior is developed and subsequently used to form an algorithm—the DCA. The abstraction process was facilitated through close collaboration with laboratory-based immunologists, who performed bespoke experiments, the results of which are used as an integral part of this algorithm. The DCA is a population-based algorithm, with each agent in the system represented as an "artificial DC". Each DC has the ability to combine multiple data streams and can add context to data suspected as anomalous. In this chapter, the abstraction process and details of the resultant algorithm are given. The algorithm is applied to numerous intrusion detection problems in computer security including the detection of port scans and botnets, where it has produced impressive results with relatively low rates of false positives.

5.1 Introduction

The dendritic cell algorithm (DCA) is a biologically inspired technique, developed for the purpose of detecting intruders in computer networks. This algorithm belongs to a class of biologically inspired algorithms known as "artificial immune systems" (AIS) [de Castro and Timmis, 2002]. Such algorithms use abstract models of the immune system to underpin algorithms capable of performing some useful computational task [Forrest et al., 1994]. The human immune system is a rich source of inspiration as it provides a high level of protection for the host body without causing harm to the host [Coico et al., 2003].

J. Greensmith
School of Computer Science, University of Nottingham, Jubilee Campus, Wollaton Road, Nottingham, NG8 1BB, UK
email: jqg@cs.nott.ac.uk

A. Schuster (ed.), *Robust Intelligent Systems,* DOI: 10.1007/978-1-84800-261-6_5,
© Springer-Verlag London Limited 2008

As the name suggests, the DCA is based on a metaphor of naturally occurring dendritic cells (DCs), a type of cell that is native to the innate arm of the immune system. DCs are responsible for the initial detection of intruders, including bacteria and parasites, through responding to the damage caused by the invading entity. Natural DCs receive sensory input in the form of molecules that can indicate if the tissue is healthy or in distress. These cells have the ability to combine these various signals from the tissue and to produce their own output signals. The output of DCs instructs the responder cells of the immune system to deal with the source of the potential damage. DCs are excellent candidate cells for abstraction to computer security as they are the body's own intrusion detection agents.

The DCA is a multi-sensor data fusion and correlation algorithm that can perform anomaly detection on ordered data sets, including real-time and time-series data. The signal fusion process is inspired by the interaction between DCs and their environment. In a similar manner, the DCA uses a population of agents, each representing an individual DC that can perform fusion of signal input to produce their own signal output. The assessment of the signal output of the entire DC population is used to perform correlation with "suspect" data items. Further details of this mechanism and of the function of the DCA are presented in Section 5.4.

This chapter presents the history of the development of the DCA, including a brief overview of the abstract biology used to underpin the algorithm. This is followed by a detailed description of a generic DC-based algorithm, including pseudocode and worked example calculations. This chapter concludes with a discussion of the applications of the algorithm to date, and application areas to which the algorithm could be applied are suggested.

5.2 Biological Inspiration

5.2.1 Danger, Death, and Damage

The immune system is a decentralized, robust, complex adaptive system. It performs its function through the self-organized interaction between a diverse set of cell populations. Classically, immunology has focused on the body's ability to discriminate between protein molecules belonging to "self" or "non-self", through the careful selection of cells during fetal and infant stages. This theory has underpinned the research performed in immunology since its conception by Paul Ehrlich in 1891 [Silverstein, 2005]. However, numerous problems have been uncovered with this paradigm. For example, if the immune system is tuned to respond only to non-self, then why do autoimmune diseases occur, such as multiple sclerosis and rheumatoid arthritis? Or, why do intestines contain millions of bacteria, yet the immune system does not react against these colonies of non-self invaders?

In 1994, immunologist Polly Matzinger controversially postulated that the immune system's objective is not to discriminate between self and non-self, but to react to signs of damage to the body. This theory is known as the "Danger

Theory" [Matzinger, 1994]. This theory postulates that the immune system responds to the presence of molecules known as danger signals, which are released as a by-product of unplanned cell death (necrosis) [Edinger and Thompson, 2004]. When a cell undergoes necrosis, the cell degrades in a chaotic manner, producing various molecules (collectively termed "the danger signals"), formed from the oxidation and reduction of cellular materials. Dendritic cells are sensitive to increases in the amount of danger signals present in the tissue environment, causing their maturation, which ultimately results in the activation of the immune system [Gallucci et al., 1999].

There are two sides to the danger theory: activation and suppression. Whereas the presence of danger signals is sufficient to activate the immune system, the presence of a different class of signal can prevent an immune response. This mechanism of suppression arises as a result of apoptotic cell death, which is the normal manner in which cells are removed from the body. When a cell undergoes this process of apoptosis, it releases various signals into the environment. DCs are also sensitive to changes in concentration of this signal. DCs can combine the danger and safe signal information to decide if the tissue environment is in distress or is functioning normally. The danger theory states that the immune system will only respond when damage is indicated and is actively suppressed otherwise [Mahnke et al., 2007].

In addition to the danger theory related signals, one other class of signal is processed as environmental input by DCs. These signals are termed PAMPs (pathogenic associated molecular patterns) and are a class of molecule that are expressed exclusively by microorganisms such as bacteria. The "infectious non-self" theory of immunology, developed by Janeway in the late 1980s [Janeway, 1989], states that the immune system will respond by attacking cells that express PAMP molecules. PAMPs are biological signatures of potential intrusion.

5.2.2 Introducing Dendritic Cells

Dendritic cells are the immune cells that are sensitive to the presence of danger signals in the tissue [Mosmann and Livingstone, 2004]. In addition to danger signals, DCs are also sensitive to two other classes of molecule, namely PAMPs and "safe" signals. PAMPs are molecules produced by microorganisms and provide a fairly definitive indicator of pathogenic presence. Safe signals are the opposite of danger signals and are released as a result of controlled, planned cell death. In response to the collection of signals, the DC produces its own set of output signals—the relative concentrations of the output signals is dependent on the relative concentrations of the input signals over time. It is the combination of external signals and current internal state that results in what is defined in this work as "context".

In addition to the processing of environmental signals, DCs also collect proteins termed "antigen". DCs have the ability to combine the signal information with the collected antigen to provide "context" for the classification of antigen. If the antigen are collected in an environment of mainly danger and PAMP signals, the context of the cell is "anomalous" and all antigen collected by the cell are deemed as potential intruders. Conversely, if the environment contains mainly safe signals, then the context of the cell is "normal" and all collected antigen are deemed as non-threatening. This theory contrasts the classical self/non-self theory as the structure of the antigen proteins is not used as a basis of classification; the context is used to determine if an antigen is derived from a potential invader. The structure of the antigen is important for the subsequent response, but the processing performed by DCs involves the examination of the tissue "context" and are unaffected by the structure of the antigen.

In the natural system, this antigen-plus-context information is passed on to a class of responder cells, termed T-cells. The T-cells translate the information given to them by the local DC population. If sufficient DCs present a particular antigen to T-cells in an anomalous context, then the immune system responds by eliminating any cell containing that antigen. It is noteworthy that this is a simplified description of a highly complicated immune function. For more information on the action of T-cells, please refer to a standard immunology text such as Janeway [Janeway, 2004].

The description above is a simplified description of the events that occur "in vivo". For readers interested in the exact mechanism of DC function, refer to Lutz and Schuler [Lutz and Schuler, 2002]. In this chapter, these principles are abstracted to form a model of DC behavior (described in Section 5.3).

5.3 Abstract Model

5.3.1 The Approach

The DCA has been developed as part of an interdisciplinary project, known as the "Danger Project" [Aickelin et al., 2003], which comprised a team of researchers including practical immunologists, computer scientists, and computer security specialists. The aim of the project was to bring together state-of-the-art immunology with artificial immune systems to improve the results of such systems when applied to computer network intrusion detection [Twycross and Aickelin, 2008]. The abstract model presented in this section is the result of the collaboration between the computer scientists and immunologists. Thorough analysis of the literature assisted the interdisciplinary collaboration, facilitating the performance of the immunological research that contributes to the results of the abstraction process. After this important development, key published findings from DC biology were collated.

To meet the needs of the development of the algorithm and to further research in immunology, aspects of DC function are investigated. This includes the characterization of signals and the effects of DCs on the responder cells. Various wet-lab experiments have been performed using natural DCs to determine this necessary information, results of which assist in clarifying certain aspects of DC function. This research is performed following intense discussion and debate between computer

Fig. 5.1 A depiction of the abstraction process used in this chapter, and the relationship between abstraction and immunology

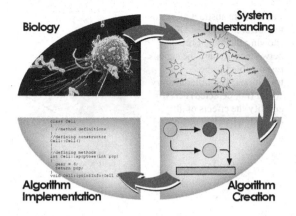

scientists and immunologists and is mutually beneficial. A diagram of the process used to develop the DCA is shown in Fig. 5.1.

5.3.2 Abstract DC Biology

As explained in Section 5.2, the biological function of DCs is as a natural intrusion detector. The mechanisms by which DCs perform this function are complex, numerous, and still debated within immunology [Matzinger, 2007]. To produce an algorithm (the DCA), the disparate information regarding DC biology must be combined to form an abstract model. The developed abstract model forms the basis of the DCA. Several key properties of DC biology are used to form the abstract model. These properties are compartmentalization, differentiation, antigen processing, signal processing, and populations.

Compartmentalization: This property provides two separate areas in which DCs perform sampling and analysis. The processing of input signals and collection of antigen occur in "tissue", which is the environment monitored by DCs. Upon maturation, DCs migrate to a processing center, termed a lymph node. While in the lymph nodes, DCs present antigen coupled with context signals, which is interpreted and translated into an immune response. In nature, this is designed to keep potentially deadly T-cells away from direct contact with the tissue until it is required.

Differentiation: In this model, DCs exist in one of three states, termed its state of differentiation: immature, semi-mature, and mature (see Fig. 5.2). Transitions to semi-mature and mature occur through the differentiation of the immature DC. This transformation is initiated upon the receipt of input signals. The resultant DC state is determined through the relative proportions of input signal categories received by the immature cell. The terminal state of differentiation dictates the context of antigen presentation where "context" is an interpretation of the state of the signal environment. Semimature implies a "safe" context and mature implies a "dangerous" context. This is a pivotal decision mechanism used by the immune system and is the cornerstone of this abstract model.

Fig. 5.2 An abstract model of
the differentiation of DCs,
showing the transformation
between states and the signals
responsible for the
transitions. The inflammatory
signal (not depicted) acts to
amplify the effects of all
other signals

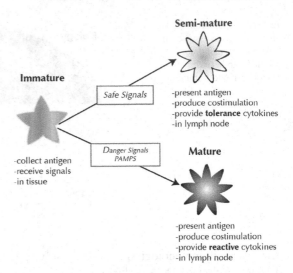

Antigen processing: The processing of antigen through collection and presentation is vital to the function of the system. The pattern matching of the antigen structure is not used in this model unlike previous AIS models [Balthrop et al., 2002]. The collection of antigen is not responsible for the activation of the immune system although it is necessary for antigen to be sampled in order to have an entity to classify. This is analogous to sampling a series of "suspects" or data to classify. The process of an immature DC collecting multiple antigen forms the sampling mechanism used by the DCA. Each DC collects a subset of the total antigen available for sampling.

Signal processing: Dendritic cells perform a type of biological signal processing. DCs are sensitive to differences in concentration of various molecules found in their tissue environment. Safe signals are the initiators of maturation to the semi-mature state. Danger signals and PAMPs are responsible for maturation to the fully-mature state. Simultaneous receipt of signals from all classes increases the production of all three output signals, though the safe signal reduces the expected amount of mature output signal generated in response to danger and PAMP signals. Output signals are generated at concentrations proportional to the input signals received.

Dendritic cells do not perform their function in isolation, residing in tissue as a population. Each member of the population can sample antigen and signals. This multiplicity of DCs is an important aspect of the natural system. Multiple DCs are required to present multiple copies of the same antigen type in order to invoke a response from the adaptive immune system. This is an error-tolerant component of DC behavior as it implies that a misclassification by one cell is not enough to stimulate a false-positive error from the immune system. Using a population of DCs also means that diversity can be generated within the population, such as assigning each DC its own threshold values, if desired. Such diversity may also add robustness to the resultant process presented in Fig. 5.3.

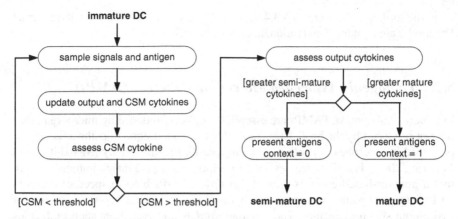

Fig. 5.3 A UML activity diagram representing the key features of DC biology, presented in a systemic manner. The processes on the left occur in the tissue and the processes on the right in the lymph node

5.3.3 Signals and Antigen Overview

As this model is in part inspired by the danger theory, various signals drive the system. In natural systems, the signals are a reflection of the state of the environment. Four categories of signal are used in this abstract model, inclusive of PAMPs, danger signals, safe signals, and inflammation. The various categories of signal direct the DC population down two distinct pathways, one causing the activation of the immune system, and one responsible for generating peripheral tolerance. Upon examination of the relevant biology, it appears that DCs process all categories of signal stated above to produce their own output signals [Lutz and Schuler, 2002]. The output signals include a costimulation signal (CSM), which shows that the cell is prepared for antigen presentation and two context signals, the mature and semi-mature output signals. An overview of the names and functions of the biological signals and their abstracted counterparts is given in Table 5.1.

Table 5.1 Biological signal functions and their abstracted counterparts

Signal	Biological Property	Abstract Property	Computational Example
PAMP	Indicator of microbial presence	Signature of likely anomaly	Error messages per second
Danger signals	Indicator of tissue damage	High levels indicate "potential" anomaly	Network packets per second
Safe signals	Indicator of healthy tissue	High levels indicate normally functioning system	Size of network packets
Inflammation	Indicating general tissue distress	Multiplies all other input signals	User physically absent

In the forthcoming Sections 5.3.4 to Section 5.3.8, all signals used in the abstract DC model are explained and rationalized individually.

5.3.4 Pathogenic Associated Molecular Patterns (PAMPs)

In a biological context, PAMPs are essential products produced by microorganisms but not produced by the host. These molecules are not unique to pathogens but are produced by microbes, regardless of their potential pathogenicity [Medzhitov and Janeway, 2002]. PAMP molecules are a firm indicator to the innate immune system that a nonhost-based entity is present. Specific PAMPs bind to specific receptors on DCs (termed pattern recognition receptors), which can lead to the production of two output signal molecules. These output signals are termed envision molecules (CSM) and the "mature" output signal. Both of these chemical outputs can indicate a likely presence of a foreign entity. In this abstract model, a PAMP is interpreted as a signal that is a confident indicator of an abnormality. An increase in the strength of the PAMP input signal leads to an increase in two of three potential output signals, namely the CSM signal and the mature output signal, produced by the artificial DCs in the abstract model.

In the abstract model, PAMPs are certain indicators of an anomaly. This is based on their role in vivo as signatures of bacterial presence. In this research, this is translated as mapping to a signature of intrusion, or abnormally high rate of errors when the DCA is applied to computer security problems. For example, when applied to the detection of scanning activity, a high frequency of networking errors is translated as a high value of PAMP signal [Bakos and Berk, 2002].

5.3.5 Danger Signals

In the human immune system, danger signals are released as a result of unplanned cell death. Specifically, danger signals are the by-product of cellular degradation in an uncontrolled manner. The constituent components of danger signals are formed from the erratically decomposing macromolecules normally found inside the cell, encapsulated by the cell membrane. They are indicators of damage to tissue, which the immune system is trying to protect. In a similar manner to PAMPs, the receipt of danger signals by a DC also causes differentiation to the fully mature state. However, the resultant effect on DCs through danger signals is less than that of PAMPs. This means that a higher concentration of danger signal molecules are needed in order to elicit a response of the same magnitude as with a similar concentration of PAMPs, where concentration is the number of molecules of signal per unit volume.

Within the context of the abstract model, danger signals are indicators of abnormality but have a lower value of confidence than associated with the PAMP signal. The receipt of danger signals also increases the amount of CSMs and mature output signals produced by the DC. The receipt of danger signals causes the presentation of antigen in a "dangerous context". This can ultimately lead to the activation of the adaptive immune system. In a computational context, for example to detect scanning activity on a computer network, the danger signal can be derived from the rate of sent/received network packets per second. A high rate of sending of packets may be indicative of an anomaly at high levels but at low levels is likely to indicate normal system function.

5.3.6 Safe Signals

Within natural immune systems, certain signals are released as a result of healthy tissue cell function. This form of cell death is termed apoptosis—the signals of which are collectively termed "safe signals" in this work. The receipt of safe signals by a DC results in the production of CSMs in a similar manner to the increase caused by PAMPs and danger signals. In addition, the "semi-mature" output signal is produced as a result of the presence of safe signals in the tissue. The production of the semi-mature output signal indicates that antigen collected by this DC was found in a normal, healthy tissue context. Tolerance is generated to antigen presented in this context.

The secondary effect of safe signals is their influence on the production of the mature output signal. In the situation where tissue contains cells undergoing both apoptosis and necrosis, the receipt of safe signals suppresses the production of the mature output signal in response to the danger and PAMP signals present in the tissue. This appears to be one of many regulatory mechanisms provided by the immune system to prevent the generation of false positives. This is a key mechanism of suppression of the response to antigen not directly linked to a pathogen. The balance between safe and danger signals and the resultant effects on the production of the mature output signal is incorporated in the signal processing mechanism. The incorporation of this mechanism is significant for the danger project as its use was facilitated by the close collaboration achieved with the team of laboratory-based immunologists.

Within this abstract model, input signals that indicate normality are termed "safe signals". This signal is interpreted as data that indicates normal system/data behavior and a high level of this signal will increase the output signal value for the "semi-mature signal". In line with the biological effect of this signal, subsequent receipt of a high safe signal value will reduce the cumulative value of the "mature" output signal, incremented by the receipt of either PAMPs or danger signals. The interaction between these signals is shown in Fig. 5.4.

In a computational context, for example to detect scanning activity on a computer network, the safe signal is an indicator of normal machine behavior, which can also be derived from the rate of sent/received network packets per second. In previous work [Greensmith and Aickelin, 2007], it is identified that scanning activity produces highly "regular" and small network packet sizes. Therefore, the safe signal value is produced in proportion to the average packet size, with a high safe signal value created if the average packet size is sufficiently larger than the expected size.

Fig. 5.4 An abstract model of
DC signal processing. The
inflammatory signal (not
pictured) acts as a general
amplification signal

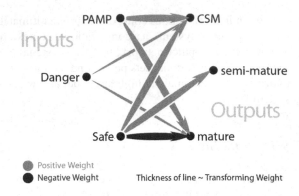

5.3.7 Inflammation

As shown in [Sporri and Caetano, 2005], the presence of inflammatory signals in
human tissue is insufficient to initiate maturation of an immature DC. However, the
presence of inflammation not only implies the presence of inflammatory cytokines
(cytokines are biological signals that act as messenger molecules between cells) but
also that the temperature is increased in the affected tissue. Additionally, the rates of
reaction are increased because of this increasing heat, plus inflammatory cytokines
initiate the process of dilating blood vessels, recruiting an increased number of cells
to the tissue area under distress.

A variant of this concept is employed in the abstract model, where inflammation
has the effect of amplifying the other three categories of input signal, inclusive of
safe signals. The resultant effect of the amplification is an increase in the artificial
DC's output signals. An increase in inflammation implies that the rate of DC migration will increase, as the magnitude of the CSMs produced by the DC will occur over
a shorter duration, hence resulting in a shortened DC life span in the tissue compartment. It is important to stress, however, that the presence of inflammatory signals
alone is insufficient to instruct the immune system how to behave appropriately.

5.3.8 Output Signals

From examination of the biological literature, it is evident that DCs produce a set of
output signals as a result of exposure to the environmental input signals experienced
in the tissue. By process of abstraction, three signals in particular are selected to be
the output signals of the DCs:

1. CSM output: limits the life span of a DC through being assessed against a
   "migration threshold".
2. Semi-mature: output incremented in response to safe signals.
3. Mature: output incremented in response to PAMP and danger signals; reduced in
   response to safe signals.

In the natural system DC CSM production is combined with production of another receptor that attracts the DC to the lymph node for antigen presentation, where the DCs present their antigen to a responder cell. This mechanism is complicated and is abstracted to a simpler version for use within an algorithm. In the abstract model, an increased amount of CSMs increases the probability of a DC leaving the tissue and entering the lymph node for analysis. This is abstracted into a model through the assignment of a migration threshold (described in detail in Section 5.4). In the abstract model, if this threshold is exceeded, the state of the cell changes from immature to either semi-mature or mature. The cell then enters the "antigen presentation stage" where its context is assessed.

In nature, the presence or absence of these two chemicals controls the response of the responder cells. In the presented model, these responder cells do not feature, and therefore, the information provided through the use of these context signals is used in a different manner. The context of the DC in the abstract model is controlled by the relative proportions of the semi-mature signal to the mature signal. The DCs context is assigned by whichever of the two output signals is greater upon presentation of antigen by the DC. A larger value of semi-mature signal implies the presented antigen was collected in a primarily "normal" context, whereas a larger value of the mature output signal would imply that the presented antigen was collected in a potentially "anomalous" context,

5.3.9 Signal Summary

Table 5.2 gives the various synonyms for the various terms at different levels of abstraction, from the actual biological terms to the terms used in the general model of a DC-based algorithm.

A state chart showing the influence of the various signals and the corresponding output signals is presented in Fig. 5.5, where IL-12 and IL-10 are the mature and semi-mature output signals, respectively.

5.3.10 Accounting for Potency: Signal Processing

The actual mechanisms of internal DC signal processing are vastly complex and are termed signal transduction mechanisms. For the purpose of the abstract model and resultant algorithm, a simplified version of signal processing can be implemented without compromising the underlying metaphor. An abstracted model of signal

Table 5.2 Biological and abstract computational terms for the input signals

Biological	Abstract
PAMP	PAMP
Necrotic products	Danger signals
Apoptotic cytokines	Safe signals
Inflammatory cytokines	Inflammation

Fig. 5.5 A state chart
showing various DC states
and the featured input and
output signals, where
responder cells are termed
T-cells

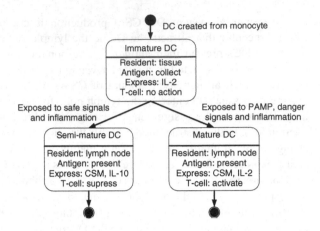

transduction is developed that accounts for the magnitude of responses but does not involve the intricacies of a signaling network. This interaction is simplified to a weighted sum equation, which is performed for the transformation of input signals to output signals. A representation of this process is shown in Fig. 5.4. The influence of a signal on a cell, the potency, is translated as the weight value given to each signal, and efficacy represented as either a positive or negative weight value. In the system presented in this chapter, the weight values given above are used as an integral part of the system, and it is repeatedly shown that these values suit the chosen applications. However, these weights are given as a guideline—other values may be more suitable for different applications. This may become apparent as the DCA is applied to a more diverse set of applications.

5.3.11 Abstract Antigen

The combination of signals provides the basis of classification that can be used for the purpose of anomaly detection. The processing of signals would be sufficient to indicate if the tissue is currently in distress or under attack, but it would not yield any information regarding the originator of the anomaly, namely the culprit responsible. Antigen is required in order to link the evidence of the changing behavior of tissue with the culprits that may have caused this change in behavior. Antigen is necessary: it is the data that is to be classified, with the basis of classification derived not from the structure of this antigen but from the relative proportions of the three categories of input signal, processed across a population of DCs.

It is important to note that a single antigen of a specific structure will not be sufficient to elicit any response from the immune system. Concentrations of antigens with identical structures are found in tissue and processed by the DCs. In selecting suitable data, multiple items with the same structure should be used, forming an "antigen type". Aggregate sampling of multiple antigens is a key property of the system and may provide some robustness and tolerance against rogue signal processing of a small number of DCs. In this abstraction, no processing of antigen is performed as the focus is on the treatment of the different categories of input signal.

5.3.12 Assumptions and Simplifications

As part of this abstraction process, various assumptions and simplifications are made, as the purpose of this process is to derive a feasible algorithm and not to produce a realistic simulator of DC biology. It is assumed that no other type of immune cells are required for this algorithm to function. Unlike the approach of [Twycross, 2007], DCs in the DCA function in isolation and the T-cell component is replaced with a statistical technique. This is possible as system changing responses do not form part of this model. It is also assumed that no inter-cell communication occurs and that individual DCs do not communicate with one another. This can be assumed as no adaptation is present in this system.

It is assumed that four signal categories exist, and that the DC does not respond to any other signal. Of course, DCs express a plethora of receptors for various molecules. In this abstraction, only the molecules responsible for immune activation are used. In a similar manner, it is assumed that three output signals are produced. It is also assumed that DCs are impervious to unexpected death, unlike in the human immune system. In this model, a single tissue compartment is used.

The above assumptions are used to make the abstraction clearer and the resultant algorithm simpler to understand. There are also various assumptions in this abstraction that are made due to the lack of understanding of natural DCs within immunology. In this abstraction, it is assumed that each DC has a fixed size capacity for antigen storage. This is assumed as there is no biological data available to confirm the antigen capacity of DCs. In a similar manner, it is unknown which agent is responsible for limiting the sampling period of the DCs within the tissue. In this abstraction, measurement of CSMs against a migration threshold determines the duration of the DCs life span. As the objective of this work is to produce an algorithm (and not an accurate simulation), it is acceptable to make such assumptions, provided they are useful in leading to a feasible algorithm.

5.4 The Dendritic Cell Algorithm

5.4.1 Algorithm Overview

The development of an abstract model of DC behavior is one step in the development of a danger theory inspired intrusion detection system. To transform the abstract model of DC biology into an immune-inspired algorithm, it must be formalized into the structure of a generic algorithm and into a series of logical processes. It must also be expressed appropriately so that the DCA can be implemented feasibly. A generic form of the algorithm is given in this section. For further details of the algorithm and for information regarding its implementation as a real-time anomaly detection system, please refer to Greensmith et al. [Greensmith et al., 2008].

The purpose of a DC algorithm is to correlate disparate data-streams in the form of antigen and signals. The DCA is not a classification algorithm but shares properties with certain filtering techniques. It provides information representing how anomalous a group of antigen is, not simply if a data item is anomalous or not. This is achieved through the generation of an anomaly coefficient value, termed the "mature context antigen value" (MCAV). The labeling of antigen data with a MCAV coefficient is performed through correlating a time-series of input signals with a group of antigen. The signals used are pre-normalized and pre-categorized data sources, which reflect the behavior of the system being monitored. The signal categorization is based on the four signal model, based on PAMP, danger, safe signals, and inflammation. The cooccurrence of antigen and high/low signal values forms the basis of categorization for the antigen data.

This overview, though technically correct, is still somewhat abstract. To cement the ideas that form the DCA, a generic representation of the algorithm is presented. A formal description of the algorithm and details of its implementation are presented in [Greensmith, 2007, Greensmith et al., 2008]. To further elaborate on the workings of a DC-based algorithm, each key component is described in turn. The primary components of a DC-based algorithm are as follows:

1. Individual DCs with the capability to perform multi-signal processing.
2. Antigen collection and presentation.
3. Sampling behavior and state changes.
4. A population of DCs and their interactions with signals and antigen.
5. Incoming signals and antigen, with signals pre-categorized as PAMP, danger, safe, or inflammation.
6. Multiple antigen presentation and analysis using "types" of antigen.
7. Generation of anomaly coefficient for various different types of antigen.

5.4.2 An Individual DC

As aforementioned, each DC in the system is represented by an object, capable of executing its own behavioral instructions. DCs process input signals to form a set of cumulatively updated output signals in addition to the collection of antigen throughout the duration of the sampling stage. Each DC can exist in one of three states at any point in time. These states are immature, semi-mature, or mature. The differences in the semi-mature and mature state is controlled by a single variable, determined by the relative differences between two output signals produced by the DCs. The initiation of the state change from immature to either mature or semi-mature is facilitated by sufficient exposure to signals, limited by the cell's "migration threshold". Pseudocode of a generic DC object is given in Algorithm 1.

Algorithm 1: Pseudocode of the functioning of a generic DC object.

---

input : signals from all categories and antigen
output: antigen plus context values

initializeDC;
while *CSM output signal < migration Threshold* **do**
> get antigen;
> store antigen;
> get signals;
> calculate interim output signals;
> update cumulative output signals;

end
cell location update to lymph node;

if *semi-mature output > mature output* **then**
> cell context is assigned as 0;

else
> cell context is assigned as 1;

end
kill cell;
replace cell in population;

While in the immature state, the DC has the following three functions, which are performed each time a single DC is updated:

1. *Sample antigen*: the DC collects antigen from an external source (in this case, from the "tissue") and places the antigen in its own antigen storage data structure.
2. *Update input signals*: the DC collects values of all input signals present in the signal storage area.
3. *Calculate interim output signals*: at each iteration, each DC calculates three temporary output signal values from the received input signals, with the output values then added to form the cell's cumulative output signals.

The signal processing performed while in the immature state is suggested to be in the form of a weighted sum equation, bypassing the modeling of any biologically realistic gene regulatory network or signal transduction mechanism. A simple weighted sum equation is used in order to reduce any additional computational overheads, with the intended DCA application being real-time anomaly detection. In the generic algorithm, the only crucial component of this procedure is the ability of the end user to map raw input data to one of the four categories of input signal (PAMP, danger, safe, and inflammation). The general form of the signal processing equation is shown in equation (5.1)

$$Output = (P_w \sum_i P_i + D_w \sum_i D_i + S_w \sum_i S_i)*(1 + I) \qquad (5.1)$$

where P_w are the PAMP-related weights, D_w for danger signals, etc., and each output value is then cumulatively added over time for future assessment.

In the generic form of the signal processing equation (5.1), P_i, D_i, and S_i are the input signal value of category PAMP (P), danger (D), or safe (S) for all signals (i) of that category, assuming that there are multiple signals per category. In the equation, I represents the inflammation signal. This sum is repeated three times, once per output signal. This is to calculate the interim output signal values for the CSM output, the semi-mature output, and mature output signals. These values are cumulatively summed over time.

The weights used in this signal processing procedure are derived empirically from immunological data, generated for the purpose of the model development. From past experience, these are combinations that have worked well, shown through sensitivity analysis to work for the chosen applications—though they are not fundamental to the algorithm. The actual values used for the weights can be user defined, though the relative values determined empirically are kept constant. The relative weight values are presented in Table 5.3.

These signals are used to assess the state of the DC upon termination of the sampling phase of a DC's life span. The three output signals of a DC perform two roles, to determine if an antigen type is anomalous and to limit the time spent sampling data. A summary of the three output signals and their function is given in Table 5.4.

Within the Danger Project, the word "context" is used extensively. The word context refers to the circumstances in which an event occurs. Context means a representation of the signal circumstances in which an antigen is processed. The context used to categorize antigen is not achieved with one DC for one antigen, but rather the aggregate total of contexts across a population of DCs and a set of antigen. Nevertheless, each member of the DC population is assigned a context upon its state transition from immature to a matured state. Each DC makes a binary choice, as an individual cell can only be either mature or semi-mature, but not both.

Diversity and feedback in the DC population is maintained through the use of variable migration thresholds. This concept is touched upon in Section 5.3, but what implications does it actually have for the algorithm, and what exactly is a variable migration threshold? The natural mechanism of DC migration is complex and not particularly well understood, involving the up and down regulation of many interacting molecules. Instead of using a model of what is ascertainable from the natural system, a surrogate mechanism that shows similar end results is implemented.

Table 5.3 Derivation and interrelationship between weights in the signal processing equation, where the values of the PAMP weights are used to create all other weights relative to the PAMP weight. $W1$ is the the weight to transform the PAMP signal to the CSM output signal, and $W2$ is the weight to transform the PAMP signal to the mature output signal

Signal	PAMP	Danger	Safe
CSM	$W1$	$\frac{W1}{2}$	$W1 * 1.5$
Semi-mature	0	0	1
Mature	$W2$	$\frac{W2}{2}$	$-W2 * 1.5$

Table 5.4 Cumulative output signals and their associated implications for the DCA

Output Signal	Function
Costimulatory signal	Assessed against a threshold to limit the duration of DC signal and antigen sampling, based on a migration threshold.
Semi-mature signal	Terminal state to semi-mature if greater than resultant mature signal value.
Mature signal	Terminal state to mature if greater than resultant semi-mature signal value.

In this algorithm, multiple DCs are used to form a population, each sampling a set of signals within a given "time window". Each DC in the population is assigned a "migration threshold value" upon its creation. Following the update of the cumulative output signals, a DC compares the value it contains for CSMs with the value it is assigned as its migration threshold. If the value of CSM exceeds the value of the migration threshold, then the DC is removed from the sampling area and its life span is terminated upon analysis in the "lymph node" area, which is a different compartment than is tissue.

Each member of the DC population is randomly assigned a migration threshold upon its creation. The range of the random threshold is a user definable parameter, with this range being applicable to the whole DC population. From previous experience with the DCA, the median point about which the migration thresholds are assigned equates to a DC sampling for two iterations when the signal strengths are half the expected total input signal maximum. This process discounts the use of inflammation in this derivation. Additionally, the range of the random assignment is $\pm 50\%$ of the median value of a uniform distribution. A derivation of this is shown in equation (5.2).

$$t_{median} = 0.5 * ((max_p * weight_{pc}) + (max_d * weight_{dc}) + (max_s * weight_{sc}))$$
(5.2)

In this equation, max_p is the maximum observed level of PAMP signal, and $weight_{pc}$ is the corresponding transforming weight from **PAMP** to **CSM** output signal. In a similar manner, max_d and max_s, and $weight_{dc}$ and $weight_{sc}$ are equivalent values for danger signal and safe signal. Inflammation is not included in this derivation.

The net result of this is that different members of the DC population "experience" different sets of signals across a time window. If the input signals are kept constant, this implies that members of the population with low values of migration threshold present antigen more frequently and therefore produce a tighter coupling between current signals and current antigen. Conversely, DCs with a larger migration threshold may sample for a longer duration, producing a more relaxed coupling between potentially collected signal and context. Having a diverse population, who all sample different total sets of signals, is a positive feature of this algorithm, demonstrated through results presented in [Greensmith et al., 2008].

Algorithm 2: Context assessment for a single DC.

---

input : semi-mature and mature cumulative output signals
output: collected antigen and cell context

if *semi-mature output > mature output* **then**
| cell context is assigned as 0;
else
| cell context is assigned as 1;
end
print collected antigen plus cell context

Once the cell has migrated, its role is to then present the antigen and output signals it has collected throughout its life span. As part of this process, the kinds of signal it was exposed to over its life span are assessed and transformed into a binary value—this is termed the DC context. This can be achieved through a simple comparison between the remaining two outputs signals, which are resultant cumulative values. These two values (semi and mature output signals) are compared directly with each other using the relationship described in Algorithm 2.

The context is vital to assign any collected antigen with the context in which the cell performed its collection. Another important feature of the algorithm is that each DC can sample multiple antigens per iteration and can store these antigens (up to a certain capacity) internally for presentation upon maturation.

To summarize, each DC has the ability to process and collect signals and antigen. Through the generation of cumulative output signals, the DC forms a cell context that is used to perform anomaly detection in the assessment of antigen. The life span of the DC is controlled by a threshold, termed the migration threshold, which is randomly assigned to each DC in the population (within a given range). Upon migration, the cumulative output signals are assessed and the greater of semi-mature or mature output signal becomes the cell context. This cell context is used to label all antigen collected by the DC with the derived context value of 1 or 0. This information is ultimately used in the generation of an anomaly coefficient.

5.4.3 Populations, Tissue, and Assessment—The Macroscopic Level

The DCA is a population-based algorithm, based on an agent-like system of artificially created cells that interact with an artificially created environment. This consists of a tissue compartment and a lymph node compartment. In the tissue compartment, signals and antigen are stored for use by the DC population. DCs are transferred to the lymph node compartment for analysis upon migration. It is in the lymph node where the antigen plus context values are logged for analysis.

The interaction between cells and environment (termed here as tissue) is crucial and drives the system. From a DC's perspective, the enviroment/tissue is what it can sense. In the case of natural DCs, they sense the world around them through activation or deactivation of receptors found on the surface. Indeed, the DCs outlined in the section above have a similar system of being able to sense the signal data present in the tissue and to respond through the generation of output signals.

In addition to sensing signals, DCs also interact with antigen. This is performed through the transfer of antigen from its store in the tissue compartment to the internal storage for antigen within the sampling DC. For use in a DC-based algorithm, the environment for a DC in the sampling population consists only of signals and antigen. Therefore, in a generic DC-based algorithm, tissue is comprised of signals and antigen as this is what the cell population can respond to and process.

It is proposed that the updates of antigen, signals, and cells are performed independently. The dictated timing of when entities are updated is left to the user. In the real-time implementations described in this chapter, cells are updated once per second. In the implemented system, signals are also updated at a rate of once per second, with antigen updated as soon as the data becomes available. The rate of update is dependent upon the requirements of the user and the nature of the input data and application. The exact nature of the update mechanisms are not specific to the algorithm, it can be up to the user or dictated by the nature of the data processed by the algorithm.

However, it is noteworthy that each of the three updates need not occur simultaneously: this temporal correlation between asynchronously arriving data is performed by the processing of the cells themselves (see Fig. 5.6 for the current discussion).

The population dynamics are used to perform the actual anomaly detection. The ultimate classification of a particular type of antigen is derived not from a single DC but from an aggregate analysis produced across the DC population over the duration of an experiment.

The derived value for the cell context is assigned to each antigen (if indeed any) collected by the assessed DC. This information is used to derive the MCAV (mature context antigen value) anomaly coefficient for a particular type of antigen. This relies on the fact that during their time as sampling entities, the DCs sample both antigen and signals. This is also dependent upon the use of "antigen types". This means that the input antigen are not unique in value but belong to a population in themselves. In the numerous experiments in this chapter, the ID value of a running

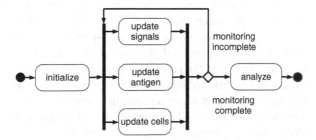

Fig. 5.6 A UML overview of the processes at the tissue level of the program, showing the asynchronous update of cells, signals, and antigen. It also shows the two main stages of update and initialization and subsequent analysis

---

Algorithm 3: The generation of MCAV coefficients for each antigen type sampled by the DC Algorithm.

---

input : total list of antigen plus context values per experiment
output: MCAV coefficient per antigen type

for *all antigen in total list* **do**
 increment antigen count for this antigen type;
 if *antigen context equals* 1 **then**
  | increment antigen type mature count;
 end
end
for *all antigen types* **do**
 | MCAV of antigen type = mature count / antigen count;
end

---

program is used to form antigen, with each antigen generated every time the program sends an instruction to the low-level system. Therefore a population of antigen is used, linked to the activity of the program, and all bearing the same ID number.

Each DC can sample multiple antigens per iteration and can store a fixed maximum amount of antigen within while sampling signals. It is the consensus value for an entire antigen type that gives rise to the anomaly detection within this algorithm. The MCAV is the mean value of context per antigen type. Pseudocode for the generation of the MCAV is given in Algorithm 3.

The closer the MCAV is to one, the more likely it is that the majority of the antigen existed in the tissue at the same time as a set of signals. This is similar to the principle of guilt by association, which has a temporal basis. If more than one tissue compartment were used, this association would also be spatial. The "cause and effect" means of classification is facilitated by the temporal correlation produced through the use of DCs that sample signals and antigen over different durations.

5.4.4 Generic DC Algorithm Summary

An overview of the DCA is presented in Fig. 5.7. In Section 5.4, a generic description of the algorithm is presented, outlining its key features and mechanisms for processing data, filtering, and detecting anomalous antigen. At a cell level, the DC is a signal processing unit, which makes a binary (yes/no) decision as to whether the antigen it has collected during its life span was collected under anomalous conditions. At a population level, the greater DC population is used to perform anomaly detection based on the consensus opinion of the collection of cells. This behavior produces a robust method of detection through the incorporation of multiple antigen and signal sampling across a population of artificial cells all with variable life spans. This forms a filter-based correlation algorithm that includes a "time window" effect that reduces false positive errors [Greensmith, 2007].

Fig. 5.7 Illustration of the DCA showing data input, continuous sampling, the maturation process, and aggregate analysis

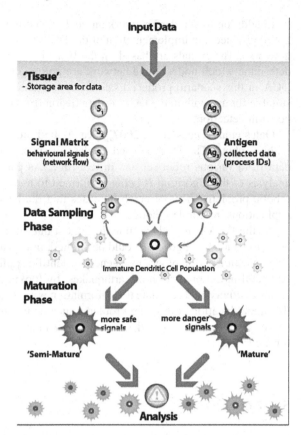

5.5 Applications: Past and Present

The DCA is designed with the objective of its ultimate application to problems in network intrusion detection, through reducing the high rates of false positives previously seen with anomaly detection systems [Aickelin et al., 2004]. While the DCA has been applied to such problems [Greensmith et al., 2006], it has also enjoyed some preliminary successes in sensor networks and mobile robotics.

Early work with the algorithm involved its application to a standard machine learning data set [Greensmith et al., 2005], where it was shown that the algorithm can process classification data but is sensitive to the data order. Once the algorithm was deemed feasible through its application to the machine learning data set, the DCA has also been applied to the detection of port scans and scanning based activity [Greensmith et al., 2008], which produced high rates of true positives and low rates of false positives. In the case of the port scan experiments, signals are taken as behavioral attributes, and system calls are used to form antigen. This research is ongoing and now encompasses the detection of other forms of malicious mobile code, such as botnets and scanning worms.

In addition to standard network anomaly detection tasks, Kim et al. [Kim et al., 2006] produced an implementation of the DCA for detecting misbehavior in sensor networks. The signals are based on the behavior of packet sending and is used to determine which nodes in the network are potentially under attack. The use of the DCA in this scenario produced satisfactory results. In conclusion, this problem is suitable for use with in the DCA as data fusion from disparate sources is required to perform detection.

Oates et al. [Oates et al., 2007] have applied the DCA to object detection using mobile robots. The DCA is used to classify specific objects based on combining data from various robot sensors in real-time. As part of this research, theoretical analysis of the algorithm is being performed to assist in its application to difficult robotic problems. This research indicates that the DCA is a suitable algorithm for applications in mobile robotics.

As the DCA can analyze time-dependent data in real-time, there are numerous areas to which the algorithm could be applied, both within computer network intrusion detection and in other more general scientific applications. For example, it may be useful in the prediction of earthquakes, by looking for "danger" in the form of seismic activity, and correlate this information with location, encoding antigen. Similar signal/location correlating problems such as the analysis of radio anomalies in space and the analysis of real-time medical data may be potential applications areas for the DCA.

5.6 Conclusions

In this chapter, the dendritic cell algorithm is presented as an immune-inspired algorithm. This algorithm is based on an abstract model of the biological dendritic cells (DCs), which are key decision-making cells of the human immune system. The abstract model presented in this chapter shows the key properties of the natural system, and such properties are presented to form a model. From this model, a generic DC-based algorithm is presented. This algorithm forms the DCA and is capable of performing multi-sensor data fusion on the input signals, combined with a correlation component, linking signals to antigen data. The process by which the signals are used and combined is detailed, in combination with a description of the behavior for each artificial cell within the algorithm.

The DCA has enjoyed success so far in its application to the detection of port scans and is shown in the related work to be a robust and decentralized algorithm. The key to the robustness lies in the "time-window effect", where different members of the population sample input data across different durations. This effect is thought to decrease the number of false-positive results produced by the algorithm.

Future developments with the DCA include the addition of a "responder cell" component to calculate the MCAV anomaly coefficient dynamically. This would potentially increase the sensitivity of the system. Understanding the exact workings of the DCA is a non-trivial task. So far, the majority of its characterization has been performed empirically, through sensitivity analysis and parameter modification. However, in the future, a more theoretical approach to its analysis will be taken, through the use of various theoretical tools such as constraint satisfaction. Perhaps through the performance of this analysis it can be shown exactly why this algorithm produces the good rates of detection in a robust manner.

References

Aickelin, U., Bentley, P., Cayzer, S., Kim, J., and McLeod, J. (2003). Danger theory: The link between AIS and IDS. In *Proceedings of the 2nd International Conference on Artificial Immune Systems (ICARIS'03), LNCS 2787*, pages 147–155. Springer, Berlin, Heidelberg.

Aickelin, U., Greensmith, J., and Twycross, J. (2004). Immune system approaches to intrusion detection–a review. In *Proceedings of the 3rd International Conference on Artificial Immune Systems (ICARIS), LNCS 3239*, pages 316–329. Springer, Berlin, Heidelberg.

Bakos, G. and Berk, V. (2002). Early detection of internet worm activity by metering ICMP destination unreachable messages. In *Proceedings of the SPIE Conference on Sensors, and Command, Control, Communications, and Intelligence (C3I) Technologies for Homeland Defense and Law Enforcement (SPIE Vol. 4708)*, pages 33–42, Orlando, Florida, April.

Balthrop, J., Esponda, F., Forrest, S., and Glickman, M. (2002). Coverage and generaliszation in an artificial immune system. In *Proceedings of the Genetic and Evolutionary Computation Conference (GECCO'02)*, pages 3–10, New York, 9–13 July. Morgan Kaufmann Publishers

Coico, R., Sunshine, G., and Benjamini, E. (2003). *Immunology: A Short Course*. Wiley-Liss, New York.

de Castro, L. and Timmis, J. (2002). *Artificial Immune Systems: A New Computational Approach*. Springer-Verlag, London.

Edinger, A. and Thompson, C. (2004). Death by design: apoptosis, necrosis and autophagy. *Current Opinion in Cell Biology*, 16(6):663–669.

Forrest, S., Perelson, A., Allen, L., and Cherukuri, R. (1994). Self-nonself discrimination in a computer. In *Proceedings of the IEEE Symposium on Security and Privacy*, pages 202–209, Oakland, California, 16–18 May. IEEE Computer Society, Washington, DC.

Gallucci, S., Lolkema, M., and Matzinger, P. (1999). Natural adjuvants: endogenous activators of dendritic cells. *Nature Medicine*, 5(11):1249–1255.

Greensmith, J. (2007). *The Dendritic Cell Algorithm*. PhD thesis, School of Computer Science, University of Nottingham.

Greensmith, J. and Aickelin, U. (2007). Dendritic cells for SYN scan detection. In *Proceedings of the 9th Annual Conference on Genetic and Evolutionary Computation (GECCO'07)*, pages 49–56, London, England, UK, 7–11 July. ACM, New York.

Greensmith, J., Aickelin, U., and Cayzer, S. (2005). Introducing dendritic cells as a novel immune-inspired algorithm for anomaly detection. In *Proceedings of the 4th International Conference on Artificial Immune Systems (ICARIS'05), LNCS 3627*, pages 153–167. Springer, Berlin, Heidelberg.

Greensmith, J., Aickelin, U., and Tedesco, G. (2008). Information Fusion for Anomaly Detection with the DCA. *Journal of Information Fusion*. In print.

Greensmith, J., Aickelin, U., and Twycross, J. (2006). Articulation and clarification of the dendritic cell algorithm. In *Proceedings of the 5th International Conference on Artificial Immune Systems (ICARIS'06), LNCS 4163*, pages 404–417. Springer Berlin, Heidelberg.

Janeway, C. (1989). Approaching the asymptote? Evolution and revolution in immunology. *Cold Spring Harbor Symposia on Quantitative Biology*, 54:1–13.

Janeway, C. (2004). *Immunobiology*. Garland Science Publishing, New York, 4th edition.

Kim, J., Bentley, P., Wallenta, C., Ahmed, M., and Hailes, S. (2006). Danger is ubiquitous: detecting malicious activities in sensor networks using the dendritic cell algorithm. In *Proceedings of the 5th International Conference on Artificial Immune Systems (ICARIS'06), LNCS 4163*, pages 390–403. Springer, Berlin, Heidelberg.

Lutz, M. and Schuler, G. (2002). Immature, semi-mature and fully mature dendritic cells: which signals induce tolerance or immunity? *Trends in Immunology*, 23(9):991–1045.

Mahnke, K., Johnson, T., Ring, S., and Enk, A. (2007). Tolerogenic dendritic cells and regulatory T-cells: a two-way relationship. *Journal of Dermatologic Science*, 46(3):159–167.

Matzinger, P. (1994). Tolerance, danger and the extended family. *Annual Reviews in Immunology*, 12:991–1045.

Matzinger, P. (2007). Friendly and dangerous signals: is the tissue in control? *Nature Immunology*, 8(1):11–13.

Medzhitov, R. and Janeway, C. (2002). Decoding the patterns of self and nonself by the innate immune system. *Science*, 296:298–300.

Mosmann, T. and Livingstone, A. (2004). Dendritic cells: the immune information management experts. *Nature Immunology*, 5(6):564–566.

Oates, R., Greensmith, J., Aickelin, U., Garibaldi, J., and Kendall, G. (2007). The application of a dendritic cell algorithm to a robotic classifier. In *Proceedings of the 6th International Conference on Artificial Immune Systems (ICARIS'07), LNCS 4628*, pages 204–215. Springer, Berlin, Heidelberg.

Silverstein, A. (2005). Paul Ehrlich, archives and the history of immunology. *Nature Immunology*, 6(7):639–639.

Sporri, R. and Caetano, C. (2005). Inflammatory mediators are insufficient for full dendritic cell activation and promote expansion of CD4+ T cell populations lacking helper function. *Nature Immunology*, 6(2):163–170.

Twycross, J. (2007). *Integrated Innate and Adaptive Artificial Immune Systems Applied to Process Anomaly Detection*. PhD thesis, University of Nottingham.

Twycross, J. and Aickelin, U. (2008). Information fusion in the immune system. *Journal of Information Fusion*, In print.

Chapter 6
Non-invasive Brain-Computer Interfaces for Semi-autonomous Assistive Devices

Bernhard Graimann, Brendan Allison, Christian Mandel, Thorsten Lüth, Diana Valbuena, and Axel Gräser

Abstract A brain-computer interface (BCI) transforms brain activity into commands that can control computers and other technologies. Because brain signals recorded non-invasively from the scalp are difficult to interpret, robust signal processing methods have to be applied. Although state-of-the-art signal processing methods are used in BCI research, the output of a BCI is still unreliable, and the information transfer rates are very small compared with conventional human interaction interfaces. Therefore, BCI applications have to compensate for the unreliability and low information content of the BCI output. Controlling a wheelchair or a robotic arm would be slow, frustrating, or even dangerous if it solely relied on BCI output. Intelligent devices, however, such as a wheelchair that can automatically avoid collisions and dangerous situations or a service robot that can autonomously conduct goal-directed tasks and independently detect and resolve safety issues, are much more suitable for being controlled by an "unreliable" control signal like that provided by a BCI.

6.1 Introduction

Ever since the first human brain waves were recorded by the German scientist Hans Berger in the late 1920s, it was speculated that EEG (electroencephalogram) technologies could be used to decipher thoughts or to control external devices. The idea of using brain waves to produce control signals—to establish a direct interface between the human brain and a machine or computer—also appeared early in the science fiction genre. Early television series like *Star Trek* and movies like *Firefox* envisaged such applications. At that time, limitations in computing power, signal processing techniques, and cognitive neuroscience kept such ideas in the realm of science fiction. However, improvements in these technologies have led to the first publications about brain-computer communication in the early 1970s,

B. Graimann
Institute of Automation, University of Bremen, Otto-Hahn Allee 1, 28359 Bremen, Germany
e-mail: graimann@iat.uni-bremen.de

A. Schuster (ed.), *Robust Intelligent Systems,* DOI: 10.1007/978-1-84800-261-6_6,
© Springer-Verlag London Limited 2008

which demonstrated a proof of principle [Vidal, 1973]. About 15 years later, ongoing improvements in relevant technologies paved the way for BCIs that could yield more than just proof of principle results [Farwell and Donchin, 1988, Wolpaw et al., 1991].

Direct communication from man to machine has now advanced well beyond science fiction. Brain-computer interfaces (BCIs), which are tools that allow communication and control via direct measures of brain activity, have been widely described in the literature. Most BCI research efforts focus on developing communication tools for people who need them most—persons with severe physical disabilities that prevent them from communicating via other means [Wolpaw et al., 2002]. However, although BCIs exhibit serious drawbacks relative to other interfaces, very recent research developments suggest that BCIs may soon become much more powerful, flexible, and usable tools, providing improved communication to severely disabled users and opening new applications and new user groups [Allison et al., 2007b, Allison et al., 2007a, Birbaumer and Cohen, 2007, Graimann et al., 2007].

This chapter initially reviews the foundations of modern BCI systems. The chapter then presents a discussion of the limitations of current BCIs. After a general discussion of BCI signal processing, the chapter presents the Bremen SSVEP BCI as an example of an easily applicable and robust BCI. The chapter also introduces new BCI applications that are about to become possible through intelligent assistive devices (e.g., rehabilitation robots). A section in this text discusses future BCI directions, and the chapter finally shows how the BCI technologies developed at Bremen, as well as other recent research developments, can compensate for many BCI limitations and adumbrate new BCI users and applications.

6.2 Modern Brain-Computer Interfaces

6.2.1 Mental Strategies and Brain Patterns

A BCI detects, interprets, and classifies specific patterns of activity in ongoing brain signals that are associated with specific intentions, tasks, or events. These tasks or events can be either exogenous or endogenous. Correspondingly, one may differentiate between exogenous and endogenous BCIs [Kleber and Birbaumer, 2005]. Exogenous systems rely on activity elicited in the brain by external stimuli, such as visual evoked potentials or auditory evoked potentials. In contrast, endogenous systems do not require an external stimulus. Through neurofeedback training, users learn to voluntarily modulate specific brain patterns. The length of the training varies with the mental strategy used, feedback and pattern classification parameters, the subjects' goals, the training environment, and other factors.

Most BCIs rely on either *selective attention* or *motor imagery*. Commonly used brain patterns are the SSVEP (steady state visual evoked potential), P300 (the 300-ms component of an evoked potential), and ERD/ERS (event-related desynchronization and synchronization). In a selective attention task, the user focuses attention on a particular stimulus. The stimulus may oscillate at a frequency from 5 to 50 Hz, or flash infrequently. Rapidly oscillating stimuli produce SSVEP activity in the brain at corresponding frequencies. This SSVEP activity becomes larger if subjects focus attention on a specific stimulus, and thus SSVEP BCI users can communicate which stimulus is of interest to them [Middendorf et al., 2000]. Transient stimuli that a user silently counts (rather than ignores) will produce a P300 [Donchin et al., 2000]. Some BCIs that rely on selective attention instead utilize auditory [Sellers and Donchin, 2006] or tactile [Müller et al., 2003a] stimuli. Because all BCIs based on selective attention require external stimuli, these BCIs are all exogenous. BCIs based on motor imagery do not require any external stimulus and therefore belong to endogenous BCIs. Motor imagery is the imagination of motor movements such as left-hand or right-hand movement without actually moving these limbs. In other words, instead of performing the motor activity such as hand movement, this movement is only mentally performed (imagined performance). Motor imagery BCIs work because ERD/ERS activity changes when people imagine or perform movement. Thus, people can imagine different movements and thereby produce ERD/ERS changes that convey user intent [Pfurtscheller et al., 2006b].

All BCI patterns can be characterized in the time and frequency domain as well as according to the topography. The relation between mental tasks and the corresponding brain patterns produced are shown in the concept map in Fig. 6.1.

The main difference between BCIs and other human-computer interaction systems is that BCIs require no muscle activity or physical movement. Unlike other

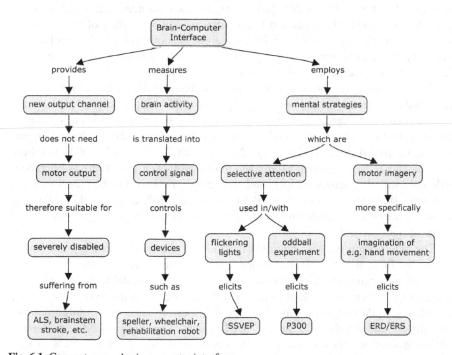

Fig. 6.1 Concept map—brain-computer interface

systems, which require muscle activity, BCIs provide "non-muscular" communication or require only little muscular activity such as gaze shifting. One of the most important reasons that this is significant is that the main application of current BCI systems is to provide assistive devices for people with severe disabilities. Some people have a medical condition called locked-in syndrome (caused by diseases that affect the neuromuscular pathways such as brainstem stroke or amyotrophic lateral sclerosis) and thus have lost all ability to communicate. Their cognitive functions, however, are mostly or completely intact. BCIs provide those patients the only possibility to interact with their environment. Although BCIs allow only limited communication capabilities compared with conventional interfaces, as pointed out in the next section, BCIs are essential for people with severe disabilities preventing them from communicating through other means.

6.2.2 Limitations of Brain-Computer Interfaces

Most non-invasive BCIs measure brain signals via electrodes mounted on the scalp. These signals are stochastic and nonstationary, have a small signal-to-noise ratio, a poor spatial resolution, and are very susceptible to external and internal interferences. Moreover, the underlying probability distributions are unknown, and the data samples available for machine learning and statistical inference are usually very limited. Therefore, robust signal processing methods are needed to reliably detect and classify voluntarily generated brain patterns. Although state-of-the-art signal processing methods are applied in BCI research, the output of a BCI is still unreliable, and the information transfer rates are very small compared with conventional human interaction interfaces such as keyboard and mouse.

BCIs are notorious for poor information throughput. Although online BCI systems have exhibited performance slightly above 60 bits per minute [Gao et al., 2003], such performance is not typical of most users in real-world settings. Other recent publications have described information throughput between 30 and 60 bits per minute [Blankertz et al., 2007, Friman et al., 2007b, Gao et al., 2003], but these still may not reflect average performance in real-world settings. There is often considerable variation across subjects and BCI usage sessions. Further, a minority of subjects exhibit little or no control [Blankertz et al., 2007, Guger et al., 2003]. The reason is not clear, but even long sustained training cannot improve performance for some of these subjects.

The information transfer rate also depends on the mental strategy employed. Typically, BCIs with selective attention strategies are faster than those using, for instance, motor imagery. Unfortunately, there is no study available that investigated the average information transfer rate for different BCI systems over a larger user population. Only one study has evaluated BCI performance over a large number of subjects, and it only used an ERD BCI system. This study found considerable variation across the 99 subjects tested. In a two target task, about 6% to 7% of subjects attained average accuracy above 90%, about the same percentage of subjects exhibited accuracy between 50% and 60%, and remaining subjects attained intermediate performance. Most BCI studies use twelve or fewer subjects [Guger et al., 2003]. Additional research exploring how different people perform with different BCI approaches, and correlations between performance and subject background is needed to explore this issue further.

Information throughput, in BCIs or any communication channel, depends on the number of selections available to the user, the probability of correctly identifying the selection that corresponds with user intent, and the number of selections possible per minute. Although some BCIs present subjects with only two selections (e.g., [Wolpaw et al., 1991, Pfurtscheller et al., 2006a]), other BCIs (e.g., [Allison and Pineda, 2003, Sellers et al., 2006]) allow 36 or more selections. BCI accuracy varies considerably, but modern BCIs can attain performance above 85% with most subjects. Further, any BCI can improve accuracy at the expense of selections per minute by using longer periods of brain activity or response verification [McFarland et al., 2003]. BCIs typically offer about 10 selections per minute, though this varies widely as well.

Both the hardware and software currently available for brain-computer communication is more suitable for experiments in the lab than for practical applications in real-world environments like user homes. The hardware needed for an EEG BCI requires a trained expert to precisely position the EEG cap, scrape the skin where each electrode will go, apply gooey electrode gel, further abrade the skin, and continue this process until all electrodes (often a large number of elec trodes is necessary) produce a clean signal. This process is not painful, but not exceptionally pleasant either. After each BCI usage session, the cap and the user's hair must be washed. BCIs not only require an expert to help set up the necessary hardware but also to configure and adapt key software parameters [Allison et al., 2007b]. Hence, BCI users are dependent on expert help to set up, clean, and configure their BCI. The conclusions and future prospects section below presents some avenues toward making BCIs more intelligent, self-adaptive, reliable, and practical.

6.2.3 BCI Signal Processing

The building blocks of a BCI are signal acquisition, signal processing, and the application interface. Figure 6.2 shows the basic scheme of a BCI.

A BCI analyzes and assesses the activity of the brain and transforms this activity, often through complicated signal processing techniques, into control signals that operate assistive devices. Brain activity suitable for a BCI can be monitored or recorded in various ways. The recording methods can be invasive or non-invasive and can record electrical activity or metabolic brain responses. The most prevalent non-invasive method is the EEG, which records the brain's electrical activity. EEG recording is relatively simple, readily available, inexpensive, and non-invasive. However, it also has some disadvantages such as poor signal-to-noise ratio and

Fig. 6.2 Basic scheme of a
BCI (adapted from
[Graimann, 2006])

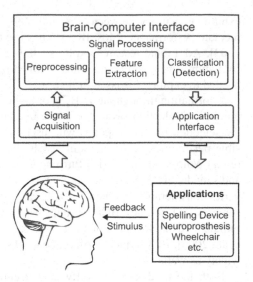

very limited spatial resolution. Invasive methods such as intracortical recordings or electrocorticogram (ECoG) alleviate the limitations of the EEG. The ECoG, which records activity from the surface of the cortex and unlike intracortical recordings does not penetrate brain tissue, is considered to be less invasive. The spectro-temporal properties of ECoG signals are similar to EEG signals, but the signal quality in terms of SNR and spatial resolution is much better. Besides EEG and ECoG, intra-cortical recordings capturing spiking activity from single neurons or neuron assemblies or methods for measuring metabolic activation (blood oxygena-tion) are other ways of recording brain activity. This chapter focuses on EEG, because this is the most common and practical tool for BCIs. Typically, BCI signal processing is subdivided in "preprocessing", "feature extraction", and "detection or classification".

Preprocessing

Preprocessing aims at improving the spatial resolution and signal-to-noise ratio (SNR) of the recorded signals. Spatial filters, which instantaneously linearly com-bine samples of different channels, are often used in BCI preprocessing. Orthog-onal source derivation is a classical spatial filter in EEG processing. Because of its simplicity and efficacy, the small Laplacian, a simplified form of orthogonal source derivation, is often used in ERD/ERS based BCIs [Pfurtscheller et al., 2006a, McFarland et al., 1997]. More advanced spatial filters can be derived from prin-cipal component analysis (PCA) or independent component analysis (ICA). PCA seeks uncorrelated components with maximal variance, and ICA tries to decompose signals into statistically independent components. ICA, PCA, and combinations of both methods have been applied to BCIs based on SSVEP, P300, and ERD/ERS [Friman et al., 2007b, Hill et al., 2007, Naeem et al., 2006]. A method that has been applied particularly successfully to discriminate ERD/ERS patterns is Common Spatial Patterns (CSP) (e.g., see [Ramoser et al., 2000, Dornhege et al., 2004, Graimann and Pfurtscheller, 2006]) and its various extensions as in the work of [Lemm et al., 2005, Dornhege et al., 2007]. In contrast with previously mentioned spatial filters, CSP is a supervised method and thus requires labeled data (class information). It is based on the simultaneous diagonalization of two matrices—the variance matrices of the two populations—and finds projections with the biggest difference in variance between the two classes.

Feature Extraction

Feature extraction is the second step in the BCI signal processing chain. Sometimes preprocessing and feature extraction are seen as one unit. The reason is that both preprocessing and feature extraction have the same aim, to simplify the problem for the subsequent detection or classification task. Both units are supposed to improve signal quality, i.e., improve signal-to-noise ratio and spatial resolution, by extracting discriminant information from the signal while simultaneously eliminating redundant and disturbing information. However, the signal processing methods for preprocessing and feature extraction are considerably different, and therefore they are treated as individual blocks here. Most feature extraction methods employed produce features characterized either in the time or in the frequency domain, and their statistics is of first or second order (i.e., mean or variance) [Pfurtscheller et al., 2006a]. Examples are simple averaging for extracting evoked potentials or calculating the variance (power) of the signal over the entire signal or specific frequency ranges. Variance features are derived from simple bandpass filters, wavelet filters, or of parametric and non-parametric spectrum estimators [Graimann et al., 2004, Pfurtscheller et al., 2006a].

Detection and Classification

A BCI essentially transforms a brain signal into a control signal. This transformation can be seen as a mapping from the high-dimensional input signal to a signal of considerably reduced dimension. In this view, a BCI is basically a classifier that maps the input to classes of which each class corresponds with a command. Robust behavior is an essential feature in BCI signal processing. This is the reason why linear classifiers such as Fisher linear discriminant (FDA) or support vector machines (SVM) with linear kernels are most often used in BCIs [Müller et al., 2004, Pfurtscheller et al., 2006a]. They are less prone to outliers and show better generalization than do non-linear classifiers. Both FDA and SVM are binary classifiers but can be easily extended to multiple classes by applying a one-vs-one or one-vs-rest scheme. In order to further reduce overfitting and improve the robustness of the classifiers, regularization has been suggested for the training of BCI classifiers [Müller et al., 2004]. The influence of outliers is demonstrated in Fig. 6.3.

Fig. 6.3 Influence of outliers
on Fisher linear discriminant
analysis as classifier

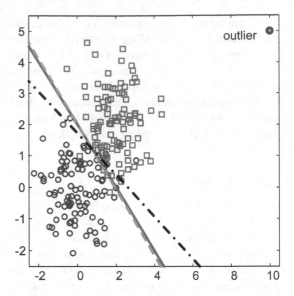

Figure 6.3 shows samples of two Gaussian distributions with the same variance but different means. The solid straight line represents the optimal linear decision function, the dashed line is the result of FDA, whereas the outlier in the upper right corner has been neglected; and the dotted line represents the result of FDA without neglecting the outlier. Obviously, the impact of the outlier is large and can change the decision function represented by the straight lines in Fig. 6.3 considerably. The standard way for calculating FDA is to maximize the ratio of the between-class variance to the within-class variance:

$$J(\mathbf{w}) = \frac{(m_2 - m_1)^2}{(s_1)^2 + (s_2)^2} = \frac{\mathbf{w}^T \mathbf{S}_B \mathbf{w}}{\mathbf{w}^T \mathbf{S}_W \mathbf{w}}, \qquad (6.1)$$

where $\mathbf{w}$ is the weight vector (linear projection vector), m_c and s_c denote the means and standard deviations for each class, $c \in \{1, 2\}$, and $\mathbf{S}_B$ and $\mathbf{S}_W$ are the between-class covariance matrix and the within-class covariance matrix, respectively. The solution for this optimization problem is [Fukunaga, 1990]:

$$\mathbf{w} = \mathbf{S}_W^{-1}(m_2 - m_1). \qquad (6.2)$$

Applying this solution on the data shown in Fig. 6.3 gives the defective result represented by the dashed line if the outlier is included in the data. In the presence of outliers, a more robust result can be obtained when regularization is used. A possible regularization when the problem is defined as a mathematical programming approach [Müller et al., 2003b]:

$$\min_{\mathbf{w}, b, \zeta} \|\mathbf{w}\|_2^2 + \frac{\lambda}{K} \|\zeta\|_2^2, \qquad (6.3)$$

subject to the constraint:

$$y_k(\mathbf{w}^T \mathbf{x}_k + b) = 1 - \zeta_k \quad \text{for} \quad k = 1, \ldots, K, \tag{6.4}$$

with ζ the slack variables, $\mathbf{x}_k$ the k-th sample vector (feature vector) of K samples, y_k is the corresponding class label (-1 or 1), and b is the bias that defines together with $\mathbf{w}$ the decision boundary. The slack variables are implicitly determined by the quadratic programming machine, which is usually used to solve this constrained optimization problem. The regularization coefficient λ, however, has to be determined for each data set explicitly. It is a so-called hyperparameter. Like other parameters, hyperparameters have to be adjusted to the data, but there are no direct optimization methods to do that. They are usually determined by an iterative process embedded in a cross-validation procedure, where the results on a subset of the data (training set) are cross-validated with the results obtained on another subset (test set).

Parameter Optimization and Evaluation

The parameters used to identify and classify brain activity in a BCI are typically calculated from off-line data. That is, the setup of the classifier is done on data recorded in a previous BCI session. The new classifier determined in the off-line analysis is then used in the next session. In order to obtain good generalization, the classifier has to be validated carefully. The data has to be divided into training and test set. All parameters, including the hyperparameters of a method, have to be determined on the training set. The evaluation has to be done on the test set. It is essential that the test data is not involved in any way before the parameters are defined, otherwise the generalization would be compromised and less robust results would be achieved [Müller et al., 2003b, Dornhege et al., 2007]. One way to perform proper cross-validation is to split the data in three disjunct sets: training, validation, and test set. The parameters are determined on the training and validation set, and the final evaluation, i.e., the estimation of the generalization error, is performed on the test set. In BCI signal processing, however, the available data for the training of classifiers is typically very limited. It is important to note that the absolute number of samples available is not important, but rather the number of independent data samples is important. In a recording sampled with 1000 Hz where the subject performed 50 mental tasks, the amount of available and statistically independent data for training a classifier is essentially the same as in the recording sampled with 250 Hz. It is the number of trials that is important and not the number of samples, provided the sampling theorem is satisfied. This is the reason why splitting the data in three portions is seldom an option in BCI signal processing. A solution for this dilemma is the use of nested cross-validation [Müller et al., 2004, Dornhege et al., 2007]. In this procedure, the training set is again split in inner-training and inner-test sets. On these inner sets, an inner cross-validation is performed to determine the parameters of the signal processing approach. The generalization error is determined on the normal (outer) cross-validation. In this way, a robust setup of the parameters can be achieved.

6.3 A Robust BCI Based on SSVEP

A high information transfer rate is very important in BCIs. Other characteristics of a BCI are also very important for a robust and practically applicable BCI:

- The BCI system should be minimally prone to artifacts and external interferences.
- The number of electrodes required should be small.
- An exact electrode placement is not necessary.
- The number of parameters that have to be optimized for each individual user should be as small as possible.
- The system should account of the inherent non-stationarity of brain signals.

Almost all BCI systems currently available combine only one or two of these practical features. One notable exception is the Bremen BCI, which is based on SSVEP and implements a robust signal processing methodology that provides high information transfer rates and also the five desirable characteristics mentioned above [Friman et al., 2007b, Friman et al., 2007a].

As mentioned previously, SSVEP patterns are elicited in a visual selective attention task in which BCI users focus their attention on light sources that flicker with frequencies above 5 Hz. The SSVEP is best described in the frequency domain, as it consists of frequency components that have the same fundamental frequency as the stimulation but also includes higher harmonics. This is seen in Fig. 6.4(A) where the spectral density of a 20-second period with repetitive stimulation with a flickering light of 11 Hz is shown.

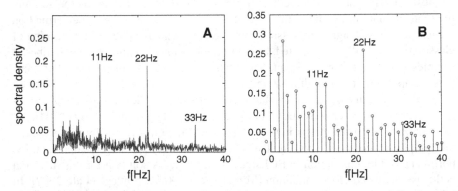

Fig. 6.4 Steady state visual evoked potentials. Figure 6.4(A) shows the spectral density of a 20-second period. Figure 6.4(B) shows the spectral density where only a 1-second period of the 20-second period was used

The SSVEP is clearly visible at the fundamental frequency of 11 Hz and the harmonic frequencies at 22 and 33 Hz. In this case, the SSVEP could be discriminated from the neighboring frequency components that indicate the ongoing background activity. However, in a real-time BCI, the user cannot wait 20 seconds for a response. The processing time frames have to be much shorter. The spectral density depicted in Fig. 6.4(B) is calculated from a 1-second period and shows that the discrimination is not so simple anymore.

In this case, more complicated signal processing methods have to be employed to achieve robust detection of the SSVEP components and also to discriminate between different SSVEP patterns evoked from different stimulation frequencies.

In a typical BCI application, flickering lights with different frequencies are used as stimuli. Each flickering light and its corresponding SSVEP are associated with a certain control command of the BCI application. The BCI system must reliably detect SSVEPs in the ongoing brain signal to identify which command the user wants to convey. For high information transfer rates, three parameters are important: the accuracy of detection, the speed of detection, and the number of frequencies that can be discriminated. These three parameters are not independent of each other. In fact, they are closely related. As indicated in Fig. 6.4, shorter time segments speed up the detection time but also reduce the accuracy. Reduced accuracy also influences the number of frequencies that can be differentiated reliably. Instead of trying to improve each of these three parameters individually, the information transfer rate can also be improved by increasing the signal-to-noise ratio in general.

The Bremen BCI implements such an approach. The brain signal is modeled as a composite of SSVEP response, background brain activity, and noise. Short time principle component analysis is used to create a spatial filter that linearly combines the signals of all electrodes in a way that the background activity and noise is minimized. The algorithm is briefly outlined in the following. More details can be found in [Friman et al., 2007b]. The assumed model of the brain signal of a channel i is:

$$y_i(t) = \sum_{k=1}^{N_h} a_{i,k} \sin(2\pi k f t + \phi_{i,k}) + \sum_j b_{i,j} z_j(t) + e_i(t), \qquad (6.4)$$

where the first part is the SSVEP modeled as sinusoidals with the fundamental frequency f and its harmonics $k \cdot f (k > 1)$, and the corresponding amplitude $a_{i,k}$ and phase $\phi_{i,k}$. The number of harmonics considered is described by N_h. The second part describes the background activity as a sum of background brain activity and nuisance signals. The last part, $e_i(t)$, describes the noise component in the measurement. Assuming a time frame of N_t samples and a number of N_y channels, the model can be written as [Friman et al., 2007b]:

$$\mathbf{Y} = \mathbf{XA} + \mathbf{ZB} + \mathbf{E}, \qquad (6.5)$$

where $\mathbf{Y} = [y_1, \ldots y_{N_y}]$ is a $N_t \times N_y$ matrix with the channel signals in the columns, $\mathbf{X}$ contains the sine and cosine pairs from the SSVEP model in its columns, $\mathbf{Z}$ the background activity, $\mathbf{A}$ and $\mathbf{B}$ contain the corresponding amplitudes, and $\mathbf{E}$ is the noise matrix.

In order to minimize activity that is not related to the SSVEP, a linear combination is sought that reduces the variance in the background activity and in the noise component of equation (6.5). To this end, any potential SSVEP activity is removed from the electrode signals. This is done by orthogonal projection.

$$\widetilde{\mathbf{Y}} = \mathbf{Y} - \mathbf{X}(\mathbf{X}^T\mathbf{X})^{-1}\mathbf{X}^T\mathbf{Y}. \tag{6.6}$$

The remaining signal $\widetilde{\mathbf{Y}}$ contains approximately only background activity and noise, i.e.,:

$$\widetilde{\mathbf{Y}} \approx \mathbf{Z}\mathbf{B} + \mathbf{E}. \tag{6.7}$$

The linear combination, i.e., the weight vector $\mathbf{w}$, for minimizing the variance of $\widetilde{\mathbf{Y}}$, is found by optimizing

$$\min_{\mathbf{w}} \|\widetilde{\mathbf{Y}}\mathbf{w}\|^2 = \min_{\mathbf{w}} \mathbf{w}^T\widetilde{\mathbf{Y}}^T\widetilde{\mathbf{Y}}\mathbf{w}, \tag{6.8}$$

which has the solution in the eigenvector that corresponds with the smallest eigenvalue of the covariance of $\widetilde{\mathbf{Y}}$. The solution is known as principal component analysis (PCA). However, in PCA, the components with the largest variance are usually used. Here, the components with the smallest variances—also known as the minor components—are needed. To increase the robustness, not only the eigenvector of the smallest eigenvalue but also those eigenvectors of the next largest eigenvalues, so that altogether about 10% of the variance of the data is included, are used to construct the spatial filter $\mathbf{W}$. The spatially filtered signal is then:

$$\mathbf{S} = \mathbf{Y}\mathbf{W}. \tag{6.9}$$

The test statistic, which is an average of the signal-to-noise ratio over all N_s spatially filtered components and all N_h SSVEP frequencies (including harmonics), is calculated by:

$$T = \frac{1}{N_s N_h} \sum_{l=1}^{N_s} \sum_{k=1}^{N_h} \frac{P_{k,l}}{\sigma_{k,l}^2}, \tag{6.10}$$

where $P_{k,l}$ is the power in the kth SSVEP harmonic frequency in the spatially filtered signal l; $\sigma_{k,l}^2$ is the corresponding estimate of the background and noise activity.

In a BCI application with several stimuli, a test statistic for each fundamental frequency of the flickering light is calculated from data blocks of a length of 1 second. Each statistic is compared with an empirically determined threshold. If a test statistic exceeds the threshold, then the corresponding frequency is detected, and the control command associated with this frequency is initiated.

This algorithm is simple to apply and gives reliable and robust results. As shown in [Friman et al., 2007b], only a few channels (6 channels or even less) are necessary to achieve good results. The exact electrode placement is not critical, as the spatial filter is adaptively calculated for each data block. This is also the reason why the algorithm is able to account for the non-stationarity in the data. The influence of artifacts is small, because the algorithm considers only information from very narrow frequency bands (SSVEP fundamental frequency and harmonics). Also, only one parameter, the detection threshold, has to be determined. This is straightforward and typically only requires less than a minute. Most importantly, however, the algorithm is also able to achieve high information transfer rates. This has been shown in [Friman et al., 2007a], where the system was applied in two different BCI spelling tasks. In this study, the subjects navigated the cursor in a matrix-like arrangement of letters or selected columns and rows of a letter matrix by selective attention on five flickering lights. Each light encoded either cursor movement commands (left, right, up, down, and select) or the indices of the columns or rows of the letter matrix. Eleven subjects participated in this study and produced information transfer rates between 11 and 43 bits/min, with an average of about 27–30 bits/min. The average classification rate was about 97.5%. The best subject was able to write 9 letters per minute. Although higher information transfer rates have been reported [Gao et al., 2003], these results are remarkable as no subject specific optimization of the BCI was performed and only five flickering lights were used. The information transfer rates could be easily improved, at least for those subjects showing prominent SSVEPs, by increasing the number of flickering lights.

6.4 New Semi-autonomous Applications for BCIs

Most BCIs have been used to control computer applications such as spelling devices, simple computer games, limited environmental control, and generic cursor control applications as in the work by [Pfurtscheller et al., 2006a, Sellers and Donchin, 2006, Blankertz et al., 2007]), for example. Only a limited number of systems have also allowed control of more sophisticated devices, including orthoses, robotic arms, and mobile robots [Allison et al., 2007b, Müller-Putz et al., 2005, Millan et al., 2004]. It appears that BCIs can control any application that other interfaces can control, provided these applications can function effectively with the low information throughput of BCIs. BCIs are not well suited for controlling more complex details of demanding applications because of two reasons: (a) complex applications increase the mental workload of the user and can thus negatively affect BCI performance, and (b) complicated tasks require a number of subtasks, which, when controlled on a low-level basis, can be time consuming, fatiguing, and frustrating. This underscores the importance of reducing the burden on BCI users through effective goal-oriented protocols. Goal-oriented or high-level BCI control means the BCI simply communicates the user's goal (the task) to the intelligent application device, which autonomously performs all necessary subtasks to achieve the goal.

In contrast, low-level control means the BCI manages all the intricate interactions involved in achieving the task or goal [Wolpaw, 2007].

In any interface, users should not be required to control unnecessary low-level details of system operation. This is especially important with BCIs; allowing low-level control of a wheelchair or robot arm, for example, would not only be slow and frustrating but also dangerous. Therefore, developing robust BCI applications capable of providing effective real-world control requires developing intelligent mechanisms that can mediate between the user's goals and the individual actions needed to implement those goals.

Wolpaw [Wolpaw, 2007] compares low-level control to actions of the spinal cord. In a healthy person, the brain is primarily responsible for identifying goals, and the peripheral nervous system bears more responsibility for determining how to best implement these goals. Once a person decides on the goal of drinking water, low-level details of how to move individual muscle groups to attain that goal are identified and implemented without conscious processing. If a BCI system aims to effectively replace the peripheral nervous system, the BCI system including the BCI application must also be able to generate low-level commands as needed to attain specific goals. This idea may also be interpreted through Marr [Marr, 1982], who discusses the three stages necessary to accomplish a task: theory (or goal), algorithm, and implementation. Any BCI can offload the "implementation" component, but only a goal-oriented BCI in cooperation with intelligent assistive devices can also identify the algorithmic details necessary to attain a goal.

An intelligent BCI system should, however, also provide the user with the option of implementing lower-level commands if desired. This is necessary if the high-level commands do not contain the exact goal that a user seeks to attain. An assistive robotic system that automatically pours water if the user conveys thirst may not satisfy a user who instead wants soda, juice, or wine. In these cases, the user might not mind the additional time required to perform tasks that are not preprogrammed. An ideal intelligent system would identify frequently issued command sequences and adapt accordingly, perhaps developing a new option to get juice if the user often does so. On the other hand, many current BCI applications that only provide low-level control would benefit if they would provide high-level control as well. BCI spellers, for instance, could accept high-level commands to prepare letter templates, which are then filled in by the user with low-level commands for spelling the individual words.

A related component of a robust intelligent BCI is application flexibility. Current BCIs support only specifically designed applications. A speller application designed for one BCI cannot be controlled by a different BCI. The large number of assistive devices available with well-defined standard interfaces but not specifically designed for BCI has been largely neglected by BCI research so far. Instead of using already existing devices that have been developed and improved over years, assistive applications for BCI are often "reinvented" and tailored for a particular system. Future BCIs should strive to provide users with increased application flexibility through a straightforward, usable interface that can effectively control a range of already existing assistive devices, software, and appliances. By leveraging existing protocols designed to allow control of common appliances, such as X10, UPNP, or Zigbee, BCI systems could provide greatly increased flexibility without extensive new developments.

In summary, much of the focus in the published literature and popular media is on new BCI signal processing and applications. While these initial validation efforts are important and promising, it is also crucial to follow up on these efforts by developing improved interfaces through more intelligent, flexible systems. In the following section, two robust intelligent systems developed and investigated at the University of Bremen are introduced and discussed.

6.4.1 Rehabilitation Robot

The term rehabilitation robot describes a broad range of assistive devices including powered orthotic or prosthetic devices, exoskeletons, powered feeding devices, automatic guided vehicles such as intelligent wheelchairs, and wheelchairs with mounted manipulators (robot arms) [Hillman, 2003]. As assistive devices, they are designed to meet the requirements of and address the problems confronted by people with disabilities. The scale of disabilities can range from slightly disabled to most severely disabled people. Depending on user's impairment (scale of disability), various forms of input mechanisms are used to control rehabilitation robots. Joystick, keyboard, and mouse are typical input devices for less severely disabled people. Sip/puff switches, interpretation of voice or head position, eye gaze, and electromyographic activity are input modalities for people with disabilities that prevent them from using other interfaces [Cook and Hussey, 2002]. Control by BCIs is usually the last resort for the most severely disabled people.

The rehabilitation robot FRIEND II (Functional Robot Arm with User Friendly Interface for disabled People) developed at the Institute of Automation at the University of Bremen is a semi-autonomous system designed to assist disabled people in activities of daily living [Ivlev et al., 2005]. The main components of FRIEND II are a conventional wheelchair, a manipulator (robot arm) with 7 degrees-of-freedom, a gripper with force/torque sensor, a stereo camera system mounted on a pan-tilt head, a smart tray with tactile surface and weight sensors, and a computing unit consisting of three independent industrial PCs. Figure 6.5 shows the FRIEND II system and an able-bodied user who controls the system with a BCI.

The stereo camera system and the smart tray form a robust and redundant system that is able to reliably localize objects on the tray largely independent from lighting conditions. FRIEND II is able to perform certain operations completely autonomously. An example of such an operation is a "pour in beverage" scenario. In this scenario, the system detects the bottle and the glass both located at arbitrary positions on the tray, grabs the bottle, moves the bottle to the glass while automatically avoiding any obstacles on the tray, fills the glass with liquid from the bottle while continuously controlling the fill level of the glass, and finally puts the bottle back in its original position—again avoiding any possible collisions.

Fig. 6.5 Rehabilitation robot
FRIEND II controlled by the
Bremen BCI

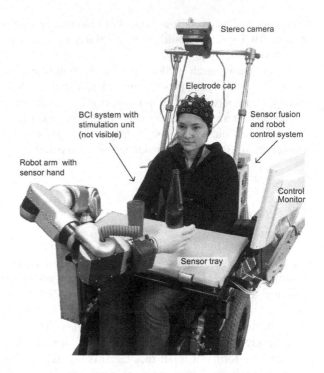

Besides this goal-oriented, high-level control approach for autonomously performed tasks, FRIEND II also provides the option to perform low-level control. This is necessary because the system operates in an unstructured environment, and uncertainties in sensor data can, in rare cases, result in slightly erroneous estimation of the position of objects. In such cases, the user can take over the control of the manipulator and adjust the gripper location. This is done in an intuitive manner using Cartesian commands and with support from the system, which controls the redundancy of the manipulator in parallel to simplify the task for the user. After gripper adjustment by the user, the system can proceed with the execution of the remaining tasks in an autonomous mode [Lüth et al., 2007].

This flexibility in providing goal-oriented, high-level commands and also low-level, direct control commands is facilitated by the robot control architecture MASSiVE (Multilayer Architecture for Semi-Autonomous Service Robots with Verified Task Executions) [Prenzel et al., 2007]. In order to enable user involvement in task execution, the MASSiVE architecture consists of four modules, shown in Fig. 6.6.

The reactive-layer abstracts the hardware specific functionality of sensors and actuators. The sequencer is responsible for task planning, and the human-machine interface (HMI) governs user interactions and provides feedback. A task is selected and started through an input device. At present, keyboard, mouse, joystick, voice, and BCI control are supported. The HMI manages the different input devices. A selected high-level task is sent from the HMI to the sequencer, which plans the task according to pre-defined task knowledge and Petri-nets. This produces is a

Fig. 6.6 Robot control architecture MASSiVE

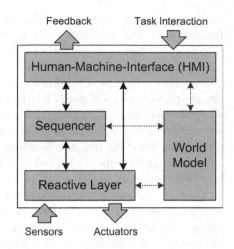

Feedback   Task Interaction

Human-Machine-Interface (HMI)

Sequencer

World Model

Reactive Layer

Sensors   Actuators

list of subtasks that the reactive layer will execute. If a problem occurs during the execution of these subtasks and the user has to be involved, the sequencer calls a special user interaction subtask using its interface to the HMI. The situation can then be addressed by the user [Prenzel et al., 2007]. From the sequencer's point of view, these user interaction subtasks are like normal subtasks executed by hardware components. This approach reduces the complexity of the semi-autonomous system. In the context of planning and execution, the world model acts as a knowledge base that stores data for different levels of abstraction. On one hand, the sequencer needs data describing objects during the task planning process (e.g., what kind of objects are involved in the task scenario) without further knowledge (symbolic data). On the other hand, detailed information about those objects is needed during execution of an already planned task in the reactive layer (subsymbolic data). Hence, the sequencer operates on the symbolic, the reactive layer on the subsymbolic part of the world model. The connection between both kinds of data is established via object anchoring [Prenzel, 2005]. The directed connection between the world model and HMI evolves from the need to give feedback to the user during execution of a user interaction subtask. Thus, the HMI only operates on the subsymbolic part of the world model.

In order to investigate the feasibility of controlling the rehabilitation robot by a brain-computer interface, the Bremen SSVEP BCI was connected to the robot control architecture. Communication between the BCI system and MASSiVE was established by a simple TCP/IP connection. Four flickering lights with frequencies 13 Hz, 14 Hz, 15 Hz, and 16 Hz and encoding four commands (select next, select previous, start task, cancel task) were used to select goal-oriented, high-level tasks performed by FRIEND II. Seven subjects in the age range of 25 to 35 years, and without previous BCI experience participated in this study. Each user was asked to perform a predefined sequence of 10 commands to select high-level robot commands. Errors made and the time required to complete the command sequence was measured. The experiment was conducted in an office-like environment without any

special shielding or other precautions to avoid or reduce external noise or interferences from other electronic devices, power lines, or routine background activity
such as people talking or performing common work tasks. Two of the seven subjects
were not able to produce a sufficiently strong SSVEP response and thus were not
able to perform the task. The other five subjects achieved on average a classification
rate of 96% and selection speed of 4.61 seconds per command. After the experiment,
all participants were asked if the task was fatiguing, if the flickering lights caused
any inconvenience, and if the selection task required considerable mental load. All
participants found the task non-fatiguing. None reported about any inconvenience
concerning the flickering lights, and none found that the task required a high mental
load [Valbuena et al., 2007].

These results demonstrate that goal-oriented control of a rehabilitation robot with
a BCI is possible. It also demonstrates the robustness of the Bremen BCI system,
because the test environment was (unlike most other BCI studies) not a shielded
room with ideal conditions for EEG recording. The fact that two out of seven subjects were not able to produce SSVEP cannot be accounted to the inefficiency of
the BCI system. Rather, this is a result of using untrained subjects for this study.
Although many subjects can perform selective attention tasks without any training, some subjects need training to learn to perform the task of selective attention
effectively.

6.4.2 Smart Wheelchairs

In this section, another type of rehabilitation robot, a smart wheelchair, is considered as a potential intelligent application for BCI control. A smart wheelchair is
an assistive device that provides mobility to individuals who have trouble using a
powered wheelchair due to motor or other impairments. Smart wheelchairs employ
artificial control systems that augment or replace user control. Smart wheelchairs
may employ sensors, such as sonar or infrared sensors, or laser range finders to
detect obstacles or map the topography of the environment. Together with sophisticated algorithms including path planning, behavior-based control, and artificial
reasoning, this sensor information is used to provide obstacle avoidance, safe object
approach, straight path maintenance, and solutions for other navigational issues.
Smart wheelchairs can thereby considerably reduce the motor and cognitive requirements needed for operating a wheelchair [Levine et al., 1999].

Wheelchairs may allow different levels of control. At a low level, the user is
responsible for path planning and most of the navigational activities, and the smart
wheelchair provides collision-avoidance. This operating level works well with reliable continuous input modes such as a joystick. For discrete input commands such as
voice control or BCI input, more intelligent wheelchair behavior is required. In these
cases, the system should assist the user with path planning decisions and provide
semi-autonomous control. For an even higher level of control—real goal-oriented
control—where the user only supplies the target destination, the artificial control

system has to plan the path completely and navigate to the destination autonomously [Simpson, 2005].

The Bremen semi-autonomous wheelchair Rolland III has been developed by the Institute of Computer Science at the University of Bremen. It features a conventional motorized wheelchair equipped with two laser range finders. The wheelchair can deal with a number of input modalities such as low-level joystick control or high-level discrete control. Autonomous and semi-autonomous navigation is supported. This flexibility is achieved by continuous local mapping of the environment in real-time and sophisticated path planning and obstacle avoidance algorithms [Mandel and Frese, 2007]. Figure 6.7 shows the smart wheelchair controlled by the Bremen BCI.

For BCI control, Rolland currently operates in a semi-autonomous mode and accepts the following set of commands: go straight ahead, go left, go right, turn around. It projects these specific instructions onto a route graph representation of the surrounding environment [Kricg-Brückner et al., 2005]. The route graph is a multilayered and graph-structured representation of the environment in which each graph layer describes the workspace on a different level of abstraction. To interpret the BCI instructions, the Voronoi layer of the graph representation, which includes metrical and topological information of the free and occupied space of the surrounding, is evaluated. This comprehensive spatial representation is first searched for all navigable routes that might move the wheelchair to the periphery of the visible neighborhood. Next, the set of navigable routes is evaluated against the given directional command by searching the route that best fits the actual instruction. This

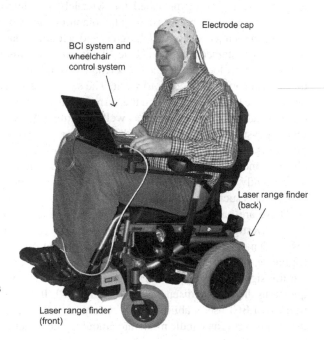

Fig. 6.7 Bremen autonomous wheelchair Rolland III controlled by the Bremen BCI

Electrode cap

BCI system and wheelchair control system

Laser range finder (back)

Laser range finder (front)

process employs fuzzy spatial relations that were first introduced to interpret coarse verbal route descriptions [Mandel et al., 2006]. The process assesses the branching angle between two consecutive segments of a given route. The best route is finally passed to the obstacle avoiding navigation module.

Initial pilot research has been conducted to assess the Bremen SSVEP BCI with Rolland. This pilot work sought to show that a BCI based on selective attention can effectively control an intelligent device even if the user is distracted by other tasks like observing the surrounding environment, interacting with other people, and planning next navigational steps. There are many reasons why this might be challenging or impossible. Because SSVEP BCIs require users to focus attention on specific stimuli, any task that distracts the user could reduce BCI performance. Furthermore, navigation is a difficult task, even with assistance via the intelligent behavior of the wheelchair. The time constraints in a navigation scenario, such as the need to convey the "turn left" command before the next possible left turn, could further increase the user's stress and workload.

Only three subjects have been assessed to date. They successfully drove Rolland through the hallway area of a typical office building with a speed of 0.56 m/s. No effort was made to reduce external noise sources such as electronic devices, 50 Hz current, or fluorescent lighting. Control relied on selective attention to one of four LEDs representing the wheelchair control commands described above. The subjects sent about 40 navigation commands with classification accuracy above 92%. The subjects sent commands over a period of about 30 minutes but frequently paused to talk to colleagues, and thus effective information throughput is difficult to measure. Hence, this pilot work shows that an SSVEP BCI can robustly control a wheelchair in a real-world setting provided the wheelchair is intelligent enough to provide obstacle avoidance and assist in path planning. However, toward the end of the session, the subjects reported fatigue, and accurate classification required longer periods of sustained attention. One likely cause of this fatigue is that the stimulation unit was located on the wheelchair tray (above the subject's lap), and thus the subject had to look down to see it. The subjects also had to frequently shift gaze between the LED apparatus and the surrounding environment. This required considerable head and eye movement, as well as frequently switching attention, that could make a system both fatiguing and difficult or impossible to use for persons with motor disabilities. Thus, improved display parameters might eliminate the need for physical movements and significantly reduce fatigue. Several such improvements are currently explored, along with and their effective integration with other display components such as feedback from the BCI.

These are only initial findings, and many other avenues for improvement are being investigated. Although the subject could control the wheelchair, the initial results demonstrated that the ongoing distraction from different sources affects performance. Allison et al. [Allison and Pineda, 2006] reported that background activity did not significantly impair SSVEP BCI performance, but that answering complex questions did require disengaging from the BCI. It is very likely that training could improve a BCI user's ability to effectively multitask, just as experienced keyboard users or drivers can handle moderate amounts of distraction better than novices.

Currently, the Bremen BCI communicates only unidirectionally with both FRIEND II and Rolland. That is, goal-oriented, high-level commands are sent to the intelligent assistive device, but no direct information from this device is sent back to and used by the BCI. However, the overall system (BCI and intelligent application) could greatly benefit from bidirectional communication. Because direct brain-computer communication is unreliable, BCI decisions are always associated with uncertainty. In the Bremen SSVEP BCI used for controlling Rolland, for instance, four commands are possible, each corresponding with a different LED. When a command is generated, the most likely command out of the four is selected. This likelihood is determined from the signal-to-noise ratio (SNR) of the SSVEP components that correspond with LED frequencies. Sometimes, it is difficult to determine which LED the user is focused on, as the SNR of two or more SSVEP components may be similar. Without further information, the BCI may select the wrong command. However, if additional information provided by the assistive device is available, e.g., that a certain command is not plausible in the current context, a more appropriate decision could be made. For example, the BCI system would not select a command to move forward if it knew (through sensors) that the wheelchair was facing a wall and could not move forward. This would lead to more robust decisions and improved information transfer rates. This idea is conceptually similar to incorporating context to determine which navigation command is sent to a mobile robot [Millan et al., 2004].

6.5 Conclusion and Future Prospects

It is unlikely that BCIs with dramatically better information throughput will be developed in the near future. Current tools for measuring brain activity are simply not powerful enough. The EEG, for example, allows a fairly low bandwidth signal that only reflects a tiny percentage of the brain's activity. Signals from different brain areas and mental processes often overlap, are badly smeared by the scalp, and are difficult to distinguish from background brain activity that is not relevant to BCI control. EEG activity is stochastic, nonstationary, and often inconsistent across subjects and within and across usage sessions. Electrical noise from other physiological signals, movements, and outside devices further degrades signal quality. Improved robust signal processing approaches can improve throughput [Friman et al., 2007b, Blankertz et al., 2007, Pfurtscheller et al., 2006a], but significant new neuroimaging technology is also needed.

However, providing the user with the desired application(s) and choices can make a huge difference in the *effective* information throughput. A patient may prefer a slow BCI that allows changing bed position over a faster BCI that only allows spelling. Similarly, intelligent systems that manage unnecessary details of system operation can substantially improve effective information throughput. For example, a wheelchair and robotic arm system that requires BCI users to control each movement would be slow, frustrating, and possibly even dangerous. Such a system would only be practical if the user could instead select from common goals, such as opening a door, getting water, or making coffee [Valbuena et al., 2007, Wolpaw, 2007]. Effective interfaces, error detection and correction, word and sentence completion, display parameters that do not produce fatigue or eyestrain, and other mechanisms can further increase the robustness of BCI systems and effectively improve information throughput.

BCI hardware and software are quickly becoming more usable, and the need for expert assistance—or indeed any assistance—may be eliminated. Recent work has described dry EEG electrodes that do not require gel, precise positioning, nor skin abrasion [Fonseca et al., 2007]. Dry electrode systems might require no expert assistance for setup or cleanup and could be easily integrated into a baseball cap or headband. High-impedance amplifiers and electrodes, combined with wireless recordings, could make BCIs even more robust in noisy environments. Further, the need for expert help to configure each BCI might be addressed through intelligent software that runs each new user through a series of tests. These tests would provide information that an automated expert system could use to configure the best BCI for each user. Ideally, this expert system could utilize a variety of pattern classification tools, stimulus and/or feedback parameters, and user queries to identify the best BCI for each user. The system would have to be robust to changes in each user's EEG over time, requiring self-adaptive mechanisms [Dornhege et al., 2007]. Because performance may differ widely across BCI approaches [Birbaumer and Cohen, 2007], this software should also examine P300, SSVEP, and ERD approaches. These tools would require substantial development work but (in concert with dry electrodes) might eliminate one of the biggest obstacles to BCI use: dependence on other persons, specifically experts. Thus, new intelligent algorithms capable of replacing human experts could make BCI systems much more robust and practical to individual users. Systems such as the Bremen SSVEP BCI, which can adapt itself according to different facets of each users' EEG activity, are important steps in this direction.

In summary, some BCI limitations are quite trenchant, such as the fundamental limitations of modern brain imaging technology. On the other hand, although modern BCIs are difficult to use, not very robust, and require outside expert help, these drawbacks may become substantially less potent over the next several years. As a result, BCIs will become more useful to typical users—people with severe motor disabilities—and may become useful to other users in some situations. Robust BCIs in combination with intelligent BCI applications that effectively integrate goal-oriented protocols and are able to largely compensate the limitations of direct brain-computer communication will play a crucial role in this next generation of BCI systems.

Advances in BCI technology will make BCIs more appealing to new user groups. BCI systems may provide communication and control to users with less severe disabilities and even to healthy users in some situations. BCIs may also provide new means of treating stroke, autism, and other disorders [Birbaumer and Cohen, 2007, Graimann et al., 2007]. These new BCI applications and groups will require new intelligent BCI components to address different challenges, such as making sure that users receive the appropriate visual, proprioceptive, and other feedback to best recover motor function.

As BCIs become more popular with different user groups, increasing commercial possibilities will likely encourage new applied research efforts that will make BCIs even more practical. Consumer demand for reduced cost, increased performance, and greater flexibility and robustness may contribute substantially to making BCIs into more mainstream tools.

References

Allison, B., Graimann, B., and Gräser, A. (2007a). Why use a BCI if you are healthy? In *Proceedings of the International Conference on Advances in Computer Entertainment*, pages 7–11, Salzburg, Austria, 13–15 June.

Allison, B. Z. and Pineda, J. A. (2003). ERPs evoked by different matrix sizes: implications for a brain computer interface (BCI) system. *IEEE Transactions on Neural Systems and Rehabilitation Engineering*, 11(2):110–113.

Allison, B. Z. and Pineda, J. A. (2006). Effects of SOA and flash pattern manipulations on ERPs, performance, and preference: implications for a BCI system. *International Journal of Psychophysiology*, 59(2).127–140.

Allison, B. Z., Wolpaw, E. W., and Wolpaw, A. R. (2007b). Brain-computer interface systems: progress and prospects. *Expert Review of Medical Devices*, 4(4):463–474.

Birbaumer, N. and Cohen, L. G. (2007). Brain-computer interfaces: communication and restoration of movement in paralysis. *Journal of Physiology-London*, 579(3):621–636.

Blankertz, B., Dornhege, G., Krauledat, M., Müller, K. R., and Curio, G. (2007). The non-invasive Berlin brain-computer interface: fast acquisition of effective performance in untrained subjects. *Neuroimage*, 37(2):539–550.

Cook, A. and Hussey, S. (2002). *Assistive Technologies: Principles and Practice*. Mosby, St. Louis, 2nd edition.

Donchin, E., Spencer, K. M., and Wijesinghe, R. (2000). The mental prosthesis: assessing the speed of a P300-based brain-computer interface. *IEEE Transactions on Rehabilitation Engineering*, 8(2):174–179.

Dornhege, G., Blankertz, B., Curio, G., and Müller, K. R. (2004). Boosting bit rates in noninvasive EEG single-trial classifications by feature combination and multiclass paradigms. *IEEE Transactions on Biomedical Engineering*, 51(6):993–1002.

Dornhege, G., Millan, J., Hinterberger, T., McFarland, D. J., and Müller, K. R., editors (2007). *Toward Brain-Computer Interfacing*. MIT Press, Cambridge, MA.

Farwell, L. and Donchin, E. (1988). Talking off the top of your head: toward a mental prosthesis utilizing event-related brain potentials. *Electroencephalography and Clinical Neurophysiology*, 70(6):510–523.

Fonseca, C., Cunha, J., and Martins, R. (2007). A novel dry active electrode for EEG recording. *IEEE Transactions on Biomedical Engineering*, 54:162–165.

Friman, O., Lüth, T., Volosyak, I., and Gräser, A. (2007a). Spelling with steady-state visual evoked potentials. In *Proceedings of the 3rd International IEEE/EMBS Conference on Neural Engineering (CNE'07)*, pages 510–523, Hawaii, 2–5 May 2007.

Friman, O., Volosyak, I., and Gräser, A. (2007b). Multiple channel detection of steady-state visual evoked potentials for brain-computer interfaces. *IEEE Transactions on Biomedical Engineering*, 54(4):742–750.

Fukunaga, K. (1990). *Introduction to Statistical Pattern Recognition*. Computer Science and Scientific Computing. Academic Press, Boston, 2nd edition.

Gao, X., Xu, D., Cheng, M., and Gao, S. (2003). A BCI-based environmental controller for the motion-disabled. *IEEE Transactions on Neural System and Rehabilitation Engineering*, 11(2):137–140.

Graimann, B. (2006). *Event-related (de)synchronization in bioelectrical brain signals and its use in brain-computer communication*. PhD thesis, Habilitationsschrift: Graz University of Technology.

Graimann, B., Allison, B., and Gräser, A. (2007). New applications for non-invasive brain-computer interfaces and the need for engaging training environments. In *Proceedings of the International Conference on Advances in Computer Entertainment*, pages 25–28, Salzburg, Austria, 13–15 June.

Graimann, B., Huggins, J. E., Levine, S. P., and Pfurtscheller, G. (2004). Toward a direct brain interface based on human subdural recordings and wavelet-packet analysis. *IEEE Transactions on Biomedical Engineering*, 51(6):954–962.

Graimann, B. and Pfurtscheller, G. (2006). Quantification and visualization of event-related changes in oscillatory brain activity in the time-frequency domain. In Neuper, C. and Klimesch, W., editors, *Event-related Dynamics of Brain Oscillations.*, Progress in Brain Research, pages 79–97. Elsevier, Amsterdam.

Guger, C., Edlinger, G., Harkam, W., Niedermayer, I., and Pfurtscheller, G. (2003). How many people are able to operate an EEG-based brain-computer interface (BCI)? *IEEE Transactions on Neural Systems and Rehabilitation Engineering*, 11(2):145–147.

Hill, J., Lal, T., Tangermann, M., Hinterberger, T., Widman, G., and Elger, C. (2007). Classifying Event-Related Desynchronization in EEG, ECoG, and MEG Signals. In Dornhege, G., Millan, J., Hinterberger, T., McFarland, D. J., and Müller, K. R., editors, *Toward Brain-Computer Interfacing*, pages 235–259. MIT Press, Cambridge, MA.

Hillman, M. (2003). Rehabilitation robotics from past to present–a historical perspective. In *Proceedings of the 8th International Conference on Rehabilitation Robotics (ICORR'03)*, pages 101–105, Daelon, Korea.

Ivlev, O., Martens, C., and Gräser, A. (2005). Rehabilitation robots FRIEND-I and FRIEND-II with the dexterous lightweight manipulator. In *Prcoeedings of the 3rd International Congress on Restoration of (Wheeled) Mobility in SCI Rehabilitation*, volume 5, pages 111–123, Amsterdam, The Netherlands, 19–21 April.

Kleber, B. and Birbaumer, N. (2005). Direct brain communication: neuroelectric and metabolic approaches at Tübingen. *Cognitive Processing*, 6:65–74.

Krieg-Brückner, B., Frese, U., Lüttich, K., Mandel, C., Mossakowski, T., and Ross, R. (2005). Specification of an ontology for route graphs. In Freska, C., Knauff, M., Krieg-Brückner, B., Nebel, B., and Barkowsky, T., editors, *Spatial Cognition IV*, volume 3343 of *Lecture Notes in Artificial Intelligence*, pages 390–412. Springer, Berlin, Heidelberg.

Lemm, S., Blankertz, B., Curio, G., and Müller, K. R. (2005). Spatio-spectral filters for improving the classification of single trial EEG. *IEEE Transactions on Biomedical Engineering*, 52(9):1541–1548.

Levine, S. P., Bell, D. A., Jaros, L. A., Simpson, R. C., Koren, Y., and Borenstein, J. (1999). The NavChair assistive wheelchair navigation system. *IEEE Transactions on Rehabilitation Engineering*, 7(4):443–451.

Lüth, T., Ojdanic, D., Friman, O., Prenzel, O., and Gräser, A. (2007). Low-level control in a semi-autonmous rehabilitation robotic system via a brain-computer interface. In *Proceedings of the 10th International Conference on Rehabilitation Robotics (ICORR'07)*, pages 721–728, Noordwijk, Netherlands, 13–15 June.

Mandel, C. and Frese, U. (2007). Comparison of wheelchair user interfaces for the paralysed: head-joystick vs. verbal path selection from an offered route-set. In *Proceedings of the 3rd European Conference on Mobile Robots (ECMR'07)*, pages 217–222, Freiburg, Germany, 19–21 September.

Mandel, C., Frese, U., and Roefer, T. (2006). Robot navigation based on the mapping of coarse qualitative route descriptions to route graphs. In *Proceedings of the IEEE/RSJ International Conference on Intelligent Robots and Systems (IROS'06)*, pages 205–210, Beijing, China, 9–13 October.

Marr, D. (1982). *Vision: a computational investigation into the human representation and processing of visual information.* W.H. Freeman, San Francisco.

McFarland, D. J., McCane, L. M., David, S. V., and Wolpaw, J. R. (1997). Spatial filter selection for EEG-based communication. *Electroencephalography and Clinical Neurophysiology,* 103(3):386–394.

McFarland, D. J., Sarnacki, W. A., and Wolpaw, J. R. (2003). Brain-computer interface (BCI) operation: optimizing information transfer rates. *Biological Psychology,* 63(3):237–251.

Middendorf, M., McMillan, G., Calhoun, G., and Jones, K. S. (2000). Brain-computer interfaces based on the steady-state visual-evoked response. *IEEE Transactions on Rehabilitation Engineering,* 8(2):211–214.

Millan, J., Renkens, F., Mourino, J., and Gerstner, W. (2004). Noninvasive brain-actuated control of a mobile robot by human EEG. *IEEE Transactions on Biomedical Engineering,* 51(6): 1026–1033.

Müller, G. R., Neuper, C., Rupp, R., Keinrath, C., Gerner, H. J., and Pfurtscheller, G. (2003a). Event-related beta EEG changes during wrist movements induced by functional electrical stimulation of forearm muscles in man. *Neuroscience Letters,* 340(2):143–147.

Müller, K., Krauledat, M., Dornhege, G., Curio, G., and Blankertz, B. (2004). Machine learning techniques for brain-computer interfaces. *Biomed Tech,* 49(1):11–22.

Müller, K. R., Anderson, C. W., and Birch, G. E. (2003b). Linear and nonlinear methods for brain-computer interfaces. *IEEE Transactions on Neural Systems and Rehabilitation Engineering,* 11(2):165–169.

Müller-Putz, G. R., Scherer, R., Pfurtscheller, G., and Rupp, R. (2005). EEG-based neuroprosthesis control: a step towards clinical practice. *Neuroscience Letters,* 382(1–2):169–174.

Naeem, M., Brunner, C., Leeb, R., Graimann, B., and Pfurtscheller, G. (2006). Separability of four-class motor imagery data using independent components analysis. *Journal of Neural Engineering,* 3(3):208–216.

Pfurtscheller, G., Graimann, B., and Neuper, C. (2006a). EEG-based Brain-Computer Interface Systems and Signal Processing. In Akay, M., editor, *Encyclopedia of Biomedical Engineering,* volume 2, pages 1156–1166. John Wiley & Sons, Hoboken, NJ.

Pfurtscheller, G., Müzsller-Putz, G. R., Schlogl, A., Graimann, B., Scherer, R., Leeb, R., Brunner, C., Keinrath, C., Lee, F., Townsend, G., Vidaurre, C., and Neuper, C. (2006b). 15 years of BCI research at Graz University of Technology: current projects. *IEEE Transactions on Neural Systems and Rehabilitation Engineering,* 14(2):205–210.

Prenzel, O. (2005). Semi-autonomous object anchoring for service-robots. *Methods and Applications in Automation,* 1:57–68.

Prenzel, O., Martens, C., Cyriacks, M., Wang, C., and Gräser, A. (2007). System-controlled user interaction within the service robotic control architecture MASSiVE. *Robotica,* 25(2):237–244.

Ramoser, H., Müller-Gerking, J., and Pfurtscheller, G. (2000). Optimal spatial filtering of single trial EEG during imagined hand movement. *IEEE Transactions on Rehabilitation Engineering,* 8(4):441–446.

Sellers, E. W. and Donchin, E. (2006). A P300-based brain-computer interface: initial tests by ALS patients. *Clinical Neurophysiology,* 117(3):538–548.

Sellers, E. W., Krusienski, D. J., McFarland, D. J., Vaughan, T. M., and Wolpaw, J. R. (2006). A P300 event-related potential brain-computer interface (BCI): the effects of matrix size and inter stimulus interval on performance. *Biological Psychology,* 73(3):242–252.

Simpson, R. (2005). Smart wheelchairs: a literature review. *Journal of Rehabilitation Research and Development,* 42(4):423–436.

Valbuena, D., Cyriacks, M., Friman, O., Volosyak, I., and Gräser, A. (2007). Brain-computer interface for high-level control of rehabilitation robotic systems. In *Proceedings of the 10th International Conference on Rehabilitation Robotics (ICORR'07),* pages 619–625, Noordwijk, Netherlands, 13–15 June. IEEE Press.

Vidal, J. J. (1973). Toward direct brain-computer communication. *Annual Review of Biophysics and Bioengineering,* 2:157–180.

Wolpaw, J. R. (2007). Brain-computer interfaces as new brain output pathways. *Journal of Physiology,* 579(Pt 3):613–619.

Wolpaw, J. R., Birbaumer, N., McFarland, D. J., Pfurtscheller, G., and Vaughan, T. M. (2002). Brain-computer interfaces for communication and control. *Clinical Neurophysiology*, 113(6):767–791.
Wolpaw, J. R., McFarland, D. J., Neat, G. W., and Forneris, C. A. (1991). An EEG-based brain-computer interface for cursor control. *Electroencephalography and Clinical Neurophysiology*, 78(3):252–259.

Chapter 7
Robust Learning of High-dimensional Biological Networks with Bayesian Networks

Andreas Nägele, Mathäus Dejori, and Martin Stetter

Abstract Structure learning of Bayesian networks applied to gene expression data has become a potentially useful method to estimate interactions between genes. However, the NP-hardness of Bayesian network structure learning renders the reconstruction of the full genetic network with thousands of genes unfeasible. Consequently, the maximal network size is usually restricted dramatically to a small set of genes (corresponding with variables in the Bayesian network). Although this feature reduction step makes structure learning computationally tractable, on the downside, the learned structure might be adversely affected due to the introduction of missing genes. Additionally, gene expression data are usually very sparse with respect to the number of samples, i.e., the number of genes is much greater than the number of different observations. Given these problems, learning robust network features from microarray data is a challenging task. This chapter presents several approaches tackling the robustness issue in order to obtain a more reliable estimation of learned network features.

7.1 Overview

Since the mapping of the human genome by the Human Genome Project, the DNA sequence underlying the plan of human life is known and publicly available [Venter et al., 2001]. Despite this fact, mankind is far away from understanding human life. In the postgenomic era, biomedical research has focused on a functional understanding of the life processes encoded in the DNA sequence. One focus lies on the elucidation of mutual and regulatory relationships between molecules in the cellular system. Because it is assumed that all cellular processes are guided by the states of the underlying interactions between genes, proteins, and other small molecules,

A. Nägele

Department of Computer Science, Technical University Munich, Boltzmannstr. 3, 85748 Garching, Germany
Siemens Corporate Technology, Department of Information & Communications, Otto-Hahn-Ring 6, 81730 Munich, Germany
e-mail: andreas.naegele.ext@siemens.com

A. Schuster (ed.), *Robust Intelligent Systems,* DOI: 10.1007/978-1-84800-261-6_7,
© Springer-Verlag London Limited 2008

the understanding of these molecular interactions and their effect on diseases or other phenotypic outcomes is crucial, in particular for the detection of diagnostic and therapeutic biomarkers or the development of new and highly effective drugs. A part of the whole interaction network is composed of the interactions between genes and proteins, forming the so-called gene regulatory network. With the advent of high-throughput methods such as microarrays, it became possible to measure the expression status, more precisely the amount of mRNA, of thousands of genes in parallel, which allows a closer look at the complex interaction network [Schena et al., 1995]. Various methods have been developed to analyze these expression measurements. For example, microarray data are used to detect genes that act differently in healthy and diseased cells. Clustering approaches can be used to detect genes showing a similar expression behavior or to group patients with similar expression profiles [Yeoh et al., 2002]. Patients can be classified according to their state of health, risk of cancer recurrence, or other phenotypic characteristics [Yeoh et al., 2002, Huang et al., 2003, Ma et al., 2004].

In recent years, the reconstruction of the genetic network with graphical models, in particular Bayesian networks, from microarray data has shown promising results [Friedman et al., 2000, Dejori and Stetter, 2003, Dejori et al., 2004]. Bayesian networks (BN) belong to a class of graphical models that describe the dependencies between a set of random variables in a probabilistic as well as graph theoretic way. BNs can represent both, the quantitative distribution as well as the structural dependencies between the variables. Regarding genetic network reconstruction with BNs, the genes are represented as variables (nodes) in the network, and edges between the variables describe relationships between genes. In general, learning BNs from microarray data produces two major types of problem: first, with BNs one learns an abstract gene-gene dependency network that might not reflect the true underlying molecular interaction network. And second, the high dimensionality and sparseness, which is typical for microarray data, brings up several problems concerning algorithm scalability and the robustness of learned network features. This chapter investigates the latter type of problem. For the first type of problem, the interested reader is directed to [Dejori and Stetter, 2003].

Because of the NP-completeness of structure learning, learning the full abstract gene-gene interaction network with about 25,000 human genes in total is impossible for current learning methods considering the computational power available today [Chickering et al., 1994]. When learning in such large domains, one typically restricts the feature dimensions on a feasible subset of relevant variables (genes) that are of high interest [Friedman et al., 2000]. As a result, a typical pipeline for learning BNs from high-dimensional data could be stated as as a two-step process [Stetter et al., 2007]: (1) Based on a statistical method, choose a number of highly relevant variables, and (2) learn a Bayesian network with the set of variables selected in step 1. Even though the structure learning becomes feasible, the restriction on a small set of variables for learning is a potentially problematic step that can lead to a strongly corrupted estimation of the true structure because (a) edges incident to missing variables cannot be learned by definition, and (b) additional false-positive edges might be learned to explain statistical dependencies that cannot be represented by a dependence on the missing variables (see Fig. 7.1 later in this chapter). To evaluate the extent of the subnetwork-based structural shifts in the learned networks, this work simulates the reduction of variables with a new method called "subnetwork learning". This approach systematically estimates the network structure of the whole network stepwise using small subnetworks. According to the method used to obtain small networks, this approach puts variables together in one subnetwork that are statistically dependent on each other. Results obtained from subnetwork learning show that the fears of getting corrupted network structures are partially justified: the amount of false-positive edges increases markedly.

In benchmark cases with known network structure, subnetwork learning can be used to estimate the influence of learning partial networks of moderate size based on the features of the network structure. To minimize the error induced by subnetworks in real-world cases with unknown true network structure, this chapter proposes a robustness assessment algorithm, called "dimensional bootstrap". In order to achieve this, the approach learns the structure of a small subnetwork iteratively. However, with each iteration, a somewhat different set of variables is added to the subnetwork in such a way that even weakly dependent variables can evolve their influence on the estimated network structure.

Another problem associated with microarray data arises from their sparseness. One one hand, microarray data sets contain the measurements of thousands of genes. On the other hand, the data sets contain usually only a small number of samples. For example, the GEO database contains only six data sets with more than 1,000 samples, whereas the vast majority contains less than 100 samples [GEO, 2007]. A common approach to deal with sparse data and the therein contained fluctuations is the non-parametric data bootstrap [Efron and Tibshirani, 1993]. This method enables the assessment of those dependencies that are caused by the underlying true dependency structure between the variables and not by statistical fluctuations in the data [Friedman et al., 1999a, 2000]. However, in very large but sparse domains, there might be several variables that are highly dependent on each other only because of such fluctuations. By restricting the learning on a subnetwork with highly related variables, the presence of fluctuations in the small subdata set can be higher than average. To estimate the influence of such fluctuations, this chapter proposes a surrogate data analysis. The approach performs the same steps used for structure learning with artificially generated data that contain no dependencies between the variables at all.

7.2 Methods

7.2.1 Bayesian Network Structure Learning

This text provides only a brief summary of learning Bayesian networks (BNs). For additional information, the interested reader is directed to the following resources [Heckerman, 1995, Friedman, 1997, 1998, Spirtes et al., 2001, Neapolitan, 2003, Tsamardinos et al., 2006a]. Bayesian networks can be used to describe the joint probability distribution of n random variables $\mathbf{X} = \{X_1, X_2, X_3, \ldots, X_n\}$. As mentioned earlier, a Bayesian network $B = (G, \Theta)$ consists of two parts. The first part is the network structure, which is a directed acyclic graph (DAG) G with each variable X_i represented as a node. The edges in the DAG represent statistical dependencies between the variables. The second part is a set of parameters. With the independence statements encoded in the DAG, the joint probability function over $\mathbf{X}$ can be decomposed into the product form

$$p(X_1, X_2, \ldots, X_n) = \prod_{i=1}^{n} p(X_i | \mathbf{Pa}_i, \Theta, G), \tag{7.1}$$

where $\mathbf{Pa}_i$ are the parents of variable X_i in the DAG G.

Learning the structure and the parameters of a Bayesian network from a data set $\mathbf{D}$ can be formulated as the following problem: Given a finite data set $\mathbf{D} = (\mathbf{d}^1, \ldots, \mathbf{d}^N)$ with N different independent observations, where each data point $\mathbf{d}^l = (d_1^l, \ldots, d_n^l)$ is an observation of all n variables, find the graph structure G and the parameters Θ that best match data set $\mathbf{D}$ by maximizing the scoring function

$$S(G|\mathbf{D}) = \frac{p(\mathbf{D}|G)p(G)}{p(\mathbf{D})}, \tag{7.2}$$

where $p(G)$ is the prior for the structure, $p(\mathbf{D})$ is a normalization constant, and $p(\mathbf{D}|G)$, the marginal likelihood of $\mathbf{D}$ given model graph G.

Finding the best structure is an NP-hard optimization problem, which leads to the need for a heuristic search method to determine efficiently a Bayesian network close to the optimum [Chickering et al., 1994]. This work uses simulated annealing [Kirkpatrick et al., 1983] as a local search strategy because it has been shown that it yields to better solutions in practice than the less time consuming greedy hill climbing method [Dejori and Stetter, 2003].

7.2.2 Robustness Assessment

Because of the sparseness of data and the heuristic search method, it is uncertain to what extent a learned model represents the underlying true network structure. Hence, it would be preferential to make predictions using the full Bayesian approach, i.e., using all possible Bayesian networks weighted by their likelihoods. However, this approach is intractable due to the large amount of different network structures.[1] Instead, this work uses a set of good models given by their likelihood for a better estimation of the true network. To describe the variations in the structure of several Bayesian networks, the framework of "feature partial directed graphs"

---

[1] The number of possible Bayesian network structures grows super-exponentially with the number of network variables.

(fPDAG) [Dejori, 2005] that is based upon the work in [Friedman et al., 1999a] is used. A fPDAG can deal with structural uncertainties by assigning a belief value to the features "edge presence" and "edge direction".

Several structurally different Bayesian networks may encode the same probability distribution and, thus, achieve the same score. In fact, these networks have the same edges, however these edges may have different directions. All statistically indistinguishable networks are called Markov Equivalent and form a class of equivalent network structures [Verma and Pearl, 1991]. Each equivalence class can be graphically represented by a partial directed acyclic graph (PDAG), which is identical to the DAG structure of a BN, but all edges with a statistically uncertain direction are encoded as undirected edges in the PDAG. Before creating a fPDAG, all Bayesian networks forming the estimation of the underlying network are transformed into their PDAG representation [Chickering, 1995].

Topological features that are used to create a fPDAG are edge presence or absence and direction of the edge. For simplicity, the forthcoming sections are restricted to the binary feature "edge presence" for simplicity. Other features like "edge direction" are not further considered.

The confidence in an edge is defined as

$$p_{i \leftrightarrow j} = \frac{1}{Q} \sum_{g=1}^{Q} f_{i \leftrightarrow j}(BN_g),$$ (7.3)

where $f_{i \leftrightarrow j}(BN_g)$ has the value one if there is an edge between X_i and X_j in the g-th network, otherwise it is zero.

The fPDAG of Q Bayesian networks with corresponding Bayesian network structures BN_g, $g \in \{1, \ldots, Q\}$ is a graph that contains all variables that are present in the Bayesian networks. The edge between each pair of variables X_i and X_j is weighted with its confidence $p_{i \leftrightarrow j}$, which is the fraction of networks having this edge. Thus, unlike Bayesian networks or PDAGs, the structure of fPDAGs is neither an acyclic directed nor a partially directed acyclic graph. Instead, it has undirected edges between related variables, and these edges are labeled with $p_{i \leftrightarrow j}$.

This work considers partially overlapping Bayesian networks, i.e., there are Bayesian networks that do not have all variables in common. Hence the probability of a feature becomes

$$p_{i \leftrightarrow j} = \frac{1}{Q_{X_i, X_j}} \sum_{g=1}^{Q} f_{i \leftrightarrow j}(BN_g),$$ (7.4)

where Q_{X_i, X_j} is the number of Bayesian networks that contain both variables X_i and X_j. It is necessary to point out that this calculation of an edge confidence can lead to a poor estimation of the confidence because an improbable edge could be assigned a confidence of one when only one subnetwork contains both variables X_i and X_j. An edge between two variables that appears in 90 of 100 networks that contain both incident variables would have less confidence. It seems apparent that this edge is more likely than the edge between X_i and X_j. However, the good estimation of the network structure with the fPDAG framework (as presented later in Section 7.3.2) shows that the approximation of the confidence given in equation 7.4 seems to be quite reasonable.

7.2.3 Subnetwork Learning

Because of the NP-hardness of Bayesian network structure learning, it is unfeasible to learn networks containing up to tens of thousands of variables in general. Although there is an approach to deal with very large networks (up to hundreds of thousands of variables) [Goldenberg and Moore, 2004], it is restricted to binary variables and a very sparse network structure. The sparseness is also used in other approaches for large network learning [Friedman et al., 1999b, Tsamardinos et al., 2006a, Nägele et al., 2007].

One possibility to get networks of moderate size is the down-scaling of the network size by removing some variables. The general idea behind it is the assumption that very large networks can be reduced in size by omitting unimportant variables. Usually, the variables are ranked according to their association with an experiment-relevant condition, and low-ranked variables are removed until a computationally manageable set of variables remains [Friedman et al., 2000, Pe'er et al., 2001, Hartemink et al., 2001, Imoto et al., 2002, Dejori et al., 2004, Stetter et al., 2007]. This procedure can be motivated by the assumption that if two variables X and Y are almost independent in the data $\mathbf{D}$, it is unlikely that X and Y are directly linked by an edge in the Bayesian network. So Y might be removed if one wants to estimate the network structure around X. This is only a heuristic approach as both variables can be marginally independent but have a strong dependence given another variable. One example is a network with X as XOR of Y and Z [Friedman et al., 1999b]. In most cases, however, it is a reasonable assumption that such dependencies do not occur.

The dependency structure between the remaining variables may change dramatically, caused by the removal of variables. The potential influence of one missing variable on the structure is shown in Fig. 7.1 [Binder et al., 1997].

The removal of one important variable (here X_7) can disrupt the structure of the Bayesian network. The direct relationships that pass originally through X_7 in the left network must be represented by indirect relationships between the remaining variables in the subnetwork to the right, which leads to a massive appearance of false-positive edges.

To estimate the influence of learning partial networks on the estimated network structure, this work models this constraint by learning a set of partially overlapping subnetworks with data drawn from benchmark networks. All the learned subnetworks are afterwards compared with the structure of the "original" benchmark network and to a learned network structure that covers the whole domain without

Fig. 7.1 The Bayesian
network to the left is an
example for a complete
Bayesian network; the
network to the right is the
simplest Bayesian network
that encodes the same
probability distribution, but
without the missing variable
X_7. Note that the variables
X_4, X_5, and X_6 are no longer
independent given their
parents

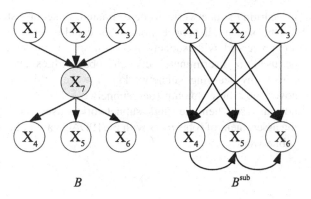

missing variables. By comparing these networks, it is possible to draw conclusions
to what extent relying on subnetworks affects the estimated structure and therewith
the appearance of false-negative and false-positive edges.

Starting from one single variable, the approach selects the variables that are statistically most dependent on this variable. As a measure for the dependency, the
approach uses mutual information. The dependent variables are henceforth referred
to as a "neighborhood". The variable and its neighborhood together form one subnetwork. By creating the subnetwork with one central variable and the variables
that are statistically most dependent on this variable, the approach emulates the
real-world case where the variables of one network are selected by their statistical
dependencies. To measure the mean influence of learning subnetworks, the approach
does not choose only one central variable but instead creates one subnetwork for
each variable in the large-scale data set.

The general algorithm can be outlined as follows: In the first step, for each vari-
able $X_i \in \mathbf{X}$, where $\mathbf{X}$ is the set of all variables in the original network, a Bayesian
subnetwork with variables $\mathbf{M}_i$ is put together, where $\mathbf{M}_i$ is the neighborhood of X_i
and X_i itself. As mentioned before, mutual information is used as a measure for
the neighborhood between X_i and X_j. The most strongly dependent variable that
is not contained in the neighborhood $\mathbf{M}_i$ of X_i is added to that neighborhood. This
procedure (adding of a variable) is iterated until $\mathbf{M}_i$ contains a predefined number
of variables. The second step involves the learning of the BN on the small local
subnetwork $\mathbf{M}_i$ of the complete network:

```
for each variable X_i ∈ X do
    M_i := {X_j | X_j neighbour of X_i} ∪ {X_i};
    learn Bayesian network B_i = (M_i, Θ_i);
end
```

In order to test the structural robustness of learning subnetworks, a comparison
is undertaken between the structure of each single subnetwork and the corresponding part of the original network by applying different distance measures
(see Section 7.3). The difference in performance between the subnetwork learning
and the learning of the complete network allows the structural shifts introduced

by learning subnetworks to be estimated. A second step creates a fPDAG formed by the set of all subnetworks. This enables assessment of robust features that are preserved with subnetwork learning, in particular the edge confidence can be used to discriminate between robust edges and those edges that are only caused by learning subnetworks. However, this implies that the subnetworks cover the whole domain (one subnetwork for each variable), which is definitely not the case when one single subnetwork is used for dependency estimation. Thus, the assessment of robustness with the fPDAG cannot be utilized with only one single subnetwork.

7.2.4 Dimensional Bootstrap

In order to assess the quality of a subnetwork, this work introduces a bootstrap approach, called dimensional bootstrap. With dimensional bootstrap, one can asses the robustness of edges against missing variables that do not occur in the subnetwork. Especially in very large domains, this bootstrap can support a robust estimation of the dependency structure between a manageable subset of variables.

Based on a set of interest (SOI) of variables, the approach tries to detect true direct relationships between variables of the SOI while false-positive edges (as shown in Fig. 7.1) should be avoided. The SOI, thereby, can be created by a user, by using a statistical criterion as described above, or by any other suitable method. Based on the assumption that variables outside the SOI that are highly dependent on variables inside the SOI might have a high impact on the learned structure, this study dynamically adds missing variables that are highly dependent on variables in the SOI. These variables are added in such a way that, on the one hand, false-positives are avoided, and, on the other hand, the size of the network is kept moderately small. The set of variables that is added to the SOI for learning is henceforth referred to as the set of additionals (SOA). After structure learning, only the edges between the variables of the SOI remain in the network, all other edges and the SOA are removed. Thus, all direct relationships inside the SOI remain as edges in the network. However, those indirect relationships between variables of the SOI that can be explained by a cascade of direct relationships passing over the SOA are removed, leading to a lower amount of false-positive edges and, thus, to a better estimation of the network structure.

In general, there might be a large number of variables highly related to the SOI and, thus, also a large number of variables that might have an impact on the learned network structure. The adding of all those variables again turns into an intractable computational problem. To avoid this problem, this work proposes a method whose general idea is based upon the bootstrap method [Efron and Tibshirani, 1993]. However, the approach does not resample data points, but resamples the variables that should be included in the network for structure learning, and with it resamples the dimensions of the data set. In practice, this means a random selection of a few variables as SOA and the combination of these variables with the SOI to learn the structure. This procedure is applied several times, each time with a different SOA. The general algorithm with given SOI can be outlined as following:

```
R := variables that are related to the SOI;
for i = 1...k
    SOAᵢ := choose subset of R randomly;
    learn Bayesian network Bᵢ with SOI ∪ SOA as variables;
    restrict Bᵢ on SOI;
end
create fPDAG comprised of all Bᵢ, i = 1...k;
```

Based on the k bootstrap networks B_i, the confidence of an edge is calculated as the fraction of networks in which this edge occurs. Edges that represent direct relationships between variables of the SOI should appear in almost every network independently of the variables in the SOA. Thus, they should be rated with a high confidence level in the fPDAG. On the other hand, false-positive edges that are caused by indirect relationships should not appear if the variables that allow the indirect relationships to be explained by direct relationships are integrated into the SOA. If these variables are contained repeatedly in the SOA by means of the boot-strap procedure, the confidence of false-positive edges can be decreased. Thus, using an appropriate threshold for the edge confidence should allow the true-positive and false-positive edges to be separated.

However, if the SOA is sampled from a fairly large set of variables by using an equal probability for each variable to be selected, the dimensional bootstrap approach might fail, because variables, highly related to variables in the SOI, could appear only in a few bootstrap networks. In contrast, the majority of the variables in the SOA might be weakly related to the SOI and, hence, have only marginal influ-ence on the learned network structure. For that reason, this work presents two meth-ods of choosing the SOA in such a way that these negative effects are avoided. Both methods rank all variables that are not part of the SOI according to their dependency on the SOI. More precisely, the maximum of the mutual information of a variable is taken with each of the variables of the SOI as the measure for dependency, and the variables are ranked in descending order. Thus, the values form a monotonically decreasing distribution.

The first approach goes through the list of variables in descending order, selects a variable with a given probability p_{sel} and includes it in the SOA, until the size of the SOA reaches a given maximum. Because the approach starts with the most dependent variable in the list, the highly dependent variables are added to the SOA with a probability of p_{sel}. However, the probability of variables at the end of the list to be included in the SOA is very low, if it is assumed that the total number of variables is large compared with the size of the SOA. All the variables in the list that can contribute to the variables in the SOA, ranging from the most dependent variable in the list to the least dependent variable that is added to the SOA, are henceforth denoted as base quantity. The size of this base quantity has an expecta-tion of $\frac{max\ size\ of\ SOA}{p_{sel}}$. That means that mainly the first $\frac{max\ size\ of\ SOA}{p_{sel}}$ variables con-tribute to the SOA, whereas the probability for the subsequent variables decreases rapidly. Thus, with the parameter p_{sel}, one can indirectly control the size of the set of variables that should be used as base quantity for the bootstrap selection of the SOA. Using this approach to define the variability of the SOA raises a question: How should the parameter p_{sel} set to reach an optimal estimation of the network? Of course, this value should be smaller than one, as a selection probability of one would lead to a relegated dimensional bootstrap and would imply that the bootstrap procedure serves no purpose. The value, however, should be large enough to restrict the base quantity on the relevant variables, avoiding the inclusion of a large amount of variables that have no impact on the structure. Here, a value of 0.5 was found to be useful, motivated by the following simplifying argument: A structural shift caused by one single latent variable is avoided in about 50% of all networks, as this variable is present in about 50% of the learned bootstrap networks. Similarly, a shift caused by two missing variables affects 75% of all networks, because only 25% of all bootstrap networks contain both variables, and so on. Thus, only high confident edges (confidence of 80% or above) are supposed to be robust against hidden variables.

The second approach for SOA selection makes a direct use of the distribution of the dependency values. This dependency distribution therefore is treated as an unnormalized probability distribution to sample the variables of the SOA. Consequently, the probability for a variable to be selected depends directly on its dependency on the SOI and represents exactly the normalized dependency value of the variable, at which the normalization factor constitutes the sum of the dependency values of all variables not already contained in the SOA or SOI. As a result, highly dependent variables, which are supposed to be important for the network structure, occur much more often in the SOA compared with only weakly dependent variables. Experimental investigations lead to the finding that having a large amount of variables that are only weakly dependent on the SOI can lead to an SOA with many variables that show no strong dependency on the SOI. Thus, in general, it is practical to restrict the base quantity for the bootstrap selection depending on the maximal size of the SOI. This is evident as the bootstrap procedure has to cover the whole space of dependent variables several times to be able to make a good estimation of the network structure. For example, consider a variable that is not contained in the SOI but causes one false-positive edge. This variable has to occur several times in the SOA to lead to a decreased confidence in this false-positive edge. Otherwise, the difference between the confidence of the edge in this example and the confidence of true-positive edges might be too small to separate between those edges. Hence, the remainder of this chapter chooses a value for the size of the base quantity that is four times higher than the maximal size of the SOI. Other values might be suitable as well, but they are not considered in this chapter.

7.2.5 Sparse Data Analysis

The high dimensionality that automatically leads to another problem, namely that of sparse data, strongly impacts the quality of structure learning. For example, statistical test methods to narrow down the amount of variables might be negatively affected by fluctuations in the data set. There might be variables that have no relevance for the tested condition, but instead they are selected because of fluctuations that in turn influence the quality of structure learning. A common approach to deal with sparse data and the therein contained fluctuations is the non-parametric data bootstrap [Efron and Tibshirani, 1993]. This approach produces a "perturbed" version of the available data and learns the network from the perturbed version. Perturbed in this case means that a new data set with the same size is generated by drawing samples with replacement from the original data set. Edges that have a high confidence in the fPDAG comprised by the perturbed networks are shown to be rarely false-positives [Friedman et al., 2000, 1999a]. This result is based on observations on small-scale networks like the Alarm network consisting of 37 variables and 46 edges. However, to the best of our knowledge, no one has tested the effect if several hundred variables are selected by a statistical method from a large set of variables. This study expects that there appear more false-positives, in particular with sparse data.

To estimate the influence of the fluctuations of sparse data, this study proposes to perform the two-step process (reduction in dimensionality and structure learning) two times, one time with the original data and a second time with surrogate data. Figure 7.2 illustrates the generation of surrogate data by scrambling the data.

Based on an original data set (left-hand side in the figure), the observations are randomly interchanged variable-wise. Thus, all higher-order statistics are destroyed in the surrogate data (right-hand side) and all variables are independent from each other, while the variable-wise marginal probabilities are kept stable. Because the variables are independent from each other, all edges that are learned from surrogate data are false-positives.

By comparing the number and confidences of edges in both cases (original and surrogate data), it is possible to quantify the fraction of edges that are caused by fluctuations in sparse data sets. As a measure this study defines the "predictive value" as the number of edges in the original case divided by the number of all edges (original and surrogate). A value of one implies that all learned edges are originated by dependencies that are not caused by the sparseness of the data. A high predictive value, however, does not imply all edges to be true-positives. In fact, a high value only indicates that there are more dependencies in the data than in a randomly

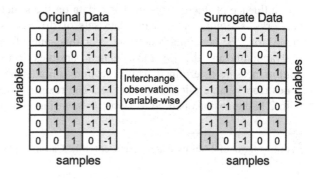

Fig. 7.2 Procedure of surrogate data generation (scrambling): The observations for each variable in the original data set (left-hand side) are interchanged randomly. The resulting data set without any higher-order statistics is referred to as "surrogate data set" (right-hand side)

chosen data set. A differentiation between true-positives and false-positives is not considered here.

A lower predictive value of 0.5 means that the learned edges have no meaning at all because the same amount occurs in the surrogate case. For this reason, the original data set contains relationships that are probably contained in any artificial (surrogate) data set by chance. Hence, the predictive value quantifies the structural shift that can be caused by data fluctuations.

7.3 Results

The standard way for assessing the accuracy of a learning method is to draw samples from a known Bayesian network, then to apply structure learning on the artificial data and to finally compare the learned structure with the original one. To benchmark the methods, this work investigates their performance on artificial data with real-world characteristics focusing on data with a large number of variables but sparse in the number of samples. As current real-world benchmark data are not large enough in the number of variables, the current study used the tiling method proposed by Tsamardinos [Tsamardinos et al., 2006b] to artificially enlarge benchmark networks. Two large networks were generated using the Causal Explorer software package [Aliferis et al., 2003] with the Alarm network [Beinlich et al., 1989] as a tile. The Alarm_50 network with 1,850 variables results from a 50-fold tiling of the Alarm network, whereas the Alarm_270 network with 9,990 variables emerges from 270 tiles.[2] In addition, a biologically motivated network that is based on microarray data was also generated. The genes that contribute to the network were selected by the 1,000 genes that are most relevant for acute lymphoblastic leukemia, ranked by the p-value of the t-test between the subtypes of the leukemia [Yeoh et al., 2002]. From the discretized microarray data that is restricted on the 1,000 genes, one single Bayesian network, called ALL_benchmark_1000 network, was learned. For all of the benchmark networks, data sets of various sizes were drawn by applying Gibbs sampling on the benchmark networks.

7.3.1 Sparse Data Analysis

The influence of fluctuations in sparse data on the structural robustness of learned networks is simulated by using data sets of different sizes that are drawn from the Alarm_270 benchmark network. For this, one of the 9,990 variables is chosen randomly and the 199 most related variables according to the mutual information measure determined. This procedure imitates the preselection of a subset of genes from a large microarray data set. The resulting data set ("Subset Data Set") with 200 dimensions is used to learn 40 Bayesian networks with a non-parametric

[2] A tiling factor of 2 was used as a parameter for the Causal Explorer software tiling component.

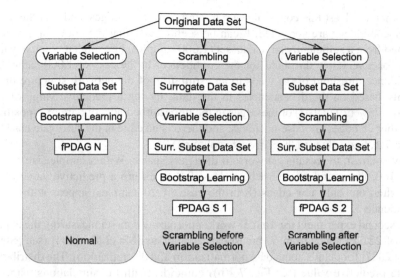

Fig. 7.3 Workflows for sparse data analysis: The general workflow of learning small networks in large domains is shown on the left-hand side ("Normal" case). The "Scrambling before Variable Selection" method imitates the "Normal" case, but with surrogate data. The learning from a small data set is imitated by the "Scrambling after Variable Selection" method

bootstrap approach ("Bootstrap Learning"). An overview over the workflow is given in Fig. 7.3 on the left-hand side ("Normal" case).

In addition, the same steps are performed similarly, but using surrogate data instead of the data sets that are drawn from the Alarm_270 network (see Fig. 7.3, "Scrambling before Variable Selection" case).

Figure 7.4(a) illustrates the predictive value for different data sizes. The predictive values are calculated for several thresholds for the edge confidence, whereas all

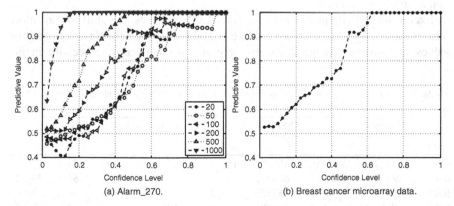

(a) Alarm_270.

(b) Breast cancer microarray data.

Fig. 7.4 Predictive values against different sample sizes and thresholds for the confidence level for (a) the Alarm_270 benchmark network and (b) the breast cancer microarray data set

edges with at least this confidence are treated as learned edges, and all others with lower confidence are neglected. It can be seen clearly that the bootstrap networks learned from a sufficiently large data set (1,000 samples) have high predictive values even for a very low threshold for the confidence. In the case of 1,000 samples, a confidence threshold of 0.4 leads to an estimation of the network structure that is mainly based on the dependencies in the data, having a predictive value of one. Almost 75% (79 of 107) of the edges in the unperturbed network are true-positives, the other 28 edges are false-positives, and there is no edge in the surrogate case (see Table 7.1, first values in the surrogate columns).

By contrast, the results get worse if data gets sparse. With a sample size smaller than 100, the confidence must be at least 0.8 to ensure a predictive value of 0.9 or higher, but only few edges (8 in the case of 20 samples) appear with such a confidence.

A second experiment used a real-world microarray data set measuring the expression of 22,575 genes from 60 breast cancer patients [Ma et al., 2004] (see [Stetter et al., 2007] for details about data normalization and discretization). The distribution of the predictive value (see Fig. 7.4(b)) coincides with the simulations using the Alarm_270 benchmark data with similar sample sizes (50 samples in the benchmark case and 60 samples in breast cancer microarray data). In accordance with the benchmark case, only eight edges remain if a threshold of 0.8 for edge confidence is assumed (see Table 7.1).

In other work, the robustness of bootstrap learning of small networks was shown [Friedman et al., 1999a]. However, the difference between learning an originally small network and an originally large network that was reduced in size by feature selection has not been investigated. To measure the influence of this dimensionality reduction, results are compared with the results obtained from an originally small data set. To generate such a data set, this work applied scrambling after the restriction to 200 variables rather than before to generate surrogate data (see Fig. 7.3, "Scrambling after Variable Selection" case). Then, 40 bootstrap networks were learned from this surrogate data. Results are shown in Table 7.1, second values in the surrogate columns.

Except for the Alarm_270 network with 1,000 samples, the shift toward more false-positive edges when the scrambling is applied before variable selection (first values in surrogate columns) can be seen in all other cases, especially in the

Table 7.1 Number of learned edges and number of true-positives (in brackets) for some of the configurations shown in Fig. 7.4. Numbers are shown for the normal (N), and surrogate case (S)

Conf	20 samples		200 samples		1000 samples		Microarray	
	N	S	N	S	N	S	N	S
0.2	132 (22)	161–100	186 (35)	147–114	129 (82)	1–8	375	268–228
0.4	28 (12)	20–20	64 (32)	21–11	107 (79)	0–0	81	33–21
0.6	13 (9)	2–2	44 (32)	4–2	106 (79)	0–0	30	3–0
0.8	8 (8)	0–0	36 (30)	0–0	101 (77)	0–0	8	0–0
1.0	4 (4)	0–0	24 (21)	0–0	88 (67)	0–0	2	0–0

microarray case. The explanation for this observation lies in the dimensionality of the data set. With many variables, data fluctuations bias the variable preselection process, resulting in a set of selected variables that are not independent from each other.

The results indicate that the commonly used method to preselect variables for network learning leads to a biased estimation of the network with occurrence of false-positive edges. Because the bias is dependent on the sparseness and dimensionality of the original data, this study proposes to perform the surrogate data analysis each time when dimensionality reduction is applied. By presetting a predictive value, one gets a confidence threshold for a discrimination between edges that might be originated from data fluctuations and edges mainly representing true dependencies in data.

7.3.2 Subnetwork Learning

The final section shows the influence of sparse data in addition to the variable preselection on structural shifts in learned networks. Now, the problem of sparse data is omitted. Based on subnetwork learning, the study investigates the influence of learning small subnetworks that are composed by a statistical method on the quality of the learned network structure. The investigation uses the Alarm_50 and ALL_benchmark_1000 networks with 500 samples for learning. The subnetwork learning was performed for subnetwork sizes of 20, 50, and 100. The study was not carried out for larger sizes because of the enormous computational time that would be needed for such configurations. The study also did not use data bootstrap as it was used for the surrogate data analysis before.

Each learned subnetwork is compared with the original, true network structure on the basis of several distance measures. To avoid the penalization of structural differences that cannot be statistically distinguished, the measures are based on the PDAG representation of the Bayesian networks. A first measure used is the structural hamming distance (SHD), which is defined as the number of the following operations to make the PDAGs match [Tsamardinos et al., 2006a]: (1) insert or remove an undirected edge or (2) insert, reverse or remove a directed edge. Secondly, the study introduces a modification of SHD, the undirected structural hamming distance, called USHD, that does not consider mismatches in the direction of edges. The number of true-positives (TP), false negatives (FN), and false-positives (FP) are additionally presented, as well as sensitivity and the positive predictive value (PPV). The study uses PPV instead of specificity because specificity is almost one in all cases.[3] All of those measures are calculated for each single subnetwork and normalized by the division by the total number of subnetworks, i.e., the measures denote the mean performance of learning a single subnetwork.

---

[3] Specificity is defined as $\frac{\sharp\ true\ neg.}{\sharp\ true\ neg. + \sharp\ false\ pos.}$. Because the number of true negatives is much greater than the number of false-positives in sparse domains, the specificity is almost one.

In addition, 40 Bayesian networks were learned with all variables included and the same measures calculated. To obtain comparable values for the globally learned networks as well as for the subnetworks, the study calculated the measures for the global network in the same way as for the subnetworks. Thus, for each previously learned subnetwork, the study selected the corresponding variables in the global network, calculated the measures for each of the selected regions, and averaged the results. Thus, these measures indicate the performance if networks are learned as a whole, but their values are transformed to be comparable with the subnetwork measures. Table 7.2 summarizes the performance of the subnetwork method by means of the previously mentioned evaluation measures (values for the complete network case are written in brackets).

One can see clearly that the subnetwork method produces significantly more false-positive edges, often two to three times higher compared with the complete network case. The structural hamming distance is much higher, as well. For example, a subnetwork size of 100 for the Alarm_50 network leads to a distance of 29 while there are only 32 true-positive edges. This high value results from false-positive edges, but also from a considerable number of edges directed in the wrong direction. On the other hand, the number of true-positives (TP), false-positives (FP), false negatives (FN), and the sensitivity values are almost equal in the subnetwork and in the complete case for both benchmark networks. This means that all edges that can be detected when learning the complete network can also be detected if only a small subnetwork is learned. However, they are sometimes learned with the wrong direction.

For a further robustness assessment, all Alarm_50 subnetworks of equal size are combined to one fPDAG, as are the 40 complete learned networks. Based on these fPDAGs, the study calculated the sensitivity values and the positive predictive values (PPV) for several confidence thresholds. In Fig. 7.5(a), the sensitivity values are plotted against the PPV for different subnetwork sizes and the complete network, with better performance indicated by more points in the top left of the graph. The figure clearly shows that learning subnetworks performs worse than learning the network on a whole. However, if one restricts on those edges that reach a high confidence level, namely a level of 0.8 or above, the difference almost vanishes

Table 7.2 Performance of subnetwork learning for different sizes of the subnetworks (20, 50, and 100). The values in brackets denote the performance of learning the complete network as a whole

Measure	Alarm_50 (1850 vars)			ALL_benchmark_1000 (1000 vars)		
	20	50	100	20	50	100
SHD	6.4(3.1)	13.0(5.7)	29.0(11.8)	8.0(4.0)	24.6(13.9)	52.6(30.6)
FP	1.2(0.3)	3.5(0.5)	9.6(0.9)	3.5(1.1)	12.0(4.4)	27.5(10.4)
FN	0.7(0.6)	1.3(1.4)	3.2(3.3)	1.6(1.8)	6.2(6.7)	13.9(14.8)
TP	9.3(9.4)	16.5(16.4)	32.0(31.9)	12.5(12.3)	29.3(28.8)	57.8(56.9)
USHD	1.9(1.0)	4.9(1.9)	12.7(4.2)	5.1(2.9)	18.2(11.1)	41.4(25.2)
Sens	.93(.94)	.92(.92)	.91(.91)	.89(.87)	.83(.81)	.81(.79)
PPV	.88(.97)	.82(.97)	.77(.97)	.78(.92)	.71(.87)	.68(.85)

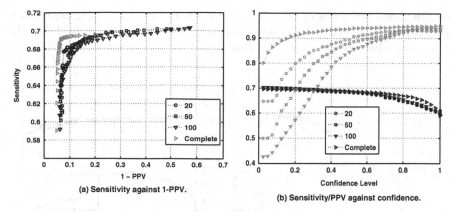

(a) Sensitivity against 1-PPV.

(b) Sensitivity/PPV against confidence.

Fig. 7.5 Benchmark results for the Alarm_50 network based on the fPDAG representation of all subnetworks. In the figure, (a) shows the sensitivity against the positive predictive value for several sizes of the subnetworks and the complete case. In (b), the sensitivity values (black) and positive predictive values (gray) are plotted for different levels of the edge confidence

(see Fig. 7.5(b)). Many of the false-positive edges that are learned in the subnetwork case have a low confidence in the fPDAG and therefore can be eliminated by introducing a suitable threshold for the confidence. It is remarkable that, for a small confidence threshold, the subnetwork learning with a small subnetwork size (20 in this example) performs much better than with larger network sizes (50 or 100). A reason for this could be that the selection method for one subnetwork—taking variables that are related to one single central variable—is suitable for detecting the structure "around" the central variable, however, edges between other variables very often seem to be false-positives as these variables lack their neighborhood required for learning.

7.3.3 Dimensional Bootstrap

The results of subnetwork learning clearly show that the learning of subnetworks leads to a number of false-positive edges that cannot be neglected. To avoid such edges, this work proposes the dimensional bootstrap approach. A performance test of this approach uses the Alarm_50 benchmark network with a data set containing 500 observations sampled from the network. From the variables in this network, the study selected three different sets of interest (SOI) each with 200 variables. To generate a SOI, one variable was chosen by chance and added its 199 most related variables, determined by the value of the mutual information. The results shown in this section are the averaged results of the three cases.

This study has chosen different settings of learning to benchmark the dimensional bootstrap method. At first, the dimensional bootstrap with a selection probability of 0.5 was used. Henceforth, this setting is referred to as "DB 0.5", where 0.5 stands for the selection probability. The alternative method based upon the distribution of the

neighborhood is denoted by "DB D". In addition, to enable a suitable comparison
with the learning without dimensional bootstrap, the SOA was kept fixed (i.e., the
selection probability was set to 1.0). This study refers to this setting as "FNS". For

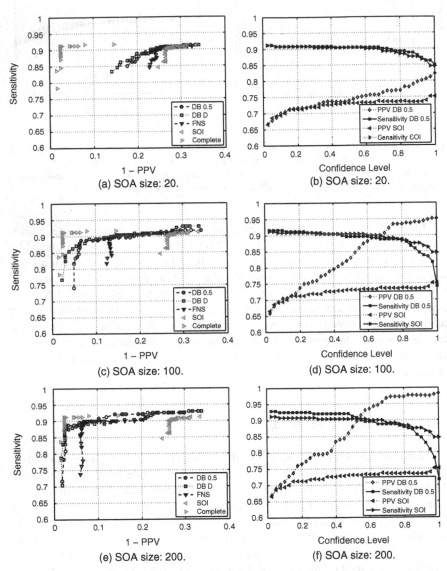

Fig. 7.6 Benchmark results for the dimensional bootstrap method for different sizes of the SOA.
For the dimensional bootstrap (DB), the study uses a selection probability of 0.5 ("DB 0.5"), and
the method based on the neighborhood distribution is denoted by "DB D". The left-hand side
shows the sensitivity against the positive predictive value (PPV). The right-hand side illustrates the
sensitivity and PPV plotted against the confidence threshold. For comparison, the results for the
simple subnetwork case ("SOI") are also plotted

the sake of completeness the study also shows how the learning without SOA performs, including only the set of interest (denoted by "SOI") and the case when the complete network was learned without missing variables ("Complete"). All cases learned 40 networks and created the fPDAG to determine the edge confidences.

As performance criteria, the study calculated the sensitivity and the positive predictive values (PPV) of the network dependent on the confidence threshold. In Fig. 7.6(a), the resulting sensitivity values are plotted against the PPV for a size of 20 for the SOA.

For a better comparison, the result for the complete learned network is plotted as well. One can see clearly that the "SOI"-method is outperformed by any other method, i.e., the PPV is markedly smaller for a given sensitivity level. With a fixed SOA ("FNS"-method), the PPV increases, however it is markedly outperformed by both bootstrap approaches ("DB 0.5" and "DB D"). With the best method, in this case the "DB D", one can achieve a sensitivity of 0.85 with a specificity up to 0.84. This means the approach is able to detect 85% of all edges with only about 15% false-positives, compared with 25% false-positives in the "SOI" case. With an increasing size of the SOA (Fig. 7.6(c) and Fig. 7.6(e)), all three methods that depend on the size of the SOA perform better. However, both dimensional bootstrap methods outperform the "FNS" method in all cases.

On the right hand side of Fig. 7.6, the sensitivity (squares) and the PPV (diamonds) of the "DB 0.5" method are plotted against several confidence thresholds. For comparison, the sensitivity (right-pointing triangles) and PPV (left-pointing triangles) of the "SOI" case are plotted in addition. One can see clearly that the dimensional bootstrap method substantially outperforms the simple case of learning a subnetwork especially for high values (0.8 and above) for the edge confidence. Whereas the sensitivity changes only marginally, the PPV increases dramatically in the bootstrap case, particularly for large sizes of the SOA (see Fig. 7.6(d) and Fig. 7.6(f)).

7.4 Conclusion

Graphical models, and in particular Bayesian networks, are very useful models for inferring genetic networks by learning the dependency structure from microarray data. However, when learning BN structures in large-scale domains such as the genetic network, one faces the problem of NP-hardness. Thus, microarray data sets are usually reduced in their dimensionality by ranking the genes according to their statistical dependency, and network learning is applied on a small subset of potentially dependent genes [Friedman et al., 2000, Dejori and Stetter, 2003, Dejori et al., 2004]. This chapter evaluated the robustness of Bayesian network learning if such a reduction in dimensionality is applied by means of artificial benchmark data.

Initially, the chapter investigated the additional influence of sparse data on the robustness of edge features. A common approach to deal with the fluctuations in sparse data is the non-parametric data bootstrap [Efron and Tibshirani, 1993], which assesses those dependencies that are caused by the underlying true dependency structure between the variables and not by statistical fluctuations in the data [Friedman et al., 2000, 1999a]. To estimate the influence of the variable-preselection on this assessment, the chapter combined the data bootstrap with a surrogate data analysis. In the surrogate data set, all true dependencies between the variables are destroyed. Thus, dependencies that do occur in data are caused by statistical fluctuations.

The chapter defined a measure, called predictive value, indicating the fraction of edges caused by true patterns in the data but not by fluctuations. Results from benchmark cases show that these fluctuations can have a significant influence on the learned network structure. Whereas edges with a low confidence might not represent true dependencies but also fluctuations, edges with a high confidence are likely to represent true dependencies in the data. For a trade-off between the number of detected relationships and the fraction of false dependencies, one can choose a predictive value leading to a threshold for the edge confidence that fulfills the given predictive value. Because the influence depends mainly on the sparseness of the data and increases with its dimensionality, the chapter proposes to perform the surrogate data analysis each time when dimensionality reduction is applied to control the influence of fluctuations.

The chapter also introduced subnetwork learning as an approach to benchmark the learning of subnetworks in a structured way. Therefore, for each variable in the complete network, the approach learns a subnetwork, where the variables in the subnetwork are determined by their dependency on the central variable. Results from a benchmark case show that the fPDAG formed by all subnetworks is a reasonable representation of the true underlying network structure, if only edges with high confidence are considered. However, each single subnetwork contains several false-positive edges and many edges with a wrong direction, on average. Whereas such false-positive edges can be neglected in the fPDAG because of their low confidence, they can disrupt the network of a single subnetwork. Although these results can probably be transferred to networks that have a similar topology as the benchmark network used here, the robustness of learning subnetworks should be benchmarked on other networks with the subnetwork algorithm, too, because networks with different topological features can also have a different performance. For example, the subnetwork method is known for not being applicable to fully or almost fully connected networks, because the variables cannot be reasonably divided into subnetworks. However, genetic networks are supposed to be scale-free [Jeong et al., 2000, Barabási and Bonabeau, 2003] and are therefore only sparsely linked.

To avoid the disruptions arising from learning subnetworks on the one hand, but to enable networks with moderate size without learning the complete network on the other hand, the chapter introduced the dimensional bootstrap approach. Thereby, the network structure between a set of variables (set of interest: SOI) is estimated by learning several networks containing the SOI and randomly chosen variables (SOA) that are highly dependent on variables contained in the SOI. At each iteration, a different set of dependent variables (SOA) is combined with the SOI for learning. The chapter has shown by means of a benchmark network that networks estimated by the dimensional bootstrap procedure are much closer to the original network structure than networks learned only based on the SOI. The bootstrap networks also have a better structural estimation than networks of same size with a fixed set of dependent variables. Particularly with regard to very large domains where the reduction in dimensionality is commonly used, the dimensional bootstrap approach can boost a more robust estimation of subparts in the complete dependency structure.

References

(2007). GEO. Gene Expression Omnibus Website. http://www.ncbi.nlm.nih.gov/geo/, last accessed September.

Aliferis, C. F., Tsamardinos, I., Statnikov, A., and Brown, L. E. (2003). Causal Explorer: A Causal Probabilistic Network Learning Toolkit for Biomedical Discovery. In Valafar, F. and Valafar, H., editors, *Proceedings of the International Conference on Mathematics and Engineering Techniques in Medicine and Biological Scienes (METMBS'03)*, pages 371–376. CSREA Press.

Barabási, A.-L. and Bonabeau, E. (2003). Scale-Free Networks. *Scientific American*, 288:60–69.

Beinlich, I. A., Suermondt, H. J., Chavez, R. M., and Cooper, G. F. (1989). The ALARM Monitoring System: A Case Study with Two Probabilistic Inference Techniques for Belief Networks. In Hunter, J., Cookson, J., and Wyatt, J., editors, *Second European Conference on Artificial Intelligence in Medicine*, volume 38, pages 247–256, London, Great Britain. Springer-Verlag, Berlin.

Binder, J., Koller, D., Russell, S., and Kanazawa, K. (1997). Adaptive Probabilistic Networks with Hidden Variables. *Machine Learning*, 29(2–3):213–244.

Chickering, D. M. (1995). A Transformational Characterization of Equivalent Bayesian Network Structures. In Besnard, P. and Hanks, S., editors, *Proceedings of the 11th Conference on Uncertainty in Artificial Intelligence*, pages 87–98, San Mateo, CA. Morgan Kaufmann Publishers, Inc.

Chickering, D. M., Geiger, D., and Heckerman, D. (1994). Learning Bayesian Networks is NP-Hard. Technical Report MSR-TR-94-17, Microsoft Research, Redmond, WA.

Dejori, M. (2005). *Inference Modeling of Gene Regulatory Networks*. PhD thesis, TU München, Garching, Germany.

Dejori, M., Schürmann, B., and Stetter, M. (2004). Hunting Drug Targets by Systems-Level Modeling of Gene Expression Profiles. *IEEE Transactions on Nanobioscience*, 3(3):180–191.

Dejori, M. and Stetter, M. (2003). Bayesian Inference of Genetic Networks from Gene-Expression Data: Convergence and Reliability. In Arubnia, H., Joshua, R., and Mun, Y., editors, *Proceedings of the 2003 International Conference on Artificial Intelligence*, pages 321–327. CSREA Press.

Efron, B. and Tibshirani, R. J. (1993). *An Introduction to the Bootstrap*. Monographs on Statistics and Applied Probability. Chapman & Hall, New York.

Friedman, N. (1997). Learning Belief Networks in the Presence of Missing Values and Hidden Variables. In Fisher, D. H., editor, *Proceedings of the 14th International Conference on Machine Learning*, pages 125–133, San Francisco, CA. Morgan Kaufmann Publishers Inc.

Friedman, N. (1998). The Bayesian structural EM algorithm. In Cooper, G. and Moral, S., editors, *Proceedings of the 14th Conference on Uncertainty in Artificial Intelligence (UAI'98)*, pages 129–138, San Francisco, CA. Morgan Kaufmann Publishers Inc.

Friedman, N., Goldszmidt, M., and Wyner, A. J. (1999a). On the Application of The Bootstrap for Computing Confidence Measures on Features of Induced Bayesian Networks. In *Proceedings of 7th International Workshop on Artificial Intelligence and Statistics*.

Friedman, N., Linial, M., Nachman, I., and Pe'er, D. (2000). Using Bayesian networks to analyze expression data. In Shamir, R., Miyano, S., Istrail, S., Pevzner, P., and Waterman, M., editors,

The 4th Annual International Conference on Computational Molecular Biology (RECOMB), pages 127–135, New York. ACM.

Friedman, N., Nachman, I., and Pe'er, D. (1999b). Learning bayesian network structure from massive datasets: The sparse candidate algorithm. In Laskey, K. B. and Prade, H., editors, *Proceedings of the 15th Conference on Uncertainty in Artificial Intelligence (UAI'99)*, pages 206–215, San Francisco, CA. Morgan Kaufmann.

Goldenberg, A. and Moore, A. (2004). Tractable Learning of Large Bayes Net Structures from Sparse Data. In *Proceedings of the 21st International Conference on Machine Learning (ICML'04)*, page 44, New York. ACM Press.

Hartemink, A. J., Gifford, D. K., Jaakkola, T., and Young, R. A. (2001). Using graphical models and genomic expression data to statistically validate models of genetic regulatory networks. In Altman, R. B., Dunker, K. A., and Hunker, L., editors, *Pacific Symposium on Biocomputing*, pages 422–433. World Scientific Publishing.

Heckerman, D. (1995). A Tutorial on Learning With Bayesian Networks. Technical report, Microsoft Research, Redmond, WA.

Huang, E., Cheng, S. H., Dressman, H., Pittman, J., Tsou, M. H., Horng, C. F., Bild, A., Iversen, E. S., Liao, M., Chen, C. M., West, M., Nevins, J. R., and Huang, A. T. (2003). Gene expression predictors of breast cancer outcomes. *Lancet*, 361(9369):1590–1596.

Imoto, S., Goto, T., and Miyano, S. (2002). Estimation of Genetic Networks and Functional Structures Between Genes by Using Bayesian Networks and Nonparametric Regression. In *Pacific Symposium on Biocomputing*, pages 175–186.

Jeong, H., Tombor, B., Albert, R., Oltvai, Z., and Barabási, A.-L. (2000). The large-scale organization of metabolic networks. *Nature*, 407:651–654.

Kirkpatrick, S., Gelatt, C. D., and Vecchi, M. P. (1983). Optimization by Simulated Annealing. *Science*, 220(4598):671–680.

Ma, X.-J., Wang, Z., Ryan, P. D., Isakoff, S. J., Barmettler, A., Fuller, A., Muir, B., Mohapatra, G., Salunga, R., Tuggle, J. T., Tran, Y., Tran, D., Tassin, A., Amon, P., Wang, W., Wang, W., Enright, E., Stecker, K., Estepa-Sabal, E., Smith, B., Younger, J., Balis, U., Michaelson, J., Bhan, A., Habin, K., Baer, T. M., Brugge, J., Haber, D. A., Erlander, M. G., and Sgroi, D. C. (2004). A two-gene expression ratio predicts clinical outcome in breast cancer patients treated with tamoxifen. *Cancer Cell*, 5(6):607–616.

Nägele, A., Dejori, M., and Stetter, M. (2007). Bayesian substructure learning–approximate learning of very large network structures. In Kok, J. N., Koronacki, J., de Mántaras, R. L., Matwin, S., Mladenic, D., and Skowron, A., editors, *Machine Learning: ECML 2007. 18th European Conference on Machine Learning*, volume 4701 of *Lecture Notes in Computer Science*, pages 238–249. Springer, Berlin.

Neapolitan, R. E. (2003). *Learning Bayesian Networks*. Prentice Hall, Englewood Cliffs, NJ, first edition.

Pe'er, D., Regev, A., Elidan, G., and Friedman, N. (2001). Inferring subnetworks from perturbed expression profiles. *Bioinformatics*, 17 Suppl 1.

Schena, M., Shalon, D., Davis, R. W., and Brown, P. O. (1995). Quantitative Monitoring of Gene Expression Patterns with a Complementary DNA Microarray. *Science*, 270(5235): 467–470.

Spirtes, P., Glymour, C., and Scheines, R. (2001). *Causation, Prediction, and Search*. The MIT Press, Cambridge, MA, second edition.

Stetter, M., Nägele, A., and Dejori, M. (2007). GeneSim: Intelligent IT Platform for the Biomedical World. In Schuster, A., editor, *Intelligent Computing Everywhere*, pages 171–194. Springer, Berlin.

Tsamardinos, I., Brown, and Constantin, A. (2006a). The max-min hill-climbing Bayesian network structure learning algorithm. *Machine Learning*, 65(1):31–78.

Tsamardinos, I., Statnikov, A. R., Brown, L. E., and Aliferis, C. F. (2006b). Generating realistic large bayesian networks by tiling. In Sutcliffe, G., Goebel, R., Sutcliffe, G., and Goebel, R., editors, *Proceedings of the 19th International Florida Artificial Intelligence Research Society Conference*, pages 592–597, Menlo Park, CA. AAAI Press.

Venter, J. C., Adams, M. D., and et al. (2001). The Sequence of the Human Genome. *Science*, 291(5507):1304–1351.

Verma, T. S. and Pearl, J. (1991). Equivalence and synthesis of causal models. In Bonissone, P. P., Henrion, M., Kanal, L. N., and Lemmer, J. F., editors, *Proceedings of the 6th Annual Conference on Uncertainty in Artificial Intelligence (UAI'90)*, pages 255–268, North Holland. Elsevier Science Publishers B.V., Amsterdam.

Yeoh, E.-J., Ross, M. E., Shurtleff, S. A., Williams, W. K., Patel, D., Mahfouz, R., Behm, F. G., Raimondi, S. C., Relling, M. V., Patel, A., and et. al., C. C. (2002). Classification, subtype discovery, and prediction of outcome in pediatric acute lymphoblastic leukemia by gene expression profiling. *Cancer Cell*, 1(2):133–143.

Part III
Robustness in Artificial Intelligence Systems

Chapter 8
Robustness in Nature as a Design Principle for Artificial Intelligence

Alfons Schuster

Abstract Robustness is a feature in many systems, natural and artificial alike. This chapter investigates robustness from a variety of perspectives including its appearances in nature and its application in modern environments. A particular focus investigates the relevance and importance of robustness in a discipline where many techniques are inspired by problem-solving strategies found in nature—artificial intelligence. The challenging field of artificial intelligence provides an opportunity to engage in a wider discussion on the subject of robustness.

8.1 Introduction

Robustness is one of those concepts that are relatively easy to understand via examples but very difficult to define. The problem is quite obvious when we consider that to this day, no generally acknowledged definition for robustness exists. It is possible, however, to share a common view that describes robustness as "a robust system is a system that tolerates faults". Robustness is not an entirely new concept. It has been recognized as an omnipresent feature in many systems, natural and artificial alike, for some time. It is only recently that scientists in various fields are intrigued to study this interesting concept more rigorously, more formally, and more deeply.

This chapter aims to contribute to this effort in several ways. Its main goals are to identify fundamental strategies (e.g., redundancy, granularity, adaptation, repair, and self-healing) nature applies to make systems robust and to study their relevance and value as general design principles for artificial intelligence.

In order to achieve this task, we use Section 8.2 to provide a more general introduction into the topic of robustness. Section 8.3 then uses a number of selective

A. Schuster
School of Computing and Mathematics, Faculty of Computing and Engineering, University of Ulster, Shore Road, Newtownabbey, Co. Antrim BT37 0QB, Northern Ireland
e-mail: a.schuster@ulster.ac.uk

A. Schuster (ed.), *Robust Intelligent Systems*, DOI: 10.1007/978-1-84800-261-6_8,
© Springer-Verlag London Limited 2008

examples in order to extract salient features of robustness in the natural world. Section 8.4, which is a cental part of this chapter, reviews appearances of robustness in artificial intelligence (AI) as well as its potential for problem-solving in this field. Section 8.5 reports on appearances of robustness in various other fields, and Section 8.6 ends the chapter with a summary.

8.2 Robustness

A defining feature of our time is the continuous and often spectacular advances in technology. We recognize that modern technology, such as modern computing, for example, touch, interfere, and influence many areas of everyday human life and human endeavor on increasingly more sophisticated and intellectually challenging levels. We also recognize that robustness is an important and omnipresent feature in many of these systems. Think about the robustness of a large telecommunication network, for example. Actually, it is fair to say that the importance of robustness as a 'principle' cannot be underestimated. For instance, reliability, availability, safety, and security are important requirements in many systems. Simply think about software systems applied in medical domains, air traffic control, life support systems, or the uninspiring field of warfare. The importance of robustness is even more palpable in nature where it often directly relates to survival. For example, biological brains and the genetic code, which are both extremely robust systems, play fundamental roles in the survival of biological organisms. As we are going to see in more detail in forthcoming sections, there are many other interesting facets to robustness. In a school of fish, for example, we find robustness on an individual level (one single fish), but also on a collective level (the entire school), which indicates that robustness can appear in different forms and levels of complexity, serving different goals and purposes.

Despite an intuitive understanding of robustness, we need to come back to the fact again that robustness is very difficult to define. In recent times, this contradiction of ease of understanding, omnipresence, and notorious difficulty to define created a great interest among scientists from many fields to research robustness more rigorously and more formally. For example, scientists in biology and genomics study the robustness of the genetic code [Hayes, 2004], the robustness exhibited by biological brains and artificial neural networks excites neuroscientists and psychologists [Shema et al., 2007], and AI practitioners [Schuster, 2007b], and telecommunication engineers apply error detection and error correction codes to confirm or protect information transmitted over communication channels in order to make telecommunication systems fault tolerant or robust [Jones and Jones, 2000]. The well-known Santa Fe Institute (USA) with its motto of "transcending the usual boundaries of science to explore the frontiers of knowledge" also features robustness high on its current agenda. In addition, many AI techniques and application areas (e.g., artificial neural networks, genetic algorithms, robotics, and autonomic computing) draw inspiration from problem-solving strategies found in nature. Often, these strategies incorporate robustness-related features (e.g., redundancy, granularity, adaptation, repair, and self-healing). The forthcoming sections explore the relevance and importance of robustness as we find it in nature in various challenging areas. Among other things, we are interested in fundamental strategies nature applies to make systems robust and in the value of these strategies as general design principles for AI. It is obvious that it is impossible to cover all facets of robustness in one chapter. The forthcoming sections therefore are selective, and we can only apologize in case areas favored by some readers are omitted in this text.

8.3 Robustness In Nature

The previous section mentioned a few examples featuring robustness already. This section aims to move a bit deeper into the subject. One of our goals is to derive some of the main shapes and disguises in which robustness can appear in the natural word around us. Initially, we concentrate on a single example system. We then provide several other examples in which robustness plays essential roles. This approach should provide us with a reasonable introduction to the topic. The introductory system investigated is the human eye. Figure 8.1 illustrates a cross-sectional view of a human eye.[1]

Essentially, a human eye is an organ that detects light. In a typical scenario, light enters the eye from an external medium through the corona through the lens. The lens focuses the light onto the retina. The retina is layered with photosensitive nerve cells and neurons and it is there where light is transformed into electric signals. The so-called blind spot is the point where the optic nerve contacts the nerve cells of the retina. From there the signals travel on the optic nerve toward the inside of the human brain. The human eye, so it seems, is a wonderful piece of nature in many ways. It is also a useful starting point for our investigation over the next few sections where we identify characteristic features of robustness in the world around

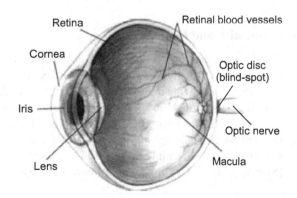

Fig. 8.1 Cross-sectional view of a human eye

---

[1] Credit to National Eye Institute of the U.S. National Institutes of Health (NIH).

us. Note that the forthcoming list of features is not exhaustive and also that some of the examples may be naive. Forthcoming sections mention other features, and those mentioned here are important in Section 8.4 where they relate to some of the work we have undertaken in AI.

Redundancy and Mechanical Robustness

Our first observation is trivial—humans have two eyes. An injury to one eye, maybe in an accident, may impact a person's vision, but the person may not lose the ability to see completely. This type of robustness may be called "safety in numbers" or "redundancy". Robustness through redundancy appears again when we imagine an object in front of the eye. This object may send a huge number of information carriers (photons) to the eye. If some photons do not make it into the eye (e.g., because of an obstacle), the object may still be recognizable to the eye to a satisfactory degree. In addition, even if for some reason a small number of the photosensitive nerve cells on the retina cease to function, the overall information processed may still suffice to produce the correct result in the brain after all. Robustness through redundancy is one design strategy we find in the human eye, but there are others of course. From the human body perspective, part of the eye is directly exposed to the outside. This exposure increases the likelihood of injury. Other parts of the eye such as the optic nerve, for instance, are less exposed and therefore less prone to injury because they are located on the inside of the eye. Other organs such as the human brain and heart demonstrate this aspect too. They are less exposed and protected by a skull, skin, muscle tissue, and a rib cage. We may call this type of robustness "mechanical robustness". A real-world example for this type of robustness can be found in system control and autonomous system design. In NASA space shuttles, for example, it is common practice to combine the outcomes of multiple computers in decision-making processes.[2] In order to avoid systematic errors, it is usual for individual components to be of different make or design, for example different hardware or software (e.g., see [Lussier et al., 2004]).

Restoration and Recovery

The eye example reveals more. We mentioned earlier that in some cases it may not be possible to visually recognize (see) an object in its entirety. For example, imagine some children playing hide and seek. One of the children may hide behind a tree, but unfortunately part of one leg is visible to the seeker. In this situation, the child seeker may be able to somehow "restore" (complete) the visual image of the child behind the tree. Without going into details about the brain and processes happening on a cognitive level, we simply may call this feature "restoration". Work by Shema et al. [Shema et al., 2007] provides an interesting example. Shema's study investigates

---

[2] For example, "Personal observations on the reliability of the Shuttle," http://www.fotuva.org/feynman/index.html

neural mechanisms underlying long-term memory persistence in the brain. The study leads to the idea of deleting information in a brain in a controlled way, but also the opposite, restoring and maybe backing-up information memorized in a brain. On a more physical (visible) level, we may relate restoration to another capacity related to robustness in natural systems—"recovery" (related, similar terms could be healing, self-healing, repair, or self-repair). For example, a biological organism may be robust if it can recover from injury. In case of a minor injury, imagine a little cut on the skin, a human being may recover by growing a new layer of skin over a wound.

Compensation

It is interesting here to mention another relationship between recovery and redundancy. The recovery (self-healing) process just mentioned applied to one single individual (a skin injury by a human). On the other hand, a collective of biological organisms may be robust (in terms of recovery from injury or loss) for different reasons. Ant colonies, bee swarms, or human societies are typical examples where the collective may still achieve its global aims and goals even though some individuals may have lost their lives due to natural disaster, intrusion of natural foes, or natural death. In a way, here redundancy seems to encapsulate recovery. For example, in case of loss of a few members in a collective, redundancy may provide a time-window in which new members may immediately replace previous members, alternatively, new members may be born and then grow into the role of previous members. The time-window therefore may allow a collective to restore itself to its former glory by recovering as a whole. Of course, during replacement of an entity in a collective, we also observe that although many individuals share common features, no two individuals are "exactly" identical. A forthcoming section refers to this as "variety". An interesting situation is the loss of a central element (e.g., the queen in an ant colony). In this case, the damage to the colony can be substantial, even fatal. The human realm is not indifferent to this phenomenon. For example, the outcome of historical battles was often decided by the capture or violent death of a leader or champion (e.g., Napoleon in the Battle of Waterloo, or Hector in Troy). In some cases, systems may have the means and mechanisms needed to regenerate and restore themselves, but this is not always the case. For example, there is a large body of work examining the stability (rise and decline) of large, social constructs such as human settlements, empires, or civilizations. Recent work shows that the great medieval temple of Angkor Wat in Cambodia is part of the pre-industrial world's most extensive urban complex [Young, 2007]. Proposals trying to explain the collapse of this system mention that factors (creation of an extensive water management system leading to environmental damages and food shortages) that may have led to the flourishing and rise of this complex may be ultimately responsible for its downfall. Anyway, we summarize our observations in this paragraph by calling this particular type of interplay between redundancy and recovery—"compensation".

Granularity

In addition to the recovery/redundancy relationship mentioned before, we often encounter another interplay, namely that between redundancy and "granularity". Although the redundancy versus granularity interplay is not an entirely new discovery, it is interesting to mention that these two principles seem to stand in an inverse relationship again (high redundancy—low granularity, and vice versa). In terms of appearances, the relationship can be found in many shapes and areas (biology, technology, etc.). A pride of lions and an ant colony present a case in biology. Obviously, lions are much larger beasts (high granularity) than ants (low granularity), but an ant colony contains many more individuals (high redundancy) than a pride of lions (low redundancy). However, the extent of granularity and redundancy, accompanied by other features and behaviors of each type of animal, makes each group of animals robust in its own way for survival. The granularity-redundancy interplay therefore counts as an elemental survival (design) strategy in nature.

Interesting information relevant to this discussion comes from a recent article by Carbone et al. [Carbone et al., 2007]. Carbone's study categorizes mammalian carnivores into two broad dietary groups: smaller carnivores ($< 20\,kg$) and larger carnivores ($\geq 20\,kg$), with the smaller animals feeding on very small prey (invertebrates and vertebrates) and the larger specializing in feeding on larger vertebrates. A main focus of the study is a theoretical model for predicting mass-related energy budgets and limits of carnivore size. According to the authors, one outcome of the study is that the "net energy gain based eating behavior" of these animals is related to their size. Larger carnivores achieve higher net gain rates by concentrating on larger animals and smaller carnivores by concentrating on smaller prey. Eating habits also differ in intake timing. Larger animals make the occasional kill with longer periods of rest in between, whereas smaller animals favor an anytime, everywhere, on-the-fly eating regime. The model also predicts an upper bound in terms of body weight ($1100\,kg$) for these animals (with about $800\,kg$, polar bears are the largest mammalian carnivores on Earth). Above this value, the energy obtained by a prey is not sufficient to cover the energy required to hunt and kill the prey. So far so good, but what about the dinos? According to the article, these animals had a different metabolism. This is an interesting observation. It demonstrates that in order to achieve something new, nature (we) may need to go back to the drawing board and come up with something entirely new (e.g., a different metabolism).

Cohesion and Coupling

Granularity leads straightaway to two more interesting concepts: "(high) cohesion" and "(low) coupling". We could take the previous lion and ant example again, but just for the sake of it, we use a context of society, say that of a family and a nation. Compared with the whole group, a family member demonstrates a higher degree of granularity within the group 'family' than a single person in the group 'nation'. Further, within an intact family, we may assume a high degree of cohesion, whereas between various, perhaps non-related families, we may assume only weak relations (low coupling). The observation actually scales up quite well too. Individuals of a nation show high cohesion in the group 'nation' but two nations may show low coupling between them. There are many more examples featuring cohesion and coupling (e.g., software development and design [Allen et al., 2001]), and indeed, forthcoming sections are going to mention these concepts in several contexts. For now, there remain only two more features we want to introduce in this section— "versatility" and "variety".

Versatility and Variety

Examples in previous sections relied on contexts such as biology and society. In order to emphasize the omnipresent character robustness holds, we introduce versatility in the rather intellectual and playful context provided by the game of chess. Chess is a highly dynamic game (a player needs to constantly re-asses, respond, and adapt to new situations) and involves pieces of different value and potential, and a queen has the highest value and potential among all pieces. The difference in value largely stems from the fact that a queen has the highest degree of maneuverability of all pieces on a chess board. For example, rooks move in straight lines (up to 15 squares, forward and backwards); pawns move forward only (1 or 2 squares straight or one square diagonal). In comparison, a queen can move in all directions, any number of squares, forward, backwards, and diagonal. Clearly, the advantage in maneuverability is an instance of versatility. From the discussion so far, it is clear that loss of a queen has a major impact on the outcome of a game. It may be similar to the loss of a major organ in an organism, which may affect the robustness of this organism to various degrees. From this point of view, the game of chess is even more illustrative. Even when a queen is lost, the game allows one to re-instantiate (recovery) a new queen (high granularity) by succeeding in moving one of eight pawns (redundancy, low granularity) onto an opponent's baseline. In nature, this may be similar to an organ recovering, or a collective having an opportunity to install (nurture, raise, or hedge) a new (maybe stronger, leading) entity (e.g., a bee queen).

Naturally, the current elaboration on the game of chess may direct our thoughts toward fields such as game theory, economics, or AI. We shall report on some of these areas later. For the moment, we try to finish this section by commenting on the issue of variety. We may remain in the chess domain and point at degrees of variety among several pieces of the same type. Rooks, for example, show zero variety. It is possible to imagine one rook being in or obtaining the same position held by its partner rook, despite having different positions at the start of a game. The same cannot be said for the two bishops available to a player. Although both bishops can move diagonally, one bishop can only move on white squares and the other only on black squares. It is relatively easy to connect these simple examples to nature. In a fish swarm, for instance, individuals may be highly similar, but no two individuals are identical. Forthcoming sections provide further discussions on some of the concepts identified in the previous paragraphs. Initially, Table 8.1 takes stock of our findings.

Table 8.1 Some of the forms and disguises in which robustness may appear in the world around us

○ Redundancy (safety in numbers)	○ Granularity
○ Mechanical robustness	○ Cohesion
○ Restoration (cognitive)	○ Coupling
○ Recovery, self-healing, self-repair (physical)	○ Versatility
○ Compensation	○ Variety

Table 8.1 is not a complete list by any means, and much more could be said about robustness of course. Also, other work may call some of the aspects of robustness mentioned here differently, it may mention other aspects altogether, or deal with the term robustness more analytically, defining boundaries and overlaps with other terms and areas (e.g., see work by Lussier et al. [Lussier et al., 2004] on fault tolerance and robustness in autonomous systems). We also want to mention that the chapter omits rigorous mathematical definitions of robustness, which should not create the false impression that the field lacks such attempts. For example, information theory, which is a corner stone of telecommunication systems, provides a sound framework for error detection and error correction mechanisms [Jones and Jones, 2000], and a paper by Beyer [Beyer and Schwefel, 2007] provides a similarly rigorous treatment in a survey on robust design optimization. Unfortunately, a detailed presentation of this mathematical treatment of robustness is beyond the scope and space of this chapter.

8.4 Robustness in Artificial Intelligence

The goal in this section is to identify features of robustness in AI. It is not possible again to address all areas and applications featuring aspects of robustness in AI. This section therefore focuses on a few selected areas only. A promising field in this regard is that of soft computing and its applications. The field itself is huge and includes techniques such as artificial neural networks, fuzzy logic systems, chaos theory, Bayesian networks, and evolution inspired computation such as genetic algorithms, genetic programming, and swarm intelligence, for instance. The forthcoming sections deal with some of these techniques. In particular the section describes two studies we have undertaken in the past. These studies are related to artificial neural networks [Schuster, 2007a,b] and robotics [Schuster, 2006].

8.4.1 Robust Artificial Neural Network Architectures

Artificial neural networks (ANNs) are one of the success stories in AI. The vast literature generated in the field demonstrates this quite well. This literature (e.g., see [Mehrotra et al., 1997]) has dealt with robustness in various ways already. Often, these dealings involve looking at network robustness (in terms of classification accuracy) from a data quality perspective (noisy data, missing data, over- and under-training, or quality and size of data sets for training and testing, etc.). Compared with the data perspective, issues concerning network architecture are usually (sometimes) minor. The number of neurons in hidden layers is typically an issue but the number of network inputs and outputs typically does not produce too much headache. The focus in this section is different to this because it is architecture driven. For example, Fig. 8.2 illustrates a typical, traditional ANN architecture. Let us refer to such a traditional ANN architecture as architecture "A_0". We also say that the network has a robustness factor ($R_{architecture}$) of $R_{A0} = 0$.

We investigated the robustness of the network in Fig. 8.2 by artificially generating "systematic" and "random" errors in the data input during network training [Schuster, 2007b]. We modeled systematic errors (sys) by replacing one or more values in an input record with the value "0.0". Random errors (ran) were created by always replacing one or more values in a record with a value drawn from the interval [0, 1]. A random selection procedure decided in both cases which values in a record are affected by an error. Imagine the following input record: {0.222, 0,824, 0.067, 0.041}. A single, systematic error may replace the second value in this record with the value 0.0, producing the erroneous record {0.222, **0.0**, 0.067, 0.041}. Here, the error affects one of four values, which is equivalent to an error rate of 25%. Without commenting too much on the application domain (Fisher's Iris Plant data set) and testing procedures applied in [Schuster, 2007b], Fig. 8.3 illustrates a performance graph for the traditional network in Fig. 8.2.

In a nutshell, Fig. 8.3 illustrates that the error-free network classifies around 91% (90.9%) of all test records correctly. The figure then indicates that network performance decreases with increasing error rates. For example, a systematic error (♦) of 25%, which corresponds with always setting one of the four input values in a test record to the value 0.0, degrades classification correctness from 90.9% to 47.7%, which is a significant drop. On the other hand, a random error (•) of the same magnitude reduces classification correctness to 59.5%, which is also a significant drop

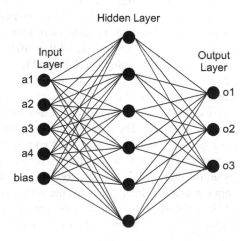

Fig. 8.2 Traditional ANN architecture of type "A_0". The network has one input layer with five inputs (attributes a_1 to a_4, plus a bias), one hidden layer with six neurons, and one output layer with three output neurons (o_1 to o_3). The question is: "How robust is this network?" (source [Schuster, 2007b])

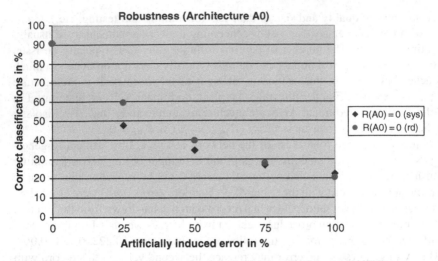

Fig. 8.3 Performance graph for the network in Fig. 8.2 (source [Schuster, 2007b])

of more than 30%. For maxim error (100%), both types of error converge toward values in the lower 20% range.

Overall, Fig. 8.3 conveys the important message that a traditional network architecture can be quite vulnerable to error. Even an error affecting a single input neuron only may impact network performance severely. Figure 8.3 also indicates that there may be differences between systematic and random errors. The network seems to react better to random errors rather than to systematic errors. The forthcoming sections query whether these results can be improved by more robust network architectures. Figures 8.4 and 8.5 illustrate two architectures we investigated. Both architectures are inspired by our observations in Section 8.2. They demonstrate, in particular, the features of safety in numbers (redundancy) and granularity.

For example, compared with the network in Fig. 8.2, the network in Fig. 8.4 has two additional neurons in the hidden layer and also one additional copy of all input attributes (a_1 to a_4) in its input layer (the bias is not duplicated). The motivation for this is our intention to model the safety in numbers (redundancy) aspect mentioned earlier. For example, related to Fig. 8.4, we may think of a scenario where an object transmits information to the eye. In this scenario, the input layer in Fig. 8.4 may correspond with the eye retina where we have a large number of photosensitive nerve cells and neurons, and where nearby neurons may receive similar (in Fig. 8.4 identical) signals. The output layer may be part of the retina and could be viewed as a gateway, similar to the blind-spot, connecting the retina to the optic nerve. Anyway, we refer to a network architecture similar to that illustrated in Fig. 8.4 as architecture "A_1". We also refer to the number of copies of a complete set of input values (excluding bias) as the architecture dependent robustness factor "R_{A1}" of the network. Based on this convention, the network in Fig. 8.4 has a robustness factor of $R_{A1} = 1$, whereas the traditional network in Fig. 8.2 has $R_{A1} = 0$.

Fig. 8.4 Network architecture type "A_1". The network has a robustness factor of $R_{A1} = 1$ (source [Schuster, 2007b])

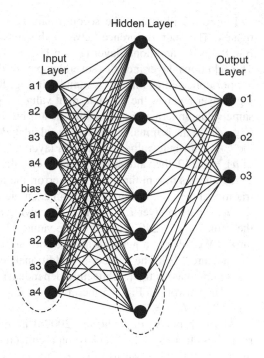

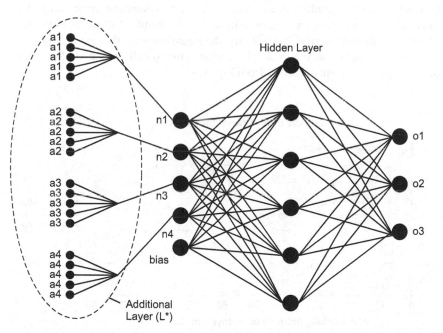

Fig. 8.5 Network architecture type "A_2". The network has a robustness factor of $R_{A2} = 4$ (source [Schuster, 2007b])

Figure 8.5 illustrates the second main type of (robust) architecture we investigated. The main difference between this network and the traditional network in Fig. 8.2 is the additional layer (L^+ in Fig. 8.5) in front of the original input layer. This additional layer includes several copies of the original input attributes (the bias is not duplicated again). For example, in Fig. 8.5, input neuron $n1$ in the original input layer receives the original input value $a1$ plus $k = 4$ additional copies of the same value. In terms of processing, the attribute (e.g., $a1$) value arriving at a neuron (e.g., $n1$) in the original input layer is calculated by taking the average of the sum of the $k + 1$ attribute values arriving on layer L^+. For example, for an attribute value of $a1 = 0.240$, the value arriving on $n1$ calculates to: $\frac{(k+1)*0.240}{(k+1)} = \frac{5*0.240}{5} = 0.240$. This indicates that in the absence of error, the network in Fig. 8.5 behaves like the traditional network in Fig. 8.2. For an example including error, imagine two of the five $a1$ inputs in layer L^+ in Fig. 8.5 receiving an erroneous value of "0.0". Taking the value $a1 = 0.240$ again, now the value $\frac{(k+1-2)*0.240}{(k+1)} = \frac{3*0.240}{5} = 0.144$ arrives on $n1$. We refer to a network architecture similar to that illustrated in Fig. 8.5 as architecture "A_2". The number of "additional" copies for a particular input variable (excluding bias) is the (architecture dependent) robustness factor "R_{A2}" of the system. The network in Fig. 8.5 therefore has $R_{A2} = 4$, and the traditional network in Fig. 8.2 has $R_{A2} = 0$.

Although our work [Schuster, 2007b] is more comprehensive (e.g., we tested robustness factors of 1, 5, and 10 on architecture A_1 and factors of 1, 10, and 100 on architecture A_2), we use Fig. 8.6 to representatively summarize our findings. Figure 8.6 illustrates results for architecture R_{A1} and systematic errors only. The results for random errors are similar and so are the results for architecture R_{A2} (systematic and random errors). For clarity, the figure connects data points via helplines. To ease comparison, the figure also includes the so-called (dotted) "baseline" $R_{A0} = 0$ (sys) for systematic errors from Fig. 8.3.

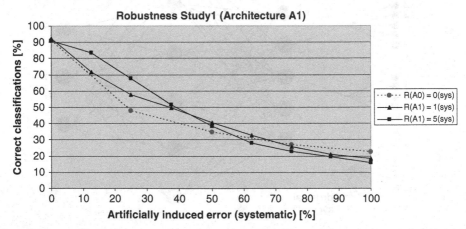

Fig. 8.6 Performance graph: architecture A_1, systematic error, robustness factors of 0 (traditional network), 1, and 5 (based on [Schuster, 2007b])

Figure 8.6 illustrates that even the smallest robustness factor, $R_{A1} = 1$ (sys), immediately generates a positive contribution to classification correctness. Up to the 50% mark, $R_{A1} = 1$ (sys) always stays clearly above baseline $R_{A0} = 0$ (sys). In the same region, $R_{A1} = 5$ (sys) dominates the baseline even more clearly. We observe, in particular, a significant performance improvement associated with robustness factor $R_{A1} = 5$ (sys) in the 25% range. For example, for an error of 25%, $R_{A1} = 5$ (sys) improves performance by 20% from 47.7% to 67.7%. For a 12.5% error, the network does even better by achieving 83.3%, which is relatively close to the 90.9% in the error-free network. Here we need to mention that for $R_{A1} = 5$ (sys), a 12.5% error affects 3 of 24 inputs. This is important, because in the tradition network an error affecting three inputs is equivalent to an error rate of 75%.

As mentioned before, these results stand representatively for our investigation. We found the same performance improvements for systematic as well as random errors in both types of (robust) network architecture. Our most important finding therefore is that the approach behind our investigation leads to significant performance improvements and hence significantly more robust networks. This outcome is quite positive in our eyes because it indicates that (for particular errors) it is possible to significantly increase the robustness of traditional ANN architectures. Our work shows that this gain in performance is due to special network topologies. These topologies are inspired by design principles found in nature, a finding that is crucial for our work. In particular, we identify two major design principles at work. "Redundancy" is the obvious one but there is also "granularity". As we identified earlier, the two principles seem to stand in an inverse relationship. For example, networks of architecture type A_1 have relatively small robustness factors (low redundancy) but they typically are larger networks (high granularity) because of the number of added neurons. Networks of architecture type A_2, on the other hand, always uses the basic network structure in Fig. 8.2 (low granularity), and seem to attain their robustness via the many (high redundancy) additional copies of input values.

It is also important to emphasize again the difference in which both robust architectures accommodate minor errors. The traditional network reacted quite heavily even to the smallest possible error. The failing of one single input already represents an absolute error of 25.0%. In contrast, one of our studies using an A_2 topology with a robustness factor of 100 and errors on one single neuron generated an absolute error of about 1% only! From this perspective, it is reasonable to mention that our work also addresses the IT philosophy of "graceful degradation" [Bentley, 2005]. For instance, compared with traditional ANN architectures, our robust architectures behave more stably in case of minor errors and degrade more gracefully when larger errors occur. Finally, although our work has aspects that are quite specific, we suggest that our work has some general value for AI. For example, autonomic computing, ambient computing, and pervasive computing all entertain the analogy between hugely complex, intelligent systems equipped with a multitude of sensors and actuators and biological brains. With some imagination, it is possible to view the robust ANN architectures in this section as mini brains (systems) where each attribute going into an ANN may be a sensor reading. Our work contributes to the robustness of such systems but how the approach scales up to larger, real-life systems is an open question at this stage.

8.4.2 Robust Robotics

Robustness plays a crucial role in modern robotics for several reasons. The availability of cheap and powerful hardware and software in general is one of them. So is the availability of extremely powerful and sophisticated robot kits and platforms. Some of these kits may be commercial off-the-shelf packages, and other systems may be open source projects. Irrespective of their origin, these systems are usually sophisticated, professional, and integrated robot development environments of high quality. The surge in robotics also reflects the challenging move from "micro-worlds" to "macro-worlds". Essentially, this move means that many AI applications work well in small micro-worlds but may fail to generalize in more complex and elaborate situations and environments. For example, there is a considerable gap between an AI-based checkers or chess program running on a PC in an office and a real humanoid robot taking a penalty kick against a human goalkeeper in the well-known RoboCup competition, or a real autonomous vehicle participating in any of the now famous DARPA (Defense Advanced Research Projects Agency) Grand Challenges. Sometimes, this trend appears under the term "new AI" as opposed to traditional AI (e.g., see [Brighton and Selina, 2003, pp. 128–155]). A crude distinction between the two terms could be that traditional AI investigates intelligence and cognition from an algorithmic, computational point of view, whereas new AI investigates intelligence from the viewpoint of a creative interplay between one or more entities, so-called agents, and a complex, real-world environment [Pfeifer and Scheier, 2000]. New AI cornerstones include robustness, scalability, real-time processing, embodiment, and situatedness. The remainder of this section considers some of these issues (with a focus on robustness) in the context of our earlier work related to the *RobSim* robot control system [Schuster, 2006]. *RobSim* is a hybrid system that incorporates several techniques from the field of soft computing. Figure 8.7 provides a high-level view of the system.

Although the current realization of the system is simple, Fig. 8.7 illustrates that *RobSim* communicates with an environment using a variety of sensors. Our previous

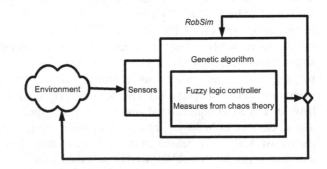

Fig. 8.7 High-level view of the *RobSim* robot control system (source [Schuster, 2006])

work, which exists as a software simulation, shows that *RobSim* reacts to incoming signals in a meaningful way. *RobSim* employs a particular problem-solving strategy to achieve this task. Figure 8.7 illustrates that this strategy involves a fuzzy logic controller, a component using measures from chaos theory, and a genetic algorithm. The next few paragraphs describe how robustness features in these components.

Robustness in Fuzzy Logic Control Component

We use several figures to introduce adaptive fuzzy sets, their use in *RobSim*, and how they relate to robustness. We begin with Fig. 8.8, which illustrates a typical fuzzy logic scenario.

The figure shows a set of five fuzzy sets (*very small, small, normal, large,* and *very large*) of common shape (trapezoidal, triangular) model a particular domain variable (*Speed*) over a particular range ([0, 160] miles per hour). Such an arrangement may be useful for modeling the "speed of a car". In case the range changes to [0, 25], it may be useful for the context "speed of a bicycle". The interesting observation here is that the arrangement of the fuzzy sets remains unchanged (five fuzzy sets distributed evenly over a certain range)—the only thing changing (adapting) is the range for *Speed*. The model is even more flexible. For example, it allows the creation of entirely different contexts without too much effort. Just imagine the range in Fig. 8.8 altered to [10, 100] and the new context "height of building in meters". It is important to mention that such a degree of flexibility and dynamics is extremely desirable in many AI areas.

The *RobSim* robot control system goes even further. The system considers situations where a predefined, initial range may change or where there is some uncertainty about the exact boundaries of a range. For instance, imagine an agent exploring an unknown environment, a temperature context, and an initial range setting of [0, 50] degree, Celsius. As long as the temperature remains within this range, this setup is sufficient, but as soon as the temperature exceeds or goes below the boundary temperatures, then the setup fails. *RobSim* deals with these situations by dynamically updating a range according to newly recorded values and by distributing the current number of fuzzy sets evenly over the new range. Figure 8.9 illustrates how this is realized in *RobSim*.

It is important to emphasize that this solution strives for a maximum of context independence (robustness) in terms of representation for the sake of acquiring

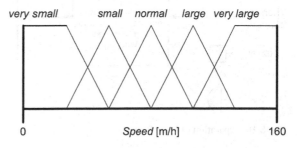

Fig. 8.8 Arrangements of fuzzy sets demonstrating the concept of adaptive fuzzy sets and their relationship to robustness

Fig. 8.9 Robust adaptive
fuzzy sets

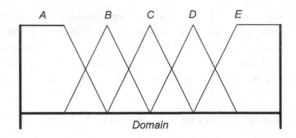

a maximum in context adaptation flexibility. Essentially, *RobSim* achieves this by doing away with labels. For example, Fig. 8.8 uses the labels *very small*, *small*, *normal*, *large*, and *very large* for the domain *Speed*. As we saw earlier, with relative ease these settings may be used for a car or a bicycle context. However, the same terms may be used for several other contexts such as height of buildings, size of coins, temperature, or blood pressure, for instance. The question of what a label actually is also exists. For example, the physical object house does not change by calling it house, maison, or Haus. *RobSim* takes this aspect into account by giving each fuzzy set a simple label only (*A*, *B*, *C*, etc. in Fig. 8.9). In proper design terminology, *RobSim* separates "logic" from "data". For example, all Fig. 8.9 needs is input data. This data may be a particular sensor reading or other input. Figure 8.10 illustrates the more general scenario.

In Fig. 8.10, sensor readings come from various types of sensors (an antenna, a light source, a thermal element, a buzzer, or a bell). Eventually, actual signals may be converted into electronic signals (e.g., a particular Voltage) in a particular interval $[x, y]$. In simple terms, the logic part receiving these signals does not need to "know" what a sensor "is". All it needs to know is what it has to do with the signal (Voltage level) it receives. It is important to understand that the separation between data and logic is a general, well-known, and widely applied design principle. For

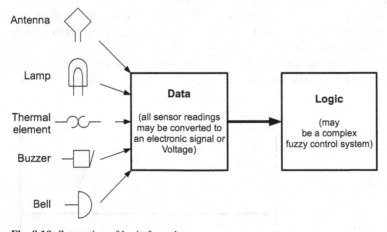

Fig. 8.10 Separation of logic from data

example, it is found in software design and development where it is a fundamental aspect of object oriented programming and design, and where it is also recognized as an important factor contributing to the production of robust software products [Lussier et al., 2004, Beyer and Schwefel, 2007].

In summary, *RobSim* demonstrates that the adaptive fuzzy set approach is highly flexible, dynamic, and versatile. We found that the approach is very well suited for systems where it is a key requirement to be able to function and adapt to changing environments and contexts, which is an essential feature of successful robust systems.

Robustness in Genetic Algorithm Component

The principles of genetic algorithms (GAs) are well-known, and in *RobSim* there are no significant deviations from standard procedures. The GA in Fig. 8.7 generates a start population with a predefined number of fuzzy control systems (FCSs). The fitness function in *RobSim* uses measures from chaos theory to establish the problem-solving potential (i.e., the fitness) of each FCS in a population. Our previous work documents the usefulness of these measures in more detail [Schuster et al., 2002]. The GA iterates through a loop with predefined exit conditions. The GA determines the quality of every FCS in each loop. *RobSim* uses well-known GA procedures (selection, crossover, mutation, etc.) to select and modify solutions that indicate as being better than other solutions in order to achieve further improvement. The GA stops when predefined exit conditions are met.

It is relatively easy to identify several of the design strategies for robustness mentioned earlier in GAs in general and in *RobSim* in particular. The first strategy that comes to mind may be redundancy (safety in numbers). A GA is an iterative process. Each iteration generates a pool of candidate solutions usually called "chromosomes". These potential solutions are selected, assessed, maybe modified, and forwarded into the next generation. It is important to mention that several parameters (e.g., crossover rate, mutation rate, number of iterations, size of a population, etc.) who have an influence on the performance of a GA usually undergo fine-tuning in order to optimize a GA. Another feature of robustness in the same context relates to the number of fuzzy sets for the representation of a variable. For example, five fuzzy sets model the variable *Speed* in Fig. 8.7. In *RobSim*, the number of fuzzy sets used for the representation of a variable is determined by a random procedure and may be any number from the set $\{3, 4, \ldots, 8\}$. These boundary values are motivated by comments by Chen and Hwang [Chen and Hwang, 1992] who indicate that it is nearly always possible to describe FCS applications in completely different domains with a relatively small number of very often similar fuzzy sets. Miller [Miller, 1965] supports this observation by identifying the number 7 ± 2 as a benchmark in many complex situations. For example, instead of lengthy explanations, book reviews in newspapers often only mention a small number of key points of a book. This line of thought provides a link to granularity and robustness. For example, four fuzzy sets for a variable is a smaller junk than eight fuzzy sets for the same variable. Interestingly, we found several times that there is little difference in performance between systems with larger numbers of fuzzy sets (high granularity) and those with smaller numbers (low granularity). Although the boundary values three (lower bound) and eight (upper bound) for the number of fuzzy sets for a domain variable are not chosen entirely arbitrarily (e.g., see [Miller, 1965]), these findings may suggest to study more systematically the upper and lower bounds in which *RobSim* operates best.

We also find restoration and recovery in a GA. In a GA run it is possible for a chromosome to do both, to improve its fitness but also to decline. On average, however, a GA improves the average fitness of the chromosomes in a population [Negnevitsky, 2005, pp.222–234]. Another observation relates to the genetic code itself. The blueprint for GAs is nature, the study of evolutionary strategies nature applies, and in particular the genetic code [Beyer and Schwefel, 2002]. Despite major efforts to better understand this code, there are still significant challenges to be overcome. For example, for some time researchers assumed that the genetic code maximizes information density, but nowadays the view that the code maximizes robustness also prevails [Hayes, 2004, Giulio Di, 2005]. The genetic code also shows a degree of versatility. A major challenge for any system (including AI systems) is to react in a meaningful way in unfamiliar or new situations. The genetic code contains large portions of redundant information or information whose purpose is still unknown. One interpretation for these redundant pieces of code may be to look at them as a multipurpose construction and/or repair kit. This kit may be similar to a box of LEGO. From an Aristotelian view, it may be possible to say that individual LEGO blocks alone may be useless. However, whenever there is a "need" or "urge", they may be arranged to fulfil a particular (maybe new) purpose. GAs typically do not have this potential to explore entirely new contexts (problem scenarios, purposes). The related field of genetic programming, however, does. Genetic programming is motivated by the challenge to produce (computer) systems that can solve problems without being explicitly programmed to do so [Negnevitsky, 2005, pp. 245–253]. Genetic programming therefore may be a possible extension to the current *RobSim* system. It may also be a field in which robustness has a word to say.

Robustness in Chaos Theory Component

Stewart [Stewart, 1997, pp. 49–63] highlights that the study of stability has a long tradition by mentioning that in 1887, King Oscar II of Sweden offered a prize of 2,500 crowns for an answer to the following fundamental question in astronomy—Is the solar system stable? As it turns out, an answer to this question is rather difficult. We therefore use a simpler example for our purposes (Fig. 8.11).

For one scenario in Fig. 8.11, imagine a ball sitting at the bottom of a bowl. For the other scenario imagine the ball sitting on top of the bowl turned upside down. If the ball is slightly perturbed, then the ball in the bowl comes to rest in approximately the same position after swinging back and forth for a couple of times. The behavior in the second case is different. Most likely, the system does not move back into its initial state, perhaps not even approximately. The ball may just roll off, where, is hard to tell. Obviously, the first system is more stable or robust with regard to (minor) changes (perturbations, influences).

Fig. 8.11 It is easy to
understand which system is
more stable

Dynamic systems have been studied for a long time, simple ones as well as very complex ones. In the late 1980s, chaos theory provided a new view and to some extent a new treatment of such systems. Mandelbrot sets, the Koch-Snowflake, and fractals are some of the better known outputs of this era. *RobSim* employs two concepts from chaos theory in the context of a tracking task. It uses a variation of the "Lyapunov Exponent" in chaos theory [Kaye, 1989] and a fractal dimension algorithm [Gough, 1993] for examining trajectories of moving objects in terms of their convergence and smoothness. Figure 8.12 helps to better understand these measures.

The problem in Fig. 8.12 is rather simple. An object *B* has to follow and catch an object *A*. Figure 8.12 illustrates two solutions. One solution (*t1*) is relatively smooth and the other (*t2*) more erratic. The important bit to understand is that although both trajectories provide a solution to the given task, the solution finally selected may be the solution that produces the trajectory that is less jagged (*t1*) because many systems (e.g., temperature control or flight control) prefer a behavior that converges toward a solution with some smoothness. As mentioned before, *RobSim* uses a fractal dimension algorithm for examining trajectories of moving objects in terms of their smoothness or jaggedness. Perhaps, the more relevant measure for robustness is the Lyapunov Exponent, which is used for measuring the stability (convergence) of a system. Essentially, the measure determines whether a dynamic system is (a) attracted to a stable fixed point or a stable periodic orbit, (b) the orbit is a neutral fixed point (the system is in some sort of steady state mode, like a satellite in a stable orbit), or (c) the orbit is unstable and chaotic.

Our earlier work [Schuster et al., 2002] demonstrated that the measures mentioned here can be useful for robot control and that the Lyapunov Exponent is particularly interesting in the context of this chapter.

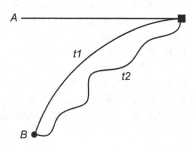

Fig. 8.12 Two solutions to a
tracking problem

8.5 Robustness Elsewhere

It is not easy to do justice to the many areas and aspects in which robustness may be discussed elsewhere. The forthcoming text therefore is selective again. However, in order to have a consistent theme in this chapter, the section reviews robustness in areas overlapping with soft computing (fuzzy, neural networks, etc.), robotics, and biology. An interesting starting point may be a paper on robot control with biological cells by Tsuda et al. [Tsuda et al., 2007]. The paper rests on the insight that there is a large gap in size, performance, adaptability, and robustness between natural and artificial information processing entities operating in real-time, "sense-think-act" situations. A central aspect of the paper is the immensely challenging problem for an agent (e.g., a robot) to operate in real-time in an uncertain, evolving, and complex environment (essentially an environment with undefined boundaries such as an ecosystem, for instance). The paper proposes a hybrid, cell-based (bio-mechanic) robot control unit on the assumption that natural systems may be better equipped for such a task than today's conventional computers are. This assumption includes the view that natural (neural and cellular) information processing mechanisms may have properties that are superior to conventional information processing on conventional computers. At its core, the paper researches a bio-hybrid architecture where "sensing" is done by a robot-kit equipped with sensors and roaming around in a macro-world. Signals are transferred from the robot via a circuit board to a multi-nuclear, single-cellular organism (*Physarum polycephalum*) for "thinking". Outgoing signals are transferred from this circuit unit back to the robot for "acting". Related to this chapter, the paper demonstrates the interdisciplinary and variation-rich aspect of robustness—the exploitation of cellular information processing capabilities in an area at the forefront of modern computing—robotics.

There are other papers in a robustness/cell context. A paper by Tann et al. [Tan et al., 2007] focuses on protein folding and the robustness of cells in metabolic networks. Proteins play a fundamental role in metabolic networks. Among other things, their shape determines a protein's function and the set of molecules it will bind to. Tann's study explores the relationship between protein folding (function and interconnection) and network robustness (the study examines robustness via random errors induced in an abstract metabolic network). The study finds that in more robust networks, function and interconnection are intertwined in a particular way and that networks where the two are independent are less robust. This is an interesting finding, because a similar relationship appears in software development and design where "cohesion" and "coupling" have a reputation to be key features [Huhns and Holderfield, 2002].

Another interesting paper comes from Teuscher [Teuscher, 2007] on self-configuration and self-replication in membrane systems (or P systems[3]). Membrane systems are abstract machines inspired by biology and chemistry and in particular by features of biological membranes. Teuscher uses the argument that the 21st

---

[3] http://psystems.disco.unimib.it.

century may be the century of bio- and nano-technology. He argues that biologically inspired computing machines may (and hopefully do) arise from this research and that, possibly, these new computing machines may have several advantages over the currently dominating von Neumann computing architecture. Teuscher focuses on several important concepts in membrane systems such as self-configuration, self-replication, and self-inspection, for example, which are all relevant in the context of this chapter. Of course, the paper is relevant to other areas, too. It addresses software and hardware design in which robustness plays a major role. It also relates to autonomic computing, a field inspired to produce large-scale computing systems that are autonomously controlled, self-organized, radically distributed, technology independent, and scale-free, and where the autonomic nervous system with its properties of self-configuration, self-healing, self-optimization, and self-protection is a key analogy [Kephart and Chess, 2003].

Some of the papers mentioned before work on a cellular level. Although this level is complex enough, some authors look at larger, possibly more holistic, systems such as biological immune systems, for example. Papers by Timmis and de Castro provide up-to-date information on the state of research in artificial immune systems [Timmis, 2007] and the role of soft computing for artificial immune systems [de Castro and Timmis, 2003]. Artificial immune systems draw their motivation from the problem-solving potential (functions, principles, and mechanisms) of biological immune systems. Although the field is permeated by soft computing techniques (e.g., fuzzy, evolutionary, neural, and hybrids), de Castro and Timmis identify a lack of an adequate framework for design, interpretation, and application in the field. The paper proposes such a framework and even more suggests the suitability of artificial immune systems as a novel soft computing paradigm. In our view, this is an interesting and meaningful suggestion, because artificial immune systems provide features that are not explicitly emphasized in other soft computing techniques. For example, fuzzy systems are appreciated for their handling of uncertainty and computing with words, but they are not known as a technique for handling self-healing, self-replication, and other aspects of robustness for which artificial immune systems stand in high regard. There is however the danger of an over-simplification. For example, this chapter has shown that fuzzy and neural systems are well capable of handling features of robustness that may be common in artificial immune systems. The proposal of a framework of an assembly of these techniques alone does not substantiate a new computing paradigm (artificial immune systems) in itself. For example, the way quantum mechanic works led to the new computing paradigm "quantum computing". What may be needed to justify the same for artificial immune systems may be the development and creation of novel computing metaphors (for example, clonal selection may be interpreted, crudely, as just another type of fitness function) that are derived from natural immune systems. Nevertheless, the work on artificial immune systems shows that the field is an inspiring area with great potential for researchers in many areas, including those with an interest in the study of robustness.

Although there are many more examples, we end this section with the overall feeling that the discussion in this section emphasized again the richness and multidisciplinary aspect of robustness. We also hope that the section created further awareness of the excitement with which robustness can be studied and the many challenges the field still holds.

8.6 Summary

The goal of this chapter is to investigate robustness from a variety of positions. Initially, the chapter identified characteristic features and appearances of robustness as it may be encountered in the natural world around us. The chapter then investigated robustness in artificial intelligence. A focus was on robust architectures for artificial neural networks and on individual components (fuzzy logic control, genetic algorithm, and chaos theory) of a hybrid robot control system. The chapter then, briefly, commented on robustness in other AI areas and the wider field of modern research and technology. Overall, the presented work indicates the important role of robustness in nature and modern technology. The chapter highlights that robustness is an exciting, interdisciplinary topic whose study may be important to many in the science community, including AI researchers.

References

Allen, E., Khoshgoftaar, T., and Chen, Y. (2001). Measuring coupling and cohesion of software modules: an information theory approach. In *Seventh International Software Metrics Symposium (METRICS'01)*, page 124. IEEE Computer Society Press.

Bentley, P. (2005). Investigations into graceful degradation of evolutionary developmental software. *Natural Computing*, 4:417–437.

Beyer, H. and Schwefel, H. (2002). Evolution strategies: a comprehensive introduction. *Natural Computing*, 1(1):3–52.

Beyer, H. and Schwefel, H. (2007). Robust optimization–a comprehensive survey. *Computer Methods in Applied Mechanics and Engineering*, 196(33–34):3190–3218.

Brighton, H. and Selina, H. (2003). *Introducing Artificial Intelligence*. Icon Books, UK.

Carbone, C., Teacher, A., and Rowcliffe, J. (2007). The costs of carnivory. *PLoS Biology*, 5(2): 363–368.

Chen, S. and Hwang, C. (1992). *Fuzzy Multiple Attribute Decision Making, Methods and Applications*. Springer-Verlag, Berlin.

de Castro, L. and Timmis, J. (2003). Artificial immune systems as a novel soft computing paradigm. *Soft Computing*, 7(8):526–544.

Giulio Di, M. (2005). The origin of the genetic code: theories and their relationships, a review. *BioSystems*, 80(2):175–184.

Gough, N. (1993). Fractal analysis of foetal heart rate variability. *Physiological Measurement*, 14(3):309–315.

Hayes, B. (2004). Ode to the code. *American Scientist*, 92:494–498.

Huhns, M. and Holderfield, V. (2002). Robust software. *IEEE Internet Computing*, 6(2):80–82.

Jones, G. and Jones, M. (2000). *Information and Coding Theory*. Springer-Verlag, London.

Kaye, B. (1989). *A Random Walk through Fractal Dimensions*. VCH, New York.

Kephart, J. and Chess, D. (2003). The vision of autonomic computing. *IEEE Computer*, 36(1): 41–50.

Lussier, B., Chatila, R., Ingrand, F., Killijian, M., and Powell, D. (2004). On fault tolerance and robustness in autonomous systems. In *3rd IARP-IEEE/RAS-EURON Joint Workshop on*

Technical Challenges for Dependable Robots in Human Environments, Lecture Notes in Computer Science, pages 7–9. Manchester, UK.

Mehrotra, K., Monan, C., and Ranka, S. (1997). *Elements of Artificial Neural Networks*. The MIT Press, Cambridge, MA.

Miller, G. (1965). The magic number seven, plus or minus two. *Psychological Review*, 63:81–97.

Negnevitsky, M. (2005). *Artificial Intelligence: A Guide to Intelligent Systems*. Addison Wesley, Harlow, England, 2nd edition.

Pfeifer, R. and Scheier, C. (2000). *Understanding Intelligence*. The MIT Press, Cambridge, MA.

Schuster, A. (2006). *Advances in Applied Artificial Intelligence*, volume 4031 of *Lecture Notes in Computer Science*, chapter A hybrid robot control system based on soft computing techniques, pages 187–196. Springer-Verlag, Heidelberg. Proceedings of 19th International Conference on Industrial, Engineering and Other Applications of Applied Intelligent Systems, IEA/AIE 2006, Annecy, France, June 27–30, 2006.

Schuster, A. (2007a). Robust artificial intelligence. In *Workshop on Artificial Intelligence for Space Applications at IJCAI'07*, Hyderabad, India.

Schuster, A. (2007b). Robust artificial neural network architectures. *IJCI International Journal of Computational Intelligence*, 4(2):98–104. World Academy of Science, Engineering and Technology.

Schuster, A., Blackburn, W., and Segui Prieto, M. (2002). A study on fractal dimensions and convergence in fuzzy control systems. *Journal of Telecommunications and Information Technology*, 3:30–36. National Institute of Telecommunications, Warsaw, Poland.

Shema, R., Sacktor, T., and Dudai, Y. (2007). Rapid erasure of long-term memory associations in the cortex by an inhibitor of PKM. *Science*, (317):951–953.

Stewart, I. (1997). *Does God Play Dice?. The New Mathematics of Chaos*. Penguin Books, Harmondsworth, England, 2nd edition.

Tan, G., Revilla, F., and Zauner, K. (2007). Protein folding and the robustness of cells. *BioSystems*, 87:289–298.

Teuscher, C. (2007). From membranes to systems: self-configuration and self-replication in membrane systems. *BioSystems*, 87:101–110.

Timmis, J. (2007). Artificial immune systems—today and tomorrow. *Natural Computing*, 6(1): 1–18.

Tsuda, S., Zauner, K., and Gunji, Y. (2007). Robot control with biological cells. *BioSystems*, 87(2–3):215–223.

Young, E. (2007). Vast ancient settlement unearthed in Cambodia. *New Scientist*, (2617):15.

Chapter 9
Feedback Structures as a Key Requirement for Robustness: Case Studies in Image Processing

Axel Gräser and Danijela Ristić

Abstract Natural as well as technical systems owe their robustness to a large extent to feedback structures. To use feedback, it is necessary to define a measurement, an actuator in the system, and a setpoint or reference—the measurement is compared with the reference and an actuator action is derived from the difference between them. This simple but powerful structure is responsible for providing the system with robustness against external influences. For a detailed discussion, the image processing system is chosen. The robustness of an image processing system is considered here to be the ability of an algorithm to achieve the desired output independently of numerous external influences such as illumination conditions, the imaging system, and imaged objects characteristics. Because of a number of problems, such as the absence of feedback from the higher to the lower processing levels, a traditional image processing system is of low robustness. This chapter presents the novel idea of the inclusion of feedback control at different processing levels to overcome the above problems of traditional image processing. The main idea behind this is to change the processing parameters in a closed-loop manner so that the current processing result at a particular processing level is driven to a reference result, providing the subsequent higher processing level with reliable input data. Presenting image processing as a new control application field, the chapter focuses on the specific features of image processing that make closed-loop control in this area different from conventional industrial control. The advantage of feedback for this advanced, prominent, and important application area is demonstrated through two examples.

9.1 Robustness Through Feedback

Robustness against parameter changes of the plant, sensitivity reduction, and disturbance rejection are among the central achievements of closed-loop control. The

A. Gräser
Institute of Automation, University of Bremen, Otto-Hahn-Allee NW1,
D-28359 Bremen, Germany
e-mail: ag@iat.uni-bremen.de

A. Schuster (ed.), *Robust Intelligent Systems,* DOI: 10.1007/978-1-84800-261-6_9,
© Springer-Verlag London Limited 2008

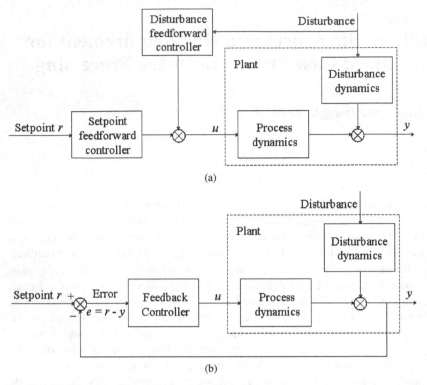

Fig. 9.1 Traditional feedforward (a) and feedback (b) control structure

basic structures of an open-loop, feedforward control and a control loop with feedback are shown in Fig. 9.1(a) and 9.1(b), respectively.

In both cases, it is the controller task to calculate the actuator control signal u, which ensures that the measured output y follows the setpoint or reference value r with minimal error. Indeed, in the completely unrealistic case where all external disturbances are known or measurable and the system to be controlled is exactly known, there is no need for feedback: optimal performance can be achieved with a feedforward controller. Feedback control is on the other hand a basic engineering strategy for ensuring that the output of a system robustly tracks its desired value independently of disturbances or variations in system parameters, which are unavoidable in real-world applications.

Classic control deals with the design of controllers for dynamic systems, to ensure stability and specified performance of the closed-loop with respect to parameter sensitivity and disturbance rejection. It is well-known that for the special class of linear, minimum phase systems, every requirement of sensitivity and disturbance rejection can be reached using feedback [Horowitz, 1993]. The price is a high bandwidth of the controller and through this a high gain at high frequencies, which may become unrealistic if measurement noise exists. It is also well-known that for disturbance rejection, there exists a trade-off between disturbance rejection and disturbance amplification and that disturbance rejection at low frequencies leads to disturbance amplification at high frequencies. Contemporary controllers are usually discrete sampling time controllers realized in some kind of computer. This leads to the introduction of a dead-time leading to non-minimum phase behavior of the system, which limits the possible control performance. Real plants are also characterized by nonlinear behavior, which makes controller design even more difficult.

The concept of robustness through feedback is not limited to technical control only, it also appears in fields as dissimilar as physics, network management, and biology. It is also well-known that it is only by virtue of internal feedback that living systems (which are highly nonlinear systems in most cases) can exist and thrive in a wide variety of environments. Blood sugar, blood pressure, respiration frequency, heart rate, and the two-legged gait of humans are just a few but very important examples for the importance of feedback control in living systems.

With the knowledge of the importance of feedback structures in natural and technical systems, the question arises whether this basic principle can be used in new applications to make them robust against all kinds of external influences. In this chapter, digital image processing is chosen as a novel application area for feedback control. It is very well-known that technical image processing lacks many abilities of image processing in biological systems, including humans, and that technical image processing usually needs a lot of adaptation and fine tuning [Lucas et al., 2006]. In this chapter, it is shown how feedback structures can overcome some of these limitations.

9.2 Robust Image Processing

A conventional digital image processing system is an open-loop chain consisting of three sequentially arranged blocks performing image acquisition, image data processing, and image understanding (Fig. 9.2).

Image data processing itself can be subdivided into two stages: low-level and high-level processing. The low-level processing consists of preprocessing and image segmentation stages whose common characteristic is that both their inputs and outputs are images. In contrast, the inputs of high-level processing feature extraction, classification, and recognition—are generally images, but their outputs are attributes extracted from those images. The reliability of the higher processing levels is strongly dependent on the correctness of the results of low-processing levels.

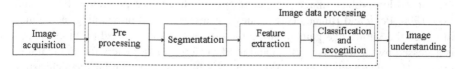

Fig. 9.2 Block-diagram of standard open-loop image processing

Nonetheless, in traditional image processing systems, the parameters of high-level algorithms are commonly designed under the assumption that the inputs are of good quality. However, in real-world applications, numerous external influences including illumination conditions, the imaging system, imaged objects characteristics, and processing algorithms parameters often cause the results of the low-processing level to be of poor quality. The progress through the image processing sequence of an uncertainty introduced by a poor-quality result may cause unreliability of the higher level processing steps, regardless of how well designed they are. Furthermore, due to the absence of feedback between the higher and lower levels, the processing at lower levels is performed regardless of the requirements of the subsequent steps, which leads to low robustness of the overall system against external influences even in the presence of reliable input image.

The improvement of robustness of vision algorithms is an emerging field of research that has been growing for the past two decades [Zhou and Shi, 2001, Mokhtarian and Suomela, 1998, Mirhmedi et al., 1997]. However, despite a number of published papers, so far, there is no precise definition for the robustness of an image processing algorithm. For this reason, in contrast with conventional control theory [Grimble, 1994], there has been until now no standardized methodology for measuring image processing robustness. According to [Wirth et al., 2006], robustness is a performance indicator that conveys the quality of an algorithm. Loosely speaking, *"robustness is the capacity of a vision algorithm for tolerating varying conditions"*. It can be said that a common characteristic of established robust image processing techniques is that they include the adaptation of processing parameters to cope with the challenges of a particular real-world application [Bhanu and Lee, 1994, Sifakis and Tziritas, 2003]. In other words, robust image processing techniques adapt the parameters to different vision conditions rather than using fixed parameter values. When considering adaptability in image processing, two types of algorithms can be distinguished.

The first group of algorithms perform so-called spatial adaptations as they deal with variability within images and adapt the processing parameters across the image [Coleman, 2005]. In contrast with spatial adaptation, so-called global adaptation involves the adaptation of global parameters (i.e., parameters that are used to process the entire image) to the different external influences [Abutableb, 1989]. Most of the published robust image processing methods adapt the parameters in a single pass, that is, in an open-loop manner. The processing parameters are calculated according to some predefined criterion using the results of the examination of the input image characteristics. Because they are open-loop methods, they are characterized by the significant disadvantage that the image processing components at high and low levels in the hierarchy of a vision system do not interact. In recent years, a few closed-loop robust image processing systems have been presented [Bhanu and Lee, 1994, Peng and Bhanu, 1998]. They are mostly based on learning techniques in which the knowledge gained during the processing of so-called training images is accessed by the adaptive system and used to suggest parameters for an incoming image. The idea behind this approach is that images with similar characteristics require similar processing parameters.

This chapter presents the novel idea of including error-based closed-loops at different levels of an image processing system to adapt processing parameters for the purpose of improving robustness against external influences without use of extensive previous knowledge. The main idea behind this is to change the processing parameters in a closed-loop manner so that the control error, the difference between a reference value and the current image processing result, is driven to zero [Ristić et al., 2005]. Hence, here, the robustness of image processing is considered to be *"the ability of a vision algorithm to achieve the desired quality of the result independently of external influences"*.

The employment of control techniques in image processing makes it a new control application field. This raises a large number of fundamental and application oriented questions including: "What are the specific features of an image processing system from a control perspective?", "What should be considered as the image processing result in the context of implementing closed-loop control?", "How should the reference value be determined?", "How should actuator and controlled variables be selected?", "How should the control action be designed?", "What improvements do feedback structures bring to image processing?". This chapter considers some of these questions and addresses their answers both generally and within the context of specific applications.

9.3 Feedback Structures in Image Processing

It is possible to include two types of closed-loops in a conventional image processing system. The first is termed here the *image acquisition closed-loop* (see Fig. 9.3). In this structure, information from a later stage of the image processing sequence is used, as feedback, to adjust the image acquisition conditions (solid lines in Fig. 9.3).

The control goal is to provide a "good" original (not-processed) image that is suitable for the processing steps subsequent to preprocessing, including the segmentation, feature extraction, and classification. The second type of closed-loop involves using feedback between the quality of the input data to a higher processing level and the parameters of the method applied at a lower level of the image processing chain (dashed lines in Fig. 9.3). This closed-loop adjusts the parameters of the applied processing algorithm according to the requirements of a subsequent image processing step and so is termed here the *parameter adjustment closed-loop*. In contrast with the image acquisition closed-loop, which represents the interaction of the

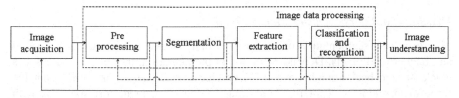

Fig. 9.3 Block-diagram of closed-loop image processing

image processing system and its environment, the parameter adjustment closed-loop is fully implemented in software.

As can be seen from Fig. 9.3, image segmentation, which is the process of segmenting the image pixels belonging to the objects of interest from the image background, has a central position in the image processing chain. Evidently, the reliability of higher processing levels, extraction of features of segmented regions, and object recognition based on extracted features is strongly dependent on the image segmentation result. On the other hand, the result of image segmentation is influenced by the correctness of the low-level processing. Therefore, the quality of a binary segmented image, which represents the result of image segmentation, has a crucial impact on the robustness of the overall image processing system. For this reason, the focus in this chapter is on the inclusion of closed-loops at different low-level processing stages in order to control the quality of binary segmented images.

9.4 Closed-Loop Image Segmentation

9.4.1 Choice of Actuator and Controlled Variables

Closed-loop control in image processing differs significantly from conventional industrial control, especially concerning the choice of actuator and controlled variables. Following general control design guidelines, the actuator variables should be those that directly influence image characteristics. Hence, for the image acquisition closed-loop, these variables can be the camera's parameters or the illumination condition, whereas for the parameter adjustment closed-loop they are the parameters of the processing algorithms. However, the choice of controlled variable is not a trivial problem. It has to be appropriate from the control as well as from the image processing point of view. From the image processing point of view, a feedback variable must be an appropriate measure of image quality. Two basic requirements of the control are that it should be possible to calculate the chosen quality measure easily from the image and the closed-loop should satisfy input-output controllability conditions. Input-output controllability primarily means that for the selected output (controlled variable), an input (actuator variable) that has a significant affect on it must exist in the image processing chain. Among the variables that affect the chosen controlled variable, one should be selected that causes rapid change of the feedback variable.

Measure of a Binary Segmented Image Quality

The result of a segmentation operation is a binary image consisting of foreground and background pixels. Depending on the implementation, the foreground color is black (0) and background is white (1) or vice versa. The assumption is that the foreground region is of interest in an image to be segmented, corresponding with an object to be recognized, being different from the image background according to a property such as color or texture. Generally, segmentation algorithms are based either on discontinuity or similarity of pixel values. The segmentation of an image by a discontinuity method is based on sharp transitions in pixel values, such as edges in an image. The result of these methods is the segmentation of the boundaries of the regions of interest and so they are known as *boundary based* segmentation methods. The principal approaches in segmentation through similarity are based on partitioning an image into regions whose pixel values are similar according to predefined criteria. Because of this, these methods are known as *region-based* segmentation methods. In both, pixel value discontinuity and similarity-based segmentation, a segmented image is said to be of good quality if all the pixels in a region of interest or of a region boundary are segmented as foreground pixels. That is, it is desired to have "unbroken" object regions or object boundaries in the segmented image. Also, there should be no pixels segmented as belonging to the object region or edges that do not actually belong there. In other words, it is desired that the segmented image is free of noise. Bearing in mind these requirements for the segmented image quality, it turns out that the number of segmented pixels may be used as a suitable quality measure. Furthermore, a measure of the connectivity of segmented pixels is necessary when assessing segmented image quality. A novel connectivity measure was introduced in [Ristić and Gräser, 2006]. It is the so-called two-dimensional entropy of the segmented pixels in a binary image, which is defined as:

$$S = -\sum_{i=0}^{8} p_{(0,i)} log_2 p_{(0,i)} \tag{9.1}$$

where $p_{(0,i)}$ is the relative frequency, that is, the estimate of the probability of occurrence of a pair $(0, i)$ representing the segmented pixel 0 surrounded with i segmented pixels in its 8-pixel neighborhood:

$$p_{(0,i)} = \frac{\text{number of segmented pixels surrounded with } i \text{ segmented pixels}}{\text{number of segmented pixels in the image}} \tag{9.2}$$

It is demonstrated in [Ristić, 2007] that the suggested entropy S has a small value when segmented pixels are well connected and a high value when segmented pixels are disconnected or scattered. In this way, the suggested entropy S can be considered also as a measure of disorder in a segmented binary image as *"the higher the value of S, the larger the disorder (noise and breaks) in a binary image is"*.

9.4.2 Choice of the Control Structure

The selection of the control configuration is a very important aspect of control system design, by which is meant the selection of a structure connecting measured (controlled) and actuated (control) variables. In classical control systems, this means the selection and placement of the actuators and sensors on the system to be controlled

[Boyd and Barratt, 1991]. In image processing, the selection of the control configuration firstly concerns the choice of a sequence of processing steps that provide achievement of the overall system goal. When designing an image processing chain, one has to have in mind that each of the individual levels has a large effect on its own on the system output. However, individual, well-designed levels cannot contribute to satisfying the overall goal if the other levels are not well designed as well. In the first place, the image acquisition hardware has to be selected so that it is able to cope with the problems arising from the nature of the imaged scene. The selected image acquisition hardware often introduces unavoidable problems such as low-contrast images so that an image processing chain has to have a contrast enhancement step in order that higher processing like segmentation is at all possible. This is discussed further in Section 9.6. In applications where it is not possible to control the illumination during the image acquisition, such as one considered in Section 9.5, the processing steps have to be chosen to overcome the problems arising from the illumination condition. At the same time, when implementing feedback structures in image processing in order to adapt the parameters of lower processing levels according to the requirements of higher levels, the selection of the processing sequence has to fulfill a number of requirements for feedback control to be effective. As described in Section 9.4.1, when selecting the image processing chain, the designer has to ensure that there are parameters available that have a large effect on the chosen controlled outputs and that can be actuated so as to drive the controlled outputs to their setpoint values. In other words, it must be ensured that there are "actuator variable-controlled variable" pairs that satisfy the conditions of input-output controllability.

In this chapter, two types of feedback connections between the chosen actuator and controlled variables in an image processing chain are proposed, forming sequential and cascade control structures. In the case of the sequential control structure, closed-loops at different levels of the image processing chain are constructed independently of each other so that their controlled variables are measured at different processing levels (or sublevels of the same processing level). Sequential closed-loops are designed so that "lower level" loops contribute to the success of subsequent "higher level" control loops and so to the reliability of the overall system. In contrast with the sequential control structure, the cascade structure is characterized by having different closed-loops whose controlled variables are measured at the same processing level. In this case, "inner" control loops provide initial improvement of the processing result while its further improvement is achieved using "outer" control loops.

9.4.3 Feedback Control Design

Two types of control law specifications are distinguished when including feedback structures at different levels of an image processing chain, depending on availability of a so-called ground truth image. In the field of computer vision, ground truth is defined as *"an ideal description of what should be obtained as the result of*

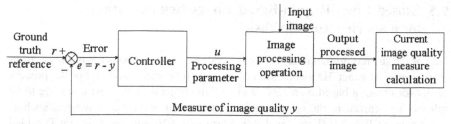

Fig. 9.4 Closed-loop image processing operation in case of available ground truth

processing of a certain image regardless of the processing algorithm". The inclusion of a proven error-based control algorithm (e.g., the PI (proportional-integral) control algorithm) is proposed in applications where a ground truth is available. The block-diagram of such a closed-loop image processing operation, which can be applied at any image processing level having an image as output, is shown in Fig. 9.4.

The idea behind this approach is to drive the current image processing result, represented through the measure of the image quality y, to the reference value r using an error-based control action u.

In applications where the ground truth is not available, the selection of a quality measure whose minimal or maximal value corresponds with the image of good quality is suggested for the controlled variable. The optimal value of the chosen controlled variable is achieved by an optimization using an appropriate extremum searching algorithm through the control structure as shown in Fig. 9.5.

Here, in principle, the feedback information on image quality y is used to choose the optimal value u_{opt} of the actuator variable u, that is, to drive the current image to one with the reference optimal quality.

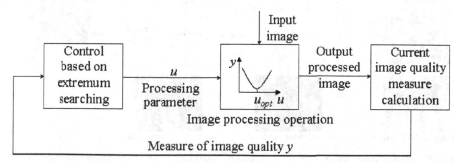

Fig. 9.5 Closed-loop image processing operation in case of not available ground truth

9.5 Closed-Loop Region-Based Image Segmentation for a Service Robotic Task

One of the key requirements of service robotics is a robust perception of the environment, aimed at exact 3D localization of objects to be manipulated. For the process of 3D localization based on a robot's vision, the objects of interest first have to be reliably recognized in the robot's camera image. Service robotic systems such as the system FRIEND II (Functional Robot arm with frIENdly interface for Disabled people), which has been developed at the Institute of Automation of the University of Bremen [Volosyak et al., 2005], are intended to support the user in daily life activities. Because of this, the object recognition must be robust enough to work effectively in different lighting conditions that arise during the day. The required robustness of the object recognition in FRIEND II is achieved by inclusion of two sequential closed-loops at the image segmentation level, thresholding and dilation closed-loop, as shown in Fig. 9.6.

The images in Fig. 9.6 correspond with a "beverage serving" scenario aimed at serving the user with a drink from a bottle. In this scenario, the task of the manipulator is to fetch the bottle located on the tray that is positioned in front of the user. To do this, the robotic system needs reliable information on the 3D location of the object of interest, the (green) bottle. The 3D location extraction module has as input information the parameters of a box that bounds the object explicitly identified as the object to be recognized. In the case of scenes in Fig. 9.6, these parameters are the principal axes and the center of the bounding ellipse. An object is identified as the object to be recognized based on object features extracted at the feature extraction stage. These features are appropriate shape descriptors of the regions of connected segmented pixels. Therefore, in order to get reliable results in feature extraction and consequently in object recognition, it is necessary to get, as the image segmentation result, a segmented image of good quality. Here, good quality means that the segmented image contains, if possible, all pixels of the object of interest forming a "full" (unbroken) and well-shaped segmented object region.

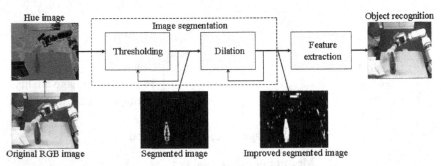

Fig. 9.6 Robust color object recognition based on closed-loop image segmentation in the robotic system FRIEND II

The first segmentation step, thresholding, is performed on the so-called Hue image, which contains the pure color information of the original RGB (red, green, blue) image of a scene from a FRIEND II working scenario. In thresholding, each pixel from the Hue image to be segmented is set to the foreground white color in the output segmented image if its pixel value belongs to a particular interval of the color values [Vuppala et al., 2007]. To further explain the thresholding operation, the Hue image is defined as a two-dimensional function $f(x, y)$, which can have values in the interval $[0, 255]$, and the object color interval as $C_l = [T_{low}, T_{high}] \in [0, 255]$ where T_{low} and T_{high} are the minimum and maximum color values across the object's pixels. Then, the thresholding operation is defined as:

$$t(x, y) = \begin{cases} 1, & \text{if } f(x, y) \in C_l \\ 0, & \text{if } f(x, y) \notin C_l \end{cases} \quad (9.3)$$

where $t(x, y)$ is the segmented binary image, 1 and 0 represent white and black color respectively, and x and y are the Hue image pixel coordinates. For the sake of clarity, an object color interval C_l in the following is referred to as an *object thresholding interval*.

The thresholding operation is highly sensitive to the illumination condition. Because of the pixel color uncertainty arising from changes in illumination during image acquisition, different thresholding intervals are needed to segment the same object at different time instances. This can be seen from Fig. 9.7, which shows the object segmentation results for the (green) bottle imaged in different illumination conditions.

The segmentation of the Hue images, corresponding with shown original RGB images, was performed using the reference thresholding interval for the (green) bottle, which was determined off-line using the so-called reference Hue image. The reference Hue image corresponds with the reference RGB image of the scene from the beverage serving scenario taken at a specific artificial illumination condition. The thresholding interval of an object of interest is determined by manually thresholding the Hue reference image. The thresholding interval is said to be a reference for the object of interest if the resulting binary image contains as many object pixels as possible.

Evidently, the segmented binary image corresponding with the image of the (green) bottle, taken in artificial light conditions is of good quality because it contains the majority of the object's pixels. In contrast, the result of segmentation of the image captured in daylight conditions is quite poor—it contains only a small number of object pixels. This is an expected result as different illumination conditions caused significant variation in the image colors. Because of this, the thresholding interval used, which is determined for the artificial light reference condition, can only yield good segmentation results for images taken in similar illumination conditions. Therefore, in order to achieve good object segmentation, it is necessary to adjust the object thresholding interval as illumination conditions change. Manual adjustment of the object thresholding interval is quite time-consuming

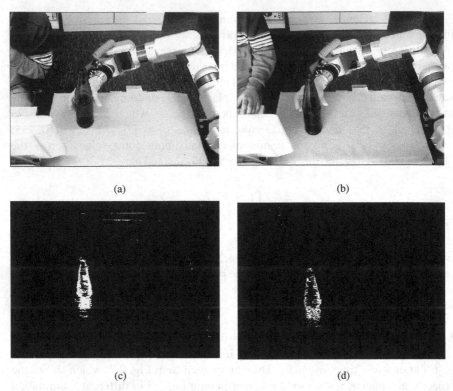

Fig. 9.7 Binary segmentation of the (green) bottle in FRIEND II environment corresponding with different lighting conditions. RGB image captured in artificial (a) and daylight illumination condition (b). Figures (c) and (d) show corresponding segmented images obtained using reference thresholding interval

and meaningless for an autonomous robot system. The implemented thresholding closed-loop provides automatic tuning of the thresholding interval so that the current number of segmented pixels is driven to the desired (reference) value.

However, due to different reflection and shadows arising during image acquisition, not all object image pixels belong to the same image color interval even though the object itself is of uniform color. As a result, the achieved reference number of segmented pixels, as said above, guarantees only the segmentation of "as many object pixels as possible". It still does not mean the achievement of the desired quality of the segmented image, which means the "full" (unbroken) well-shaped object segmented region. To overcome this problem, the dilation operation is implemented as a second segmentation step. The basic effect of the dilation operator on a binary image is to gradually enlarge areas of foreground pixels while suppressing holes within those regions. The dilation operator takes two inputs. One is the binary image to be dilated—in the presented system this is the image resulting from the thresholding closed-loop—and the other is the so-called structuring element. The structuring element is a matrix consisting of 0s and 1s. The distribution of 1s determines the shape of the structuring element and the size of the pixel neighborhood that is considered during the image dilation. The structuring element is shifted over the input image, and at each image pixel its elements are compared with the set of the underlying pixels according to some predefined operator. As a result, a black background pixel is converted to a white foreground pixel if there are white pixels in its neighborhood that are covered by the 1s of the structuring element. The effect of this "filling of segmented regions" by dilation strongly depends on the shape and size of the structuring element as well as on the number of dilations performed. Manual tuning of the dilation parameters is time-consuming and impractical for the autonomous functioning of the robotic system. In the proposed object recognition system, the included dilation closed-loop provides automatic implementation of image dilation so that the achieved two-dimensional entropy S of segmented pixels is equal to the reference one, yielding an object region of well-connected pixels.

The discrete PI controller structure used in both closed-loops is implemented in the following velocity form:

$$\Delta u(k) = K_P \left(\Delta e(k) + \frac{1}{T_I} e(k) \right) \tag{9.4}$$

where k is the discrete time index, $e(k)$ is the control error $(e(k) = r - y(k))$, $y(k)$ is controlled variable (number of segmented object pixels in the thresholding closed-loop and the two-dimensional entropy S of segmented object pixels in the dilation closed-loop), and $u(k)$ is the actuator variable (the increment to the boundaries T_{low} and T_{high} of the object thresholding interval and the height of the dilation structuring element in the thresholding and dilation closed-loop, respectively). The choice of the "actuator variable-controlled variable" pair for both closed-loops was done following the general control design guidelines described in Section 9.4.1 and the examination of the quality of the binary image at particular segmentation sublevel described above. Properly tuned proportional K_P and integral $K_I = \frac{K_P}{T_I}$ gains in equation (9.4) provide closed-loops that drive the current binary segmented images to the reference ones independently of the illumination condition during image acquisition. The reference values for both closed-loops, the reference number of segmented pixels, and the reference two-dimensional entropy S of segmented pixels respectively were determined off-line by manual thresholding and dilation of the reference image. The stopping criterion for the manual thresholding was the extraction of as many object pixels as possible without including the image noise, that is without segmenting the pixels that do not belong to the object. In the case of manual dilation, the stopping criterion for applying the dilation operation was "filling" the holes in the segmented object region without the degradation of the object contour.

Closed-Loop Versus Open-Loop Region-Based Segmentation

This subsection compares the performance of the proposed closed-loop segmentation with the performance of traditional open-loop segmentation consisting of thresholding and dilation steps. In contrast with the proposed feedback method, the open-loop method uses constant parameters of both thresholding and dilation operations. These parameters are determined off-line, as discussed above, by manual thresholding and dilation of the reference image.

In order to evaluate the performances of the two segmentation methods, the following Euclidean distance was used as a performance criterion:

$$d = \sqrt{(I_{r1} - I_1)^2 + (I_{r2} - I_2)^2}. \tag{9.5}$$

The Euclidean distance in equation (9.5) measures the closeness of the segmented object features I_i to their reference values $I_{ri}, i = 1, 2$. In the presented system, the used features are two Hu moments that uniquely describe an object of particular shape and so represent features that are appropriate for the object classification and recognition [Hu, 1962]. As region-based shape descriptors, Hu moments exploit both boundary and internal pixels of a segmented region. Hence, as demonstrated in [Vuppala et al., 2007], in order to get a reliable Hu moment value for the segmented region intended to be an object of interest and consequently the correct object classification and recognition, it is necessary to have a reliable segmented image input to the feature extraction step. The reliable segmented image corresponds with the case of having a "full" and well-shaped segmented object region whose Hu moments $I_i, i = 1, 2$ are close to their reference values. The reference Hu moments, $I_{ri}, i = 1, 2$, are calculated from the so-called ground truth image that is obtained by manually segmenting the reference image as explained above.

A set of images of the FRIEND II environment in the beverage serving scenario were taken at different times during the day. The illumination condition during the image acquisition ranged from bright artificial lighting to relatively dark natural lighting. Each captured image was segmented twice using the proposed closed-loop segmentation and the above described open-loop segmentation method. For each segmented image, the distance measure from equation (9.5) was calculated after extracting the Hu moments as relevant features of the segmented bottle object region. The results are shown in Fig. 9.8.

As can be seen, the Euclidean distance d calculated from segmented images obtained by open-loop as well as by closed-loop segmentation of bright images is almost equal to the desired zero value. This means that both of the considered segmentation methods give good segmentation result for the images captured in lighting conditions similar to the reference ones. This is expected even for the open-loop method because the used constant processing parameters are determined off-line by manual segmentation of the reference image. However, in contrast with the closed-loop method, the performance of open-loop segmentation degrades significantly with changing illumination conditions. This demonstrates the advantage of using feedback information on processing quality to adjust the processing parameters and thus to improve the system robustness with respect to external influences.

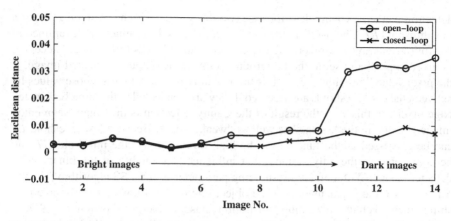

Fig. 9.8 Performance measure d of the segmentation of images captured in different illumination conditions ranging from bright to dark

9.6 Closed-Loop Boundary-Based Image Segmentation for an Industrial Application

In recent years, an extensive investigation into the development of computer vision systems to support the manual welding process has been made. The goal of the system presented in [Hillers et al., 2004] is to provide users with both an improved view of the welding scene and a view augmented with the parameters important for reliable welding. One of the research topics associated with this investigation is the extraction of object feature points (e.g., corners from the image) to provide the user with additional information about the welding task to be done. The nature of the manual welding process raises the need for cameras that are able to cope with the high brightness of the welding arc. The bright welding arc is approximately 10^3 times brighter than the average environmental illumination. Therefore, special high-dynamic range cameras are needed to allow the simultaneous observation of the welding arc and the environment. These cameras map the high dynamic range of brightness to a range of only 256 gray values. As a result, the generated image is of low contrast. Because of the low contrast, these images are very difficult to use for object boundary detection and so for most feature point extraction methods. The curvature scale space (CSS), which detects corners using the intuitive notion of locating when the contour of an object makes a sharp turn in the image, is a "state-of-the-art" corner detector [He and Yung, 2004]. However, the success of the CSS, is strongly dependent on the quality of the input boundary segmented image which is obtained by "Canny" edge detection [Canny, 1986]. The standard Canny edge detector consists of three processing stages: smoothing of the input image to reduce noise, filtering of the smoothed image with an edge detection mask to enhance the information on edges and to suppress unimportant background information, and thresholding of the obtained gray-level edge detected image to separate the true from the false detected edges. In thresholding, in contrast with other edge detection methods, Canny detector uses two thresholds, a high threshold *HT* and a low threshold *LT*. The pixels in the edge detected gray-level image are examined in the following way: if a pixel value is greater than *HT*, it is immediately accepted as an edge pixel and set to the foreground color in the output segmented image. If the pixel value lies below the *LT*, it is immediately rejected. Pixels whose values lie between the two thresholds are accepted if they are connected to the already detected edge pixels. In this way, the result of the Canny detection is the binary segmented image containing the "strong" as well as "weak" edges. Because low threshold *LT* can be expressed as the function of the high threshold *HT*, the threshold *HT* can be considered as the only variable that influences the quality of the binary edge detected image. With default thresholding parameter of the CSS algorithm [He and Yung, 2004], the segmentation of the object contour in a low contrast image of a ship corner, taken in the welding preparation phase, is poor, as shown in Fig. 9.9(a).

This under-segmented image is the result of "too high" a threshold *HT*. However, "too low" a threshold yields an over-segmented image as shown in Fig. 9.9(b). Neither an under-segmented nor an over-segmented image is a good input to the CSS corner detector—the first one allows detection of only few corners, and the latter one results in detection of too many false positives.

Evidently, it is crucial to define a threshold value that will yield reasonable and efficient segmentation of object edges as in Fig. 9.9(c). The suggested cascade control structure, shown in Fig. 9.10, aims to do this automatically before the segmentation results pass to a higher level of the CSS system.

As can be seen, beside the extension with two closed-loops in the proposed system, the open-loop CSS corner detection chain is augmented with a preprocessing, contrast enhancement, stage. The purpose of this is to improve the contrast of the input image before performing the edge detection and hence to increase the effective range of input variables that influence the quality of boundary-based segmentation [Ristić, 2007].

In contrast with the application considered in Section 9.5, here the ground truth reference segmented image is not available. This is because the imaged object is viewed from different positions, which results in different object appearances and consequently in different detected edges. Because of' this, the control actions in both control loops of the cascade structure are realized through an optimization

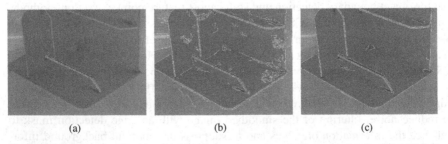

      (a)   (b)   (c)

Fig. 9.9 Original object image overlaid with the edge-contours detected using "too high" (a), "too low" (b), and optimal (c) threshold

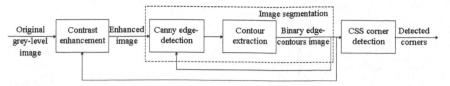

Fig. 9.10 "Cascade control structure for the control of the binary edge-contours image representing the input to the CSS corner detector

procedure, that is through an extremum searching algorithm. The control objective of the inner closed-loop is to provide a binary segmented image that is free from noise. It is accomplished by changing the threshold of the Canny edge detector, so that the measured variable, two-dimensional entropy S of edge segmented pixels, is minimized. The control goal of the outer closed-loop is to detect as many true edge-contours as possible. This is achieved by changing the parameter of a pre-processing contrast enhancement operation, so that the contrast of gray-level input image is improved, allowing segmentation of more object edges. In this way, the second output variable, the number of segmented edge pixels representing the length of the object edges, is maximized.

In [Ristić, 2007] it is demonstrated that the proposed cascade control structure provides an optimal trade-off between the edge length and noise reduction in segmented images, independent of external influences. In this way, the higher levels of the CSS corner detector are provided with reliable input data.

Closed-Loop Versus Open-Loop Boundary-Based Segmentation

In order to evaluate the performance of the proposed closed-loop segmentation technique, the binary segmented images of a stereo camera system used for corner-based stereo matching are considered. One motivation for using this application is that the benefit of good object boundary segmentation in both images of the stereo system for features point extraction is particularly significant [Zhou and Shi, 2001]. For reliable stereo matching, it is crucial that the same corners are extracted in both images of a stereo camera system, and that the extracted points are well localized. To achieve this using CSS as the corner detector, it is of key interest to first extract the same object contours in both stereo images. In order to achieve good quality for both of the binary segmented images in a stereo system, the independent optimization of left and right binary segmented images through the above cascade control structure is suggested. The reason for separate image optimization is that due to different characteristics of cameras in a stereo system, it can be the case that the left and right gray-level input images are of different quality, demanding different processing parameters.

Performing the optimization procedure for both images of the considered ship welding scenario using the cascade control structure for both segmentation processes, the following results were achieved (Fig. 9.11).

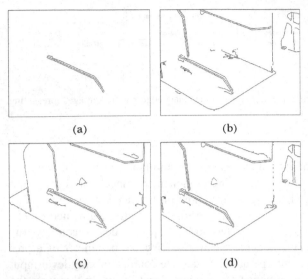

(a)   (b)

(c)   (d)

Fig. 9.11 Stereo left (a) and right (b) binary image result from the default open-loop segmentation method. Stereo left (c) and right (d) binary image result from the proposed closed-loop segmentation method

As can be seen in Fig. 9.11(a) and 9.11(c), where segmented edge pixels are shown as black and background pixels are shown as white, there is clear improvement of the left binary segmented image. From a visual inspection, there is no significant improvement of the right binary segmented image. An open-loop segmentation method based on default parameters of the Canny edge detector yielded the image with a lot of edges shown in Fig. 9.11(b). However, this image is noisier than the binary segmented image shown in Fig. 9.11(d), which resulted from the proposed closed-loop segmentation method. This subjective evaluation is confirmed by the quantitative measures of the image quality given in Table 9.1.

Evidently, the length of edges in the right binary images resulting from the two methods is almost the same. However, the two-dimensional entropy S of edges in the image resulting from the proposed method is much smaller than the one resulting from the default open-loop segmentation method, indicating that the image is less noisy. This demonstrates the benefit of using feedback information on image

Table 9.1 Length of detected edges and their two-dimensional entropy S in left and right binary images of the scene from ship welding scenario

LEFT IMAGE	S	Length (pixels)
Default open-loop method	0.1033	799
Proposed closed-loop method	0.1432	3961
RIGHT IMAGE	S	Length (pixels)
Default open-loop method	0.2374	4219
Proposed closed-loop method	0.1594	4293

quality to adjust the processing parameters. However, the most important aspect of the result, as shown in Fig. 9.11(c) and Fig. 9.11(d), is that the result in terms of detected edges is the same for both the left and the right image. The same appearance of the segmented imaged object in both stereo images is the main prerequisite for the reliable solution of the stereo matching problem.

9.7 Conclusions

This chapter presents the benefit of using feedback structures for the improvement of robustness of image processing against external influences. The focus was on feedback control of the quality of binary segmented image. The presented results demonstrate the need for closed-loop image segmentation to provide the reliable input to higher processing levels of the image processing chain and so to fully exploit the advantages of "state-of-the-art" image processing algorithms. The chapter demonstrates that in image processing, the feedback control design is application dependent. Nonetheless, the successful controller design presented here for two different applications suggests that the approach used provides a framework for inclusion of closed-loop control in a wide range of vision applications.

References

Abutableb, A. S. (1989). Automatic thresholding of gray-level pictures using two-dimensional entropy. *Computer Vision, Graphics and Image Processing*, 47(1):22–32.

Bhanu, B. and Lee, S. (1994). *Genetic Learning for Adaptive Image Segmentation*. Kluwer Academic Publishers, Norwell, MA.

Boyd, S. and Barratt, C. (1991). *Linear Controller Design—Limits of Performance*. Prentice-Hall, Upper Saddle River, NJ.

Canny, J. (1986). A computational approach to edge detection. *IEEE Transactions on Pattern Analysis and Machine Intelligence*, 8(6):679–698.

Coleman, S. A. (2005). Content-adaptive feature extraction using image variance. *Pattern Recognition*, 38(12):2426–2436.

Grimble, M. J. (1994). *Robust Industrial Control—Optimal Design Approach for Polynomial Systems*. Prentice Hall, Englewood Cliffs, NJ.

He, X. C. and Yung, N. H. C. (2004). Curvature scale space corner detector with adaptive threshold and dynamic region of support. In *17th International Conference on Pattern Recognition (ICPR'04)*, volume 2, pages 791–794, Cambridge, UK.

Hillers, B., Aiteanu, D., and Gräser, A. (2004). Augmented-reality helmet for the manual welding process. In Ong, S. and Nee, A., editors, *Virtual and Augmented Reality Applications in Manufacturing*, pages 351–370. Springer-Verlag, New York.

Horowitz, I. M. (1993). *Quantitative Feedback Design Theory (QFT)*. QFT Publications, Boulder, Colorado.

Hu, M. K. (1962). Visual pattern recognition by moment invariants. *IEEE Transactions on Information Theory*, 8:179–187.

Lucas, Y., Domingues, A., Driouchi, D., and Treuillet, S. (2006). Design of experiments for performance evaluation and parameter tuning of a road image processing chain. *EURASIP Journal on Applied Signal Processing*, 2006:1–10.

Mirhmedi, M., Palmer, P. L., and Kittler, J. (1997). Robust line segment extraction using genetic algorithms. In *6th IEE International Conference on Image Processing and its Applications*, pages 141–145, Dublin, Ireland. IEE Publications.

Mokhtarian, F. and Suomela, R. (1998). Robust image corner detection through curvature scale space. *IEEE Transactions on Pattern Analysis and Machine Intelligence*, 20(12):1376–1381.

Peng, J. and Bhanu, B. (1998). Closed-loop object recognition using reinforcement learning. *IEEE Transactions on Pattern Analysis and Machine Intelligence*, 20(2):139–154.

Ristić, D. (2007). *Feedback Structures in Image Processing, PhD Thesis*. Shaker Verlag.

Ristić, D. and Gräser, A. (2006). Performance measure as feedback variable in image processing. *EURASIP Journal on Applied Signal Processing*, 2006:1–12.

Ristić, D., Volosyak, I., and Gräser, A. (2005). Feedback control in image processing. *ATP International—Automation Technology in Practice*, 1:61–75.

Sifakis, E. and Tziritas, G. (2003). Robust object boundary determination using locally adaptive level set algorithm. In *International Conference on Image Processing*, volume 1, pages 141–144, Barcelona.

Volosyak, I., Ivlev, O., and Gräser, A. (2005). Rehabilitation robot FRIEND II—the general concept and current implementation. In *9th International Conference on Rehabilitation Robotics (ICORR'05)*, pages 540–544, Chicago, Illinois.

Vuppala, S. K., Grigorescu, S., Ristić, D., and Gräser, A. (2007). Robust color object recognition for a service robotic task in the system FRIEND II. In *10th International Conference on Rehabilitation Robotics (ICORR'07)*, pages 704–713, Netherlands.

Wirth, M., Fraschini, M., Masek, M., and Bruynooghe, M. (2006). Performance evaluation in image processing. *EURASIP Journal on Applied Signal Processing*, 2006:1–15.

Zhou, J. and Shi, J. (2001). A robust algorithm for feature point matching. *Computer and Graphics*, 26:429–436.

Chapter 10
Exploiting Motor Modules in Modular Contexts in Humanoid Robotics

Francesco Nori, Giorgio Metta, and Giulio Sandini

Abstract There is a growing interest within various research communities in modeling motor control systems with modular structures. Recent studies identified that such control structures have many interesting properties. This chapter focuses, in a robot environment, on properties that are related to the fact that specific sets of contexts can themselves be modular. In particular, the chapter shows that the adaptation of a modular control structure can be guided by the modularity of contexts, by means of interpreting a current unexperienced context as the combination of previously experienced contexts.

10.1 Introduction

Humans exhibit a wide repertoire of motor capabilities that can be performed in a wide range of different environments and situations. From the point of view of control theory, the problem of dealing with different environmental situations is nontrivial and requires significant adaptive capabilities. Even the simple movement of lifting an object can depend on quite a number of variables that can be both "internal" and "external" to the body. Examples of internal variables may be the state of the arm (e.g., joint angles and angular velocities) and its dynamic parameters (masses, moments of inertia, etc.). However, when interacting with the environment, motor commands also often need to be adapted to "external" variables that describe the interaction environment (e.g., geometrical and dynamical parameters of the objects being lifted). These variables together define what is generally called the "context" of the movement. As the context of the movement changes the input-output relationship of the controlled system, the motor commands must be tailored so as to take into account the current context. In everyday life, humans interact with a variety of different, complex, and continuously changing environments and their possible combinations. Therefore, a fundamental question in motor control is how

F. Nori
Italian Institute of Technology, via Morego 30, 16163 Genoa, Italy
e-mail: francesco.nori@iit.it

A. Schuster (ed.), *Robust Intelligent Systems,* DOI: 10.1007/978-1-84800-261-6_10,
© Springer-Verlag London Limited 2008

the control system robustly adapts to a continuously changing operating context. The adaptation of the motor control system to a continuously changing environment is a complex task. Noticeably, the dimensionality of the context space grows exponentially with the number of alternatives/variables used to describe the context itself. Therefore, this "curse of dimensionality" rules out any brute force approach for solving the context adaptation problem. Moreover, recent studies have shown that nature has found several more sophisticated, incredibly interesting solutions to this problem. Specifically, it has been proposed that the adaptation to new contexts can be achieved by means of linearly combining the knowledge about previously experienced contexts. The forthcoming sections describe, with the help of evidence gathered from experiments, this principle in detail.

10.1.1 Experimental Evidence on Modular Organization of the Motor Control System

A large amount of current literature shows that biological motor control systems are based on a continuous adaptation of internal models. These models can be seen as internal representations used by the central nervous system to handle a variety of different contexts. Within this framework, recently, there has been a major interest in modeling these internal models by means of linear combinations of a finite number of elementary modules. According to this modular architecture, multiple controllers, each suitable for a specific context, coexist. In case no controller is available for a given context, then individual controllers can be combined to generate an appropriate motor command. Therefore, even if internal models could be learned by a single module, there seem to be at least three main advantages related to their organization in multiple modules [Wolpert and Kawato, 1998]:

- **Modularity of contexts**. The contexts within which the model operates can be themselves modular. Experiences of past contexts and objects can be meaningfully combined and new situations can be often understood in terms of combinations of previously experienced contexts.
- **Modularity of motor learning**. In a modular structure, only a subset of the individual modules cooperate in a specific context. Consequently, only these modules have a part in motor learning without affecting the motor behaviors already learned by other modules. This situation seems more effective than a global structure where a unique module is capable of handling all possible contexts. Within such a global framework, motor learning in a new context possibly affects motor behaviors in other (previously experienced) contexts.
- **Dimensionality of generated motor acts**. By modulating the contribution of each module, a huge amount of new behaviors can be generated. Modules can be seen as a vocabulary of motor primitives that are the building blocks for constructing complex novel motor acts.

Remarkably, there is experimental evidence supporting the hypothesis that biological motor control systems are organized in modules. In particular, [Mussa-Ivaldi and Bizzi, 2000] have shown that this modularity is already present at the spinal cord level in the form of multiple goal-directed muscle synergies acting at the level of individual limbs. Each synergy has been described in terms of the force field generated at the extremity of the limb. Interestingly, the observed fields were limited in number (activated fields were grouped into few classes), goal-directed (the force field converged toward an equilibrium point), and linearly combinable (the simultaneous stimulation led to vector summation of the generated forces). The opinion in this chapter is that this experiment, though limited to frogs and rats, paves the way to interpret biological motor control systems (and the associated internal models) as modular structures.

In a different context, experiments with monkeys have shown that the pre-motor cortex has a modular structure, in particular area F5 has been shown to contain neurons responding to the execution of different types of grasp. They have been typically regarded as constituting a vocabulary of motor acts with populations of neurons coding and controlling the execution of a particular grasp (e.g., precision grip, full palm grasp, etc.) [Fadiga et al., 2000].

Concerning experiments with humans, there has been a growing interest in understanding whether internal models are organized modularly within the central nervous system. The existence and the adaptability of kinematic internal models [Flanagan and Rao, 1995] and dynamic internal models [Shadmehr and Mussa-Ivaldi, 1994] has been extensively proved. These two representations have been proved [Krakauer et al., 1999] to be weakly intertwined, thus revealing a first level of modularity.

A second level of modularity is revealed when considering the human capability of switching between previously learned internal models. Specifically, although the time required for adapting to a new context may extend over hours, restoring the pre-perturbation behavior is often faster [Welch et al., 1993, Brashers-Krug et al., 1996], thus suggesting the restoration of the previously acquired module.

On a third level of understanding, there is also evidence suggesting that previously acquired modules can be generalized to new situations if the new context can be interpreted as the combination of previously experienced contexts. In particular, in a kinematic scenario, it has been shown that different visuomotor mappings can be learned [Ghahramani and Wolpert,, 1997] and these maps can be interpolated to create new ones. Similarly, in a dynamic scenario, human subjects have shown the ability of combining previously acquired internal models when new contexts can be interpreted as the combination of previously acquired contexts. For example, studies revealed that after learning the correct grasping forces for lifting two different objects, subjects have displayed the ability of producing the correct force for lifting both objects simultaneously without any training [Davidson and Wolpert, 2004].

In a concluding remark, the robustness displayed by biological motor control systems seems to be the result of an extraordinary capability of adapting to continuously changing contexts. This adaptation seems to be achieved in a twofold manner:

(1) by a continuous update of existing modules, and (2) by the combination (switching) of (between) previously learned modules. Remarkably, experiments suggest that the two processes take advantage of different information: while adaptation can be attributed to performance errors [Shadmehr and Mussa-Ivaldi, 1994], switching and combination depend on sensory components of the context [Shelhamer et al., 1991].

10.1.2 Adaptive and Modular Motor Control Strategies

Based on the findings mentioned before, there has been recently a growing interest in investigating the potentialities of "adaptive" and "modular" control schemes as proposed in [Wolpert and Kawato, 1998] and [Mussa-Ivaldi, 1997]. These investigations suggest the possibility of developing humanoid robots capable of adapting to a continuously changing environment. At the current state of the art, performance error-based adaptation has been extensively studied [Sastry and Bodson, 1989, Slotine and Li, 1991]. However, modern robots still lack the capability of exploiting previous experiences on the basis of context related sensory information. Considering the previous discussion, modularity seems to play a fundamental role within this framework. Remarkably, modularity does not seem to be useful "per se" but reveals its usefulness when adapting to modular contexts. The forthcoming text in this chapter therefore aims at giving further evidence to the fact that a modular control structure is extremely useful when associated with a set of modular contexts. Within the forthcoming investigations, modularity is formalized in terms of multiple forward/inverse models.[1] Motor commands are usually obtained by combining these elementary internal models: different combinations serve different contexts. Assuming that a set of possible operational contexts has been defined, the following two fundamental questions arise:

1. Is there a way to choose the elementary internal models so as to cover all the contexts within the specified set?
2. Given a set of internal models that appropriately cover the set of contexts, how is the correct subset of internal models selected for the particular current context?

Both questions have been investigated already within the function approximation framework (e.g., see [Mussa-Ivaldi and Giszter, 1992] and [Wolpert and Kawato, 1998]). Recently, the same two questions have been considered within a novel control theoretical framework [Nori and Frezza, 2005]. This later approach has already provided interesting results for answering the first of the two questions stated before [Nori and Frezza, 2004a, Nori, 2005].

---

[1] Here a forward model is considered to be a map from motor commands to the corresponding movement. Vice versa, an inverse model corresponds with a map from desired movement to motor commands.

This work proceeds along the same line to answer the second question. Having in mind an application in the humanoid robotic field, the current work proposes a strategy to adaptively select a given set of inverse models. The selection process is based on both performance errors (Section 10.3.3) and context-related sensory information (Section 10.3.4). Remarkably, both of these measures have been shown to play a fundamental role in the module adaptation and selection processes (see Section 10.1.1). The key features of the proposed control scheme are the following:

- **Minimum number of modules.** Previous work has established the minimum number of modules that are necessary to cover all the contexts in a specified set [Nori, 2005]. Part of this chapter is going to describe how this minimality result can be fitted in the adaptive selection of the modules.
- **Linear combination of modules.** The theory of adaptive control has been widely studied since the early 1970s. Interesting results have been obtained, especially in situations where some linearity properties can be proven and exploited. In this work, linearity will be a property of the considered set of admissible contexts.

The remaining sections in this chapter are organized as follows. Section 10.2 provides a formal definition of modular motor control strategy; a simple example is analyzed and a solution is given. Section 10.3 describes a similar scenario but immersed in different contexts; a modular architecture is proposed as a possible solution to the problem of constructing the correct control strategy according to the current context (Section 10.3.1). Finally, two intertwined solutions to the context adaptation problem are proposed: a performance error-based adaptation (Section 10.3.3) to be used when nothing is known about the current context and an "error-free" adaptation that instead relies on "a priori" context-related sensory information (Section 10.3.4).

10.2 Reaching with a Modular Control Structure

This section gives a formal definition of the motor control modules. In a mathematical framework, the system to be controlled will be described by the following differential equation:

$$\dot{\mathbf{x}} = f(\mathbf{x}) + g(\mathbf{x})\mathbf{u} \tag{10.1}$$

where $\mathbf{x} \in \mathbb{R}^n$ is the system state and the vector $\mathbf{u} \in \mathbb{R}^m$ is the system input, corresponding with our control variable. Equation 10.1 describes the state evolution given the current input; its internal representation corresponds with what is usually called forward internal model. An inverse internal model, on the other hand, defines the input to be used in order to obtain a desired state evolution.

Although different definitions of modular control strategies can be given, this chapter follows the formalization [Mussa-Ivaldi and Bizzi, 2000] that was originally proposed as a mathematical description of the experimentally observed spinal fields. Practically speaking, the original control variable $\mathbf{u}$ is replaced by the linear superposition of a finite number of elementary control strategies $\{\Phi^1(\mathbf{x}), \Phi^2(\mathbf{x}), \dots, \Phi^K(\mathbf{x})\}$. Specifically:

$$\mathbf{u} = \sum_{k=1}^{K} \lambda_k \Phi^k(\mathbf{x}), \qquad (10.2)$$

where the new control variables are the mixing coefficients $\lambda_1, \lambda_2, \dots, \lambda_K$ assumed to be constant during the execution of a single movement.

To exemplify the proposed ideas, it is convenient to consider a specific task—nominally reaching (i.e., moving a limb to desired final point). Within this framework, the system to be controlled will be a mathematical model of the limb dynamics that can always be written as follows:

$$M(\mathbf{q})\ddot{\mathbf{q}} + C(\mathbf{q}, \dot{\mathbf{q}})\dot{\mathbf{q}} + g(\mathbf{q}) = \mathbf{u}, \qquad (10.3)$$

where $\mathbf{q}$ are the generalized coordinates that describe the pose of the kinematic chain (e.g., joint angles), $\mathbf{u}$ are the control variables (e.g., torques applied at the joints) and the quantities M, C, and g are the inertia, Coriolis, and gravitational components. Remarkably, equation (10.3) can always be written in the state space form equation (10.2) defining $\mathbf{x} = [\mathbf{q}, \dot{\mathbf{q}}]$.

The mathematical formulation for reaching consists in finding a time varying input $\mathbf{u}$ that drives the system configuration $\mathbf{x}$ to any desired reachable state $\mathbf{x}_f$. In case the control input were the original (time variant) input variable $\mathbf{u}$, then the problem would be solved easily by using classical control techniques [Murray et al., 1994]. In the modular structure framework, the input variables are the (time invariant) mixing coefficients $\lambda_1, \lambda_2, \dots, \lambda_K$, and therefore major attention should be given to selecting the modules. In case the functions Φ_k are not chosen carefully, some configurations (reachable by a suitable choice of the original input $\mathbf{u}$) might be no longer reachable by the new input variables. Formally speaking, the system 10.3 might lose its controllability by imposing the modular structure 10.2 on its input. More specifically, the following problem has been formulated:

Problem 1 (Synthesis of Elementary Controls for Reaching). Find a set of modules $\{\Phi^1, \dots, \Phi^K\}$ and a continuously differentiable function $\lambda(\cdot)$, such that for every desired reachable state $\mathbf{x}_f$, the input:

$$\mathbf{u} = \sum_{k=1}^{K} \lambda_k(\mathbf{x}_f) \Phi^k(\mathbf{x}) \qquad (10.4)$$

steers the system (10.3) to the state $\mathbf{x}_f$ (see Fig. 10.1).

As mentioned earlier, previous attempts [Mussa-Ivaldi and Giszter, 1992, Wolpert and Kawato, 1998] to solve the controllability problem mentioned before were based on an approximation framework. The main drawback of this approach is the large number of required modules. Such a drawback follows from a quite general

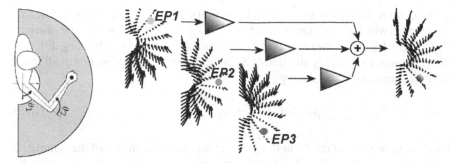

Fig. 10.1 A graphical representation of the modular reaching problem. A finite number of reaching movements (each with a specific equilibrium point EP) are used as primitives; these movements are represented with the associated force fields. Given an arbitrary point to be reached (indicated in gradient black to white), the primitives need to be linearly combined so as to obtain a new force field capable of reaching the desired point. Notice that the linear mixing coefficients (the triangles) are represented with a gradient color so as to make explicit their dependency on the desired reaching point

principle: without any "a priori" knowledge about the function to be approximated, the more modules there are, the better the approximation will be. The approach presented in this chapter follows a different solution originally proposed in [Nori and Frezza, 2004b] and based on the idea of maintaining the number of primitives as low as possible. Remarkably, the proposed solution is composed by $n + 1$ primitives,[2] that is proven to be the minimum number under suitable hypotheses (see Section A). Details on how to construct such a minimal solution for Problem 1 can be found in [Nori and Frezza, 2005].

10.3 Reaching in Different Contexts

In order to immerse the reaching action into different contexts, let us now consider reaching while holding objects with different masses and inertias. The underlying idea is to replicate a framework similar to the framework proposed in other human behavioral studies, e.g., [Krakauer et al., 1999, Davidson and Wolpert, 2004]. Within such a framework, a successful execution of the reaching movements requires a control action that should compensate for the perturbing forces. Because the controlled system[3] changes its properties with the context, suitable changes should be imposed on the control action. It is important to notice that the considered set of contexts is itself modular. In particular, two different objects can be held simultaneously, thus producing a situation that is exactly the combination of the two contexts corresponding with holding the two objects separately.

---

[2] Remember that n is the state space dimensionality, i.e., $\mathbf{x} \in \mathbb{R}^n$.

[3] Within this framework, the controlled system is composed of the arm "and" the object being held.

Once again, the dynamic system to be controlled can be expressed as a differential equation with the structure of equation (10.3). However, in this case the matrices M, C, and g depend on the context as a consequence of the fact that holding different objects results in changing the limb's dynamic parameters. Let us group all these dynamic parameters in a vector $\mathbf{p}$:

$$\mathbf{p} = [m_i \ I_1^i \ \ldots \ I_6^i \ c_x^i \ c_y^i \ c_z^i]_{i=1\ldots n}^\top, \tag{10.5}$$

where m_i is the mass of the ith link, $I_1^i, \ldots, I_6^i$ represent the entries of the symmetric inertia tensor, and $[c_x^i, c_y^i, c_z^i]^\top$ is the center of mass position. The system to be controlled therefore is:

$$M_{\mathbf{p}}(\mathbf{q})\ddot{\mathbf{q}} + C_{\mathbf{p}}(\mathbf{q}, \dot{\mathbf{q}})\dot{\mathbf{q}} + g_{\mathbf{p}}(\mathbf{q}) = \mathbf{u}, \tag{10.6}$$

where the notation explicitly indicates that the controlled dynamical system depends on the contexts by explicitly indicating the subscript $\mathbf{p}$.

10.3.1 Modules for Handling Admissible Contexts

This section answers a fundamental question that is strictly related to the problem of adapting to a continuously changing environment. In order to adapt to new contexts, do we need to adapt the primitives themselves or can we just adapt the way of combining a unique and "hardwired" set of primitives? Clearly (see Section 10.2), given a context $\mathbf{p}$, a set of primitives $\{\Phi_{\mathbf{p}}^1(\mathbf{x}), \Phi_{\mathbf{p}}^2(\mathbf{x}), \ldots, \Phi_{\mathbf{p}}^K(\mathbf{x})\}$ can be tailored for the specific context. An alternative solution consists in trying to find a unique set of primitives whose combination can handle all possible contexts. However, the existence of such a set of primitives cannot be guaranteed a priori and needs to be proven.

This section shows that such a set of primitives exists for the given set of contexts described by equations (10.5) and (10.6). Practically, a solution is proposed to the following problem where instead of controlling (10.3), the goal is to control (10.6), which is context dependent:

Problem 2 (Synthesis of Elementary Controls for Reaching in Different Contexts). Find a set of modules $\{\Phi^1, \ldots, \Phi^K\}$ and a continuously differentiable function $\lambda(\cdot, \cdot)$, such that for every desired final state $\mathbf{q}_f$ and for every possible context $\mathbf{p}$, the input:

$$\mathbf{u} = \sum_{k=1}^K \lambda_k(\mathbf{q}_f, \mathbf{p})\Phi^k(\mathbf{q}, \dot{\mathbf{q}}) \tag{10.7}$$

steers the system (10.6) to the configuration $\mathbf{q}_f$ (see Fig. 10.2).

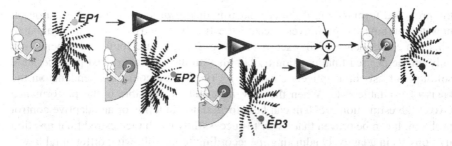

Fig. 10.2 A graphical representation of the modular reaching problem within different contexts. A finite number of reaching movements (each with a specific equilibrium point EP, and a specific context—indicated by different held objects) are used as primitives; these movements are represented with the associated force fields. Given an arbitrary point to be reached (represented in black) in a specific context (represented in gradient from black to white), the primitives need to be linearly combined so as to obtain a new force field capable of reaching the desired point in the given context. Notice that the linear mixing coefficients (the triangles) are represented with gradient and black colors so as to make explicit their dependency on the desired reaching point and the current context

Obviously, the proposed problem is related to the question posed in the introduction: is there a way to choose the elementary (inverse) models so as to cover all the contexts within a specified set? The answer turns out to be "yes". Specifically, a complete procedure for constructing a solution for Problem 2 has been proposed in [Nori, 2005]. The solution turns out to have the following structure:

$$\mathbf{u} = \sum_{i=1}^{I} \sum_{j=1}^{J} \lambda_i(\mathbf{q}_f) \mu_j(\mathbf{p}) \Phi^{i,j}(\mathbf{q}, \dot{\mathbf{q}}), \qquad (10.8)$$

where $\{\Phi^{1,j}, \dots, \Phi^{I,j}\}$ is a solution to Problem 1 for a specific context $\mathbf{p}^j$; minimality results can be easily extended within this framework.

10.3.2 Adaptive Modules Combination

Taking advantage of the results proposed in Section 10.3.1, this section faces the problem of adaptively combining a given set of primitives to a continuously changing environment. Initially, the section describes a method for adaptively adjusting module selection on the basis of performance errors. The section then shows that adaptation can be made on the basis of context-related information.

10.3.3 Performance Error Based Adaptation

In many situations, the context of a movement is not known "a priori" and therefore no previously acquired context-related sensory information can be exploited. Within the proposed formulation, if the context **p** is unknown, there is no information on how to combine the primitives because the functions $\mu_j(\mathbf{p})$ cannot be evaluated. This is a consequence of the fact that the way modules are combined depends not only on the desired final position $\mathbf{q}_f$ but also on the current context **p**. A possible solution consists in adaptively choosing μ_j (which are context dependent) on the basis of available data. When the only information available is the performance error,[4] the estimation problem can be reformulated in terms of an adaptive control problem. It can be proven that a way to successfully reach the desired final position $\mathbf{q}_f$ consists in adaptively adjusting μ_j according to the following differential law:

$$\frac{d}{dt}\mu_j = -\mathbf{s}^\top \left[\sum_{i=1}^{I} \lambda_i(\mathbf{q}_f)\Phi^{i,j}(\mathbf{q}, \dot{\mathbf{q}}) \right], \tag{10.9}$$

where **s** is the performance error (see [Kozlowski, 1998] for details). A mathematical proof of the system stability properties is out of the scope of this chapter and therefore omitted. It suffices to say that, in fact, it can be proved that (10.9) together with (10.4) and (10.6) leads to a stable system.

10.3.4 Context-Based Adaptation

The previous sections have shown how performance errors can be used to adapt inverse internal models to an unknown context. This type of adaptation is useful when no "a priori" information is available. However, its major drawback relies in the fact that adaptation takes place only in the presence of systematic errors. Moreover, every time the context is switched, a certain amount of time is required for the adaptation process (10.9) to converge. Within certain scenarios, this adaptation process might be very long and performance errors may be highly undesirable. In these situations, different adaptation strategies should be adopted.

Humans exhibit an extraordinary capability of exploiting previous experiences to plan their control actions. Consider, for instance, the problem of lifting an object. Clearly, the movement is preplanned on the basis of some "a priori" information[5] that allows one to perform actions in different contexts without systematic performance errors. How do humans create this "a priori" information when lifting an object that they have never lifted before?

---

[4] The performance error **s** measures the difference between the desired reaching trajectory $\mathbf{q}^d$ and the actual trajectory **q**. Further details can be found in [Kozlowski, 1998].

[5] A very common situation reveals that movements are preplanned on the basis of some "a priori" information. For example, imagine the movement of lifting an empty bottle. Sometimes, humans misinterpret the context, considering the bottle full and therefore using incorrect "a priori" information. In these situations, the resulting movement presents an overshoot, thus revealing that incorrect "a priori" information has been used.

"A priori" information of unknown objects can be obtained on the basis of similarity. Trivially, if an unknown object is similar to a known object, then a control action suitable for the latter should be suitable also for the former. This section shows that another way to retrieve "a priori" information consists in interpreting an unknown object as the combination of two or more known objects. However, the way of using such "a priori" information for choosing a suitable control action is nontrivial. Specifically, the modularity of the control architecture will play a fundamental role within this framework.

Modularity of Forward Models

As pointed out previously, each module is a combination of inverse and forward models. This section focuses on the forward part while leaving the discussion on the inverse part to the remainder of the chapter. In particular, it is pointed out that the modularity of contexts reflect into the modularity of the corresponding forward models. Specifically, it is shown that the forward model describing the dynamic behavior of a composed object is obtained by the linear sum of the forward models describing the component objects.

To begin with, consider the forward model associated with a limb not holding any object (10.3):

$$M(\mathbf{q})\ddot{\mathbf{q}} + C(\mathbf{q}, \dot{\mathbf{q}})\dot{\mathbf{q}} + g(\mathbf{q}) = \mathbf{u}. \tag{10.10}$$

Let us rewrite this as follows:

$$Y(\mathbf{q}, \dot{\mathbf{q}}, \ddot{\mathbf{q}}) = \mathbf{u}. \tag{10.11}$$

Let us modify this model in order to take into account an externally perturbing force $\mathbf{f}_1$. We have [Murray et al., 1994]:

$$Y(\mathbf{q}, \dot{\mathbf{q}}, \ddot{\mathbf{q}}) + Y_{\mathbf{f}_1}(\mathbf{q}) = \mathbf{u}, \quad Y_{\mathbf{f}_1}(\mathbf{q}) = J^\top(\mathbf{q})\mathbf{f}_1 \tag{10.12}$$

where J is the Jacobian matrix describing the point where the force is applied. How should 10.11 be modified when two forces $\mathbf{f}_1$ and $\mathbf{f}_2$ are simultaneously applied? Remarkably, the following holds:

$$Y(\mathbf{q}, \dot{\mathbf{q}}, \ddot{\mathbf{q}}) + Y_{\mathbf{f}_1}(\mathbf{q}) + Y_{\mathbf{f}_2}(\mathbf{q}) = \mathbf{u}, \tag{10.13}$$
$$Y_{\mathbf{f}_1}(\mathbf{q}) = J^\top(\mathbf{q})\mathbf{f}_1,$$
$$Y_{\mathbf{f}_2}(\mathbf{q}) = J^\top(\mathbf{q})\mathbf{f}_2$$

Interestingly, the addition of new forces reflects into the additivity of the corresponding forward models. Is a similar property preserved when considering the modularity of objects? To answer this question, let us rewrite (10.6) as follows:

$$Y_{\mathbf{p}}(\mathbf{q}, \dot{\mathbf{q}}, \ddot{\mathbf{q}}) = \mathbf{u}. \tag{10.14}$$

Suppose that a context $\mathbf{p}_1$ corresponds with holding an object $\mathcal{O}_1$. It can be shown that the following equation holds [Kozlowski, 1998]:

$$Y_{\mathbf{p}_1}(\mathbf{q}, \dot{\mathbf{q}}, \ddot{\mathbf{q}}) = Y(\mathbf{q}, \dot{\mathbf{q}}, \ddot{\mathbf{q}}) + Y_{\mathcal{O}_1}(\mathbf{q}, \dot{\mathbf{q}}, \ddot{\mathbf{q}}), \tag{10.15}$$

where Y describes the forward model of the limb not holding any object and $Y_{\mathcal{O}_1}$ the forces (inertial, Coriolis and gravitational) due to the held object. The importance of this decomposition is evident when our representation of the forward dynamics is itself modular. Practically, the forward dynamics of the limb holding an object ($Y_{\mathbf{p}_1}$) can be obtained by combining the module describing the limb dynamic (Y) and the module describing the object ($\mathcal{O}_1$), i.e., $Y_{\mathbf{p}_1} = Y + \mathcal{O}_1$.

Using this property, it can be shown that the effect of two different objects $\mathcal{O}_1$ and $\mathcal{O}_2$ is given by:

$$Y_{\mathbf{p}}(\mathbf{q}, \dot{\mathbf{q}}, \ddot{\mathbf{q}}) = Y(\mathbf{q}, \dot{\mathbf{q}}, \ddot{\mathbf{q}}) + Y_{\mathcal{O}_1}(\mathbf{q}, \dot{\mathbf{q}}, \ddot{\mathbf{q}}) + Y_{\mathcal{O}_2}(\mathbf{q}, \dot{\mathbf{q}}, \ddot{\mathbf{q}}), \tag{10.16}$$

which can be interpreted as the fact that additivity of forces (10.13) is preserved when considering modular objects.

The best way to exploit this compositional property consists in using a representation of the internal models that shares a similar compositionality. Remarkably, the modular representation has this property. Suppose that the internal model is represented by the linear combination of the elementary modules $\Phi^1(\mathbf{q}, \dot{\mathbf{q}}, \ddot{\mathbf{q}})$, $\Phi^2(\mathbf{q}, \dot{\mathbf{q}}, \ddot{\mathbf{q}}), \ldots, \Phi^J(\mathbf{q}, \dot{\mathbf{q}}, \ddot{\mathbf{q}})$. Two different objects $\mathcal{O}_1$ and $\mathcal{O}_2$ (corresponding with contexts $\mathbf{p}_1$ and $\mathbf{p}_2$) can therefore be represented as follows:

$$Y_{\mathcal{O}_1}(\mathbf{q}, \dot{\mathbf{q}}, \ddot{\mathbf{q}}) = \sum_{j=1}^{J} \Psi_j(\mathbf{p}_1) \Phi^j(\mathbf{q}, \dot{\mathbf{q}}, \ddot{\mathbf{q}}), \tag{10.17}$$

$$Y_{\mathcal{O}_2}(\mathbf{q}, \dot{\mathbf{q}}, \ddot{\mathbf{q}}) = \sum_{j=1}^{J} \Psi_j(\mathbf{p}_2) \Phi^j(\mathbf{q}, \dot{\mathbf{q}}, \ddot{\mathbf{q}}). \tag{10.18}$$

Given (10.16), the composition of the two objects is represented by a new internal model that is described by the same elementary modules. Specifically we have:

$$Y_{\mathcal{O}}(\mathbf{q}, \dot{\mathbf{q}}, \ddot{\mathbf{q}}) = \sum_{j=1}^{J} [\Psi_j(\mathbf{p}_1) + \Psi_j(\mathbf{p}_2)] \Phi^j(\mathbf{q}, \dot{\mathbf{q}}, \ddot{\mathbf{q}}), \tag{10.19}$$

where the new object $\mathcal{O}$ and the associated context $\mathbf{p}$ interpreted as the composition of $\mathbf{p}_1$ and $\mathbf{p}_2$ is internally represented by the composition of the associated internal model. Moreover, the modules mixing coefficients satisfy the following:

$$\Psi_j(\mathbf{p}) = \Psi_j(\mathbf{p}_1) + \Psi_j(\mathbf{p}_2) \quad j = 1 \ldots J, \tag{10.20}$$

which implies that these coefficients also share the compositional property.

Modularity of Inverse Models

The previous section has shown that the additivity of forces implies the additivity of forward models. Exploiting this property, the advantages of modular representations of forward internal models were discussed in detail. Interestingly, a similar result holds for inverse internal models. Specifically, following the procedure proposed in [Nori and Frezza, 2005], it can be shown that the modular inverse model (10.8) posses the same property described by (10.20). In particular, if a context $\mathbf{p}$ can be interpreted as the combination of the contexts $\mathbf{p}_1$ and $\mathbf{p}_2$, then the following holds:

$$\mu_j(\mathbf{p}) = \mu_j(\mathbf{p}_1) + \mu_j(\mathbf{p}_2) \quad j = 1 \dots J. \tag{10.21}$$

A proof demonstrating the correctness of the above equation falls outside the scope of this chapter and therefore is omitted here. The complete proof starts from (10.20) and uses the fact that the inverse model (10.8) depends linearly on the forward model (see [Nori and Frezza, 2005, Nori, 2005]).

10.4 Experimental Results

This section describes some experimental results that have been obtained by implementing a very simple modular control strategy on a humanoid robot that is used as a testing environment by the authors (see Fig. 10.3).

A major goal of this section is to demonstrate that equation (10.21) holds and can be used to predict the inverse model suitable in a context that is the combination of previously encountered contexts.

The experimental scenario is quite simple. The robot picks up a first object and explores its dynamic properties by learning a suitable inverse model. The robot then picks up a second object and explores this object likewise. Finally, a third object,

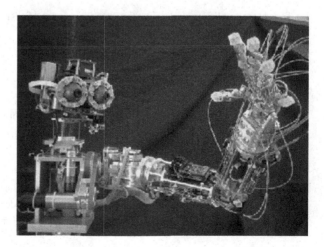

Fig. 10.3 James, a humanoid upper torso

usually the combination of the former two objects, is picked up and two alternatives are considered. The first alternative consists of exploring this third object as if it were a new object. The second alternative, on the other hand, exploits the fact that this new object is the combination of the two previously learned objects.

In order to simplify the scenario, this chapter considers a very simple inverse model corresponding with the motor torques necessary to compensate for the gravitational forces. Obviously, these torques depend on the dynamical properties of the object being grasped. The objects used in the experiment are two cylinders of different weight. The objects can be inserted one into the other so as to form a combined object.

During the exploration phase, the robot randomly moves its arm around while holding the objects. During this phase, the robot uses the first four degrees of freedom of the arm (three in the shoulder and one in the elbow). At each rest position, the motor torques necessary to support the arm are collected. The inverse model maps a given arm position $\mathbf{q}$ into the torques $\mathbf{u}$ necessary to counterbalance the gravitational forces. This model has been represented modularly as follows:[6]

$$\mathbf{u} = \sum_{j=1}^{J} \mu_j(\mathbf{p}) \Phi^j(\mathbf{q}). \tag{10.22}$$

The basis functions $\Phi^j(\mathbf{q})$ can be chosen freely. The results presented here followed a parametric strategy as proposed in [Kozlowski, 1998]. Alternative strategies could have been a support vector machine and radial basis function representations, for example. Given a collection of training pairs $(\mathbf{u}_k, \mathbf{q}_k)_{k=1}^{K}$ describing the torques to compensate gravity in a given context $\mathbf{p}$, the values for $\mu_j(\mathbf{p})$ are estimated by solving a minimum least squares problem:

$$[\hat{\mu}_1(\mathbf{p}) \ldots \hat{\mu}_J(\mathbf{p})] = \min_{\mu} \sum_{k=1}^{K} \left\| \mathbf{u}_k - \sum_{j=1}^{J} \mu_j \Phi^j(\mathbf{q}_k) \right\|^2. \tag{10.23}$$

In order to validate the estimation process, a set of testing pairs $(\mathbf{u}_l, \mathbf{q}_l)_{l=1}^{L}$ is used to compute the prediction errors $\mathbf{e}_l$:

$$\mathbf{e}_l = \mathbf{u}_l - \sum_{j=1}^{J} \hat{\mu}_j(\mathbf{p}) \Phi^j(\mathbf{q}_l). \tag{10.24}$$

The resulting mean square errors (MSE) have been computed and are reported in Table 10.1.

---

[6] This specific example is mainly interested in the context-dependent part of the inverse model. This is the reason why (10.22) differs from (10.8) where the goal dependent part was also included. Moreover, because gravity is compensated at rest, we also have $\dot{\mathbf{q}} = 0$.

Table 10.1 Mean square error results. The training set is composed of 300 samples, i.e., $K = 300$, and the test set of 100 samples, i.e., $L = 100$

Context	Training set MSE	Testing set MSE
$\mathbf{p}_1$	0.5392	0.6086
$\mathbf{p}_2$	0.5082	0.5638
$\mathbf{p}_{1\&2}$	0.6143	0.5770
$\mathbf{p}_1 + \mathbf{p}_2$	–	0.7458

Table 10.1 considers three contexts: (1) object held ($\mathbf{p}_1$); (2) object held ($\mathbf{p}_2$); and (3) both objects held ($\mathbf{p}_{1\&2}$). Finally, the bottom line in Table 10.1 corresponds with the mean square error obtained if instead of using the training data to estimate $\mu_j(\mathbf{p}_{1\&2})$ we simply use the property 10.21, i.e., $\mu_j(\mathbf{p}_{1\&2}) = \mu_j(\mathbf{p}_1) + \mu_j(\mathbf{p}_2)$. Even though the performance in this last case is not optimal, the obtained results are still interesting as they have been obtained without any learning on the training data.

10.5 Open Issues and Future Work

Modern artificial systems fail to adapt to the variety of situations that can be encountered in everyday life. Nowadays, even the most sophisticated machines are designed to work and operate within highly structured environments. Therefore, building highly interactive and adaptive systems capable of operating in a "human-like" environment seems to be a fundamental challenge in the field of robotics.

Within this context, recent studies have proposed the importance of modular control structures. Specifically, it has been argued that the big advantage of modularity lies in the possibility of combining previous experiences to handle new situations. As to this concern, this chapter demonstrated that the advantages of modularity can be exploited by interpreting the current context as the combination of previously experienced contexts. Moreover, it was pointed out that the variety of contexts in everyday life is such that every brute force adaptive strategy has to deal with the curse of dimensionality. As a consequence, innovative adaptive strategies scaling linearly with the number of contexts need to be considered. The authors believe that modularity possesses this property but also that many open issues remain before artificial systems can exploit their full potential.

The chapter focused specifically on motor control modularity, stressing its capability of adapting to modular contexts. However, the chapter did not deal with the issue of how to retrieve context-related sensory information from the environment. Clearly, acquiring this information requires sensors that are able to extract salient features from the surrounding environment. Therefore, the implementation of these ideas seems to fit perfectly within the field of humanoid robotics.

The authors are currently using a humanoid upper torso, James (see Fig. 10.3), as a testbed to further explore the potential of these ideas. The platform is currently equipped with three kinds of exteroceptive sensors: vision, force (Fig. 10.4), and touch sensors (Fig. 10.5).

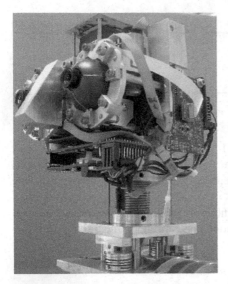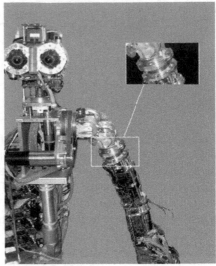

Fig. 10.4 Pictures of the vision (left) and force (right) sensors mounted on James. Vision is achieved with a stereo pair of digital cameras. External forces are measured with a six degrees of freedom force sensor placed in the forearm of the robot

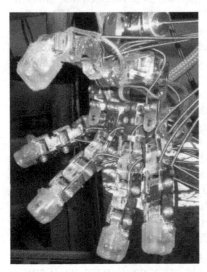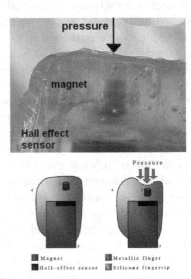

Fig. 10.5 Picture (left) and schematics (right) of the touch sensors mounted on the hand of James. Each fingertip has a couple of sensors based on a Hall effect technology. Eight more touch sensors are mounted on the phalanxes

Although, potentially, these sensors can be used to retrieve context-related information from the environment, representing this information modularly still remains an open issue to be further investigated.

Current work also explores the potential of the presented approach within the context of manipulation. Manipulating objects is a complicated task because of the high number of degrees of freedom of the hand and because of the multiplicity of objects that can be manipulated. Clearly, an exploration approach that scales exponentially with the complexity will fail within this context. The work presented here therefore also explores the modular approach as a technique to simplify the complexity of the task. Interestingly, there is evidence supporting the idea that a handful of motor synergies can be used in manipulation tasks. Finally, other ongoing research is not only investigating the potential of a smart mechanical design [Brown and Asada, 2007] but also the role of synergies in human manipulation [Santello et al., 1998, Baud-Bovy et al., 2005].

10.6 Conclusions

Modular control structures are appealing because there are contexts that can be modular as well. In order to investigate this concept, the presented work considered a simple movement (moving an arm toward a target) within different contexts (handling different objects). Intuitively, a modular control structure seems to be best suited to operate within modular contexts. In the specific problem of moving the arm while holding different objects, it was shown that the system dynamics are modular themselves. Taking advantage of this property, it was demonstrated that a modular control structure is capable of handling multiple contexts. Finally, the chapter proposed two ways for adaptively combining the modules. One adaptation is based on performance errors only. The other adaptation, which relies on the first, is used to combine the modules in unexperienced contexts that can be interpreted as the combination of previously experienced contexts.

Acknowledgments The work presented in this paper has been supported by the project ROBOT CUB (IST-2004-004370) and by the project NEUROBOTICS (IST-2003-511492). Both projects are funded by the European Union through the Sixth Framework Programme for Research and Technological Development (FP6).

A Minimum Number of Motion Primitives

A.1 Lower Bound on the Number of Elementary Controls

This section proves that any given solution of Problem 1 is composed by at least n elementary controls, i.e., $K \geq n$. Before giving the main result, it is important to recall the following lemma, claiming the injectivity of the function λ. In the following, the set of reachable states is denoted $\mathcal{X} \subseteq \mathbb{R}^n$.

Lemma 1. Let $\{\Phi^1, \ldots, \Phi^K\}$ and $\lambda : \mathcal{X} \to \mathbb{R}^K$ be a solution to Problem 1. Then $\lambda(\mathbf{x}_f)$ is injective.

Proof. Suppose by contradiction that there exist $\mathbf{x}_f^1$ and $\mathbf{x}_f^2$ such that $\mathbf{x}_f^1 \neq \mathbf{x}_f^2$ but $\lambda(\mathbf{x}_f^1) = \lambda(\mathbf{x}_f^2)$. Define:

$$\mathbf{u}^1 \overset{\triangle}{=} \sum_{k=1}^{K} \lambda_k(\mathbf{x}_f^1)\Phi^k(\mathbf{x}), \qquad (10.25)$$

$$\mathbf{u}^2 \overset{\triangle}{=} \sum_{k=1}^{K} \lambda_k(\mathbf{x}_f^2)\Phi^k(\mathbf{x}). \qquad (10.26)$$

Under the given assumption $\mathbf{u}^1 = \mathbf{u}^2$, but this contradicts the fact that $\mathbf{u}^1$ drives the system to $\mathbf{x}_f^1 \neq \mathbf{x}_f^2$. By contradiction, this proves that λ is injective. $\Diamond$

Proposition 1 *Let $\{\Phi^1, \ldots, \Phi^K\}$ and $\lambda : \mathcal{X} \to \mathbb{R}^K$ be a solution to Problem 1. Then $K \geq n$.*

Proof. Using Lemma 1, we have that $\lambda(\cdot)$ is a continuously differentiable injective function from an open subset of $\mathbb{R}^n$ to $\mathbb{R}^K$. It can be proved that this implies $K \geq n$ (see [Boothby, 2002] for details). $\Diamond$

A.2 Minimum Number of Elementary Controls

It was shown that we need at least n primitives to preserve controllability. It is here proved that n are not sufficient under suitable assumptions. Let us consider an affine nonlinear system of type 10.1. Let $\{\Phi^1, \ldots, \Phi^K\}$, $\lambda : \mathcal{X} \to \mathbb{R}^K$ be a solution to Problem 1. Moreover, define $\mathcal{X}_{\text{eq}} \subset \mathcal{X}$ to be the set of equilibrium points with $\mathbf{u} = 0$, i.e., $\mathbf{x}_f \in \mathcal{X}_{\text{eq}}$ if and only if $f(\mathbf{x}_f) = 0$. The proof of the main result requires the following additional assumption.

(HP). $\mathcal{X}_{\text{eq}} \neq \emptyset$ and $\forall \mathbf{x}_f \in \mathcal{X}_{\text{eq}}$ the solution of the following differential equation:

$$\begin{cases} \dot{\mathbf{x}} = f(\mathbf{x}) + g(\mathbf{x}) \sum_{k=1}^{K} \lambda_k(\mathbf{x}_f)\Phi^k(\mathbf{x}, t) \\ \mathbf{x}(0) = \mathbf{x}_f \end{cases}, \qquad (10.27)$$

is $\mathbf{x}(t) \equiv \mathbf{x}_f$, $\forall t \in [0, T]$. Basically, this is equivalent to requiring that if we start at an equilibrium point and we want to reach the same equilibrium point, then this is accomplished leaving the system in the same position for the entire time interval.

Theorem 2. *Let* $\{\Phi^1, \ldots, \Phi^K\}$, $\lambda : \mathcal{X} \to \mathbb{R}^K$ *be a solution to Problem 1 with dynamics given by (10.1). Moreover, assume that for the given solution, (HP) holds. Then* $K \geq n + 1$.

Proof. Suppose by contradiction that $K < n + 1$. Because it was shown that $K \geq n$, only one possibility is left out: $K = n$. Define:

$$\Phi(\mathbf{x}, t) \stackrel{\Delta}{=} [\Phi^1(\mathbf{x}, t) \ldots \Phi^n(\mathbf{x}, t)] \quad \lambda(\mathbf{x}_f) \stackrel{\Delta}{=} [\lambda_1(\mathbf{x}_f) \ldots \lambda_n(\mathbf{x}_f)]^\top \quad (10.28)$$

so that the following holds:

$$\sum_{k=1}^{n} \lambda_k(\mathbf{x}_f)\Phi^k(\mathbf{x}, t) = \Phi(\mathbf{x}, t)\lambda(\mathbf{x}_f). \quad (10.29)$$

Because the proposed primitives solve Problem 1, the following system:

$$\begin{cases} \dot{\mathbf{x}} = f(\mathbf{x}) + g(\mathbf{x}) \quad \Phi(\mathbf{x}, t)\lambda(\mathbf{x}_f) \\ \mathbf{x}(0) = \mathbf{x}_0 \in \mathcal{X} \end{cases}, \quad (10.30)$$

converges to $\mathbf{x}_f$, $\forall \mathbf{x}_f \in \mathcal{X}$ regardless of the initial condition. Consider $\mathbf{x}_f \in \mathcal{X}_{eq}$ and $\mathbf{x}(0) = \mathbf{x}_f$. Using (HP) in (10.30) we get:

$$g(\mathbf{x}_f)\Phi(\mathbf{x}_f, t)\lambda(\mathbf{x}_f) = 0, \quad \forall t \in [0, T]. \quad (10.31)$$

Now, let us use the fact that the image of $\mathcal{X}$ under $\lambda : \mathcal{X} \to \mathbb{R}^n$ is an open set in $\mathbb{R}^n$. This is consequence of the fact that λ is injective and $\mathcal{C}^1(\mathcal{X})$ with $\mathcal{X}$ open (see [Boothby, 2002] for details). If $\mathrm{Im}_\lambda(\mathcal{X})$ is open and $\lambda(\mathbf{x}_f) \in \mathrm{Im}_\lambda(\mathcal{X})$, we can always find $\mu \neq 1$ such that $\mu\lambda(\mathbf{x}_f) \in \mathrm{Im}_\lambda(\mathcal{X})$; we only need to take $|1 - \mu|$ small enough. Therefore, there always exists $\tilde{\mathbf{x}}_f \in \mathcal{X}$, such that $\lambda(\tilde{\mathbf{x}}_f) = \mu\lambda(\mathbf{x}_f)$. According to the given hypothesis, the following system:

$$\begin{cases} \dot{\mathbf{x}} = f(\mathbf{x}) + g(\mathbf{x}) \quad \Phi(\mathbf{x}, t)\lambda(\tilde{\mathbf{x}}_f) \\ \mathbf{x}(0) = \mathbf{x}_0 \in \mathcal{X} \end{cases}, \quad (10.32)$$

should converge to $\tilde{\mathbf{x}}_f$ regardless of the initial condition. However, take $\mathbf{x}_0 = \mathbf{x}_f$, and observe that the corresponding trajectory is given by $\mathbf{x}(t) \equiv \mathbf{x}_f$, $\forall t \in [0, T]$ as we have:

$$\dot{\mathbf{x}} = f(\mathbf{x}_f) + g(\mathbf{x}_f)\Phi(\mathbf{x}_f, t)\lambda(\tilde{\mathbf{x}}_f) = \mu g(\mathbf{x}_f)\Phi(\mathbf{x}_f, t)\lambda(\mathbf{x}_f) \stackrel{(10.31)}{=} 0 \quad \forall t \in [0, T]. \quad (10.33)$$

Therefore, we have found an initial condition for (10.32) that is not driven to $\tilde{\mathbf{x}}_f$. This is in contradiction to our hypothesis. $\diamondsuit$

References

Baud-Bovy, G., Rossi, S., and Prattichizzo, D. (2005). Effect of transcranial magnetic stimulaton on the grip and net force in the tripod grasp. In *Proceedings of the 1st Joint Eurohaptics Conference and Symposium on Haptic Interfaces for Virtual Environment and Teleoperator Systems (WHC'05)*, pages 120–125, Pisa, Italy, 18–20 March. IEEE Computer Society, Washington, DC.

Boothby, W. M. (2002). *An Introduction to Differentiable Manifolds and Riemannian Geometry*. Academic Press, New York, 2nd edition.

Brashers-Krug, T., Shadmehr, R., and Bizzi, E. (1996). Consolidation in human motor memory. *Nature*, 382:252–255.

Brown, C. and Asada, H. (2007). Inter-finger coordination and postural synergies in robot hands via mechanical implementation of principal components analysis. In *Proceedings of IEEE/RSJ International Conference on Intelligent Robots and Systems (IROS'07)*, pages 2877–2882, California, San Diego, CA, 29 October–2 November.

Davidson, P. and Wolpert, D. (2004). Internal models underlying grasp can be additively combined. *Experimental Brain Research*, 155(3):334–340.

Fadiga, L., Fogassi, L., Gallese, V., and Rizzolatti, G. (2000). Visuomotor neurons: ambiguity of the discharge or motor perception? *International Journal of Psychophysiology*, 35:165–177.

Flanagan, J. R. and Rao, A. K. (1995). Trajectory adaptation to a nonlinear visuomotor transformation: evidence of motion planning in visually perceived space. *Journal of Neurophysiology*, 74(5):2174–2178.

Ghahramani, Z. and Wolpert, D. (1997). Modular decomposition in visuomotor learning. *Nature*, 386(6623):392–395.

Kozlowski, K. (1998). *Modelling and Identification in Robotics*. Springer-Verlag, New York, 1st edition.

Krakauer, J., Ghilardi, M., and Ghez, C. (1999). Independent learning of internal models for kinematic and dynamic control of reaching. *Nature Neuroscience*, 2(11):1026–1031.

Murray, R. M., Li, Z., and Sastry, S. S. (1994). *A Mathematical Introduction to Robotic Manipulation*. CRC Press, Inc., Boca Raton, FL.

Mussa-Ivaldi, F. and Giszter, S. (1992). Vector field approximation: a computational paradigm for motor control and learning. *Biological Cybernetics*, 37:491–500.

Mussa-Ivaldi, F. A. (1997). Nonlinear force fields: a distributed system of control primitives for representing and learning movements. In *Proceedings of the IEEE International Symposium on Computational Intelligence in Robotics and Automation (CIRA'97)*, page 84, Los Alamitos, CA. IEEE Computer Society.

Mussa-Ivaldi, F. A. and Bizzi, E. (2000). Motor learning through the combination of primitives. *Philosophical Transactions of the Royal Society: Biological Sciences*, 355:1755–1769.

Nori, F. (2005). *Symbolic Control with Biologically Inspired Motion Primitives*. PhD thesis, Università degli studi di Padova.

Nori, F. and Frezza, R. (2004a). Biologically inspired control of a kinematic chain using the superposition of motion primitives. In *Proceedings of 43rd IEEE Conference on Decision and Control (CDC'04)*, pages 1075–1080, Atlantis, Paradise Island, Bahamas.

Nori, F. and Frezza, R. (2004b). Nonlinear control by a finite set of motion primitives. In *Proceedings of the 6th IFAC Symposium on Nonlinear Control Systems Design (NOLCOS'04)*, pages 393–398, Stuttgart, Germany, 1–3 September.

Nori, F. and Frezza, R. (2005). A control theory approach to the analysis and synthesis of the experimentally observed motion primitives. *Biological Cybernetics*, 93(5):323–342.

Santello, M., Flanders, M., and J.Soechting (1998). Postural hand synergies for tool use. *The Journal of Neuroscience*, 18(23):10105–10115.

Sastry, S. and Bodson, M. (1989). *Adaptive control: Stability, Convergence, and Robustness*. Prentice-Hall, Inc., Upper Saddle River, NJ.

Shadmehr, R. and Mussa-Ivaldi, F. A. (1994). Adaptive representation of dynamics during learning of a motor task. *Journal of Neuroscience*, 14:3208–3224.

Shelhamer, M., Robinson, D., and Tan, H. (1991). Context-specific gain switching in the human vestibuloocular reflex. *Annals of the New York Academy of Sciences*, 656(5):889–891.

Slotine, J. E. and Li, W. (1991). *Applied NonLinear Control*. Prentice-Hall International.

Welch, R., Bridgeman, B., Anand, S., and Brownman, K. (1993). Alternating prism exposure causes dual adaptation and generalization to a novel displacement. *Perception and Psychophysics*, 54(2):195–204.

Wolpert, D. and Kawato, M. (1998). Multiple paired forward and inverse models for motor control. *Neural Networks*, 11:1317–1329.

Part IV
Robustness in Space Applications

Chapter 11
Robustness as Key to Success for Space Missions

Olaf Maibaum, Sergio Montenegro, and Thomas Terzibaschian

Abstract To lead space missions to a success requires a high degree of autonomous intelligence in software and highly reliable hardware. In particular, all software and hardware components should be robust against failures, inexact measurement of data, and, ideally, unforeseen events. This chapter provides an introduction to the demanding conditions in the space environment and describes measures in hardware and software and their testing that are necessary for the development of robust systems for space missions.

11.1 Introduction

Systems for space missions require a high degree of robustness and inbuilt "intelligence" in order to complete missions successfully. This is mainly because in the event of complications, a direct intervention of a human operator is not possible as a rule. A main reason for this lies in the limited time that is available for communication and data transmission between spacecraft and ground station. This applies in particular to deep space missions. For example, a direct data transmission between Mars and ground requires approximately 10 minutes. Thus, a complete interaction with the spacecraft communicating a reaction to an unforeseen event takes about 20 minutes.

Because of these restrictions, a spacecraft must be equipped with a high degree of autonomy and robustness. The control hardware and control software are required to recognize irregularities in both, hardware and software, and have to initiate suitable measures for troubleshooting in order to guarantee the survival of a mission. This goal can only be achieved with a sufficient degree of implemented intelligence in the software and a dependable hardware platform.

O. Maibaum

German Aerospace Center, Department of Simulation and Software Technology, Lilienthalplatz 7, D-38108 Braunschweig, Germany

e-mail: olaf.maibaum@dlr.de

A. Schuster (ed.), *Robust Intelligent Systems,* DOI: 10.1007/978-1-84800-261-6_11,
© Springer-Verlag London Limited 2008

This chapter investigates how this goal may be achieved. Initially, the chapter describes some of the many challenges in space a spacecraft is required to handle autonomously. The chapter then introduces measures in hardware and software with which some of these difficult conditions in space may be met. Finally, the chapter presents, briefly, methodologies with which the control software and its robustness are tested.

11.2 Challenge Space

The ambient conditions in space pose a challenge for the requirements for a spacecraft—in particular for its electronic components. The design of a spacecraft therefore must fulfil these requirements in order to be able to lead a space mission to success. The biggest challenge for the spacecraft developers is, on this occasion, always the unknown, which may arise from incomplete data or other material about the target area (please note that [ECSS-E10-04A, 2000] provides more detailed information on this topic).

11.2.1 Temperature, Vacuum, and Launch

For example, the extreme temperatures in space are a challenge for the design of satellites. Most electronic components are in working order only in temperature ranges of −40°C to +80°C, and batteries for energy storage are in working order only in a rather limited temperature range, too. The optimum operation range for the electronic components is given at +20°C, but the normal temperature in space lies around −270°C. On irradiated surfaces, temperatures of more than +100°C can be reached by the heat radiation of the Sun and that of other planets. These temperature requirements must be taken into consideration in the temperature design of a spacecraft. For example, temperature conditions may result in the operation of a spacecraft where certain devices or surfaces of the spacecraft may not be aligned in the direction of the Sun or the ground to avoid superheating.

Operation in vacuum is another challenge for spacecrafts. For instance, the operation of electric components in vacuum complicates the removal of the heat generated by a component. Hence, on a circuit board, heat conductors that transport the generated heat off the components to a temperature emitter must also exist. However, gas inclusions or liquids in this environment can lead to damage in components. Particularly problematic in this regard are capacitors that contain liquids as a dielectric. This dielectric can resign under vacuum and destroy the component and other components by it.

Spacecraft also experience extreme vibrations at their launch. In particular, short accelerations with a multiple of the Earth's acceleration can appear. During operation in space, spacecraft with propulsion systems experience strong vibrations during the operation of these systems. For example, for fixed electronic devices, the loosening of electrically conducting components by vibration may lead to short circuits in the electronics of the spacecraft. Besides, the materials used should have no mechanical eigenfrequency in the frequency spectrum of the expected vibrations (e.g., this could lead to the rupture of boards during the launch or the operation of propulsion systems).

11.2.2 Magnetism, Cosmic Radiation, Particles, and Gravity

Another factor not to be neglected for spacecraft in low Earth orbit is magnetism. Spacecraft in low Earth orbit move within the magnetic field of the Earth. This leads to an electromagnetic charging of the spacecraft. In case of bigger satellites, differences in potential may be produced through this. On the surface of a spacecraft, differences in potential of a few volts only result, but during the approach of two spacecraft several kilovolts may be created. A sudden discharge of such differences in potential can lead to damage in the electronics of a spacecraft. One of the consequences of this is that in satellites, only materials should be used that cannot be affected by magnetism, otherwise, for example, a dipole moment may be created that influences the attitude of the satellite or disturbs the sensors of the satellite. However, both effects can also be used for satellite operation, for example, for power production or the alignment of the spacecraft.

Cosmic radiation is another key challenge for electronic systems in space [Stassinopoulos and Brucker, 1992]. Cosmic radiation consists of protons, alpha particles, heavy ions, electrons, and neutrons. These particles can cause three kinds of effects in the integrated circuits: Total Ionizing Dose (TID), Single Event Upset (SEU), and Single Event Latch Up (SEL).

- TID causes a quicker ageing of the silicon components. The ageing causes slowly—but continuously—an increase of power consumption and internal noise. If by the signal/noise ratio in a component no clear separation between the signal and the noise is permissible, then this component is constantly corrupt. TID is measured in the SI unit Gray [Gy = J/kg]. The radiation intensity depends on the orbit. For spacecraft with low Earth orbit, 30 Gy to 100 Gy per year is a good estimate. Normal electronic components survive approximately 300 Gy, and space-certified (radiation hard) components are laid out for a dose of 3 kGy. For comparison, 10 Gy is already deadly for a human.
- SEU and SEL together are also referred to as Single Event Effect (SEE). Both effects are caused on semiconductors by the impact of single particles rich in energy. The adjacent particle delivers energy to the surrounding material and causes an ionization in the material. Through this, an ion track originates in the semiconductor material. If this happens within a flip flop or a memory cell, then this can change the state of a memory cell. Thus, the saved data may also be changed (SEU). However, the components themselves are not damaged in this process. Developers should count on up to 10 SEUs per day.

- Single Event Latch Ups (SEL) are power spikes or voltage peaks that can damage a component permanently. A charged particle can cause an ion track in the semiconductor substrate and, through this, cause a high current flow on the chip surface. If these high current flows are not interrupted immediately, then circuit paths can be interrupted on the chip. However, SELs are extremely rare, and several years may pass before a SEL appears.

Besides radiation, a spacecraft may also be hit by solid particles. These particles may have a natural origin (e.g., meteorites) or originate from the use of space itself (e.g., space debris) [Mulholland and Veillet, 2004]. In any case, a collision with solid parts can lead (depending on the kinetic energies involved) to substantial structural damage in a spacecraft. Space garbage caused by the space industry is a particular concern for spacecraft in low Earth orbit. For example, space garbage with more than 10 cm edge size is registered and traced by space organizations. This information helps with the planning of the launch of a mission in order to avoid collision with these particles. On the other hand, the collision with smaller particles cannot be foreseen and thus is a potential danger for the loss of a spacecraft.

Movable components in spacecraft are a further source of danger for the failure of a space mission. Movable parts may get caught or freeze by humidity. In most cases, this humidity may originate from condensate during the launch phase in start places close to the semitropical regions and the Equator. Movable components also wear out over time. Hence, spacecraft developers usually completely renounce movable parts, or their movements for overcoming adhesion are initiated by pyrotechnics.

A lack of gravity is only challenging for mechanical components because movable parts cannot be moved or fixed by gravitational forces. For this purpose pyrotechnics, springs, or electric motors are used as a rule. For control systems, the lack of gravity is only a challenge for testing, because their effectiveness can be tested in the laboratory only under gravitational influence. Consequently, because of the lack of "true" space conditions in the laboratory, new components are also often carried along for space qualification (space qualification means that a component is tested under space conditions) as an additional payload in a satellite mission.

11.3 Robustness in the Hardware

It is possible to intercept a large number of introduced malfunctions in a space system through special hardware. This can be done, for example, via the use of special materials for the hardware or via circuits that are designed with fault-tolerance in mind.

11.3.1 Materials and Pre-treatment of Used Materials

A first measure for attaining robustness consists in the choice of materials and the pre-treatment of used materials. For example, the used components should contain no liquids or gases that can resign in vacuum and so lead to damage. For instance, capacitors should not contain liquids as a dielectric—if they do then their design must also prevent stamping out the liquid in vacuum. Aerial inclusions in integrated components also can lead to problems in vacuum. As a rule, the materials are tested several times before their installation in a vacuum chamber so that they can outgas. The high failure probability of new components is likewise reduced by this so-called "burn in". Besides this, attention is being paid on the choice of the materials such that only materials with similar thermal expansion are used (e.g., in compound components).

The choice of electric components is also limited to components that own a protection against the radiation existing in space and may be achieved by layers of gold, for example. A suitable protection reduces TID and thus also the ageing of the components. In case no adequately protected components are available, then a suitable protection must be created by the surrounding materials. For example, components that are particularly sensitive to radiation should be placed only inside the spacecraft because the surrounding components already provide some protection.

Against SEL, only the monitoring of the electric currents can be used. If a sudden rising current is registered by the latch up protection, all affected electric components are immediately separated electrically. This avoids the burning through of the electric components. More precisely, to be able to recognize the voltage peaks, it is advisable to monitor all components separated from each other.

11.3.2 Redundancy and Redundancy Management

An important principle to achieve increased reliability is the use of multiple (redundancy) components [Tanenbaum, 1995]. Here, it is necessary to distinguished between "cold" and "hot" redundancy. Cold redundant components form silent reserves that are not in operation. With a permanent failure of a component, this silent reserve is put into operation as a substitute. Hot redundant components are permanently in operation and in case of a malfunction can take over immediately the task(s) of other components. Both principles differ in the speed at which an operation of a redundant component can occur. Naturally, the introduction of a hot redundant component can occur faster than that of a cold redundant component. Nevertheless, hot redundant components have the disadvantage that they are subjected to ageing, and their power demand must be provided, too.

However, robustness cannot be achieved with the use of redundant components only. In order to achieve robustness, an "optimum redundancy management" is also required. This managing component decisively influences the design of the software and hardware of the complete spacecraft. One kind of redundancy management is the introduction of a comparative function by a so-called "voter". The voter components compare different signals with each other in order to recognize faulty signals. If two source signals are compared with each other, faults can only be recognized in the signals, but not localized. In this way, two components can be connected with

Fig. 11.1 Two modules with comparator

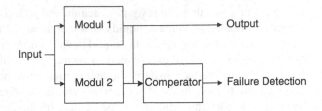

each other and the correctness of the signal determined with a comparator [Poledna, 1996]. Figure 11.1 illustrates a possible setup.

With more than two signals, it is possible to correct a faulty signal by a majority decision. The probability for two faulty signals of the same kind is extremely low, so that a correct signal of the components at the output of the voter can be accepted.

11.3.3 Fault-Recognition and Fault-Correcting Codes

Fault-recognition and fault-correcting codes are used for the protection of data storage and data transmission [Tanenbaum, 1996]. For example, parity bits that can recognize odd bit errors can be used for error detection. Faulty bytes can be recognized, for example, by the use of double data storage and a replacement of itself with the redundant bytes. Fault-correcting codes like Hamming code or Reed Solomon's code have enough redundant information within themselves to recover the original information, provided that the number of the faulty bits is not too high in an information unit [Stone et al., 1998].

The hardware mechanisms for the construction of a robust hardware platform mentioned so far are not included in standard CPUs (central processing units). This is why it can come to data falsifications in standard CPUs. Hence, the LEON central processing unit [Pouponnot, 2005], which is based on the Sparc V8 architecture, was developed by order of ESA (European Space Agency). Inside, the LEON3FT central processing unit has a fault-tolerant architecture toward SEU that is able to correct up to four bit errors per 32-bit word in the registers and the cache memory. The LEON CPU is protected, but slower than standard CPUs. Provided that the marginal conditions admit it, developers try to use normal COTS (commercial off the shelf) hardware. The required redundancy is built up externally or by software. For example, two or three CPUs can be used together and their results compared with each other in order to recognize faults.

Further, so-called "watchdogs" are used in order to recognize software running out of control by faulty data. A watchdog is a counter that triggers a reset of a component after a certain duration [Murphy, 2000]. The monitored component must announce itself to the watchdog with "Keep Alive" messages to reset the counter to its start value. If the counter of the watchdog runs off, then the watchdog triggers a reset. Watchdogs are often included in microprocessors for embedded systems. However, they can also be taken into consideration as external components in a processor board design.

11.4 Robustness in the Software

Some of the biggest disadvantages of the hardware measures mentioned earlier to build a robust system are the mass, the size, and the power consumption of additional hardware. Measures related to the increase of robustness in software do not have these disadvantages. Spacecraft design therefore aims to find a well-balanced compromise between hardware and software solutions. For example, voters may not be implemented in hardware, but can maybe be realized in software. Besides, signal processing algorithms can be realized in software instead of a realization in hardware by specially developed components. In case of hardware solutions, the big disadvantage compared with software solutions is that they cannot be customized to changing basic conditions. This may become necessary, for example, through the failure or the ageing of components, but also through incorrect assumptions about the target area of a space mission.

11.4.1 Noise, Bias, and Missing Data

A system designer also has to assume that sensor data are typically affected with noise, bias, and missing data. Noise parameters and bias values can change over the mission time, and data gaps may arise suddenly. An essential principle in dealing with sensor data therefore is that sensor data have to be monitored all the time. A suitable device for this purpose is the well-known Kalman filter [Kalman, 1960, Brammer and Siffling, 1989]. The device was originally designed for noise reduction but it also has the potential to contribute to robustness and autonomy. This is why it is presented here more explicitly with a clear focus on the topic of robustness (it is not the intention here to go into too much detail of the filter theory).

A simple example may be the determination of the Earth's magnetic field vector B by using data taken by a magnetometer. In fact, the magnetometer measures the vector of the magnetic flux density in the unit Tesla. All raw sensor data have a certain noise level. This measurement noise is assumed here to be uncorrelated and normally distributed white noise. A Kalman filter algorithm is based on the introduction of "a priori knowledge". This knowledge is introduced by mathematical models of the underlying physical processes of measurement, system dynamics, or the noise process itself. A simple model may be, for example, that the magnetic field is stationary (like in a laboratory):

$$\frac{d}{dt}B = 0 \tag{11.1}$$

Although the real magnetic field in a lab is never constant due to several disturbances, the important aspect is that the model in equation 11.1 permits a prediction of B. The model assumption of the constant magnetic field is valid on average but there are usually fluctuations. These fluctuations can be measured and described by statistical parameters. So it is possible to connect the predicted B vector with an uncertainty parameter due to the model uncertainty (the fluctuations). The prediction can start with the first measured B vector as an initial value. This initial value has the variance of the measurement noise. The prediction uncertainty is increasing with the prediction time span due to the model uncertainty. When the next B vector is measured (again with measurement uncertainty), there are two B values available—the predicted value and the measured value. The prediction uncertainty and the measurement uncertainty will be used for computing a weighted B vector. This estimated B vector incorporates the measurement process and the a priori knowledge, presented here by a simple system state equation 11.1. Its uncertainty can be better than the raw measurement variance. So it can be used as the next initial value for further prediction. This initial value can be more accurate than the first initial value, and so the next predicted value becomes more accurate than the first predicted value, and so on. In this way, the estimation accuracy usually

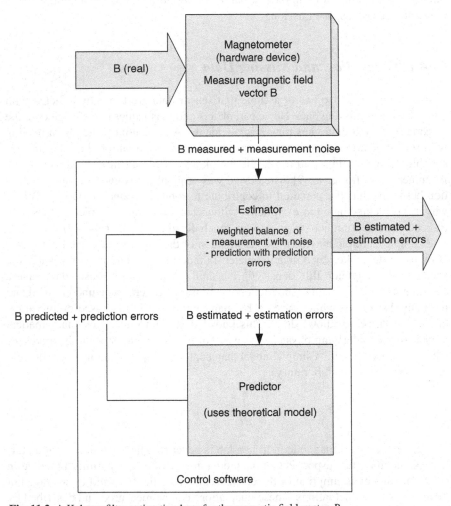

Fig. 11.2 A Kalman filter estimation loop for the magnetic field vector B

converges to an estimation accuracy that is better than the pure raw data accuracy while measurement, prediction, and estimation are running in a loop. Figure 11.2 illustrates this typical loop for a simple example.

The real B vector is measured by the magnetometer. The output is the measured vector plus measurement noise. It will be fed into the estimator where it is combined with the vector predicted for the same time. The new estimated B vector for the same time is the output of the complete sensor processing. It is usually used instead of raw data and it will be fed into the predictor, which uses the known system dynamics for a prediction to that time when the next measured vector arrives and so on.

So far, the filter is a tool for noise reduction. But some small changes of this figure lead to the topics of robustness and autonomy. This is illustrated in Fig. 11.3.

In particular, the changes are:

1. The sensor is connected to the estimator by a logical *use switch*, the sensor can be *in use* or *not in use*.
2. The estimator module itself can be *enabled* or *disabled*.
3. The estimator compares the difference between prediction and measurement (the so-called innovation) with a new threshold value.
4. The predictor can be *enabled* or *disabled*.

The complete filter module can be configured now by setting the *use switch* and by enabling or disabling the estimator and/or predictor. In fact, the used threshold value is also part of the configuration. The output now depends on the actual configuration given in Table 11.1.

The threshold evaluation is used for the identification of sensor processing problems. Unlikely deviations of measurements from predicted values indicate a problem. In this simple example, it can be used only for a signalization of the problem— the sensor would get a "not healthy flag". It only indicates that there is a problem— either with the sensor or with the estimation loop. A big improvement comes with the combination of configurable filters and redundant sensors. This combination permits the introduction of another threshold value for the direct comparison of signals from each redundant sensor. If there was a redundant sensor in a parallel processing loop, then it becomes really possible to locate the problem either at one of the two redundant sensors or at the filter algorithm. In the first case, the problematic sensor is set to "not in use" and will get the "I am not healthy" flag. But the signal processing is not really stopped. In the second case, the predictor has to be disabled and the loop is going on with raw data from both redundant sensors. In a space environment, it is quite common to have redundant sensors. In combination with the configurable Kalman filter, it gives a robust behavior, because single sensor failures can be detected automatically, and reduces only the output accuracy. Even signal gaps in two redundant sensors will not completely stop the delivery of useful output signals. Last but not least, the redundant sensors allow identification of problems in the estimator and predictor part. This is why a filter reconfiguration can automatically fix the problem. Including the right tuning of the used threshold values, it is a powerful and proven tool for automatic and autonomous fault detection, isolation, and recovery.

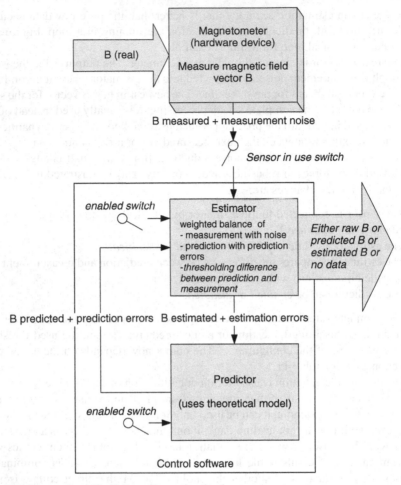

Fig. 11.3 The configurable Kalman filter estimation loop

Table 11.1 Filter configurations

Sensor	Estimator	Predictor	Output	Remark
In use	Enabled	Enabled	Estimated value	Best accuracy, threshold evaluation
Not in use	Enabled	Enabled	Predicted value	Can fill sensor gaps, accuracy is going down over time. No threshold evaluation.
Not in use	Disabled	–	No output	The complete processing is "switched off"
In use	Enabled	Disabled	Raw data	No threshold evaluation

11.4.2 Software Redundancy, N-version Programming, and Measurement Analysis

The principle of the redundancy can also be applied in software. For example, corruptions can be excluded in calculations by a SEU with the multiple calculation of a formula and the comparison of the generated arithmetic results. Through this, CPU architectures can also be used in space applications that do not dispose of redundancy to the interception of SEU.

Another redundancy principle for achieving increased levels of robustness is the use of several software versions for a calculation—so-called n-version-programming [Lyu, 1995]. The different software versions should be created by different developing teams on the basis of identical requirements and interfaces. Thus, permanent faults that may appear only under certain marginal conditions during operation may be recognized in software. However, because of multiple development expenses, this principle is seldom applied in practice.

Basically, in this approach all input data and intermediate results are to be checked for validity before their use. This principle avoids the unlimited propagation of faults. The same principle is also applied if the source of the data is a trustworthy module and, hence, no incorrect values are used. Changes of the data within control systems are possible by environmental conditions in space, even beyond the control flow.

Beside the installation of redundant sensors, it is also possible in the software to derive other physical values according to the physical principles from values measured at different times. This can be derived, for example, from two measured direction vectors, a rotation; from two positions, the speed; or from two positions and the speed, the acceleration. As a rule, these computed values have a higher inaccuracy than values of measuring apparatuses especially laid out for this purpose. However, they increase the redundancy for the measurement of some physical states. Through this, values obtained from not redundant laid-out sensors can be checked on their validity and rejected in case of unacceptable deviations.

Figure 11.4 illustrates the principle of the choice of functioning sensors.

An expected state space in which future measurement values lie without any control activities and annoying influence arises from the measured data at times

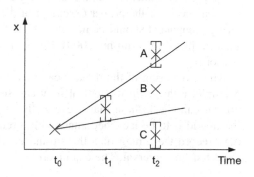

Fig. 11.4 Identification of valid sensors

t_0 and t_1 and the confidence interval of the measured value. At time t_2, values are measured by three sensors. The measurement value of sensor B lies clearly within the expected state space and consequently is accepted as valid. The value obtained by sensor C lies clearly outside the expected state space and so is evaluated as faulty. The value obtained by sensor A may lie within the measuring noise interval of the sensor and also within the expected state space and so is not evaluated as faulty but "unsafe". This principle can be used for the "in use flag" of the configurable Kalman filter in Fig. 11.3.

The measured data can be combined by calculating a weighted average of the various sensor readings. As far as possible, only valid identified values should be used. Unsafe measured data may be included with a lower weighting. The weighting of the single sensor systems takes place according to the quality of the measured data. Sensors with a high noise ratio receive a lower weight than do sensors working with high precision. In case an evaluation of the measured data detects a lot of results outside the expected state space, then an external influence or a failure in the actuators can be assumed. In this case, no evaluation of the measured data can be carried out, and all measured data are to be taken into consideration in the averaging process. If a high number of invalid measurement results is observed permanently, then the cause can be classified as an actuator defect. The sensors that supply invalid data often or permanently are to be classified by the control software as corrupt. Such sensors are to be unloaded permanently from the control system.

11.4.3 Software Flow Control

The principles mentioned so far in the control software for obtaining robustness are concerned merely with the correctness of the data being processed. Another possible source for error concerns the control flow within the software. The programmed control flow can be left by corruption in the object code or the corruption of program pointers and return addresses in the stack of the software. The consequences of such a fault cannot be predicted and can be repaired only by a reload and restart of the affected systems.

To recognize such faults, a monitoring component is required in an application that watches over the proper execution of the threads in an application. The monitoring component should be monitored itself again by a hardware watchdog of the satellite platform [Murphy, 2000]. Figure 11.5 illustrates this for idea for a single platform.

The monitoring of the threads can be achieved with different mechanisms. For example, a thread in its control flow can set marks and the "surveillance" component can check these marks cyclically. If the marks are not correctly set, then the thread is to be launched anew with a renewed object code. Another approach may record the timing of a thread and check whether this timing lies within an expected time interval. The examination of the timing also allows the checking of

Fig. 11.5 Monitoring cascade

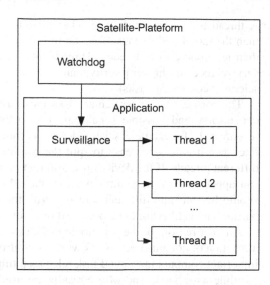

temporal dependencies between threads. This is particularly important in case of a loose coupling between threads.

In addition, the surveillance component should provide an interface for the threads where events about the threads can be announced. Possible events may be state changes in the controller, invalid measurement results of sensors, special decisions in the control flow of a thread, or the reception of messages.

With a discovered non-conformity in the execution of the threads, the surveillance component decides actively on a measure to bring the system back to a regular state. The catalogue of measures includes the recording of an irregularity in the housekeeping data, the repair of subcomponents in the application, the deactivation or exchange of components, the transition to special control strategies as for example to the safe mode (explained in more detail later), up to the restart of an application or the overall system.

The kind of measures for the removal of the non-conformity strongly depends on the requirements of the application, in particular on those of the availability of the system. The availability of the system is defined by the safety integrity level (SIL) which is defined by standards IEC 61508 [IEC 61508, 2005] and IEC 61511 [IEC 61511, 2004]. For example, in an application with SIL 4, no down-times may show. That is, a restart of the application cannot be carried out. In this case, a hot redundant subassembly must take over the control actively. For SIL 3, a cold redundant subassembly can take over the control. For SIL 2, a restart of the system is possible. Applications under SIL 4 are, for example, control systems for the flight path in manned missions. For Earth observation satellites, a reboot of the system is possible without serious consequences.

The partitioning of tasks within the software into threads and their priorities is an important design criterion. The assigned priorities for the scheduling of the threads within an application are defined by their importance and their time criticality.

A thread for the monitoring of other threads has, for example, a higher priority than the monitored threads. Threads in time-critical areas have a higher criticality than less time-critical threads. Threads involved with tasks that are important for survival receive a higher priority than other threads (e.g., threads performing simple scientific computing tasks).

The partitioning of particular tasks into threads also requires considering the dependency and possible synchronization between the tasks as well as limited resources. If, for example, several devices communicate on a single communication line, then it makes no sense to split the communication between the devices into different threads. If the devices use different communication busses and blockades can appear within the communication, then the communication with the devices should be split into different threads. With the treatment of redundant devices, a partitioning is likewise to be preferred over several threads.

Another reason for the partitioning of a task into several threads is the temporal allocation of computer resources within a controlling cycle. The interruption of an important computation-bound task releases a time slot for less important tasks that are time-wise bound and whose results are used as input data for other important tasks. Without this free time slot, the less important tasks would have to be provided with a higher priority. This, however, could lead to the blockade of the more important tasks (e.g., in the case of a high extent of utilization or a fault in the control flow within a less important task). As an alternative, it is obvious to interrupt the loop body of the important thread several times. Nevertheless, this alternative signifies an additional expenditure for the planning of the resource allocations in the system and complicates the maintenance of the software.

For the communication between different threads, basically asynchronous communication mechanisms are to be used to avoid blockades. In case of use of synchronized communication mechanisms, an inheritance of a low priority is to be avoided to a thread with high priority. This can be achieved by a communication protocol with influence on the scheduling of the threads [Rajkumar, 1991]. To prevent the appearance of deadlocks, a cycle formation between the use of protected regions to the data interchange is to be avoided. Moreover, for the entry into a protected region, the order of the entries must correspond with the priorities of the threads [Weske, 1995, Silberschatz and Galvin, 1994].

To protect the survival of a satellite, a safe mode is defined. The safe mode offers a minimum control strategy that satisfies the marginal conditions for the survival of the satellite until an intervention by ground control is possible. With this control strategy, only inexact sensors and actuators are used with a reduction of the control accuracy. The target of the control strategy is to reach a high charging current in the solar panels of the satellite to avoid an unloading of the batteries. In addition, the satellite is set by the processing of a safe mode list in a configuration with a low energy consumption. A scientific use of the satellite is not possible in this mode as a rule. These satellite control modes are always triggered when a reboot of the systems became necessary or if important sensors or actuators have fallen out and this cannot be treated any more with high reliability by the autonomous onboard software.

11.5 Testing Robustness

The testing of the used methods is essential for the development of a robust control software. Actually, different test approaches accompany the development of the control software. More specifically, these test are module test, different test approaches in the closed control loop with a simulation of the controlled system, and fault injection [Broekman and Notenboom, 2003]. The forthcoming sections describe these approaches in more detail.

The first possibility is the module test. In a test-driven development approach, the module tests are developed before the actual implementation of the module. One advantage of this process is that a developer involved in the test development gains an increased insight about the requirements for the module before the first line of code of the implementation is actually written. Eventually, the insights acquired from the development of the module test increase the quality of the implementing, in particular that of the module interfaces.

For module tests, test stubs are required that provide the dependent software modules for the module under test. The test stubs pass the input values to the module to be tested. Test cases for a module test are also to be defined. These test cases test for the normal operation, tests in margin areas, and cases with exceptions. In particular, the correct detection and handling of wrong input values should be within the scope of the tests. The test evaluation takes place within the test stubs through the examination of assurances to the module.

For the testing in the closed control loop, different approaches are used according to the development phase. In an early phase of the development, even before implementation starts, the control system is tested at first as a model. This kind of test is called "Model in the Loop" (MiL) test. On this occasion, the model of the controller is embedded in the simulated actuators, the sensors, and the natural environment. The MiL test permits one to meet statements about the quality of the control algorithms and strategies.

In the phase of the software development of the subsystems, "Software in the Loop" (SiL) tests are used. The SiL test is similar to the MiL test, only that the models of the control system are replaced with the implemented software modules to check the implementation of the model in software. In this step of the development, it is also possible to test an only partially integrated system. That is, a mixture of MiL and SiL tests is carried out. Besides, the models are replaced bit by bit with the implemented software modules.

If all software modules are implemented, then these can be integrated into an overall system and tested by a "Processor in the Loop" (PiL) test. The PiL test executes the system on the target computing platform, only the communication with actuators and sensors is carried out about stubs of the hardware drivers. This test approach offers a huge number of possibilities to test the robustness of the integrated software.

The concluding test approach is a "Hardware in the Loop" (HiL) test. This test tests the completely integrated software on the final target platform with the original drivers. The HiL test can be carried out in different forms. For example, the HiL test can be carried out with a simulation of the actuators, the sensors, and the environment. In contrast with the PiL test, the connection takes place between software to be tested and simulation, however, above the electric interfaces of the target platform. Alternatively, the HiL test can be also carried out by a laboratory sample of the target system with physical devices.

PiL test and HiL test are similar to each other. However, the PiL test offers some advantages to the testing of the robustness of the system. For example, malfunctions in the electric interfaces can be simulated in the PiL test. With a HiL test, deviations through electromagnetic effects can appear in the electric interfaces between single test runs. Because of this, HiL tests are not repeatable. The PiL test also requires no real-time simulation, provided that a synchronization of the software to be tested is executed in an artificial simulation time. The behavior of the artificial simulation time corresponds with the real timing behavior. On the one hand, this permits the application of more complicated simulation models. On the other hand, the software to be tested can be stopped any time.

Stopping the system allows fault injection. Through this, it becomes possible to test all possible malfunctions that can appear with a hardware/software system of a spacecraft. This can be, for example, a specific manipulation in the storage of an application, but also malfunctions in the simulated actuators and sensors. Ageing phenomena of the sensors and actuators can also be simulated. Moreover, the simulated sensors are manipulated in their signal to noise ratio.

Finally, in a cascade of fault cases, multiple faults can also be tested. In this case, the final state of a test case is the initial state of the dependent test case. The possibilities of the definition for test cases and their automatic execution for MiL, SiL, and PiL tests were examined and applied within the scope of the SiLEST (Software-in-the-Loop for Embedded Software Testing) project [Montenegro et al., 2006, Schumann et al., 2007, Maibaum et al., 2007].

11.6 Conclusion

This chapter investigated the topic of robustness as a key requirement for space missions. The chapter identified several of the many challenges in this exciting environment. A particular focus of the chapter was on identifying and describing measures that are used in hardware and software design in order to (ideally) guarantee the robust, safe, and successful operation of spacecraft.

The chapter found that the measures in the hardware create a dependable computer platform with a high availability, which is a basic requirement for the dependable operation of the onboard software. The chapter also found that the intelligence implemented in the onboard software enables the spacecraft to act autonomously. In particular, the software is able to make decisions in the case of malfunctions, which guarantees at least the survival of the spacecraft. Without this autonomy, the survival of the spacecraft could not be guaranteed in between the contact (communication) time with the operating team.

The chapter also contemplates that only a design with "enough" redundant systems and components—and their management—produces the robustness that is desired and needed for mission success. The finally selected design, however, may depend on several other mission requirements, including the marginal conditions in volume, measures, and technical feasibility.

Unfortunately, the chapter agrees that a certain residual risk for the success of a space mission will always remain. However, according to this chapter, a robust system design may reduce this risk to an "appropriate" level.

References

Brammer, K. and Siffling, G. (1989). *Kalman-Bucy Filters*. Artech House Communication.

Broekman, B. and Notenboom, E. (2003). *Testing Embedded Software*. Addison-Wesley.

ECSS-E10-04A (2000). *Space engineering: Space environment*. ESA-ESTEC.

IEC 61508 (2005). *Functional safety of E/E/PE safety-related systems*. International Electrotechnical Commission (IEC).

IEC 61511 (2004). *Functional safety—safety instrumented systems for the process industry sector*. International Electrotechnical Commission (IEC).

Kalman, R. (1960). A new approach to linear filtering and prediction problems. *Transactions of the ASME-Journal of Basic Engineering*, 82(Series D):35–45.

Lyu, M., editor (1995). *Handbook of Software Reliability Engeneering*. IEEE Computer Society Press.

Maibaum, O., Schumann, H., and Berres, A. (2007). Test of satellite control software with simulated faults. In Sandau, R., Röser, H.-P., and Valenzuela, A., editors, *6th IAA Symposium on Small Satellites for Earth Observation*, pages 389–392, Berlin, Germany. Wissenschaft und Technik Verlag, Berlin. Small Satellites for Earth Observation–Digest of the 6th International Symposium of the International Academy of Astronautics.

Montenegro, S., Jähnichen, S., and Maibaum, O. (2006). Simulation-based testing of embedded software in space applications. In Hommel, H., editor, *Embedded Systems–Modelling, Technology and Applications*, pages 73–82. Springer, The Netherland.

Mulholland, J.-D. and Veillet, C. (2004). A space debris primer for astronomers. *Space Debris*, 2(4):295–317.

Murphy, N. (2000). Watchdog timers. *Embedded Systems Programming*, 13(12).

Poledna, S. (1996). *Fault-Tolerant Real-Time Systems*. Springer, Berlin.

Pouponnot, A.-L.-R. (2005). Strategic use of SEE mitigation techniques for the development of the ESA microprocessors: Past, present and future. In *Proceedings of the 11th IEEE International On-Line Testing Symposium (IOLTS'05)*, pages 319–323, France, July 6–8. IEEE Computer Society, Washington, DC.

Rajkumar, R. (1991). *Synchronization in Real Time Systems—A Priority Inheritance Approach*. Kluwer Academic Publishers, Bosten, Dordrecht, London.

Schumann, H., Berres, A., Maibaum, O., and Liebezeit, T. (2007). Simulation-based testing of small satellite attitude control systems. In *6th IAA Symposium on Small Satellites for Earth Observation*, pages 151–154, Berlin, Germany. Wissenschaft und Technik Verlag, Berlin. Small Satellite Earth Observation.

Silberschatz, A. and Galvin, P. (1994). *Operating Sytem Concepts*. Addison Wesley.

Stassinopoulos, E. and Brucker, G. (1992). Shortcomings in ground testing, environment simulations, and performance predictions for space applications. Technical report, Goddard Space Flight Center. Technical paper, NASA-TP-3217, NASA.

Stone, J., Greenwald, M., Partridge, C., and Hughes, J. (1998). Performance of checksums and CRC's over real data. *IEEE/ACM Transactions on Networking*, 6(5):529–543.

Tanenbaum, A. S. (1995). *Distributed Operating Systems*. Prentice Hall, Englewood Cliffs, NJ.

Tanenbaum, A. S. (1996). *Computer Networks*. Prentice Hall, Englewood Cliffs, NJ, 3rd edition.

Weske, M. (1995). *Deadlocks in Computersystemen*. International Thomson Publishing, Bonn.

Chapter 12
Robust and Automated Space System Design

Martin Fuchs, Daniela Girimonte, Dario Izzo, and Arnold Neumaier

Abstract Over the past few years, much research has been dedicated to the creation of decisions support systems for space system engineers or even for completely automated design methods capturing the reasoning of system experts. However, the problem of taking into account the uncertainties of variables and models defining an optimal and robust spacecraft design have not been tackled effectively yet. This chapter proposes a novel, simple approach based on the *clouds* formalism to elicit and process the uncertainty information provided by expert designers and to incorporate this information into the automated search for a robust, optimal design

12.1 Introduction

The design of a spacecraft is a demanding challenge. The complexity of the task and its multidisciplinarity make it difficult to obtain a complete survey and a deep understanding of the whole design process.

In a classical approach to multidisciplinary design, each specialist would prepare a subsystem design rather independently, using stand-alone tools (cf. [Roy, 1996, Belton and Stewart, 2002]). Design iterations among the different discipline experts would take place in meetings at intervals of a few weeks. This well-established approach reduces the opportunity of finding interdisciplinary solutions and to create system awareness in the specialists. A considerable step toward a multidisciplinary approach in the early phases of space system design has been achieved by concurrent engineering where a sequential iterative routine is replaced by a parallel and cooperative procedure. Design facilities where these methodologies are implemented include the ESA Concurrent Design Facility [Bandecchi et al., 1999], the NASA

M. Fuchs
University of Vienna, Faculty of Mathematics, Nordbergstr. 15, 1090 Wien, Austria
European Space Agency, Advanced Concepts Team, ESTEC, EUI-ACT, Keplerlaan 1, 2201 AZ
Noordwijk, The Netherlands
e-mail: martin.fuchs@univie.ac.at

A. Schuster (ed.), *Robust Intelligent Systems*, DOI: 10.1007/978-1-84800-261-6_12,
© Springer-Verlag London Limited 2008

Goddard Integrated Mission Design Center [Karpati et al., 2003], and the Concept Design Center at the AeroSpace Corporation [Aguilar et al., 1998].

In these facilities, it is common practice of preliminary spacecraft design to handle uncertainties by assigning intervals, or safety margins, to the uncertain variables, usually combined with an iterative process of refining the intervals while converging to a robust optimal design. The refinement of the intervals is done by the system experts who assess whether the worst-case scenario, which has been determined for the design at the current stage of the iteration process, is too pessimistic or too optimistic. How to assign the intervals and how to choose the endpoint of the assigned intervals to get the worst-case scenario is usually not computed but assessed by a system expert. The goal of the whole iteration process includes both optimization of the design and safeguarding against uncertainties. The available uncertainty information in the early phase of a spacecraft design is often very limited. Mostly, there are only interval bounds on the uncertain variables and sometimes probability distributions for single variables without correlation information. When the amount of available uncertainty information is small, traditional methods face several problems. To make use of well-known current methods from probability theory or fuzzy theory (e.g., fuzzy clustering), more information would be required. Simulation techniques like Monte Carlo also require a larger amount of information to be reliable. The lack of information typically causes these methods to underestimate the effects of the uncertain tails of the probability distribution (cf. [Ferson, 1996]). Similarly, a reduction of the problem to an interval analysis after assigning intervals to the uncertain variables as described before (e.g., $3\,\sigma$ boxes) entails a loss of valuable uncertainty information that would actually be available but not involved in the uncertainty model. Moreover, in higher dimensions, the numerical computation of the error probabilities is very expensive, if not impossible; even when the knowledge of the multivariate probability distributions is given.

Several previous works deal with uncertainty modeling applied to space systems design. In [Pate-Cornell and Fischbeck, 1993] probability risk analysis is applied to the uncertainties in space shuttle design; an approach from fuzzy theory can be found, e.g., in [Ross, 1995]. Also, in [Thunnissen, 2005], a general qualitative and quantitative investigation of uncertainties in space design is given. The work by [Amata et al., 2004] presents studies harmonizing the interests from different disciplines in multidisciplinary design optimization; and a decision support tool for spacecraft design is implemented in [Zonca, 2004]. The attempt to incorporate both uncertainty and autonomy in the design process was made, e.g., in [McCormick and Olds, 2002] using Monte Carlo simulation techniques, or with a fuzzy logic approach in [Lavagna and Finzi, 2002]. More recently, the ESA Advanced Concepts Team in cooperation with the University of Vienna performed an Ariadna study on the application of the clouds theory in space design optimization [Neumaier et al., 2007]. This study presented an initial step on how clouds could be applied to handle uncertainties in spacecraft design. This chapter aims to go a step further in this direction.

Generally speaking, the task of robust and automated space system design cannot be regarded as a single task, but consists of two tasks that have to be accomplished concurrently. First, the design should be robust; in other words, the design should be safeguarded against uncertain perturbations. Second, the design should be found automatically; this indicates the existence of a method that is able to find the optimal design choice automatically. The optimality of a spacecraft design can depend on multiple objectives such as the cost or the mass of the spacecraft or both at the same time. Continuing the work from [Neumaier et al., 2007] to accomplish the two tasks, this chapter presents a newly developed methodology to gather all available uncertainty information from system experts, process it to a reliable worst-case analysis, and finally optimize the design seeking the optimal robust design.

The presented approach handles and processes information gathered by the clouds formalism introduced in [Neumaier, 2004a]. Clouds allow the representation of incomplete stochastic information in a clearly understandable and computationally attractive way, mediating between aspects of fuzzy set theory and probability distributions (cf. [Dubois and Prade, 2005]). The use of clouds permits an adaptive worst-case analysis without losing track of important probabilistic information. At the same time, all computed probabilities and hence the resulting designs are reasonably safeguarded against perturbations due to unmodeled and possibly unavailable information. For given confidence levels, the clouds provide regions of relevant scenarios affecting the worst-case for a given design. This work has the ambitious goal to achieve a quantification of reliability close to classical probability theory methods, but in higher dimensional spaces of uncertain scenarios so that one can deal with real-life system design.

To find a robust optimal design automatically, heuristic optimization methods were developed that take advantage of inherent characteristics of spacecraft design problems. This allows applications to investigate concrete spacecraft design problems. Figure 12.1 illustrates the basic concept of the approach.

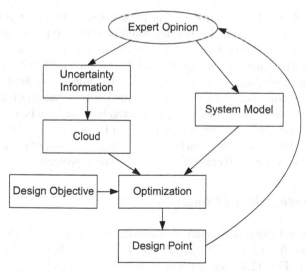

Fig. 12.1 Basic concept

The expert provides the underlying system model, given as a black-box model, and all currently available uncertainty information on the input variables of the model. The information is processed to generate a *cloud* that provides a nested collection of regions of relevant scenarios parameterized by a confidence level α, thus producing safety constraints for the optimization. The optimization minimizes a certain objective function (e.g., cost, mass) subject to the safety constraints, to account for the robustness of the design, and subject to the functional constraints, which are represented by the system model. The result of the optimization, i.e., the automatically found optimal design point and the worst-case analysis, are returned to the expert, who is given an interactive possibility to provide additional uncertainty information afterwards and reruns the procedure.

The uncertainty information can be provided, on the one hand, as bounds or marginal probability distributions on the uncertain variables. On the other hand, the engineers can adaptively improve the uncertainty model, even if their expert knowledge is only a little formalized, by adding correlation constraints to exclude scenarios deemed irrelevant. The information can also be provided as real sample data, if available.

The remainder of this chapter is organized as follows: Section 12.2 and Section 12.3 present a more detailed investigation of the uncertainty modeling and the design optimization methods. These techniques are applied to an example from spacecraft system design described in Section 12.4. Section 12.5 discusses general and detailed aspects, remarks, problems, and advantages of the approach. Section 12.6 concludes the chapter with a summary of findings and an outlook on possible future work.

12.2 Uncertainty Modeling

The concept of clouds was introduced in [Neumaier, 2004a] as a new notion for handling uncertainty. Clouds describe the rough shapes of typical samples of various size without fixing the details of the distribution. The special case of interest for large-scale models is a *potential-based* cloud. This section deals with these potential clouds, with their properties, computation, and their illustration through examples. Initially, the section gives a theoretical introduction to potential clouds, i.e., how they are defined, their probabilistic properties, and how they can be interpreted intuitively. The section then describes how they can be generated computationally, if the uncertainty information is given by marginal distributions or boxes for uncertain variables, and how they will constrain the optimization problem.

12.2.1 Potential-Based Clouds

A potential-based cloud is defined by a continuous potential V, which assigns to each scenario ε from a set $\mathbb{M} \subseteq \mathbb{R}^n$ a value $V(\varepsilon) \in \mathbb{R}^+$ defining the shape of the cloud (see e.g., Fig. 12.2), and a lower probability $\underline{\alpha}(U)$ and an upper probability $\overline{\alpha}(U)$ defining the boundary of the cloud, such that, for all $U \in \mathbb{R}^+$:

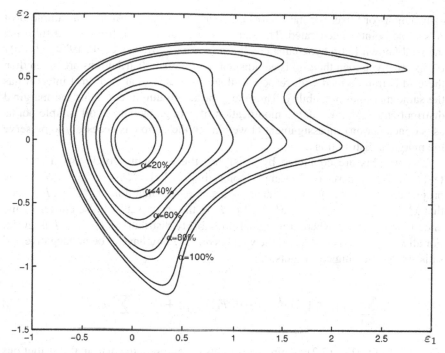

Fig. 12.2 α-cuts of a two-dimensional potential-based cloud

$$\underline{\alpha}(U) \leq \Pr(V(\varepsilon) < U) \leq \Pr(V(\varepsilon) \leq U) \leq \overline{\alpha}(U), \tag{12.1}$$

where $\varepsilon \in \mathbb{M}$ is a random variable, and $\underline{\alpha}$ and $\overline{\alpha}$ are strictly increasing continuous functions of U mapping the range of V to $[0, 1]$.

The mapping $x \rightarrow [\underline{\alpha}(V(x)), \overline{\alpha}(V(x))]$, $x \in \mathbb{M}$, is the potential-based cloud. The functions $\underline{\alpha}$ and $\overline{\alpha}$ can be interpreted as boundings on the distribution of $V(\varepsilon)$.

For a given failure probability p_{err} and $\alpha := 1 - p_{\mathrm{err}}$, the so-called α-cut describes an inner region $\underline{C}_\alpha$ (lower α-cut) of α-relevant scenarios and a (generally larger) region $\overline{C}_\alpha$ (upper α-cut) of α-reasonable scenarios. Define $\underline{C}_\alpha := \{\varepsilon \in \mathbb{M} \mid V(\varepsilon) \leq \underline{U}_\alpha\}$ if $\underline{U}_\alpha := \min\{U_\alpha \in V(\mathbb{M}) \mid \overline{\alpha}(U_\alpha) = \alpha\}$ exists, and $\underline{C}_\alpha := \emptyset$ otherwise; analogously $\overline{C}_\alpha := \{\varepsilon \in \mathbb{M} \mid V(\varepsilon) \leq \overline{U}_\alpha\}$ if $\overline{U}_\alpha := \max\{U_\alpha \in V(\mathbb{M}) \mid \underline{\alpha}(U_\alpha) = \alpha\}$ exists, and $\overline{C}_\alpha := \mathbb{M}$ otherwise. The conditions defining the cloud (i.e., $\underline{\alpha} \leq \overline{\alpha}$, $\underline{\alpha}$ and $\overline{\alpha}$ strictly increasing and monotone) guarantee that $\underline{U}_\alpha \leq \overline{U}_\alpha$, and that there is a region C_α with $\underline{C}_\alpha \subseteq C_\alpha \subseteq \overline{C}_\alpha$ containing a fraction of α of all scenarios considered possible.

12.2.2 Cloud Generation and Constraints

This text now describes a method to generate, computationally, a cloud that matches the above definition, assuming the uncertainty information is given by marginal distributions or boxes for the vector of uncertain variables. At first, a sample S of N sample points is generated. The sample points are chosen from a grid fulfilling the well-known Latin hypercube condition (see e.g., [McKay et al., 1979]). If only boxes are given then the grid is equidistant. If marginal distributions are given then the grid is transformed with respect to them, to ensure that each grid interval has the same marginal probability. Thus the generated sample represents the marginal distributions. However, after a modification of S (e.g., by cutting off sample points as is done later on), an assignment of weights to the sample is necessary to preserve the marginal distributions.

The weights are computed by satisfying the following conditions. Let $S = \{x_1, \ldots, x_N\}$ be a set of N sample points in $\mathbb{R}^n$. Let x_i^k, $i = 1, \ldots, N$ be the projection of x_i to the kth coordinate, π_k a sorting permutation of $\{1, \ldots, N\}$, such that $x_{\pi_k(1)}^k \leq x_{\pi_k(2)}^k \leq \ldots \leq x_{\pi_k(N)}^k$. Let I be the index set of those entries of the uncertainty vector ε where a marginal probability distribution $F_k, k \in I$ is given. For all $k \in I$ and $i = 1, \ldots, N$, the weights $\omega_1, \ldots, \omega_N$ have to be nonnegative and satisfy the following constraints:

$$\sum_{j=1}^{i} \omega_{\pi_k(j)} \in [F_k(x_{\pi_k(i)}^k) - d, F_k(x_{\pi_k(i)}^k) + d], \quad \sum_{i=1}^{N} \omega_i = 1. \quad (12.2)$$

The constraints (Eq. 12.2) require the weights to represent the marginal distributions with some reasonable margin d. In other words, the weighted empirical distribution of the sample projected to a margin should not differ from the given marginal probability distribution by more than d. In practice, one chooses d with Kolmogorov-Smirnov statistics.

Initially, one chooses the potential function V to be boxed shaped, i.e., $V(\varepsilon) := \max_k \frac{|\varepsilon^k - \mu^k|}{r^k}$, where $\varepsilon, \mu, r \in \mathbb{R}^n$, $\varepsilon^k, \mu^k, r^k$ are the kth components of the vectors, μ the mode, and r the radius of the sample S. With the computed weights, one achieves an empirical distribution for $\{V(\varepsilon), \varepsilon \in S\}$ approximating the distribution function of $V(\varepsilon)$. Smooth lower bounds $\underline{\alpha}(V(\varepsilon))$ and upper bounds $\overline{\alpha}(V(\varepsilon))$ are fitted for the empirical distribution (with a piecewise cubic Hermite spline, cf. Fig. 12.3) considering the size of the sample and the quality of the approximation of the distribution function of $V(\varepsilon)$, i.e., a violation of the constraints (Eq. 12.2).

The shorter the sample, or the lower the acceptable incidence of violations, the larger the width of the bounds is chosen. Having found an appropriate bounding of the distribution function of $V(\varepsilon)$, a potential cloud was generated that fulfills the conditions that define the cloud according to the remarks to Theorem 4.3 in [Neumaier, 2004a]. Thus, it represents the given uncertainty information.

As already mentioned, initially a box-shaped potential has been chosen, but the expert will have the option to cut off scenarios that are not considered relevant and thus specify the uncertainty information in the form of correlation bounds adaptively, resulting in a polyhedron-shaped potential. This iterative step imitates the procedure of decision making of real-life applications and is particularly important

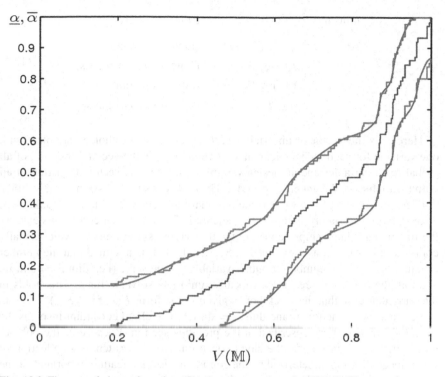

Fig. 12.3 The smooth lower bounds $\underline{\alpha}(V(\varepsilon))$ and upper bounds $\overline{\alpha}(V(\varepsilon))$. The mapping $\varepsilon \rightarrow [\underline{\alpha}(V(\varepsilon)), \overline{\alpha}(V(\varepsilon))]$ is a potential cloud (cf. Section 12.2.1)

if there is only a small amount of uncertainty information available. As soon as the cloud representing the uncertainty information is generated, one can produce the worst-case relevant region C for a given potential. For a given confidence level α, one numerically computes the solution V_α of $\overline{\alpha}(V_\alpha) = \alpha$, cf. Section 12.2.1, and defines the region $C := \{\varepsilon \mid V(\varepsilon) \leq V_\alpha\}$ if a solution V_α exists and $C := \emptyset$ otherwise, which is only the case for very low confidence levels. The next section shows that the region C can be used to constrain the design optimization problem.

12.3 Design Optimization

The focus of this section is on design optimization. The section starts with a general optimization problem formulation, points out the characteristics and difficulties that come with it, and finally gives a short introduction to the heuristic approach that was developed to solve the problem.

It is assumed that the optimization problem can be formulated as a mixed-integer, bi-level problem of the following form:

$$\min_{\theta} \max_{x,z,\varepsilon} \quad f(x) \qquad \qquad \text{(objective functions)}$$

$$\text{s.t.} \qquad z = Z(\theta) + \varepsilon \qquad \text{(table constraints)}$$

$$F(x, z) = 0 \qquad \text{(functional constraints)} \qquad (12.3)$$

$$V(\varepsilon) \leq V_\alpha \qquad \text{(cloud constraint)}$$

$$\theta \in T \qquad \qquad \text{(selection constraints)}$$

Here, ε is the vector of uncertainties, θ is the vector of choice variables (with one variable for each independent table of choices), z is the vector consisting of all global input variables and all design variables, and x is the vector consisting of all output variables of the underlying model. The table constraints assign to each choice θ a design vector z whose value is the nominal table entry $Z(\theta)$ plus its (unknown) error ε, with uncertainty specified by the cloud. The functional constraints express the functional relationships defined in the underlying system model, which usually comes as a black-box as mentioned in Section 12.1. It is assumed that the number of equations and the number of output variables is the same (i.e., $\dim F = \dim x$), and that the equations are (at least locally) uniquely solvable for x. This holds in the particular case that the black-box is given in the form $F(x, z) = \overline{F}(z) - x$ with some black-box function $\overline{F}$ and $\dim \overline{F} = \dim x$. The cloud constraint involves the potential function V as described in the previous section. Because of the polyhedral structure of our clouds, the cloud constraint can be written as a collection of linear inequalities parameterized by the confidence level, a feature important for the implementation. The selection constraints specify how many choices are allowed for each choice variable.

This optimization problem (Eq. 12.3) features difficulties of the most complex nature: it is a mixed integer nonlinear program (MINLP) with a bi-level structure that cannot be handled directly with standard optimization tools. Therefore, the problem is approached with heuristic methods that were developed to exploit the characteristics of the above design optimization problem.

12.3.1 Heuristics

The inner level of the problem (Eq. 12.3), i.e., finding the worst-case scenario for f over the polyhedron C for a fixed design choice θ, is solved using linear programming. To this end, f is linearly approximated within a box b that contains C.

To tackle the outer level of the problem (Eq. 12.3), i.e., to find the design choice θ with the minimal worst-case objective function value, two different methods are used; one based on a quadratic model, the other on separable underestimation. In the first method, one fits a quadratic model of the objective function and minimizes this model to get a guess of the optimal solution for the problem. In this approach, the discrete nature of the choice variables is ignored. The second method, on the other hand, takes advantage of the discrete nature of θ and finds a separable underestimator $q(\theta)$ for the objective of the form:

$$q(\theta) := \sum_{i=1}^{n_0} q_i(\theta^i), \qquad\qquad (12.4)$$

where n_0 is the dimension of the choice variable, and θ^i is the ith coordinate of θ. Let N_0 be the number of function evaluations $f_1, \ldots, f_{N_0}$ that have been made in advance for the design choices $\theta_1, \ldots, \theta_{N_0}$. The expression $q_i(\theta_l^i)$ is simply a constant q_{i,θ_l^i} for integer choice variables θ_l^i, and $q_i(\theta_l^i) = q_{i1} \cdot \theta_l^i + q_{i2} \cdot \theta_l^{i^2}$, with constants q_{i1}, q_{i2}, for continuous choice variables θ_l^i. The constants q_i are treated as variables q_i in a linear optimization program (LP) satisfying the constraints

$$\sum_{i=1}^{n_0} q_i(\theta_l^i) \le f_l \;\; l = 1, \ldots, N_0, \qquad\qquad (12.5)$$

and are computed by an LP solver. This ensures that many constraints in (Eq. 12.5) will be active. The underestimator $q(\theta)$ can then be easily minimized afterwards.

Finally, the minimizers that result from these methods are used as starting points for a limited global search that consists of an integer line search for the discrete choice variables and multilevel coordinate search [Huyer and Neumaier, 1999] for the continuous choice variables. Thus, the hope is to find the global optimal solution, but as heuristics are used there is no guarantee.

12.4 Case Study

This section applies the proposed robust and automated design method to a case study in spacecraft engineering, i.e., the Attitude Determination and Control Subsystem (ADCS) for the NASA's Mars Exploration Rover (MER) mission, cf. [MER, 2003, Manning et al., 2004], whose scientific goal is to investigate the history of water on Mars. The spacecraft has no main propulsion subsystem onboard and the ADCS is composed of eight thrusters aligned in two clusters. The mission sequence after orbit injection includes a number of spin maneuvers and slew maneuvers as reported in Table 12.3 (see Appendix). Spin maneuvers are required for keeping the gyroscopic stability of the spacecraft, whereas slew maneuvers serve to control the direction of the spacecraft and to fight the effects of solar torque. Fault protection is considered to correct possible errors made when performing nominal maneuvers.

The goal is to select the type of thrusters (from a set of possible candidates as listed in Table 12.4, see Appendix) considering the design objective of minimizing the total mass m_{tot}, and the worst possible performance of a thruster with respect to m_{tot}, i.e., to find the thruster with the minimal mass worst-case scenario. The total mass consists of the fuel needed for attitude control (computed as the sum of the fuel needed for each maneuver) plus the mass of the eight thrusters that need to be mounted on the spacecraft. The variable structure and the model equations to compute the fuel mass for attitude control can be found in Appendices A and B, respectively. According to the notation introduced in (Eq. 12.3), the choice variable θ, i.e., the type of thruster, can be selected as an integer between 1 and 30. The uncertainty specification for the model variables are taken from [Thunnissen, 2005] and reported in Table 12.5 of Appendix E. The number of uncertain variables in this application example is 33 plus 1 uncertain design variable.

12.4.1 Results

The cloud constraints for the optimization are generated for a confidence level of $\alpha = 95\%$ and a generated sample size of $N = 1000$. For the computation of the results, the presented methods have been implemented as MATLAB code. The study makes use of the Statistics Toolbox of MATLAB to evaluate probability distributions. The study also uses CVX [Grant and Boyd, 2007] to solve linear programs, SNOBFIT [Huyer and Neumaier, 2006] and MCS [Huyer and Neumaier, 1999] as external optimization routines, and NLEQ [Nowak and Weimann, 1990, Deuflhard, 2004] to solve systems of nonlinear equations. The results for optimization are divided into four different configurations of uncertainty handling and specifications:

a. The uncertainties are as specified in Table 12.5 (see Appendix). Here they are treated in a classical engineering way, assigning $3\,\sigma$ boxes to the uncertain variables, which corresponds with a 99.7% confidence interval for a single normally distributed variable. Then the optimal design choice is $\theta = 9$ with an objective function value of $m_{tot} = 3.24\,\text{kg}$ in the nominal case and $m_{tot} = 5.56\,\text{kg}$ in the worst case.

b. The uncertainties are again as in Table 12.5. Here we use the methods presented in the previous sections and find $V_\alpha = 0.9922$ and the optimal design choice $\theta = 9$, as in Configuration a. However, when comparing the worst-case analysis of b and a, it is apparent that the results for the $3\,\sigma$ boxes are far too optimistic to represent a reliable worst-case scenario, the value of m_{tot} is now $8.08\,\text{kg}$ instead of $5.56\,\text{kg}$ for the $3\,\sigma$ boxes.

c. This configuration does not take any uncertainties into account, generally assuming the nominal case for all uncertain input variables. The optimal design choice then is $\theta = 3$ with a value of $m_{tot} = 2.68$ kg in the nominal, but $m_{tot} = 8.75\,\text{kg}$ in the worst case, which is significantly worse than in Configuration b.

d. The uncertainties are obtained by taking the values from Table 12.5 and doubling the standard deviation of the normally distributed variables. It is interesting to report that if one increases the uncertainty in the normally distributed uncertain variables simply in this way, the optimal design choice changes to $\theta = 17$ with a value of $m_{tot} = 3.38\,\text{kg}$ in the nominal and $m_{tot} = 9.49\,\text{kg}$ in the worst case.

The results are summarized in Table 12.1, showing the optimal design choice for each configuration and the corresponding value of the objective function m_{tot} for the nominal case and for the worst case, respectively. Configuration b is our

Table 12.1 Nominal and worst-case values of m_{tot} for different design choices obtained by the four different configurations

Configuration	Design choice θ	Nominal value m_{tot}	Worst-case m_{tot}
a	9	3.24	5.56
b	9	3.24	8.08
c	3	2.68	8.75
d	17	3.38	9.49

reference configuration, as in this case we apply our new methods given the original uncertainty information from Table 12.5.

The results reported above show a number of important facts related to spacecraft design. The comparison between configurations b and d suggests that in a preliminary stage of the spacecraft systems modeling the optimal design point is quite sensitive to the uncertainty description, a fact well-known to the system engineers, who see their spacecraft design changing frequently during preliminary phases when new information becomes continuously available. The presented method captures this important dynamic and describes it in rigorous mathematical terms.

The comparison between configurations b and c suggests that the uncertainties need to be accounted for at an early stage, in order to not critically overestimate the spacecraft performances.

Finally, the comparison between configurations b and a suggests that the simple 3σ analysis of uncertainties, very frequent in real practice, produces a quite different estimation of the spacecraft performances with respect to a more rigorous accounting of the uncertainty information.

We see that Configuration b is the best approach to the goal presented in this chapter, i.e., minimizing the design worst-case while reasonably taking account of uncertainties.

12.5 Discussion

The importance of a robust design has been the starting point and main motivation of this research work, and the results obtained from a case study confirm that the optimal spacecraft design is strongly sensitive to uncertainties. At the current stage, it can be confirmed that neglecting uncertainties results in a design that completely lacks robustness, and a simplified uncertainty model (like a 3σ approach) may yield critical underestimations of worst-case scenarios.

When trying to collect the uncertainty information, it turned out to be very difficult to get useful, formalized information directly from expert engineers. To collect all information, both formalized and unformalized, an interactive dialogue between expert and computer can be realized by a graphical user interface, where the engineers can specify uncertainties, provide sample data, cut off worst-case irrelevant scenarios, and adjust the quality of the uncertainty model. It is expected that this kind of interaction is an inevitable next step in space design.

The discussion now continues with more detailed considerations on the study.

- In the theory of clouds (cf. Section 12.2.1), there is a distinction between regions of α-relevant, α-reasonable scenarios and borderline cases (which is the set difference of the α-reasonable and the α-relevant regions). In robust design, the uncertain scenarios that are possible are required to satisfy safety constraints. With respect to the presented terminology, the regions above have the following interpretation: if at least one of the α-relevant scenarios fails to satisfy the safety constraints, the design is unsafe; if all of the α-reasonable scenarios satisfy the safety constraints, the design is safe. Between these two cases there is the borderline region where no precise statement can be made without additional uncertainty information. The width of the borderline region is increasing if the width of the cloud increases and vice versa. So widening the cloud enlarges the borderline region, corresponding with a lack of uncertainty information. This fact is reflected in our approach as both a smaller sample size and an increased dimension of the uncertainty result in a wider cloud.
- The width of the cloud is defined as the difference between the mappings $\underline{\alpha}$ and $\overline{\alpha}$ (cf. Section 12.2.1). The mappings were constructed to fulfill the conditions that define a cloud with an algorithm that is non-rigorous, but can grant a high, adjustable reliability of the fulfillment of the conditions. Thus, the user of the algorithm is able to control the desired level of reliability.
- The choice of the potential function is arbitrary. Different shapes of the cloud (i.e., shapes of the potential) can make the worst-case analysis more pessimistic or optimistic. It is necessary to emphasize that a poor choice of the potential makes the worst-case analysis more pessimistic, but will still result in a valid robust design. This study allows a variation of the potential by switching from a box-shaped to a polyhedron-shaped potential, to enable the experts to improve the uncertainty model iteratively.
- A good weight computation (cf. Section 12.2.2) is the key to a good uncertainty representation with clouds. In higher dimensions, the weight computation is very expensive. To overcome this problem and to allow the adjustment of the computation time, the relaxation radius d (cf. Section 12.2.2) must be increased carefully. The presented algorithm respects the relaxation property, widening the cloud by the amount of relaxation after evaluating the quality of the weights.
- As mentioned before, this work is limited to the use of heuristic methods, as the design problem (Eq. 12.3) is highly complex and not suitable for standard optimization methods. The problem formulation here therefore asks the system to find the design with the optimal worst-case scenario. It is possible to trade off between the worst-case scenario and the nominal case of a design, but this would lead to a multi-objective optimization problem formulation.
- The number of 34 uncertain variables in the presented application example is large enough to make our problem representative for uncertainty handling in real-life applications.
- Though global optimality for the solution in the presented case study is very likely, as the choice variable is one-dimensional and discrete, the heuristical methods cannot guarantee global optimality of the problem solution in general.

- The method of separable underestimation introduced in this chapter takes advantage of the discrete nature of many of the variables involved in spacecraft design, supporting, at the same time, continuous choice variables. Details about the heuristic approach for design optimization introduced in Section 12.3 will be published elsewhere.

12.6 Conclusions and Future Work

This chapter presented a new approach to robust and automated space system design. Starting from the background of the cloud theory, the chapter developed methodologies to process the uncertainty information from expert knowledge toward a reliable worst-case analysis and an optimal and robust design. The presented approach is applicable to real-life problems of early phase spacecraft system design. At present, in most instances of the spacecraft design, reliability is only assessed qualitatively by the experts. This work presents a step forward toward quantitative statements about the design reliability.

The adaptive nature is one of the key features of the presented uncertainty model as it imitates real-life design strategies. The iteration steps significantly improve the uncertainty information, and it is possible to process the new information to an improved uncertainty model afterwards.

The presented approach is generally applicable to problems of robust design optimization, especially with discrete design choices. The advantage of achieving the optimal design automatically is undeniable. Although the new methods have already been applied to space system design problems (cf. [Neumaier et al., 2007]), one future goal is to apply them to other problem classes in order to learn from new challenges. Another aspect for future improvements of the uncertainty model with clouds is the investigation of different shapes of the potential function.

The presented approach makes it possible to process the available uncertainty information to perform a reliable worst-case analysis linked to an adjustable confidence level. An additional value of the uncertainty model is the fact that one can capture various forms of uncertainty information, even those less formalized. There is no loss of valuable information, and the methods are capable of handling the uncertainties reliably, even if the amount of information is very limited.

In summary, the presented methods offer an exciting new approach to face the highly complex problem of robust and automated system design, an approach that is easily understandable, reliable, and computationally realizable.

References

Aguilar, J. A., Dawdy, A. B., and Law, G. W. (1998). The Aerospace Corporation's concept design center. In *8th Annual International Symposium of the International Council on Systems Engineering (INCOSE'98)*, pages 26–30, Vancouver, Canada, 26-30 July.

Amata, V., Fasano, G., Arcaro, L., Della Croce, F., Norese, M., Palamara, S., Tadei, R., and Fragnelli, F. (2004). Multidisciplinary optimisation in mission analysis and design process.

GSP programme ref: GSP 03/N16 contract number: 17828/03/NL/MV, European Space Agency.

Bandecchi, M., Melton, S., and Ongaro, F. (1999). *Concurrent engineering applied to space mission assessment and design.* ESA Bulletin.

Belton, V. and Stewart, T. J. (2002). *Multiple criteria decision analysis: an integrated approach.* Kluwer Academic Publishers, Dordrecht, The Netherlands.

Deuflhard, P. (2004). *Newton Methods for Nonlinear Problems: Affine Invariance and Adaptive Algorithms*, volume 35 of *Springer Series in Computational Mathematics.* Springer-Verlag, Heidelberg.

Dubois, D. and Prade, H. (1986). *Possibility Theory: An Approach to Computerized Processing of Uncertainty.* Plenum Press, New York.

Dubois, D. and Prade, H. (2005). Interval-valued fuzzy sets, possibility theory and imprecise probability. In *Proceedings of International Conference in Fuzzy Logic and Technology (EUSFLAT'05)*, Barcelona, Spain, 8–10 September.

EADS (2007). European Aeronautic Defence and Space Company (EADS) Space Propulsion webpage: http://cs.space.eads.net/sp/.

ESA engineers (2007). Personal communication with ESA engineers.

Ferson, S. (1996). What monte carlo methods cannot do. *Human and Ecological Risk Assessment*, 2:990–1007.

Ferson, S., Ginzburg, L., and Akcakaya, R. (1996). Whereof one cannot speak: When input distributions are unknown. Risk Analysis, in press, http://www.ramas.com/whereof.pdf.

Grant, M. C. and Boyd, S. P. (2007).CVX: Matlab Software for Disciplined Convex Programming. http://www.stanford.edu/ boyd/cvx/cvx_usrguide.pdf, and http://www.stanford.edu/ boyd/cvx/.

Huyer, W. and Neumaier, A. (1999).Global optimization by multilevel coordinate search.*Journal of Global Optimization*, 14:331–355.

Huyer, W. and Neumaier, A. (2006).SNOBFIT: stable noisy optimization by branch and fit. Submitted preprint, http://www.mat.univie.ac.at/ neum/ms/snobfit.pdf, and http://www.mat.univie. ac.at/ neum/software/snobfit/.

Karpati, G., Martin, J., Steiner, M., and Reinhardt, K. (2003). The Integrated Mission Design Center (IMDC) at NASA Goddard Space Flight Center. In *Proceedings of IEEE Aerospace Conference*, volume 8, pages 3657–3667, Big Sky Montana, 8–15 March.

Kreinovich, V. (1997). Random sets unify, explain, and aid known uncertainty methods in expert systems. In Goutsias, J., Mahler, R. P. S., and Nguyen, H. T., editors, *Random Sets: Theory and Applications*, pages 321–345. Springer, Berlin.

Larson, W. J. and Wertz, J. R. (1999). *Space Mission Analysis and Design.* Microcosm Press, 3rd edition.

Lavagna, M. and Finzi, A. E. (2002). A multi-attribute decision-making approach towards space system design automation through a fuzzy logic-based analytic hierarchical process. In Hendtlass, T. and Ali, M., editors, *Proceedings of the 15th International Conference on Industrial and Engineering. Applications of Artificial Intelligence and Expert Systems*, pages 596–606, Cairns, Australia, 17–20 June. Springer-Verlag, London, UK.

Manning, R. M., Adler, M., and Erickson, J. K. (2004). Mars exploration rover: Launch, cruise, entry, descent, and landing. In *55th International Astronautical Congress of the International Astronautical Federation, the International Academy of Astronautics, and the International Institute of Space Law*, Vancouver, Canada, 6 October. Pasadena, CA: Jet Propulsion Laboratory, National Aeronautics and Space Administration, 2004.

McCormick, D. J. and Olds, J. R. (2002). A distributed framework for probabilistic analysis. In *AIAA/ISSMO Symposium On Multidisciplinary Analysis And Design Optimization*, pages AIAA 2002-5587, Atlanta, Georgia, 4–6 September.

McKay, M., Conover, W., and Beckman, R. (1979). A comparison of three methods for selecting values of input variables in the analysis of output from a computer code. *Technometrics*, 221:239–245.

MER (2003). Mars Exploration Rover Project http://marsrovers.nasa.gov/mission/spacecraft. html.

Neumaier, A. (2003). On the structure of clouds. Manuscript, http://www.mat.univie.ac. at/ neum/ms/struc.pdf.

Neumaier, A. (2004a). Clouds, fuzzy sets and probability intervals. *Reliable Computing*, 10:249–272. http://www.mat.univie.ac.at/ neum/ms/cloud.pdf.

Neumaier, A. (2004b). Uncertainty modeling for robust verifiable design. Slides, http://www.mat. univie.ac.at/ neum/ms/uncslides.pdf.

Neumaier, A., Fuchs, M., Dolejsi, E., Csendes, T., Dombi, J., Banhelyi, B., and Gera, Z. (2007). Application of clouds for modeling uncertainties in robust space system design. ACT Ariadna Research ACT-RPT-05-5201, European Space Agency. http://www.esa.int/gsp/ ACT/ariadna/completed.htm.

Nowak, U. and Weimann, L. (1990). A family of Newton codes for systems of highly nonlinear equations: Algorithm, implementation, application. Technical report, Konrad-Zuse-Zentrum für Informationstechnik Berlin. http://www.zib.de/Numerik/numsoft/CodeLib/ codes/nleq1_m/nleq1.m.

Pate-Cornell, M. and Fischbeck, P. (1993). Probabilistic risk analysis and risk based priority scale for the tiles of the space shuttle. *Reliability Engineering and System Safety*, 40(3):221–238.

Purdue School of Aeronautics and Astronautics (1998). Satellite Propulsion webpage http:// cob-web.ecn.purdue.edu/ propulsi/propulsion/rockets/satellites.html.

Ross, T. J. (1995). *Fuzzy Logic with Engineering Applications*. McGraw-Hill, New York.

Roy, B. (1996). *Multicriteria Methodology for Decision Aiding*. Kluwer Academic Publishers, London.

Shafer, G. (1976). *A Mathematical Theory of Evidence*. Princeton. University Press, Princeton, New Jersey.

Thunnissen, D. P. (2005). *Propagating and Mitigating Uncertainty in the Design of Complex Multidisciplinary Systems*. PhD thesis, California Institute of Technology, Pasadena.

Williamson, R. C. (1989). *Probabilistic Arithmetic*. PhD thesis, University of Queensland.

Zonca, A. (2004). Modelling and optimisation of space mission prephase a design process in a concurrent engineering environment through a decision-making software based on expert systems theory. ESA Stage Final Report, 9/7/04. CNR Report, 22/12/03, *Combustion Synthesis under Reduced Gravity: Parabolic Flight Technique*.

Appendix

A Model Variable Structure

The 49 variables involved in the model fall into the following four categories:

- **7 fixed parameters**.
  Input variables for the model with fixed values and no uncertainty (for the values, see Table 12.2).

1. c_0, speed of light in a vacuum
2. d, average distance from the spacecraft to the sun in AU
3. g_0, gravity constant
4. t, total mission time
5. θ_i, sunlight angle of incidence
6. χ, the specific impulse efficiency parameter is a property of a particular thruster. Lacking the specification of χ for several thrusters, we fixed χ to take the same values for all thrusters.
7. c_1, the numerical solution x of $\tan(x) - x/(1 - \chi) = 0$

Table 12.2 Values of the fixed parameters

Fixed parameter	Value
c_0	$3 \cdot 10^8$ m/s
d	1.26 AU
g_0	9.81 m/s^2
t	216 days
θ_i	$0°$
χ	0.0375
c_1	0.334

- **33 Uncertain input variables**.
  The uncertainties are specified by probability distributions for each of these variables (cf. Appendix E).

  1. A_{max}, maximal cross-sectional area
  2. J_{xx}, J_{zz}, moments of inertia
  3. R, engine moment arm
  4. δ_1, δ_2, engine misalignment angle
  5. g_s, solar constant at 1 AU
  6. κ, distance from the center of pressure to the center of mass
  7. ω_{spin_i}, spin rates, $i = 0 \ldots 3$, given in rpm
  8. ψ_{slew_i}, slew angles, $i = 1 \ldots 19$, given in$°$
  9. q, spacecraft surface reflectivity
  10. $uncfuel$, additive uncertain constant that represents inaccuracies in the equations used for the calculation of the fuel masses

- **3 Design variables**.
  Thruster specifications relevant for the model. There is uncertainty information given on one of them (the thrust).

  1. F, thrust
  2. I_{sp}, specific impulse
  3. m_{thrust}, mass of a thruster

- **6 Output variables**.
  Result variables containing the objective for the optimization m_{tot}.

  1. m_{fp}, fuel mass needed for fault protection maneuvers
  2. m_{fuel}, total fuel mass needed for all maneuvers
  3. m_{slew}, fuel mass needed for slew maneuvers
  4. m_{slew_s}, fuel mass needed for slew maneuvers fighting solar torque
  5. m_{spin}, fuel mass needed for spin maneuvers
  6. m_{tot}, total mass of the subsystem

B Model Equations

The background for the equations of the ADCS subsystem model are the equations from [Thunnissen, 2005, Chapter 9]. The basic equations are as follows:

$$c = I_{sp} \cdot g_0 \tag{12.6}$$

$$r = \sin(40°) \cdot R \tag{12.7}$$

$$F_{ideal_{tot}} = 2 \cdot F \tag{12.8}$$

$$F_{act_{tot}} = (\cos(\delta_1) + \cos(\delta_2)) \cdot F \tag{12.9}$$

To calculate the fuel mass m_{spin} needed for one spin maneuver (change in spin rate from ω_{spin_i} to $\omega_{spin_{i+1}}$, $i = 0...2$), the following equations are given:

$$\Delta\omega_{ideal} = |\omega_{spin_i} - \omega_{spin_{i+1}}| \tag{12.10}$$

$$I_{ideal} = \frac{\Delta\omega_{ideal} \cdot J_{zz}}{r} \tag{12.11}$$

$$t_{spin} = \frac{I_{ideal}}{F_{ideal_{tot}}} \tag{12.12}$$

$$I_{actual} = t_{spin} \cdot F_{act_{tot}} \tag{12.13}$$

$$m_{spin} = \frac{I_{actual}}{c} \tag{12.14}$$

To calculate the fuel mass m_{slew} needed for one slew maneuver, the following equations are given (requires the slew angle ψ_{slew} for the maneuver and the current spin rate ω_{spin} at the time the maneuver is performed):

$$t_{half\_rev} = \frac{\pi}{\omega_{spin}} \tag{12.15}$$

$$t_{on_{ideal}} = \frac{2 \cdot c_1}{\omega_{spin}} \tag{12.16}$$

$$\Delta\phi_{ideal} = t_{on_{ideal}} \cdot \omega_{spin} \qquad (12.17)$$

$$\Delta\tau = \frac{2 \cdot F_{ideal_{tot}} \cdot r}{\Delta\phi_{ideal} \cdot \sin\left(\frac{\Delta\phi_{ideal}}{2}\right)} \qquad (12.18)$$

$$H = J_{zz} \cdot \omega_{spin} \qquad (12.19)$$

$$\Delta\psi_{ideal} = \frac{\Delta\tau \cdot t_{on_{ideal}}}{H} \qquad (12.20)$$

$$n_{pulses_{ideal}} = \left\lceil \frac{\psi_{slew}}{\Delta\psi_{ideal}} \right\rceil \qquad (12.21)$$

$$\Delta\psi = \frac{\psi_{slew}}{n_{pulses_{ideal}}} \qquad (12.22)$$

$$\Delta I_{torque} = H \cdot \Delta\psi \qquad (12.23)$$

$$\Delta\phi = 2 \cdot \arcsin\left(\frac{\Delta I_{torque} \cdot \omega_{spin}}{2 \cdot F_{ideal_{tot}} \cdot r}\right) \qquad (12.24)$$

$$t_{on} = \frac{\Delta\phi}{\omega_{spin}} \qquad (12.25)$$

$$\eta = \frac{t_{on}}{t_{half\_rev}} \qquad (12.26)$$

$$c_{sd} = c \cdot \eta^{\chi} \qquad (12.27)$$

$$m_{slew} = n_{pulses_{ideal}} \cdot \frac{F_{act_{tot}} \cdot t_{on}}{c_{sd}} \qquad (12.28)$$

To calculate the total fuel mass m_{fuel} needed for all maneuvers, we compute for each maneuver to be performed the mass m_{spin} or m_{slew} (depends on the maneuver type), and achieve m_{fuel} as the sum of these masses. To calculate the total mass m_{tot}, we compute:

$$m_{tot} = m_{fuel} \cdot (1 + uncfuel) + 8 \cdot m_{thrust} \tag{12.29}$$

C MER Mission Sequence

The sequence of maneuvers for the MER mission is listed in Table 12.3.

D Thruster Specification

Table 12.4 shows the thruster specifications and the linked choice variable θ. The table entries are sorted by the thrust F. The difference between the so-called design and choice variables can be seen easily in this table: the table represents 30 discrete choices in $\mathbb{R}^3$. The 3 design variables are the 3 components of these points in $\mathbb{R}^3$. The choice variable θ is one-dimensional and has an integer value between 1 and 30. The various sources for the data contained in Table 12.4 are [Purdue School of Acronautics and Astronautics, 1998, Zonca, 2004, Thunnissen, 2005, EADS, 2007, ESA engineers, 2007].

Table 12.3 Mission sequence (cf. [Thunnissen, 2005])

Mission sequence event	Maneuver type	Parameter	Value	Unit
De-spin from 3rd stg.	Spin	ω_{spin1}	2.000	rpm
A-practice	Slew	ψ_{slew1}	5.000	°
ACS-B1	Slew	ψ_{slew2}	50.45	°
ACS-B2	Slew	ψ_{slew3}	5.130	°
ACS-B3	Slew	ψ_{slew4}	6.350	°
ACS-B4	Slew	ψ_{slew5}	2.760	°
ACS-B5	Slew	ψ_{slew6}	8.510	°
ACS-B6	Slew	ψ_{slew7}	9.880	°
ACS-B7	Slew	ψ_{slew8}	5.640	°
ACS-B8	Slew	ψ_{slew9}	5.040	°
ACS-B9	Slew	ψ_{slew10}	5.750	°
ACS-B10	Slew	ψ_{slew11}	4.470	°
ACS-B11	Slew	ψ_{slew12}	5.530	°
ACS-B12	Slew	ψ_{slew13}	5.850	°
FP: spin event	Spin	ω_{spin2}	2.750	rpm
FP: spin recovery	Spin	ω_{spin3}	7.410	rpm
FP: emergency slew 1	Slew	ψ_{slew14}	15.75	°
FP: emergency slew 2	Slew	ψ_{slew15}	15.75	°
FP: emergency slew 3	Slew	ψ_{slew16}	15.75	°
FP: emergency slew 4	Slew	ψ_{slew17}	15.75	°
FP: emergency slew 5	Slew	ψ_{slew18}	15.75	°
FP: emergency slew 6	Slew	ψ_{slew19}	15.75	°

E Uncertainty Specification

All uncertainty specifications taken from [Thunnissen, 2005] are reported in Table 12.5. The notation used for the distributions is:

Table 12.4 Thruster specifications and the linked choice variable θ: Thrust F in Newtons, specific impulse I_{sp} in seconds, mass m_{thrust} in grams

θ	Thruster	F	I_{sp}	m_{thrust}
1	Aerojet MR-111C	0.27	210.0	200
2	EADS CHT 0.5	0.50	227.3	200
3	MBB Erno CHT 0.5	0.75	227.0	190
4	TRW MRE 0.1	0.80	216.0	500
5	Kaiser-Marquardt KMHS Model 10	1.0	226.0	330
6	EADS CHT 1	1.1	223.0	290
7	MBB Erno CHT 2.0	2.0	227.0	200
8	EADS CHT 2	2.0	227.0	200
9	EADS S4	4.0	284.9	290
10	Kaiser-Marquardt KMHS Model 17	4.5	230.0	380
11	MBB Erno CHT 5.0	6.0	228.0	220
12	EADS CHT 5	6.0	228.0	220
13	Kaiser-Marquardt R-53	10	295.0	410
14	MBB Erno CHT 10.0	10	230.0	240
15	EADS CHT 10	10	230.0	240
16	EADS S10 - 01	10	286.0	350
17	EADS S10 - 02	10	291.5	310
18	Aerojet MR-106E	12	220.9	476
19	SnM 15N	15	234.0	335
20	TRW MRE 4	18	217.0	500
21	Kaiser-Marquardt R-6D	22	295.0	450
22	Kaiser-Marquardt KMHS Model 16	22	235.0	520
23	EADS S22 - 02	22	290.0	650
24	ARC MONARC-22	22	235.0	476
25	ARC Leros 20	22	293.0	567
26	ARC Leros 20H	22	300.0	408
27	ARC Leros 20R	22	307.0	567
28	MBB Erno CHT 20.0	24	234.0	360
29	EADS CHT 20	25	230.0	395
30	Daimler-Benz CHT 400	400	228.6	325

- $U(a, b)$: uniform distribution in (a, b),
- $N(\mu, \sigma)$: normal distribution with mean μ and variance σ^2,
- $L(\mu, \sigma)$: lognormal distribution, distribution parameters μ and σ (mean and standard deviation of the associated normal distribution),
- $\Gamma(\alpha, \beta)$: gamma distribution with mean $\alpha\beta$ and variance $\alpha\beta^2$.

Table 12.5 ADCS uncertainty specifications

Variable	Probability distribution	Variable	Probability distribution
A_{max}	$N(5.31, 0.053)$	ψ_{slew6}	$N(8.51, 0.4)$
J_{xx}	$U(300, 450)$	ψ_{slew7}	$N(9.88, 0.5)$
J_{zz}	$U(450, 600)$	ψ_{slew8}	$N(5.64, 0.2)$
R	$N(1.3, 0.0013)$	ψ_{slew9}	$N(5.04, 0.2)$
δ_1	$N(0, 0.5)$	ψ_{slew10}	$N(5.75, 0.2)$
δ_2	$N(0, 0.5)$	ψ_{slew11}	$N(4.47, 0.1)$
g_s	$N(1400, 14)$	ψ_{slew12}	$N(5.53, 0.1)$
κ	$U(0.6, 0.7)$	ψ_{slew13}	$N(5.85, 0.1)$
ω_{spin0}	$N(12, 1.33)$	ψ_{slew14}	$\Gamma(1.5, 10.5)$
ω_{spin1}	$N(2, 0.0667)$	ψ_{slew15}	$\Gamma(1.5, 10.5)$
ω_{spin2}	$\Gamma(11, 0.25)$	ψ_{slew16}	$\Gamma(1.5, 10.5)$
ω_{spin3}	$L(2, 0.0667)$	ψ_{slew17}	$\Gamma(1.5, 10.5)$
ψ_{slew1}	$N(5, 0.5)$	ψ_{slew18}	$\Gamma(1.5, 10.5)$
ψ_{slew2}	$N(50.45, 5)$	ψ_{slew19}	$\Gamma(1.5, 10.5)$
ψ_{slew3}	$N(5.13, 0.5)$	q	$N(0.6, 0.06)$
ψ_{slew4}	$N(6.35, 0.6)$	$uncfuel$	$N(0, 0.05)$
ψ_{slew5}	$N(2.76, 0.2)$	F	$N(F_{table}, 7/300 F_{table})$

The uncertainty information on the design variable F should be interpreted as follows: The actual thrust of a thruster is normally distributed, has the mean F_{table} ($:=$ the nominal value for F specified in Table 12.4) and standard deviation $\frac{7}{300} F_{table}$.

Chapter 13
Robust Bio-regenerative Life Support Systems Control

Jordi Duatis, Cecilio Angulo, Vicenç Puig, and Pere Ponsa

Abstract Recent developments in the international space community have shown that there is an increasing interest in the human exploration of outer space. In particular, the objective of sending a manned mission to Mars by 2030 has been settled. The feasibility of such a mission will require "life support systems" (LSSs) able to provide vital elements to the exploration crew in an autonomous, self-sustained manner, as resupply from Earth will not be possible. Bio-regenerative life support systems (BLSSs) are considered to be the LSS technology alternatives that can meet this demand. Developing effective BLSSs is a challenge for the control community because of the high degree of automation, indeterminism, non-linearity, and instability in such systems. This chapter proposes to provide "robustness" to the system for tasks such as distributed control, intelligent control, fault detection and identification, or high-level planning and supervision.

13.1 Introduction

New horizons of space exploration have opened the research community to study how to perform long-duration flights, or how to settle permanent human outposts on the Moon, Mars, or Jupiter moons [ESA, 2003, NASA, 2004, ESA, 2004]. A Moon base is planned for long stays or even continuous stay as a primary goal. The Moon is very interesting because of the fact that most of the technologies that could be used for a mission to Mars or to Jupiter moons could be first tested and validated on a Moon base.

Although several, crucial problems still need to be solved such as radiation or loss of muscle mass in micro gravity, the supply of human consumables (e.g., food, water, and oxygen) has been identified as a major concern [Hoffman and Kaplan, 1997]. In response to these challenges, a new generation of LSSs is being developed that should allow for the re-creation of an Earth environment for human survival in

J. Duatis
NTE, Can Malè, s/n 08186 Lliçà d'Amunt, Barcelona, Spain
e-mail: jordid@nte.es

A. Schuster (ed.), *Robust Intelligent Systems,* DOI: 10.1007/978-1-84800-261-6_13,
© Springer-Verlag London Limited 2008

extreme environments reproducing natural processes on a small scale. The final goal is to get as close as possible to 100% recycling of human wastes through a chain of processes that eventually will provide a breathable atmosphere, potable water, and fresh food, with the provision of an external energy supply such as the Sun.

Advanced LSSs can be thought of as a factory planning problem: several interdependent chains, sharing resources and needing continuous planning. An important aspect to be considered is fault tolerance with the objective of minimizing downtime [Blanke et al., 2003]. In the case of LSSs, downtime is not only an economic problem but a survival problem. It is mandatory to guarantee maximum reliability because humans are in the loop as a part of the system to be analyzed.

This chapter suggests to increase the "robustness" of LSSs by incorporating distributed control, intelligent control, fault detection and identification, and high-level planning and supervision in such systems [Duatis et al., 2003]. Distributed control techniques will help coordinating the different processes, dealing with sharing information, and controlling the network architecture, network communications, and network hierarchy. Distributing the process control tasks minimizes the risk of a critical failure with respect to a centralized design [Rotkowitz and Lall, 2006]. Intelligent control will define the level of autonomy for each component in the control system. The support of agents, organized in a network as a multi-agent system, provides the system with reasoning capabilities for each component, generating plans, reacting to its environment, and communicating with the hierarchy [Bussmann et al., 2004]. Fault diagnosis and identification will provide the capability of locating faults either at local and/or global levels [Simani et al., 2003]. With this issue in mind, the system being designed will be able to cope with faults and carry on its function (maybe with some degradation) but operate continuously. In order to achieve this goal, analytical and hardware redundancy will maximize the level of reliability. In addition, a supervisory system with a high level of autonomy will process the information and take high-level decisions. This supervisory system requires human intervention only when mandatory and provides the information to humans in a clear and understandable form.

The remainder of the chapter is structured as follows. Section 13.2 provides an introduction to life support systems. The section describes, in particular, the MELISSA European approach. Section 13.3 outlines the proposed BLSS architecture. Sections 13.4 and 13.5 analyze this architecture in more detail, its problems and proposed solutions. Section 13.6 involves fault tolerance, reliability, and health management, which are important aspects of LSSs. Appendix 13.7 contains a list of abbreviations used in this chapter.

13.2 Life Support Systems

Advanced LSSs are designed to provide temperature and humidity control, atmosphere control, supply and revitalization, water recovery and management, as well as waste and food management. So-called "open loop" LSSs work under the assumption that resupply of consumables is possible. Current implementations of such systems are based on physical-chemical processes. An alternative under study are "closed loop" LSSs that are based on waste recycling, conserving the mass through a complete cycle, and then maintaining an equilibrium. The latter systems are implemented using biological organisms whose biological functions conduct the recycling process (e.g., higher plants recycling CO_2 into oxygen and producing food through photosynthesis). Both approaches, however, need an external energy supply. Systems using biological organisms are called "bio-regenerative" life support systems (BLSSs). Most recent approaches combine both technologies, physical-chemical and bio-regenerative systems, in order to obtain maximum benefits from both approaches (see Fig. 13.1).

The importance of BLSSs is referenced in the "NASA Mars Reference Mission" [Hoffman and Kaplan, 1997], which states that BLSS support will be an early task to be deployed by the crew at Mars arrival. Although it is not determined as a mandatory task for crew survival, this will improve robustness of the global LSS and so will increase the autonomy of the mission.

The processes involved in BLSSs are sustained by specialized microorganisms contained in bio-reactors (which perform a first step in the degradation of wastes) and by a higher plants compartment (or greenhouse), which is the main source for fresh food. These bio-reactors are interconnected, each performing a very specific function that must be controlled and supervised. The control of these systems is rather complex because the cultures in the bio-reactors are very sensitive to changes in the operating conditions.

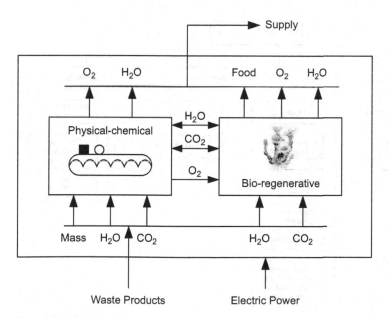

Fig. 13.1 A LSS combining physical-chemical and bio-regenerative technologies

13.2.1 An Example: MELISSA

The so-called MELISSA (Micro-ecological Life Support Alternative) project is the concept developed by the European Space Agency (ESA) jointly with a group of research and industrial organizations [Gòdia et al., 2002]. This project is devoted to promote research in artificial ecosystems with the objective of developing a BLSS to support long-term manned space missions. Figure 13.2 illustrates the magnitude of this challenge by providing a functional breakdown of the various tasks in MELISSA [Masot-Mata, 2007].

From a bird's-eye view, MELISSA is composed of five compartments, each having its own specific function (see Fig. 13.3):

- *Compartment I (CI)* is responsible for the first degradation of the wastes (i.e., feces, urea, and paper) as well as inedible biomass coming from the higher plants compartment and other inedible microbial biomass from the other compartments. This compartment is currently achieving a recycling efficiency of 70%. The outputs are volatile fatty acids, ammonium, H_2, CO_2, and minerals.
- *Compartment II (CII)* is a photo-heterotrophic compartment responsible for the elimination of the terminal products coming from compartment *CI*, mainly volatile fatty acids and H_2.
- *Compartment III (CIII)*, also called the nitrifying compartment, has the main function to oxidize NH_4 to NO_2 and NO_2 to NO_3, which is the most favorable source of nitrogen for the higher plants.

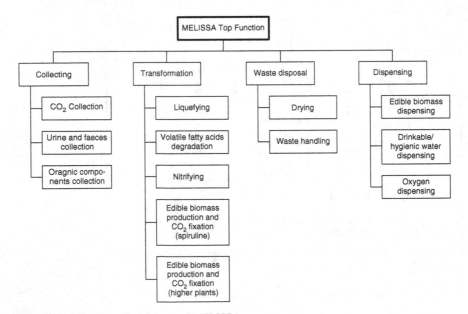

Fig. 13.2 A functional breakdown of MELISSA

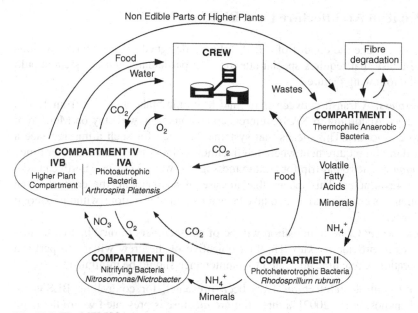

Fig. 13.3 The MELISSA loop concept

- *Compartment IV (CIV)* is divided into two different parts, the algae compartment (*CIVa*) colonized by the "spirulina platensis" and the higher plants compartment (*CIVb*). These compartments perform the photosynthesis generating edible biomass, water, and O_2.
- *Compartment V (CV)* is the crew compartment. For this compartment, atmosphere composition, temperature, pressure and humidity is controlled. The outputs of the compartment are CO_2, fecal material, urine, and residual (gray) water.

For all compartments, basic variables (e.g., pH, temperature, pressure, compounds in the gas and liquid phase, and gas and liquid flow rates) need to be controlled continuously. Complex sensors and analyzers therefore are deployed throughout the loop to obtain continuous measures over the different processes.

MELISSA is currently integrated at "Pilot Plant" level at the University (Autònoma) of Barcelona. The control system of the Pilot Plant is based on traditional programmable logic controllers in a network with a centralized supervision, implementing master control functions. Currently, the recycling efficiency at steady state is known, that is without accounting for kinetics, although some compartments have models validated incorporating kinetics. For most of the compartments, "first principle" models exist based on mass balance, describing the reactions that take place. These models have been used to create high-level controllers. For example a "model predictive control" (MPC) has been developed and validated at Pilot Plant scale to control the biomass production in compartment *CIVa* [Lobo and Lasseur, 2004]. The complete Pilot Plant is expected to have a considerable number (1000+) of variables measured and/or controlled.

13.3 Control Architecture for a BLSS

Several facts make the control of a BLSS that is designed for long-term missions in space a task that requires special attention. In particular, such a system should satisfy the following features:

- *Robustness*: A transit between Earth and Mars may take anything from 120 to 240 days. According to NASA reference mission, crew will stay on Mars from 18 to 20 months. This means that systems designed for such a mission face a long-duration requirement where the likelihood of a failure increases over time.
- *Autonomy*: The round-trip for a radio message between Mars and Earth can take up to 42 minutes. This means that in case of an incident, the crew shall be autonomous enough and able to take decisions and plan actions without external guidance.
- *Maintenance*: Crew composition will be of six members trained in crossed disciplines to provide backup. The first objective of the crew will be to perform exploration. Crew time dedicated to maintenance should be minimized.

Several control architectures have been presented for controlling BLSSs. In [Schreckenghost et al., 2002], a three-tier architecture is presented where the main elements of the system are high-level components with artificial intelligence reasoning capabilities. The system is governed by a planner and scheduler that indicates the course of action distributing the tasks among the lower layer components and monitoring its execution to reevaluate the plans. No details are given with respect to the structure of the lower level controllers. A drawback of the three-tier architecture and, in general, with the different approaches used in NASA experiments with BLSSs is the lack of cohesion in the architecture design as indicated in [Biswas et al., 2005]. The NASA approach has been to develop independent systems (e.g., the air revitalization system or the water recovery system), and to integrate them under the same high-level control system to perform experiments with humans. An important, positive aspect to be taken into account is the experience NASA/JSC (Johnson Space Center) has gained through these experiments.

This chapter proposes the use of a multi-agent system (MAS) architecture as the main driver for the design of a LSS control system. The proposal is based on the experience obtained from the implementation of the current MELISSA Pilot Plant control system [Duatis et al., 2003, Duatis et al., 2006], the study and review of current advanced control technologies, and the requirements for a system that has to be used in an extreme space environment. Up to now, only some experiments have been performed to validate various parts of this proposal, but several other tests and experiments are planned as part of ongoing research. The final objective is to end up with a new control system architecture able to fully control the MELISSA Pilot Plant, eventually being a control system covering all requirements for a future space BLSS.

The proposed multi-agent system architecture will be embedded in a hierarchical architecture combining the use of well-defined design methods for controllers where no special reasoning capabilities are needed with more complex structures, and where the system has to apply decision-making up to planning and human-centered supervision layers. This architecture conforms to a "holonic" or "heterarchical" system.

For ancillary controllers, simple PID (proportional, integrator, derivative controller) structures will be sufficient. For more complex control, with multiple inputs multiple outputs (MIMO), constraints, and probably nonlinear behavior, model predictive control (MPC) is selected as the best choice. Controllers with a more complex structure can be designed following recently introduced hybrid systems design methods [Ocampo-Martíinez et al., 2007, Ocampo-Martínez et al., 2007a]. In addition, more complex components will be used only for the high-level controllers where the universe of discourse is mainly symbolic and planning and scheduling is needed. Following this approach, the robustness of the lower level near reactive controllers is guaranteed by design. For the medium/high-level control, however, verification of the performance will be more difficult, and novel methods and tools need to be investigated [Antsaklis and Passino, 1993].

Multi-agent systems are one of these novel methods in the software engineering arena because they allow us to not only encapsulate methods and data but also behavior [Woolridge, 2002]. Main agent characteristics are:

- *Autonomy*: An agent is autonomous in the sense that it does not need external intervention (in particular human intervention) to react to some event and control its actions and internal state.
- *Reactive*: An agent receives information (signals) from its environment and reacts according to this information.
- *Proactive*: An agent will not only initiate actions in response to changes in its environment but also exhibit goal-directed behavior by taking the initiative.
- *Sociability*: An agent may require information or services from other agents (systems or humans) to accomplish its tasks.

A very important and interesting capability of agents is that they do not need to know all possible situations (states) to design a course of action.

We could think that a simple PID controller can be modeled as an agent—it is autonomous, reactive, and normally is in communication with a system that allows reconfiguration and monitoring (supervision system). If the control system is a fault-tolerant controller with, for example, several configurations depending on the fault, it can also be classified as proactive, because it reconfigures itself in abnormal situations.

According to the controlled actions, three broad classes of agents are identifiable: "reactive", "deliberative", and "mixed":

- In a reactive agent, perception is tightly coupled to action without the use of any symbolic or abstract internal model of the agent, the environment, or their time histories. For each compartment, a collection of agents will be monitoring the activity of the ancillary controllers responsible for the regulation of each loop. These lower level controllers will perform the interaction with the sensors and actuators.

- A deliberative agent system reasons and plans based on an internal model of both itself and the environment it inhabits. They are able to generate plans and evaluate them with respect to an optimization function before deciding its execution. They can hold information of their environment to generate plans but also information from other agents. They may even negotiate the optimality of a plan with other agents.
- Finally, a mixed agent is devoted to safety issues by combining aspects of both reactive and deliberative agency. The mixed agent is also hybrid because it has a hybrid control system at its core [Fregene et al., 2005].

According to agents functionality in the proposed MAS, four types of agents can be identified [Angulo et al., 2007, González et al., 2007]: the "controller agent" (CA), the "compartment control agent" (CCA), the "phase control agent" (PCA), and the "planning and supervision agent" (PSA). Figure 13.4 illustrates a hierarchical architecture for these controller agents.

In more detail, the CA will encapsulate the traditionally designed controllers providing an agent-based interface with capabilities of communicating with other controller agents in the compartment and with the CCA. The controlled dynamic processes can be modeled using space-state representation. These controllers will be interacting with sensors and actuators. The CCA will be responsible for the coordination between the ancillary loops and the main recycling processes of the compartment. The CCA will incorporate simplified models of the involved processes of the compartment and will be able to evaluate situations through the use of these models to perform simulations. This capability will be used to evaluate alternatives in the event of problems or a need for reconfiguration coming from higher layered components. The CCA will be in tight communication with the PCAs that will coordinate the generation of compounds at each phase. The PCA will use symbolic information and numeric information. Symbolic information will represent the current state communicated by the controller agent(s) (CA) in the lower layers, and numeric information will be used jointly with symbolic information for planning and decision-making. The PCA will be at the same time under command by the PSA to ensure the correct execution of the current plan.

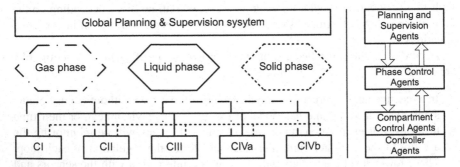

Fig. 13.4 Architecture and context for the proposed multi-agent system (MAS)

As was mentioned earlier, the production of O_2, potable water, and food are main requirements for a LSS. Therefore, each action of the system will be driven to maximize the production rates of these elements while preserving the overall system performance. Each of the compartments mentioned earlier will contribute differently to this objective. There are also intermediate functions that prepare the compounds (e.g., compartments *CI*, *CII*, and *CIII* in MELISSA) that will be finally transformed into oxygen, water, and food in the final phase (compartment *CIV*). Eventually, these final products will be consumed in the crew compartment.

13.4 The Reactive Level

A compartment can be characterized as a bio-reactor with gas and liquid input flows, a transfer of components between the two phases, and a set of (bio-)reactions in the liquid phase. At the output, there will be again gas and liquid and in some cases a solid separation system including an additional output of solids (see Fig. 13.5).

Each compartment implements a set of control loops to maintain the hosted microorganism culture(s) in optimal operating conditions, in general: *pH* control, temperature control, liquid flow control, gas flow control, and pressure control.

In general, the compensation of *pH* will be implemented as a regulation of some input compounds generated in other compartments, as for example CO_2. The control of *pH* is a main issue still to be solved because to preserve loop closure, it is not feasible to continuously supply sales to regulate *pH*, and compounds resulting from the reactions of the compartments would need to be used. Temperature control is usually performed by a cooling/heater system that maintains the temperature set-point. Liquid flow and gas flow are regulated by means of valves and pumps. Usually the compartment needs a regular provision of liquid and gas to maintain recirculation and provision of nutrients and gas components (CO_2, O_2) for the reactions. Pressure control will be related to gas and liquid flow control to maintain a constant pressure in the reactor. Normally input flow and output flow will be equal. These ancillary control loops will need continuous regulation because the bio-reactions normally

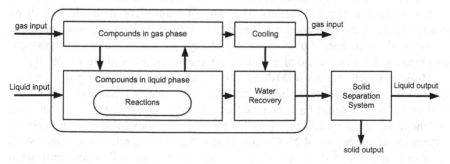

Fig. 13.5 Compartment functions

destabilize the reactor, performing temperature variations, pH variations, pressure variations (gas generation), etc.

The recycling process control will be responsible for regulating the main function of the reactor with respect to the complete loop as biomass production, oxygen production, water production, NO_2 and NO_3 production, etc. The rest of the control loops will maintain the conditions to maximize the performance of the reactor, normally measured as the "recycling efficiency". For example, for a water recycling unit, the recycling efficiency will be measured as the input flow of dirty water with respect to the output flow of clean potable water, or, in the case of oxygen production, the CO_2 input flow with respect to the O_2 output flow. Even with the correct control of the ancillary loops, the reaction efficiency will be limited by several factors such as the concentration of compounds in the liquid and gas inputs, which will not be constant, or by variations in the behavior of the cultures responsible to the recycling function. This will add uncertainty to the process, and the variation cannot be determined at control level but only fitted by statistical approximation.

The compartment might have several nominal operating modes, that is, a compartment can reduce its efficiency producing edible biomass increasing the efficiency in oxygen production, or produce a higher flow of clean non-potable water than potable water.

A greenhouse is a special case of a compartment because the level of automation required for this compartment can vary widely, from a complete manual procedure where the crew will perform the seeding, maintenance, and harvesting tasks, up to a completely autonomous compartment, that is, robotized to the point that all operations are performed automatically. More specific monitoring tasks can be envisaged for this compartment, for example, image processing to detect diseases or environmental problems (humidity, atmosphere composition, etc.) that can be observed from the color and form of the leaves of plants. However, considered as a black box, a greenhouse is not much different to any of the other compartments.

13.4.1 Controller Agents

The domain of the controller agent can be represented by dynamic processes modeled through state-space equations. The type of controllers at this level will be mainly based on modern control techniques but using the conventional approach. However, the inclusion of discrete events, always present in real control systems, eventually will imply the use of mixed dynamic and discrete systems modeling.

Model predictive control (MPC) offers a robust way of implementing the control of the processes involved in a BLSS. It is well accepted that simple PID controllers can work fine for basic control loops such as pH, flow rates, temperature, and the rest of ancillary control loops, but for more complex MIMO (multiple input outputs) systems the use of MPC controllers offers a more robust approach. MPC algorithms are designed for specific restrictions and work well under constrained conditions [Ocampo et al., 2006].

In general, these kinds of controllers are based on a model of the plant that allows us to calculate a prediction. The controller evaluates the prediction with respect to a set of objectives and adjusts the available manipulated variables to achieve these objectives. The model can be linear or nonlinear. In the linear case, the controller can be designed straightforwardly, and for the nonlinear case, normally a linear model is derived to design the controller around an operating point. One important characteristic of MPC that makes it different from other optimal control strategies is that it includes constraints of the plant in the design of the controller; that is, saturations, physical limits, etc., of the sensors and actuators that are intrinsic to the process to control.

Models of the plant used to create the MPC are usually first principle models, although models could also be derived from experiments and using system identification techniques.

Verification of the specifications of MPC controllers is guaranteed by design [Ocampo-Martínez et al., 2007b]. However, real control system implementations have several factors that can reduce the confidence, among others: changes in the operating point (in the case of linearized nonlinear controllers), changes in the mode of operation (externally commanded), perturbations on the inputs (variations on the compounds concentration), or malfunctions (detected by the "fault detection and identification module" (FDI) module). Therefore, we can consider the plant to be controlled (a compartment in this case) as a system with several state partitions. The system will be switching continuously from one partition to another. The proposed control system will need to follow these changes, adapting the controller. Normally, these cases are handled through the implementation of a set of similar controllers that are switched depending on the current situation. In this case, however, verification by design cannot be ensured even if all the single controllers are compliant with the specifications because the transitions between the different controllers are not taken into account in the traditional approach. These transitions can be identified as discrete inputs to the system.

Hybrid systems: More recently, hybrid control system (which are more similar to real implementations) received considerable attention from the research community [Glavaski et al., 2007]. Hybrid systems theory combines the areas of computer science and control theory resulting in a model for verifying controllers including discrete transitions and system constraints. Hybrid systems provide a unified framework for describing processes evolving according to continuous dynamics, discrete dynamics, and logic rules [Bemporad and Morari, 1999]. In case the process can be described in the form:

$$x(t+1) = A_i x(t) + B_i u(t)$$
$$y(t) = C_i x(t) + g_i$$
$$for \begin{bmatrix} x(t) \\ u(t) \end{bmatrix} \in \chi_i, \tag{13.1}$$

where each χ_i represents a partition of states, the process can be modeled as a "piece-wise affine" (PWA) system where dynamic equations and switching rules are linear functions of the state. According to [Bemporad et al., 2000], these systems are equivalent to "mixed logic dynamic systems" (MLD), using a set of Boolean conversions to translate switching rules to mixed integer linear inequalities. For MLD stability, controllability, and observability, tests are defined allowing the robust design for this type of controller.

Hybrid systems are characterized by having a continuous part governed by a supervisor that affects the behavior of this continuous part. The supervisor detects the occurrence of events (e.g., mode changing, malfunctions, reconfiguration) and commands the continuous part to adapt to a change (see Fig. 13.6).

Almost all real control systems are hybrid, as the presence of alarms, modes of function, and other reconfiguration procedures are widely implemented. However, when the feasibility study of the controller is performed, usually, only the continuous part is analyzed without any accounting for the counterpart discrete system.

In case the set of controllers can be designed as PWA or MLD, the solution has been already defined. But, for cases where the mode change cannot be governed by linear variations of the inputs or the states, a more complex system is required. Controllability and observability will be restricted again to the individual controllers, and only if changes are performed when the system is in steady state, the specifications of the controller can be guaranteed by design. In such a "complex hybrid system controller", the supervisor will be a critical part, implementing high-level operations as communications to the upper control levels as the switching between controllers will not be determined intrinsically by the design of a controller.

Another component closely related to the supervisor of the hybrid controller will be the fault detection and identification module in charge of analyzing the signals and detecting and identifying possible faults [Blanke et al., 2003]. In case of a fault, the new state will be reported to the CA, were a coordinated decision will be taken. Normally, a reconfiguration of the controller will be commanded to continue the control function in a degraded form. The decision will be taken at a higher level because knowledge from the CCA could be needed.

Disturbances in the Inputs

In the case of the MELISSA Pilot Plant to control biomass production in the spirulina compartment, a MPC is used that regulates the biomass concentration. The bio-reactor is implemented as two cylinders with well-known geometric

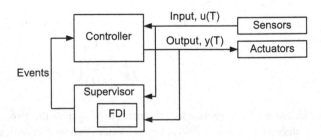

Fig. 13.6 Hybrid controller

characteristics. Using the knowledge of the light radiation influence in the cylinder and according to the biomass concentration, a first-order model has been developed to calculate the biomass production using only light as the manipulated variable. The biomass concentration is estimated by integrating along the radius of the cylinder considering the effect of the light according to the measured biomass concentration. Therefore, it depends on the biomass concentration, the light flux, and the geometric characteristics of the reactor. Other constants are obtained experimentally. The measured variable will be the biomass concentration. The model is highly nonlinear because for every step an integration is performed to calculate the light influence on the cells along the radius of the cylinder.

Also, nitrate concentration in the input will not be constant, and if it drops below acceptable margins, it can affect biomass production not allowing the system to reach the set-point, eventually causing a saturation of the light regulation and a total failure of the system because regulation of flows and temperature can collapse. To prevent this situation, a variation of the model of the MPC for biomass production would be required. In this variation, the supervisor, which is monitoring the inputs, will detect that the nitrate concentrate is below the constraints for the current controller. The supervisor will inform the upper control level about this and a change in the controller will be prepared. In case no opposing reaction is received from the upper level, the change will take place and the new controller will start to regulate biomass production in the compartment.

Commanded Mode Changing

Sometimes, it is possible that the plant is required to maximize production of oxygen instead of maximizing biomass production. In that case, the supervisor will receive the command to reconfigure the controller, if possible. Because the new controller will have a different structure, as inputs and outputs change, the switching will be performed when the system is in steady state.

Fault Detection and Recovery

It is extremely important to detect any fault in the system as early as possible. This capability will allow the starting of corrective actions and minimize the consequences. This factor has to be considered at design phase, allowing by design, the identification of faults by analytical redundancy and the minimization of the consequences by taking corrective actions [Blanke et al., 2003]. The FDI techniques can be applied from the lowest level (e.g., to identify faults in a simple device such as a valve, a pump, or a sensor) up to the highest level (e.g., detecting when a culture in a reactor is decreasing its activity and then affected by some unexpected situation) [Puig et al., 2006].

In principle, using the signature identification process from signal analysis and calculation of residuals, it will be possible to diagnose a set of faults. Again, in case of a fault, the new state will be reported by the supervisor to the upper control level were a coordinated decision will be taken. In general, it can be assumed that system redundancy has been taken into account in the design of the system and that a redundant unit will be available for the most critical parts in order to continue with the nominal function. However, due to the long expected lifetime of the system, it could be possible that a double-fault occurs, redundancy has to be provided analytically, or even that no redundancy is available. In these cases, whenever possible, a reconfiguration of the controller will be commanded to continue the control function in a degraded form. The decision will be taken at upper level because knowledge from the rest of the controllers of the compartment will be needed.

Models will be required to implement FDI, however, it has to be expected that models will be incomplete and inputs not completely defined but bounded. In this situation, forecasting techniques will be required, such as Kalman filters. Hybrid systems modeling supports these situations again [Supavatanakul et al., 2006].

All these traditionally designed controllers will be wrapped by agents. These agents together will form an agent network in the compartment. The information flows do not need to be predefined but more flexible methods such as "publish–and–subscribe" can be used. In principal, the agent that will implement the main reasoning part of the compartment will be the compartment control agent.

13.5 The Deliberative Level

13.5.1 Compartment Control Agents

The "compartment control agent" (CCA) will be in charge of:

- Reporting the current state to the upper level.
- Receiving commands from upper levels.
- Determining the next-state of the controllers in case of commanded reconfiguration.
- Evaluate situations and report results.
- Acquire compromises with the PCA about the production of specific compounds.

Clearly, the higher plants compartment will need an even more complex CCA because it can be considered as a batch process where the different activities have to be planned, scheduled, and monitored. Planting, cultivating, and harvesting tasks (robotized or not) will need to be coordinated with respect to the global system requirements. For instance, the decision on the type of crops and cultivation surface will be based on diet requirements, current food storage, time before harvesting, etc.

13.5.2 Phase Controller Agents

In BLSSs, three phases can be defined: the gas phase, the liquid phase, and the solid phase. A phase controller agent (PCA) will be implemented for each phase. The main control function at this level will be to ensure the availability of resources in a certain time horizon. Recovering the information about the state of each compartment, it will be relatively easy to obtain the instant production rates of each component of interest (e.g., O_2, water, food). However, it will be mandatory to command the system to ensure a continuous supply of the principal compounds for each compartment at a certain time horizon, devoting special attention to the crew compartment where maintaining the supply levels will be critical. Therefore, the PCA will be responsible for maintaining the required production rates in its phase. The phase controllers will also control the input and output flows of the buffers where compounds will be temporarily stored. These buffers will allow to cover, during a certain period of time, a lower concentration of a compound, or store an excess in production. The buffers will have an important function in maintaining the stability of the system. Obviously, the concentration of compounds in the flows between compartments will not be constant. For example, the crew compartment will feed CO_2 to the other compartments in a different way during daytime or nighttime, or, the main part of waste water will be transferred to the loop during specific periods (e.g., morning, midday, or at night). However, the compartments need a stable and continuous supply of compounds to maintain their expected functionality. Currently, the capacity of the buffers still needs to be defined, which will not be an easy problem to solve. Another fact that will affect the flows between compartments is the different residence times, that is, the time one compound takes to be degraded or transformed biologically into another compound. This time can vary from minutes to several hours between different compartments.

To implement the coordination between the PCA and CCA agents, the well defined FIPA Contract Net Protocol can be used.[1] This protocol defines the relation between managers and contractors. In our case, managers are the phase controllers that will populate the proposals for producing a certain amount of one compound according to the current plan. Then CCAs from the compartments that are able to produce the compound will offer their willingness of producing it, maybe requiring a certain amount from other compounds. The manager will need to harmonize the demand and the needs even with the PCA of the other phases and finally perform assignations. The manager (that is the PCA) will monitor the execution of the tasks and in case some contractor is not accomplishing the "contract", it will again issue proposals for supplying the required components from other compartments. This protocol has been tested for the purpose of regulating resources competition using "Islander" (a graphical tool that supports the specification of the rules and protocols in an "electronic institution") [Sierra et al., 2004] to create an electronic institution were agents perform according to a predefined set of protocols and rules.

The phase controllers will need a coordinated plan for their work. The plan can be defined on a daily basis for the major tasks, accounting for the special behavior

---

[1] http://www.fipa.org/specs/fipa00029/SC00029H.html, Foundation For Intelligent Physical Agents (FIPA).

of the higher plants compartment. The planning and supervision agent will interface with the crew to define the configuration on a day by day basis, taking into account extravehicular activities, workload, resting periods, and all other activities that can affect generation of CO_2 or wastes. From this first planning, requirements for the PCA will be defined, and the PCA will command the configuration of the compartment controllers.

13.5.3 Planning and Supervision Agent

The PSA (planning and supervision agent) will implement the interface with the crew to elaborate plans and allow simulations of "what-if" scenarios. The crew will be able to elaborate the planning for a period of time where activities that could affect the resources in the BLSS will be defined. The PSA will implement a powerful user interface were lists of activities and potential effects will be related to aid in the plan creation. The system will also require from the crew the allocation of time for the maintenance activities programmed to keep the system healthy. The accomplishing of these activities will be monitored, requiring the crew to confirm task completion in order to have the global state of the system.

A scenario could be that the crew plan the activities for the next day: all crew members will stay on the habitat for the complete day. Then the system is aware that a high level of clean water and oxygen production is required (in contrast with the previous day, where the crew was performing extravehicular activities). Imagine that the levels of clean water and food are correct but the levels of oxygen are low but increasing and a new harvest of lettuce is ready to be obtained from the higher plants compartment. In preparation for this situation, the PSA can suggest to leave the crops a few days longer with a reduced risk of deterioration of the harvest to allow for more oxygen generation.

At this level, it is necessary to establish the cooperation between the human and the PSA, and the cooperation between the PSA and the phase controllers (see Fig. 13.7). The cooperative relation between human and PSA is called "Human Supervisory Control" [Sheridan, 1992]. One or more human operators are intermittently programming and continuously receiving information from the PSA. In a sense, humans specify (by programming) to the computer their goals, objective trade-offs, physical constraints, models, plans, and "if-then-else" procedures, and the PSA elaborates plans and "what-if" scenarios.

Once a plan is created, the PSA will derive concrete orders for the phase controllers in order to adapt to the plan and coordinate the different phases in the compartments. Mainly, it will indicate the new production rates and the prediction of the component flows from the crew compartment. The phase controllers then will reconfigure the controllers on the lower levels and will start receiving information about the progress of the reconfiguration. In case any anomaly is detected during the reconfiguration, an event will be sent to the PSA informing about the situation. The global planning and supervision system will then decide whether crew intervention

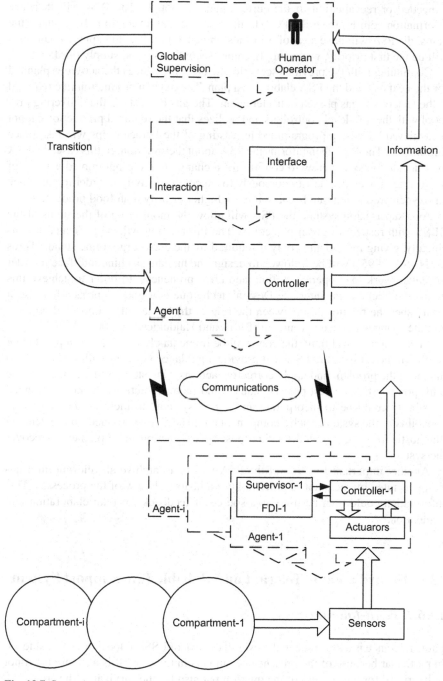

Fig. 13.7 Supervisory control inside a life support system scheme

is needed or reevaluation of the current plan is enough. The PSA will then use information coming from the PCA to monitor the plan execution. To evaluate the plans, the PSA will have a set of priorities. In general terms, atmosphere conditions will be the first priority, water supply comes second, and food supply third.

Continuing with the previous scenario, the crew introduces the activities planned for the next day and the PSA elaborates a plan. The oxygen production rate required is the task of the gas phase controller agent. The gas PCA starts the delivering protocol with the low-level controllers and realizes that the required production cannot be achieved because a programmed harvesting of the lettuce crops will take place imminently. The PCA then informs the PSA about the situation. In this case, the PSA may decide to ask the crew to confirm for a change in the programmed activity of harvesting or even decide autonomously to cancel this activity in order to guarantee an oxygen production rate because it has a higher priority than food production.

As a supervision system, the PSA will allow the monitoring of the status of the BLSS with respect to given objectives. The information will be presented hierarchically, giving more details only if required by the crew. Ergonomic standards (as in [NASA, 1995]) will be followed to design the human-machine interface in order to reduce work-load operations time and error proneness. In order to achieve this goals, the "Ecological Interface Design" technique is a good approach because it establishes the relationship between the role of the human, the controlled process, and the changes in the environment [Burns and Hajdukiewicz, 2004].

In case of a critical fault, the crew will be immediately notified. As support from Earth will be limited, the PSA will provide a guidance system to allow the crew to diagnose the problem and apply corrective actions. One step will be to identify the fault point and to suggest possible causes and recovery actions. A more advanced possibility could be to incorporate an "expert system" to increase the diagnostic capability of the system. Such a component could be able to produce a more detailed diagnostic from the symptoms and propose specific actions to implement to recover the system.

Another important function of the PSA will be to archive all relevant information generated by the plant in order to have a historical view of the processes. This information could then be used as a source of feedback for plan elaboration and simulation.

13.6 Toward a Fault-Tolerant and Reliable Life Support System

13.6.1 Fault-tolerance

Fault-tolerance is a key issue in the overall control of LSSs at local or at global level, in particular because of the presence of humans in the loop. It is a requirement not only critical for the success of the mission but also for the survival of the crew.

Tolerance at the lowest level can be embedded (see Section 13.3) in the MPC controller including the fault modes as new additional modes and using hybrid systems theory [Ocampo et al., 2006]. However, because of the hierarchical, distributed structure used to control the whole LSS presented in Section 13.1 and because fault-tolerance mechanisms require information locally and/or from other locations, they also need to be cooperative between different levels [Blanke et al., 2003]. Cooperation in this case will also be achieved by the use of agents that will allow reconfiguration of the system at all levels. These agents are able to provide FDI, decision-making, and reconfiguration on a local level. The agents communicate with each other, thus, performing coordinated behavior or even cooperation in the decision-making process.

In case of a fault at the lowest level where a valve is not working properly, the agent responsible for the loop will reconfigure itself to continue its function in a degraded form. It will inform the higher level agent in the hierarchy about the anomaly, and this agent will evaluate the situation from a different perspective. In case an optimal solution exists that increases the global performance of the system but requires interaction of several agents, the higher level agent will coordinate the communication to these agents to achieve the new objective. As several plans could be applied, the coordinator agent will need to negotiate with the other agents and finally agree on a solution. At the same time, the coordinator agent will report the anomaly to components with higher responsibility until, eventually, the planning and supervision system is alerted about the fault. If the system is not able to reconfigure itself into a (reasonably) good state, it will require (maybe by generating a high-priority alert) mandatory human intervention to cope with the problem. Although this process seems very complex, in fact, it is relatively simple. Phase control agents will have planning capabilities, and in case the affected compartment control agent cannot continue with the required performance, plans will be generated that incorporate the change on the global performance. Other compartments will be alerted about the reduction of the generation of a specific compound and required to change their configuration in order to reflect (assume) this change. If any compartment is able to supply the reduction of the compound, then the global system plan will continue, otherwise the planing and supervision agent will adjust the global plan to the new situation. Priority will be given to bio-regenerative processes, but as indicated in Section 13.1, the current trends in design of advanced LSSs is to mix physical-chemical and bio-regenerative processes. This approach adds additional redundancy because in case the bio-regenerative processes cannot cope with a fault or are unable to reach a required production rate of a compound, then the physical-chemical processes might be able to perform (temporarily) the missing function.

13.6.2 Reliability Through Predictive Maintenance: Integrated Health Management

In addition to the real-time fault-tolerance and diagnostic mechanisms already mentioned in previous sections, another very important feature to be taken into account is the maintenance program [Blanke et al., 2003]. Main objectives in maintenance of systems and equipment are ensuring safety, equipment reliability, and cost reduction. Traditionally, there have been two common maintenance philosophies employed: preventive maintenance (sometimes called schedule-based or event-based) that uses statistics to estimate the machine behavior, leading to very conservative estimates about the probability of failure; and corrective (sometimes called restorative) maintenance philosophy, with the machine running until it fails and then being restored back to good health; hence maintenance costs are reduced, but unexpected faults may result in longer than expected system down-times.[2] It seems clear that both approaches must be considered. It is a known fact that system operation decreases the reliability of a system. A well-driven maintenance program of the whole LSS will minimize faults and consequently increase system reliability. Integrated health management systems allow us to keep a record of the evolution of system reliability, pacifying maintenance actions in those subsystems/components whose reliability has decreased below a given threshold over time. On the other hand, a provision of spares also needs to be available to apply corrective maintenance when required to restore the system back to good health in case of an unexpected failure. Both conditions will have an impact on the planning capabilities of the planning and supervision system, in particular, preventive maintenance being a new source of information to account for when elaborating plans.

13.7 Conclusions

This chapter proposes a robust control architecture for bio-regenerative life support systems. The system robustness is obtained as the result of applying distributed control, intelligent control, fault detection and identification, and high-level planning and supervision. Distributed control techniques are used to coordinate the different processes, dealing with sharing information, controlling network architecture, network communication, and network hierarchy. With the support of agents, organized in a network as a multi-agent system, the proposed control architecture will be able to provide reasoning capabilities for each component for generating plans, interacting with its environment, and standardizing the communication between the different components in the network hierarchy. Fault detection, identification, and diagnosis provides the capability of detecting faults at local and global level. With these issues in mind, when the system is designed, the system will be able to cope with faults and continue its function (maybe) with some degradation but nonstop. Both analytical and hardware redundancy will maximize the level of reliability. The chapter mentioned that the system also includes a supervisory system with a high level of autonomy. This supervisory system will process information and take decisions at a high level, requiring human intervention only when mandatory and

---

[2] For an in-depth review of the state-of-the-art in vehicle health management, in particular in aerospace, visit the Web page of the First International Forum on Integrated System Health Engineering and Management in Aerospace (ISHEM) [ISHEM, 2005].

providing the information to humans in a clear and understandable form. Based on the presented research, this work suggests the proposed control architecture as a meaningful component in a real bio-regenerative LSS, such as the MELISSA Pilot Plant, for example, in order to prepare such a system for the highly demanding and challenging requirements of space technology.

Appendix A: Abbreviations in This Chapter

BLSS = Bio-regenerative life support system; CA = Controller agent; CCA = Compartment control agent; CI, CII, CIII, CIV, CIVa, CIVb, CV = Compartments; FDI = Fault detection and identification; LSS = Life support system; MAS = Multi-agent system; MELISSA = Micro-ecological life support alternative; MIMO = Multiple input multiple output system; MLD = Mixed logic dynamic system, MPC = Model predictive control; PCA = Phase control agent; PID = Proportional, derivative, and integrator; PSA = Planning and supervision agent; PWA = Piece-wise affine.

References

Angulo, C., Gonzáalez, G., Raya, C., and Català, A. (2007). An OSA-CBM multi-agent vehicle health management architecture for self-health awareness. *International Journal of Intelligent Control and Systems*, 12(12):158–166.

Antsaklis, P. and Passino, K., editors (1993). *An Introduction to Intelligent and Autonomous Control*. Kluwer Academic Publishers, Norwell, MA.

Bemporad, A., Ferrari-Trecate, G., and Morari, M. (2000). Observability and controllability of piecewise affine and hybrid systems. *IEEE Transactions on Automatic Control*, 45(10): 1864–1876.

Bemporad, A. and Morari, M. (1999). Control of systems integrating logic, dynamics, and constraints. *Automatica*, 35(3):407–427.

Biswas, G., Bonasso, P., Abdelwahed, S., Manders, E., Wu, J., Kortenkamp, V., and Bell, S. (2005). Requirements for an autonomous control architecture for advanced life support systems. In *Proceedings of the 35th SAE International Conference on Environmental Systems (ICES'05)*, Rome, Italy, 14th July.

Blanke, M., Kinnaert, M., Lunze, J., and Staroswiecki, M. (2003). *Diagnosis and Fault-Tolerant Control*. Springer-Verlag Berlin Heidelberg.

Burns, C. and Hajdukiewicz, J. (2004). *Ecological Interface Design*. CRC Press, Boca Raton, FL.

Bussmann, S., Jennings, N. R., and Wooldridge, M. (2004). *Multiagent systems for manufacturing control: a design methodology*. Series on Agent Technology. Springer-Verlag, Berlin Heidelberg.

Duatis, J., Angulo, C., and Mas, J. (2006). A new approach for advanced life-support systems control. *ERCIM News*, 65(65):18–19.

Duatis, J., Elvira, J. Mas, J., and Doulami, F. (2003). Melissa adaptation for space. In Lobo, M. and Lasseur, C., editors, *MELISA Yearly Report for 2002 Activity. Memorandum of Understanding*. ESA.

ESA (2003). European Space Agency (ESA): European framework for exploration. Paris, ESA/AURORA-BP(2003)25,rev.1.

ESA (2004). European Space Agency (ESA): The Aurora programme.

Fregene, K., Kennedy, D., and Wang, D. (2005). Toward a systems- and control-oriented agent framework. *IEEE Transactions on Systems, Man, and Cybernetics, Part B: Cybernetics*, 35(5):999–1012.

Glavaski, S., Subramanian, D., Ariyur, K., Ghosh, R., Lamba, N., and Papachristodoulou, A. (2007). A nonlinear hybrid life support system: dynamic modeling, control design, and safety verification. *IEEE Transactions on Control Systems Technology*, 15(6):1003–1017.

Gòdia, F., Albiol, J., Montesinos, J., Pérez, J., Creus, N., Cabello, F., Mengual, X., Montras, A., and Lasseur, C. (2002). MELISSA: a loop of interconnected bioreactors to develop life support in space. *Journal of Biotechnology*, 99(3):319–330.

González, G., Angulo, C., and Raya, C. (2007). A multi-agent-based management approach for self-health awareness in autonomous systems. In *Proceedings of the 4th IEEE International Workshop on Engineering of Autonomic and Autonomous Systems (EASe'07)*, pages 79–88, Tucson, Arizona, 26–29 March. IEEE Press.

Hoffman, S. and Kaplan, D. (1997). The reference mission of the NASA mars exploration study team. Lyndon B. Johnson Space Center, Houston Texas.

ISHEM (2005). First international forum on integrated system health engineering and management in aerospace. http://ic.arc.nasa.gov/projects/ishem/. Napa, CA.

Lobo, M. and Lasseur, C. (2004). The melissa partners–yearly report for the 2003 activity. ESA/EWP-2244.

Masot-Mata, A. (2007). *Engineering Photosynthetic Systems for Bioregenerative Life Support*. PhD thesis, Departament d'Enginyeria Química, Universitat Autònoma de Barcelona.

NASA (1995). Man-systems integration standards. Lyndon B. Johnson Space Center, Houston Texas.

NASA (2004). National Aeronautics and Space Administration (NASA): The vision for space exploration.

Ocampo, C., Puig, V., Quevedo, J., Ingimundarson, A., Figueras, J., and Cembrano, G. (2006). Fault-tolerant optimal control of sewer networks: Barcelona case study. *Measurement and Control*, 5(39):151–156.

Ocampo-Martínez, C., Bemporad, A., Ingimundarson, A., and Puig, V. (2007). Hybrid model predictive control of sewer networks. In Sanchez-Peña, R., Quevedo, J., and Puig, V., editors, *Identification and Control: The Gap between Theory and Practice*, pages 87–116. Springer-Verlag, London Ltd.

Ocampo-Martínez, C., Guerra, P., Puig, V., and Quevedo, J. (2007a). Fault tolerance evaluation of linear constrained MPC using zonotope-based set computations. *Journal of Systems and Control Engineering*, 6(221):915–926.

Ocampo-Martínez, C., Ingimundarson, A., Puig, V., and Quevedo, J. (2007b). Hybrid model predictive control applied on sewer networks: The Barcelona case study. In Lamnabhi-Lagarrigue, F., Laghrouche, S., Loria, A., and Panteley, E., editors, *Taming Heterogeneity and Complexity of Embedded Control*, pages 523–540. Selected papers presented at the Joint CTS-HYCON Workshop on Nonlinear and Hybrid Control, Paris IV Sorbonne, 10–12 July 2006.

Puig, V., Stancu, A., Escobet, T., Nejjari, F., Quevedo, J., and Patton, J. (2006). Passive robust fault detection using interval observers: application to the damadics benchmark problem. *Control Engineering Practice*, 6(14):621–633.

Rotkowitz, M. and Lall, S. (2006). A characterization of convex problems in decentralized control. *IEEE Transactions on Automatic Control*, 51(2):274–286.

Schreckenghost, D., Thronesbery, C., Bonasso, P., Kortenkamp, D., and Martin, C. (2002). Intelligent control of life support for space missions. *IEEE Intelligent Systems Magazine*, 17(5):24–31.

Sheridan, T. B. (1992). *Telerobotics, Automation, and Supervisory Control*. The MIT Press, Cambridge, MA.

Sierra, C., Rodríguez-Aguilar, J., Noriega, P., Esteva, M., and Arcos, J. (2004). Engineering multi-agent systems as electronic institutions. *UPGRADE The European Journal for the Informatics Professional*, V(4):33–39.

Simani, S., Patton, R., and Fantuzzi, C. (2003). *Model-Based Fault Diagnosis in Dynamic Systems Using Identification Techniques*. Springer-Verlag, New York.

Supavatanakul, P., Lunze, J., Puig, V., and Quevedo, J. (2006). Diagnosis of timed automata: theory and application to the DAMADICS actuator benchmark problem. *Control Engineering Practice*, 6(14):609–619.

Woolridge, M. (2002). *Introduction to Multiagent Systems*. John Wiley & Sons, Inc., New York.

Index